WELCOME TO OAHU

Oahu is the Hawaiian island that has it all—untouched tropical landscapes as well as a stimulating urban vibe. You can explore the beaches and gentle waves of Kailua, or take in nightlife in buzzing Honolulu (the state's capital), home to a vibrant Chinatown and burgeoning arts scene. Life is still appealingly slow-paced on the northern and eastern shores, where razor-edged mountains descend to spectacular beaches. A thriving traditional culture, plus top-notch historic sites such as the royal Iolani Palace and Pearl Harbor, spice up the mix here as well.

TOP REASONS TO GO

★ **Pearl Harbor:** This historic memorial in Honolulu is a sobering, don't-miss sight.

★ **Waikiki:** Busy but beautiful, with a perfect beach for first-time surfers.

★ **Great Food:** Simple plate lunches, fresh sushi, creative modern Hawaiian cuisine.

★ **Polynesian Cultural Center:** The famous luau provides insight into island culture.

★ **Nightlife:** From upscale jazz bars to local hangouts, Honolulu comes alive after dark.

★ **North Shore:** Shave ice, big waves, pro surfers, and a slower pace add appeal here.

Fodor's OAHU

Publisher: Amanda D'Acierno, *Senior Vice President*

Editorial: Arabella Bowen, *Editor in Chief*; Linda Cabasin, *Editorial Director*

Design: Fabrizio La Rocca, *Vice President, Creative Director*; Tina Malaney, *Associate Art Director*; Chie Ushio, *Senior Designer*; Ann McBride, *Production Designer*

Photography: Melanie Marin, *Associate Director of Photography*; Jessica Parkhill and Jennifer Romains, *Researchers*

Maps: Rebecca Baer, *Senior Map Editor*; David Lindroth, Ed Jacobus, William Wu, with additional cartography provided by Henry Columb, Mark Stroud, and Ali Baird, Moon Street Cartography, *Cartographers*

Production: Linda Schmidt, *Managing Editor*; Evangelos Vasilakis, *Associate Managing Editor*; Angela L. McLean, *Senior Production Manager*

Sales: Jacqueline Lebow, *Sales Director*

Marketing & Publicity: Heather Dalton, *Marketing Director*; Katherine Punia, *Senior Publicist*

Business & Operations: Susan Livingston, *Vice President, Strategic Business Planning*; Sue Daulton, *Vice President, Operations*

Fodors.com: Megan Bell, *Executive Director, Revenue & Business Development*; Yasmin Marinaro, *Senior Director, Marketing & Partnerships*

Writers: James Cave, Lesa Griffith, Trina Kudlacek, Chris Oliver, Catherine E. Toth, Anna Weaver

Editors: Douglas Stallings

Production Editor: Elyse Rozelle

5th Edition

ISBN 978-0-8041-4216-8

ISSN 1559–0771

All details in this book are based on information supplied to us at press time. Always confirm information when it matters, especially if you're making a detour to visit a specific place. Fodor's expressly disclaims any liability, loss, or risk, personal or otherwise, that is incurred as a consequence of the use of any of the contents of this book.

SPECIAL SALES

This book is available at special discounts for bulk purchases for sales promotions or premiums. For more information, e-mail specialmarkets@randomhouse.com

PRINTED IN COLOMBIA

10 9 8 7 6 5 4 3 2 1

CONTENTS

ABOUT
THIS GUIDE

Fodor's Recommendations

Everything in this guide is worth doing—we don't cover what isn't—but exceptional sights, hotels, and restaurants are recognized with additional accolades. **Fodor's**Choice★ indicates our top recommendations; and **Best Bets** call attention to notable hotels and restaurants in various categories. Care to nominate a new place? Visit Fodors.com/contact-us.

Trip Costs

We list prices wherever possible to help you budget well. Hotel and restaurant price categories from **$** to **$$$$** are noted alongside each recommendation. For hotels, we include the lowest cost of a standard double room in high season. For restaurants, we cite the average price of a main course at dinner or, if dinner isn't served, at lunch. For attractions, we always list adult admission fees; discounts are usually available for children, students, and senior citizens.

Hotels

Our local writers vet every hotel to recommend the best overnights in each price category, from budget to expensive. Unless otherwise specified, you can expect private bath, phone, and TV in your room. For expanded hotel reviews, facilities, and deals visit Fodors.com.

Restaurants

Unless we state otherwise, restaurants are open for lunch and dinner daily. We mention dress code only when there's a specific requirement and reservations only when they're essential or not accepted. To make restaurant reservations, visit Fodors.com.

Credit Cards

The hotels and restaurants in this guide typically accept credit cards. If not, we'll say so.

Top Picks
★ **Fodor's**Choice

Listings
⊠ Address
⊠ Branch address
☎ Telephone
🖷 Fax
⊕ Website
✉ E-mail
🎫 Admission fee
🕐 Open/closed times
Ⓜ Subway
✛ Directions or Map coordinates

Hotels & Restaurants
🏨 Hotel
🛏 Number of rooms
🍽 Meal plans
✗ Restaurant
☝ Reservations
👔 Dress code
▭ No credit cards
$ Price

Other
⇨ See also
☞ Take note
⛳ Golf facilities

EXPERIENCE OAHU

WHAT'S WHERE

1 Honolulu. The vibrant capital city holds the nation's only royal palace, free concerts under the tamarind trees in the financial district, and the art galleries, hipster bars, and open markets of Nuuanu and Chinatown. It also encompasses Waikiki—dressed in lights at the base of Diamond Head, famous for its world-class shopping, restaurants, and surf—and Pearl Harbor, Hawaii's largest natural harbor and the resting place of the USS *Arizona*, sunk on December 7, 1941.

2 Southeast Oahu. Honolulu's main bedroom communities crawl up the steep-sided valleys that flow into Maunalua Bay. Also here are snorkelers' favorite Hanauma Bay and a string of wild and often hidden beaches.

3 Windward Oahu. The sleepy neighborhoods at the base of the majestic Koolau Mountains offer a respite from the bustling city with long stretches of sandy beaches, charming eateries, ancient Hawaiian fishponds, and offshore islands to explore.

4 The North Shore. Best known for its miles of world-class surf breaks and green sea-turtle sightings, this plantation town also boasts farms, restaurants, and hiking trails.

Waialee

NORTH SHORE 4

Waimea Bay

83

Waialua Bay

Haleiwa

930

Dillingham Airfield

KAENA POINT

WAIANAE

Yokohama Bay

803

Kaala

80

6

Wahiawa

WEST OAHU 5

Makaha

93

Waianae

Mililani Town

Maili

Palikea

Puu Manawahua

750

Nanakuli

0   5 mi

0   5 km

93

H1

76

Ko Olina Resort & Marina

Ewa

Kapolei

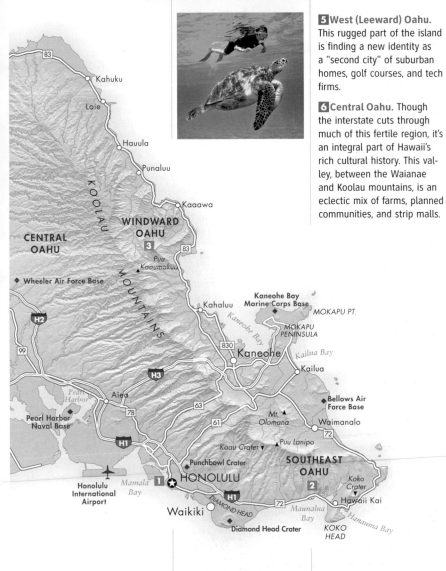

5 West (Leeward) Oahu.
This rugged part of the island
is finding a new identity as
a "second city" of suburban
homes, golf courses, and tech
firms.

6 Central Oahu. Though
the interstate cuts through
much of this fertile region, it's
an integral part of Hawaii's
rich cultural history. This valley, between the Waianae
and Koolau mountains, is an
eclectic mix of farms, planned
communities, and strip malls.

83

Kahuku

Laie

Hauula

Punaluu

Kaaawa

**WINDWARD
OAHU**

K O O L A U

3

83

Puu
Kaaumakua

**CENTRAL
OAHU**

M
O
U
N
T
A
I
N
S

◆ Wheeler Air Force Base

Kahaluu

Kaneohe Bay
Marine Corps Base ◆

MOKAPU PT.

H2

*MOKAPU
PENINSULA*

99

830

Kaneohe

Kaneohe Bay

Kailua Bay

H3

Kailua

*Pearl
Harbor*

Aiea

78

63

61

Mt.
Olomana ▲

◆ **Bellows Air
Force Base**

**Pearl Harbor
Naval Base**

Kaau Crater ▼

Puu Lanipo ▲

Waimanalo

72

H1

Punchbowl Crater ▼

**SOUTHEAST
OAHU**

*Koko
Crater*

2

HONOLULU

1 ✪

◆ **Honolulu
International
Airport**

*Mamala
Bay*

Hawaii Kai

DIAMOND HEAD

H1

72

Waikiki

*Maunalua
Bay*

Hanauma Bay

Diamond Head Crater

*KOKO
HEAD*

OAHU AND HAWAII TODAY

Nicknamed "The Gathering Place," Oahu is the third-largest Hawaiian island and has 75% of the state's population. Honolulu is the perfect place to experience the state's indigenous culture, the hundred years of immigration that resulted in today's blended society, and the tradition of aloha. The museums and historic and cultural sites will ground you, at least a bit, in Hawaii's history. Honolulu has everything from award-winning restaurants to farmers' markets, from legendary surf breaks to trendy nightclubs. But Oahu is not just Honolulu and Waikiki. It's looping mountain trails on the western Waianae and eastern Koolau ranges. It's monster waves breaking on the golden beaches of the North Shore. It's country stores and beaches where turtles are your swimming companions.

Hawaiian culture and tradition here have experienced a renaissance over the last few decades. There's a real effort to revive traditions and to respect history as the Islands go through major changes. New developments often have a Hawaiian cultural expert on staff to ensure cultural sensitivity and to educate newcomers.

Nonetheless, development remains a huge issue for all Islanders—land prices are skyrocketing, putting many areas out of reach for the native population. Traffic is becoming a problem on roads that were not designed to accommodate all the new drivers, and the Islands' limited natural resources are being seriously tapped. The government, though sluggish to respond at first, is trying to make development in Hawaii as sustainable as possible.

Sustainability

Although sustainability is an effective buzzword and authentic direction for the Islands' dining establishments, 90% of Hawaii's food and energy is imported.

Most of the land was used for mono-cropping of pineapple or sugarcane, both of which have all but vanished. Sugarcane is now produced in only two plants on Kauai and Maui, while pineapple production has dropped precipitously. Dole, once the largest pineapple company in Hawaii, closed its plants in 1991, and after 90 years, Del Monte stopped pineapple production in 2008. The next year, Maui Land and Pineapple Company also ceased its Maui Gold pineapple operation, although in early 2010 a group of executives took over one third of the land and created a new company. Low cost of labor and transportation from Latin American and Southeast Asian pineapple producers are factors contributing to the industry's demise in Hawaii. Although this proves daunting, it also sets the stage for great agricultural change to be explored.

Back-to-Basics Agriculture

Emulating how the Hawaiian ancestors lived and returning to their simple ways of growing and sharing a variety of foods has become a statewide initiative. Hawaii has the natural conditions and talent to produce far more diversity in agriculture than it currently does.

The seed of this movement thrives through various farmers' markets and partnerships between restaurants and local farmers. Localized efforts such as the Hawaii Farm Bureau Federation are collectively leading the organic and sustainable agricultural renaissance. From home-cooked meals to casual plate lunches to fine-dining cuisine, these sustainable trailblazers enrich the culinary tapestry of Hawaii and uplift the Islands' overall quality of life.

Tourism and the Economy

The over-$10 billion tourism industry represents a third of Hawaii's state income. Naturally, this dependency causes economic hardship as the financial meltdown of recent years affects tourists' ability to visit and spend.

One way the industry has changed has been to adopt more eco-conscious practices, as many Hawaiians feel that development shouldn't happen without regard for impact to local communities and their natural environment.

Belief that an industry based on the Hawaiians' *aloha* should protect, promote, and empower local culture and provide more entrepreneurial opportunities for local people has become more important to tourism businesses. More companies are incorporating authentic Hawaiiana in their programs and aim not only to provide a commercially viable tour but also to ensure that the visitor leaves feeling connected to his or her host.

The concept of *kuleana*, a word for both privilege and responsibility, is upheld. Having the privilege to live in such a sublime place comes with the responsibility to protect it.

Sovereignty

Political issues of sovereignty continue to divide Native Hawaiians, who have formed myriad organizations, each operating with a separate agenda and lacking one collectively defined goal. Ranging from achieving complete independence to solidifying a nation within a nation, existing sovereignty models remain fractured and their future unresolved.

The introduction of the Native Hawaiian Government Reorganization Act of 2009 attempts to set up a legal framework in which Native Hawaiians can attain federal recognition and coexist as a self-governed entity. Also known as the Akaka Bill after Senator Daniel Akaka of Hawaii, this pending bill has been presented before Congress and is still awaiting a vote at the time of this writing.

Rise of Hawaiian Pride

After Hawaii became a state in 1959, a process of Americanization began. Traditions were duly silenced in the name of citizenship. Teaching Hawaiian language was banned from schools and children were distanced from their local customs.

But Hawaiians are resilient people, and with the rise of the civil rights movement they began to reflect on their own national identity, bringing an astonishing renaissance of the Hawaiian culture to fruition.

The people rediscovered language, hula, chanting, and even the traditional Polynesian arts of canoe building and wayfinding (navigation by the stars without use of instruments). This cultural resurrection is now firmly established in today's Hawaiian culture, with a palpable pride that exudes from Hawaiians young and old.

The election of President Barack Obama definitely increased Hawaiian pride and inspired a ubiquitous hope for a better future. The president's strong connection and commitment to Hawaiian values of diversity, spirituality, family, and conservation have restored confidence that Hawaii can inspire a more peaceful, tolerant, and environmentally conscious world.

OAHU PLANNER

When You Arrive

Honolulu International Airport is 20 minutes (40 during rush hour) from Waikiki. Car-rental companies have booths at baggage claim; shuttle buses then take you to the car pickup areas. An inefficient airport taxi system requires you to line up to a taxi wrangler who radios for cars (about $35–$40 to Waikiki). Other options include the city's reliable bus system ($2.50) with stops throughout Honolulu and Waikiki, or the Roberts Hawaii shuttle ($13), which transports you to any hotel in Waikiki. Ask taxi drivers to take Interstate H1, not Nimitz Highway, or your introduction to paradise will be via Honolulu's industrial back side.

Visitor Information

Hawaii Visitors and Convention Bureau ⊠ *2270 Kalakaua Ave., Suite 801, Waikiki, Honolulu* ☏ *800/464–2924 for brochures* ⊕ *www.gohawaii.com.*

Getting Here and Around

You can get away without renting a car if you plan on staying in Waikiki. But if you want to explore the rest of the island, there's no substitute for having your own wheels. Avoid the obvious tourist cars—candy-colored convertibles, for example—and never leave anything valuable inside, even if you locked the car. Get a portable GPS navigator, as Oahu's streets can be confusing.

Reserve your vehicle in advance, especially when traveling during the Christmas holidays and summer breaks. This will not only ensure that you get a car but also that you get the best rates. ⇨ *See "Travel Smart Oahu" for more information on renting a car and driving.*

Island Driving Times

Don't let maps fool you. While the distance between Waikiki and, say, the North Shore is roughly 40 miles, it may take more than an hour to get there, thanks to heavy traffic, construction, and other factors. Many of Oahu's main roads are a single lane in each direction, with no alternate routes. So if you're stuck behind a slow-moving vehicle, you may have no other choice than to hope it turns soon. Heavy traffic moving toward downtown can begin as early as 6 am, with after-work traffic starting at 3 pm.

Here are some average driving times—without traffic—that will help you plan your excursions.

Waikiki to Ko Olina	1 hour
Waikiki to Haleiwa	45 minutes
Waikiki to Hawaii Kai	25 minutes
Waikiki to Kailua	30 minutes
Waikiki to downtown Honolulu	10 minutes
Waikiki to airport	25 minutes
Kaneohe to Turtle Bay	1 hour
Hawaii Kai to Kailua	25 minutes
Haleiwa to Turtle Bay	20 minutes

Money-Saving Tips

A vacation to Hawaii doesn't have to break the bank. Take advantage of coupons in the free publications stacked at the airport and in racks all over Waikiki. Online sources like Groupon or Living Social offer discounted rates for everything from dinner cruises to massages.

Access to beaches and most hiking trails on the island is free to the public. For inexpensive fresh fruit and produce, check out farmers' markets and farm stands along the road—they'll often let you try before you buy.

For cheap and quick lunches, consider a food truck. Part of the culinary landscape of Oahu for generations, these lunch wagons—which rove around downtown and other areas—charge substantially less than restaurants.

Dining and Lodging on Oahu

If you want to see Hawaii's cultural blending, look no further than its cuisine. From traditional local-style plate lunches to sushi bars to high-end steak houses, there's no shortage of interesting flavors and cuisines.

Whether you're looking for a quick snack or a multicourse meal, turn to Chapter 8 to find the best eating experiences the island has to offer. And bring your appetite.

Choosing vacation lodging is a tough decision, but fret not—our expert writers and editors have done most of the legwork.

Looking for a tropical forest retreat, a luxurious resort, or a private vacation rental? Chapter 9 will give you all the details you need to book a place that suits your style.
Quick tips: Reserve your room far in advance. Be sure to ask about discounts and special packages. (Some hotel Web sites have Internet-only deals).

Seeing Pearl Harbor 1

Pearl Harbor is a must-see for many, but there are things to know before you go.

Consider whether you want to see only the USS *Arizona* Memorial, or the USS *Bowfin* and USS *Missouri* as well. Allow approximately an hour and 15 minutes for the USS *Arizona* tour, which includes a 23-minute documentary of the Pearl Harbor attack and a ferry ride to the memorial itself.

Plan to arrive early—tickets for the USS *Arizona* Memorial are free and given out on a first-come, first-served basis. They can disappear within an hour. Take some time to enjoy the newly upgraded visitor center, which houses two exhibits using state-of-the-art technology to tell the story of the attack on December 7, 1941.

Strict security measures prohibit purses, backpacks, diaper bags, and camera cases (although cameras are allowed). Strollers are allowed in the visitor center but not in the theaters or on the shuttle boats. Baggage lockers are available for a small fee. Also, don't forget your ID.

Children under four years of age are not allowed on the USS *Bowfin* for safety reasons, and may not enjoy the crowds or waiting in line at other sights.

Older kids are likely to find the more experiential, hands-on history of the USS *Bowfin* and USS *Missouri* memorable.

For more information, visit ⊕ www.nps.gov/valr.

OAHU
TOP ATTRACTIONS

That Beach

(A) Kailua is the beach you came to Hawaii for—and the reason why many have never left. This popular stretch of white, sandy beach on Oahu's windward side is wide and inviting, with several small offshore islands perfect for exploring on kayaks. The waves are gentle and forgiving, and the beach is within walking distance of small convenience stores and friendly eateries.

Finding Shangri La

(B) Built atop the cliffs of Diamond Head, Shangri La is the lavish oceanfront home of American philanthropist Doris Duke. It houses an extensive collection of Islamic art, much of which was collected during her world travels. But the sprawling 5-acre estate—with its sweeping views, exotic gardens, and 75-foot saltwater pool—is an architectural wonder in its own right. It's open to the public for small group tours.

Oahu After Hours

(C) Nightlife in Hawaii may conjure up visions of mai tais by the hotel pool at sunset. But in the multicultural metropolis of Honolulu, there's so much more to it than that. Sip one of 17 different sparkling wines at Brasserie Du Vin in downtown Honolulu. Nosh on deep-fried potato cakes at Genius Lounge Sake Bar & Grill in Waikiki. Sing karaoke and munch on fried pork chops at the Side Street Inn near the Ala Moana Center. Or listen to jazz with a glass of wine—and maybe some artichoke-and-crabmeat fondue on crostini—at Formaggio Wine Bar.

Hiking to Kaena Point

(D) On the westernmost point of the island, magical Kaena Point is one of the last intact dune ecosystems in the Hawaiian Islands and is home to a growing population of wedge-tailed shearwaters and other rare and endangered seabirds. Hawaiian green sea turtles and monk seals often rest along the shore, and in winter you can often see migrating humpback whales offshore. While you can't access all 850 acres of this culturally significant place—this area has long been known as the leaping place of souls—you can walk or bike along the coastline. A trek through this protected area may change your mind about Oahu being "too crowded."

Catching a Wave

(E) Since the turn of the 20th century, Waikiki beach boys like the famed Duke Kahanamoku have been teaching visitors how to ride the waves. Even today you can walk the beach along Kalakaua Avenue and find a tanned instructor to get you up on your board. Waikiki is one of the best spots to catch that first wave. The surf here is rolling and gentle (except during south swells in the summer). You might forget the name of the break, but you'll never forget the feeling of catching that first wave.

Exploring Chinatown

(F) Over the past few years, Chinatown has been transformed into the center of Oahu's arts scene. This vibrant neighborhood, which pours into downtown Honolulu, boasts art galleries, eclectic restaurants, hip bars, trendy boutiques, and the historic Hawaii Theatre. There are a few guided tours of the cultural attractions, but you can easily wander the area on your own. Every first Friday of the month there's a block party of sorts, when art galleries and restaurants stay open late and bars feature live music. It's well worth the cab fare.

Hula with Heart

(G) Professional hula dancers—the ones in poolside hotel shows and dinner extravaganzas—are perfection: hands like undulating waves, smiles that never waiver. But if you want to experience hula with heart, scan the newspapers for a hula school fundraiser or ask the activities desk about local festivals. You may see some missteps and bumbles, but you'll also experience different hula styles and hear songs and chants deeply rooted in the culture, all the while surrounded by the scents of a hundred homemade lei.

A Sail on the Wild Side

(H) Who wouldn't want these memory snapshots to take home: the unblinking and seemingly amused eye of a spinner dolphin as it arcs through the wake of the catamaran in which you're riding; the undulating form of an endangered Hawaiian green sea turtle swimming below you; the slap and splash and whoosh of a humpback whale breaching in full view on indigo seas. Wild Side Specialty Tours can't promise these specific encounters, but their ecologically conscious daily excursions in a quiet, uncrowded catamaran do guarantee good memories.

A Day on the North Shore

(I) Head north along Oahu's eastern coastline toward the famed North Shore, where professional surfers nab some of the world's best waves. You'll pass through quaint residential areas and fruit stands on the side of the road. (Stop and buy bananas in Kahuku.) While you'll be tempted to try one of the famous shrimp trucks—plates of garlic shrimp hover around $20—consider the variety of eats on the North Shore, from old-school bakeries to burger joints to sit-down restaurants. In Haleiwa town, cool off at Matsumoto Shave Ice or Aoki's Shave Ice. If you're visiting in the summer, head to Three Tables or Shark's Cove for some stellar snorkeling. Or spend a lazy day at Sunset Beach, good book optional.

A Trip to Japan

(J) Little known outside Oahu's growing community of Japanese nationals is a class of small restaurant-bars called *izakaya,* or

Japanese taverns. Grilled, fried, and raw dishes are perfect with beer, sake, or *shochu* (a liquor distilled from barley, sweet potato, or rice). Even newer on the scene are *okonomi*, hip spots that specialize in Osaka-style grilled omelets and potent Japanese spirits. Both are like a visit to Japan, minus the long plane ride. They are a must-notch in any foodie's belt.

A Plate-Lunch Picnic

(K) Grab a plate lunch—typically meat with two scoops of macaroni salad and two scoops of white rice—and head to the nearest beach or park. Eat, *talk story* (local slang for chatting), and relax. You can find plate lunches at restaurants or from lunch wagons all over town. Some options: Rainbow Drive-In on Kapahulu Avenue; Sugoi on Kalani Street in Kapalama; Dean's Drive-Inn in Kaneohe; and Diamond Head Market and Grill near Kapiolani Park.

Walking in the Rain Forest or to a Waterfall

(L) Wend your way through the hillside neighborhood of Aiea, northwest of Honolulu, and suddenly you're in a cool, green park, scented with astringent eucalyptus. This is the 3½-mile Aiea Loop Trail, and if you're committed to squeezing a hike into a short Oahu stay, you couldn't do better for glimpses of hidden valleys and the experience of an island forest.

(M) If waterfalls are more your speed, then head straight to the back of Manoa Valley, 3 miles *mauka* (toward the mountains from Waikiki) and you'll find a 1½-mile trail along a well-worn path following Manoa stream through native trees and flowers to the Manoa Falls.

GREAT ITINERARIES

To experience even a fraction of Oahu's charms, you need a minimum of four days and a bus pass. Five days and a car is better: Waikiki is at least a day, Honolulu and Chinatown another, Pearl Harbor the better part of another. Each of the rural sections can swallow a day each, just for driving, sightseeing, and stopping to eat. And that's before you've taken a surf lesson, hung from a parasail, hiked a loop trail, or visited a botanical garden. The following itineraries will take you to our favorite spots on the island.

First Day in Waikiki

You'll be up at dawn due to the time change and dead on your feet by afternoon due to jet lag. Have a dawn swim, change into walking gear, and head east along Kalakaua Avenue to Monsarrat Avenue toward Diamond Head. Either climb to the summit (about 1½ hours round-trip) or enjoy the view from the lookout. After lunch—there are plenty of options along Monsarrat—take a nap in the shade, do some shopping, or visit the nearby East Honolulu neighborhoods of Moiliili and Kaimuki, rife with small shops and quaint restaurants. End the day with an early and inexpensive dinner at one of these neighborhood spots.

Southeast and Windward Exploring

For sand, sun, and surf, follow H1 east to the keyhole-shaped Hanauma Bay for picture-perfect snorkeling, then round the southeast tip of the island with its windswept cliffs and the famous Halona Blowhole. Watch bodysurfers at Sandy Beach or walk up the trail leading to the Makapuu Point Lighthouse. If you like, stop in at Sea Life Park. In Waimanalo, stop for local-style plate lunch or punch on through to Kailua, where there's intriguing shopping and good eating.

Lounge at Lanikai Beach until sunset, then grab dinner at one of the area's many restaurants.

The North Shore

Hit H1 westbound and then H2 to get to the North Shore. You'll pass through pineapple fields before dropping down a scenic winding road to Waialua and Haleiwa. Stop in Haleiwa town to shop, enjoy shave ice, and pick up a guided dive or snorkel trip. On winding Kamehameha Highway, stop at famous big-wave beaches, take a dip in a cove with a turtle, and buy fresh island fruit from roadside stands.

Pearl Harbor

Pearl Harbor is almost an all-day investment. Be on the grounds by 7:30 am to line up for USS *Arizona* Memorial tickets. Clamber all over the USS *Bowfin* submarine. Finally, take the free trolley to see the "Mighty Mo" battleship. If it's Wednesday, Saturday, or Sunday, make the five-minute drive *mauka* (toward the mountains) for bargain-basement shopping at the sprawling Aloha Stadium Swap Meet.

Town Time

If you are interested in history, devote a day to Honolulu's historic sites. Downtown, see Iolani Palace, the Kamehameha Statue, and Kawaiahao Church. A few blocks east, explore Chinatown, gilded Kuan Yin Temple, and artsy Nuuanu with its galleries. On the water is the informative Hawaii Maritime Center. Hop west on H1 to the Bishop Museum, the state's anthropological and archaeological center. And 1 mile up Pali Highway is Queen Emma Summer Palace, whose shady grounds were a royal retreat. The Foster Botanical Garden is worth a visit for plant lovers.

WHEN TO GO

Long days of sunshine and fairly mild year-round temperatures make Hawaii an all-season destination. Most resort areas are at sea level, with average afternoon temperatures of 75°F to 80°F during the coldest months of December and January; during the hottest months of August and September, the temperature often reaches 90°F. Higher upcountry elevations typically have cooler and often misty conditions. Only at mountain summits does it reach freezing.

Moist trade winds drop their precipitation on the north and east sides of the Islands, creating tropical climates, whereas the south and west sides remain hot and dry with desertlike conditions. Rainfall can be high in winter, particularly on the north and east shores.

Most travelers head to the Islands in winter, specifically from mid-December through mid-April. This high season means that fewer travel bargains are available; room rates average 10% to 15% higher during this season than the rest of the year.

Winter on Oahu is whales (November through March) and waves (surf competitions December through February). In September, the Aloha Festivals celebrate island culture. In summer, the Islands honor the king who made them a nation, Kamehameha I, on June 11, with parades and events on all islands. Oahu's one-of-a-kind Pan-Pacific Festival follows the Kamehameha Day, bringing together hundreds of performers from Japan's seasonal celebrations. And summer swells bring waves (and surf contests) to southern beaches.

Hawaiian Holidays

If you happen to be in the Islands on March 26 or June 11, you'll notice light traffic and busy beaches—these are state holidays not celebrated anywhere else. March 26 recognizes the birthday of Prince Jonah Kuhio Kalanianaole, a member of the royal line who served as a delegate to Congress and spearheaded the effort to set aside homelands for Hawaiian people. June 11 honors the first island-wide monarch, Kamehameha I; locals drape his statues with lei and stage elaborate parades. May 1 isn't an official holiday, but it's the day when schools and civic groups celebrate the quintessential Island gift, the flower lei, with lei-making contests and pageants. Statehood Day is celebrated on the third Friday in August (admission to the Union was August 21, 1959). Most Japanese and Chinese holidays are widely observed. On Chinese New Year, homes and businesses sprout bright-red good-luck mottoes, lions dance in the streets, and everybody eats *gau* (steamed pudding) and *jai* (vegetarian stew). Good Friday is a state holiday in spring, a favorite for family picnics.

Climate

The following are average maximum and minimum temperatures for Honolulu; the temperatures throughout the Hawaiian Islands are similar.

°F   HONOLULU, O'AHU   °C

KIDS AND FAMILIES

With dozens of adventures, discoveries, and fun-filled beach days, Hawaii is a blast for kids of all ages. Even better, the things to do here do not appeal only to small fry. The entire family, parents included, will enjoy surfing, discovering a waterfall in the rain forest, and snorkeling with sea turtles. And there are plenty of organized activities for kids that will free parents' time for a few romantic beach strolls.

Choosing a Place to Stay

Resorts: All the big resorts make kids' programs a priority, and it shows. When you are booking your room, ask about *keiki* (children's) menus at restaurants, free activities on the property, and pools and water parks built specifically for the younger set.

In Waikiki, your best bet for kids is the Hilton Hawaiian Village, where there's a large beach and loads of kids' programs. Another good choice is the Waikiki Beach Marriott Resort, which has a variety of programs for kids as well. Other options include the Waikiki Beach Hotel and the Sheraton Princess Kaiulani.

Condos: Condo and vacation rentals are a fantastic value for families vacationing in Hawaii. You can cook your own food, which is cheaper than eating out and sometimes easier (especially if you have a finicky eater in your group), and you'll get twice the space of a hotel room for about a quarter of the price. If you decide to go the condo route, be sure to ask about the size of the complex's pool (some try to pawn off a tiny soaking tub as a pool) and whether barbecues are available. One of the best parts of staying in your own place is having a sunset family barbecue by the pool or overlooking the ocean.

For the ultimate condo experience on Oahu, Marriott's Ko Olina Beach Club can't be beat. Sheltered beaches, four pools, barbecues, and children's play areas, combined with large kitchens and an on-site grocery store make this the best condo option for families. In Waikiki, the Castle Waikiki Shore is the only beachfront condo property. Outrigger Luana Waikiki offers barbecues, a pool, and recreational areas near Fort DeRussy on Waikiki Beach.

Ocean Activities

Hawaii is all about getting your kids outside—away from TV and video games. And who could resist the turquoise water, the promise of spotting dolphins or whales, or the fun of body boarding or surfing?

On the Beach: Most people like being in the water, but toddlers and school-age kids tend to be especially enamored of it. The swimming pool at your condo or hotel is always an option, but don't be afraid to hit the beach with a little one in tow. There are several beaches in Hawaii that are nearly as safe as a pool—completely protected bays with pleasant white-sand beaches and staffed by lifeguards. As always, use your judgment, and heed all posted signs and warnings.

In Waikiki, your best bets for young children are Kuhio Beach Park and Fort DeRussy Beach Park. Both are protected from a strong shore break and offer a wide stretch of sand. (And lifeguards are on duty.) On the windward side, your best bets are Kailua Beach Park, with its shady trees and good bathroom and shower facilities, or laid-back Lanikai Beach. North Shore beaches are recommended for children only in the summer months, and of these, Waimea Bay, with its wide stretch of sand and good facilities, ranks as the best for kids. (Don't let your kids jump off the rock—a popular but very dangerous pastime.) On the leeward side of the island, KoOlina's protected coves are great for families with small children.

On the Waves: Surf lessons are a great idea for older kids, especially if mom and dad want a little quiet time. Beginner lessons are always on safe and easy waves and last anywhere from two to four hours.

Waikiki is *the* place for everyone to learn to surf, including kids. Some hotels, including the Waikiki Beach Marriott Resort & Spa, offer in-house surf schools. Or, for a unique experience, try Hawaiian Fire. These off-duty Honolulu firefighters teach water safety in addition to surfing in their two-hour lessons near Barber's Point (starting at $99).

The Underwater World: If your kids are ready to try snorkeling, Hawaii is a great place to introduce them to the underwater world. Even without the mask and snorkel, they'll be able to see colorful fish darting around coral reefs, and they may also spot endangered Hawaiian green sea turtles and dolphins at many of the island beaches.

On Oahu the quintessential snorkeling experience can be had at Hanauma Bay. After viewing an educational film about Hawaii's underwater world, and descending into a half-submerged volcano, kids have an opportunity not only to see hundreds of species of fish in protected waters but to enjoy a wide stretch of beach as well. In summer months only, Shark's Cove on the North Shore is an interesting experience for older kids who have learned the basics of snorkeling at Hanauma Bay.

Land Activities

In addition to beach experiences, Hawaii has rain forests, botanical gardens, numerous aquariums (Oahu and Maui take the cake), and even petting zoos and hands-on children's museums that will keep your kids entertained and out of the sun for a day.

Oahu is fortunate to have the largest variety of land-based experiences in the Islands. Kids can visit the Honolulu Zoo for a sleepover, touch fishy friends at the Waikiki Aquarium, help in a dolphin training session at Sea Life Park, or even learn to husk a coconut at the Polynesian Culture Center. For kids who need some room to roam, Hoomaluhia Botanical Garden offers wide-open spaces and a pond complete with ducks, while Kualoa Ranch is the place for horseback riding.

After Dark

At night, younger kids get a kick out of luau, and many of the shows incorporate young audience members, adding to the fun. The older kids might find it all a bit lame, but there are a handful of new shows in the Islands that are more modern, incorporating acrobatics, lively music, and fire dancers. If you're planning on hitting a luau with a teen in tow, we highly recommend going the modern route.

OAHU'S BEST BEACHES

The best thing about Oahu's beautiful beaches? Like snowflakes, no two are exactly alike. Some are wide, others are narrow. Some are protected by fringing reefs, and others have huge waves breaking right on shore. *All* are special.

Here are some of our favorite stretches of sand, where you can make your home away from home:

Best for Families

KoOlina, West (Leeward) Oahu. Four man-made lagoons are totally protected and offer great grassy spots to grab a nap. Plus, Disney's new resort is nearby if the kids get restless and need a Mickey fix.

White Plains, West (Leeward) Oahu. Not only are there are bathrooms, barbecues, and picnic tables here—there are even sleeping seals. What more could a kid want?

Best for Big Waves

Waimea Bay, the North Shore. In summer, snorkeling is great at this beach. But in winter, surf's up, so be careful if you don't know what you're doing. Pros flock here for contests—"the Eddie," a competition honoring big-wave-surfer Eddie Aikau, is held here only when waves are at least 20 feet—and fans flock to watch. Come early in the morning when there are waves and claim your seat on the dunes.

Haleiwa Alii Beach Park, the North Shore. The Vans Triple Crown of Surfing kicks off at this beach in November, and the small town of Haleiwa is a surf mecca. From board shops to galleries devoted to inside-the-tube photos, you'll experience the full range of surf lifestyle.

Best for Flying a Kite

Sandy Beach, Southeast Oahu. If you're afraid you'll break your neck bodysurfing in the waves here, retire to the shoreline and watch kites perform acrobatics in the gusts.

Kualoa Regional Park, Windward Oahu. This expansive park gives campers and others plenty of space to spread out and take advantage of the wind with two-handed kites. Chinaman's Hat, an offshore island, provides a great backdrop.

Best for Soft Sand

Ala Moana Beach Park, Honolulu. Just steps away from food and shopping outlets, this beach offers extraordinarily fine sand, though there's little shade. When you get warm, the equally smooth water beckons.

Lanikai Beach Park, Windward Oahu. This spot and adjacent Kailua Beach Park have powdery white sand and some trees for shade. But good luck finding a parking spot on weekends.

Best for Watching the Sun Rise and Set

Bellows Beach, Southeast Oahu (Sunrise). Try camping out (weekends only) at this east-ward-facing beach so you can catch the earliest rays. Nearby Waimanalo Beach Park offers another option.

Sunset Beach, the North Shore (Sunset). The name says it all. From here, you can see all the way down the North Shore toward Kaena Point in the west, and enjoy the last rays before the sun dips below the horizon.

OAHU'S BEST OUTDOOR ADVENTURES

In a place surrounded by the ocean, water sports abound. Surfing. Snorkeling. Scuba diving. Hawaii has it all—and more. But that's just the sea. Interior mountains and valleys offer a never-ending stream of other outdoor adventures. Here are our picks for the best water and land adventures.

Take in the View atop Diamond Head

You won't get off the beaten path on this hike, but the well-worn route to the top of Hawaii's most famous crater will get your heart racing, especially when you reach the steep stairs near the top. The views are worth the climb—on clear days you'll gaze over Honolulu, Waikiki, and the Pacific Ocean. Bring water, as this trail is hot and sunny.

Dive and Snorkel at Shark's Cove

Some of the best things in life require a wait. That's the case with Shark's Cove—you have to wait for summer until it's safe to enter the water and swim with an amazing array of marine life, thanks to the large boulders and coral heads dotting the seafloor and forming small caves and ledges. This is both a spectacular shore dive and snorkeling destination in one—perfect for the diver–snorkeler couple.

Bike the Aiea Loop Trail

This 4.5-mile, single-track loop trail offers some of the most fun mountain biking in central Oahu. Although it's listed as an intermediate trail, some sections are a bit technical, with steep drop-offs. We recommend it for the weekend warrior who has a bit more experience. Caution: do not attempt in wet weather.

Golf at Luana Hills Country Club

Carved out of the middle of a tropical rain forest, this peaceful setting offers an antidote to the hustle and bustle of Waikiki. Bring your A game and a full bag, because club selection is key here. You'll want to hit every fairway.

Learn to Surf at Waikiki Beach

You've heard the age-old saying that goes, "When in Rome, do as the Romans do"? Well, when in Hawaii, surf. Surfing was once reserved for *alii* (royalty), but today it knows no class barrier. And there is no better place to learn than Waikiki, with its long and gentle rolling swells.

Hike to Kaena Point

For a raw and rugged look at Oahu's coastline, head to hot, dry Kaena Point. The 5-mile round-trip hike—you can also bike it—ends at the westernmost tip of the island, known in Hawaiian culture as the jumping-off point for souls departing this world for the next. Today, Laysan albatrosses nest here.

Watch Monster Waves at Waimea Bay

This is the beach that makes Hawaii famous every winter when monster waves and the world's best surfers roll in. Show up to watch, not partake. If the rest of us want to get in the water here, we have to wait until summer when the safe onshore break is great for novice bodysurfers.

THE HAWAIIAN ISLANDS

Oahu. The state's capital, Honolulu, is on Oahu; this is the center of Hawaii's economy and by far the most populated island in the chain—976,000 residents add up to 71% of the state's population. At 597 square miles Oahu is the third largest island in the chain; the majority of residents live in or around Honolulu, so the rest of the island still fits neatly into the tropical, untouched vision of Hawaii. Situated southeast of Kauai and northwest of Maui, Oahu is a central location for island hopping. Pearl Harbor, iconic Waikiki Beach, and surfing contests on the legendary North Shore are all here.

Maui. The second-largest island in the chain, Maui is northwest of the Big Island and close enough to be visible from its beaches on a clear day. The island's 729 square miles are home to only 150,000 people but host more than 2 million tourists every year. With its restaurants and lively nightlife, Maui is the only island that competes with Oahu in terms of entertainment; its charm lies in the fact that although entertainment is available, Maui's towns still feel like island villages compared to the heaving modern city of Honolulu.

Hawaii (The Big Island). The Big Island has the second-largest population of the Islands (almost 190,000) but feels sparsely settled due to its size. It's 4,038 square miles and growing—all the other Islands could fit onto the Big Island and there would still be room left over. The southernmost island in the chain (slightly southeast of Maui), the Big Island is home to Kilauea, the most active volcano on the planet. It percolates within Volcanoes National Park, which draws nearly 3 million visitors every year.

Kauai. The northernmost island in the chain (northwest of Oahu), Kauai is, at approximately 622 square miles, the fourth largest of all the Islands and the least populated of the larger Islands, with 68,000 residents. Known as the Garden Isle, this island is home to lush botanical gardens as well as the stunning Napali Coast and Waimea Canyon. The island is a favorite with honeymooners and others wanting to get away from it all—lush and peaceful, it's the perfect escape from the modern world.

Molokai. North of Lanai and Maui, and east of Oahu, Molokai is Hawaii's fifth-largest island, encompassing 260 square miles. On a clear night, the lights of Honolulu are visible from Molokai's western shore. Molokai is sparsely populated, with about 7,300 residents, the majority of whom are Native Hawaiians. Most of the island's 79,000 annual visitors travel from Maui or Oahu to spend the day exploring its beaches, cliffs, and former leper colony on Kalaupapa Peninsula.

Lanai. Lying just off Maui's western coast, Lanai looks nothing like its sister Islands, with pine trees and deserts in place of palm trees and beaches. Still, the tiny 140-square-mile island is home to about 3,200 residents and draws an average of 75,000 visitors each year to two resorts (one in the mountains and one at the shore), both operated by Four Seasons, and the small, 11-room Hotel Lanai.

Hawaii's Geology

The Hawaiian Islands comprise more than just the islands inhabited and visited by humans. A total of 19 islands and atolls constitute the State of Hawaii, with a total landmass of 6,423.4 square miles.

The Islands are actually exposed peaks of a submersed mountain range called the Hawaiian Ridge-Emperor Seamounts chain. The range was formed as the Pacific plate moves very slowly (around 32 miles every million years—or about as much as your fingernails grow in one year) over a hot spot in the Earth's mantle. Because the plate moves northwestwardly, the Islands in the northwest portion of the archipelago (chain) are older, which is also why they're smaller—they have been eroding longer and have actually sunk back into the sea floor.

The Big Island is the youngest, and thus the largest, island in the chain. It is built from five different volcanoes, including Mauna Loa, which is the largest mountain on the planet (when measured from the bottom of the sea floor). Mauna Loa and Kilauea are the only Hawaiian volcanoes still erupting with any sort of frequency. Mauna Loa last erupted in 1984. Kilauea has been continuously erupting since 1983.

Mauna Kea (Big Island), Hualalai (Big Island), and Haleakala (Maui) are all in what's called the post-shield-building stage of volcanic development—eruptions decrease steadily for up to a million years before ceasing entirely. Kohala (Big Island), Lanai (Lanai), and Waianae (Oahu) are considered extinct volcanoes, in the erosional stage of development; Koolau (Oahu) and West Maui (Maui) volcanoes are extinct volcanoes in the rejuvenation stage—after lying dormant for hundreds of thousands of years, they began erupting again, but only once every several thousand years.

There is currently an active undersea volcano to the south and east of the Big Island called Kamaehu that has been erupting regularly. If it continues its current pattern, it should breach the ocean's surface in tens of thousands of years.

Hawaii's Flora and Fauna

More than 90% of native Hawaiian flora and fauna are endemic (they evolved into unique species here), like the koa tree and the yellow hibiscus. Long-dormant volcanic craters are perfect hiding places for rare native plants. The silversword, a rare cousin of the sunflower, grows on Hawaii's three tallest peaks: Haleakala, Mauna Kea, and Mauna Loa, and nowhere else on Earth. Ohia trees—thought to be the favorite of Pele, the volcano goddess—bury their roots in fields of once-molten lava, and one variety sprouts ruby pom-pom–like lehua blossoms. The deep yellow petals of ilima (once reserved for royalty) are tiny discs, which make elegant lei.

But most of the plants you see while walking around aren't Hawaiian at all and came from Tahitian, Samoan, or European visitors. Plumeria is ubiquitous; alien orchids run rampant on the Big Island; bright orange relatives of the ilima light up the mountains of Oahu. Though these flowers are not native, they give the Hawaiian lei their color and fragrance.

Hawaii's state bird, the nene goose, is making a comeback from its former endangered status. It roams freely in parts of Maui, Kauai, and the Big Island. Rare Hawaiian monk seals breed in the northwestern Islands. With only 1,500 left in the wild, you probably won't catch many lounging on the beaches, though they have been spotted on the shores of Kauai in recent years. Spinner dolphins and sea turtles can be found off the coast of all the Islands; and every year from November to April, the humpback whales migrate past Hawaii in droves.

HAWAIIAN HISTORY

Hawaiian history is long and complex; a brief survey can put into context the ongoing renaissance of native arts and culture.

The Polynesians

Long before both Christopher Columbus and the Vikings, Polynesian seafarers set out to explore the vast stretches of the open ocean in double-hulled canoes. From western Polynesia, they traveled back and forth between Samoa, Fiji, Tahiti, the Marquesas, and the Society Isles, settling on the outer reaches of the Pacific, Hawaii, and Easter Island, as early as AD 300. The golden era of Polynesian voyaging peaked around AD 1200, after which the distant Hawaiian Islands were left to develop their own unique cultural practices and subsistence in relative isolation.

The Islands' symbiotic society was deeply intertwined with religion, mythology, science, and artistry. Ruled by an *alii*, or chief, each settlement was nestled in an *ahupuaa*, a pie-shaped land division from the uplands where the *alii* lived, through the valleys and down to the shores where the commoners resided. Everyone contributed, whether it was by building canoes, catching fish, making tools, or farming land.

A United Kingdom

When the British explorer Captain James Cook arrived in 1778, he was revered as a god. With guns and ammunition purchased from Cook, the Big Island chief, Kamehameha the Great, gained a significant advantage over the other *alii*. He united Hawaii into one kingdom in 1810, bringing an end to the frequent interisland battles that dominated Hawaiian life.

Tragically, the new kingdom was beset with troubles. Native religion was abandoned, and *kapu* (laws and regulations) were eventually abolished. The European explorers brought foreign diseases with them, and within a few short decades the Native Hawaiian population was decimated.

New laws regarding land ownership and religious practices eroded the underpinnings of pre-contact Hawaii. Each successor to the Hawaiian throne sacrificed more control over the Island kingdom. As Westerners permeated Hawaiian culture, Hawaii became more riddled with layers of racial issues, injustice, and social unrest.

Modern Hawaii

In 1893, the last Hawaiian monarch, Queen Liliuokalani, was overthrown by a group of Americans and European businessmen and government officials, aided by an armed militia. This led to the creation of the Republic of Hawaii, and it became a U.S. territory for the next 60 years. The loss of Hawaiian sovereignty and the conditions of annexation have haunted the Hawaiian people since the monarchy was deposed.

Pearl Harbor was attacked in 1941, which engaged the United States immediately into World War II. Tourism, from its beginnings in the early 1900s, flourished after the war and naturally inspired rapid real estate development in Waikiki. In 1959, Hawaii officially became the 50th state. Statehood paved the way for Hawaiians to participate in the American democratic process, which was not universally embraced by all Hawaiians. With the rise of the civil rights movement in the 1960s, Hawaiians began to reclaim their own identity, from language to hula.

HAWAII AND THE ENVIRONMENT

Sustainability—it's a word rolling off everyone's tongues these days. In a place known as the most remote island chain in the world (check your globe), Hawaii relies heavily on the outside world for food and material goods—estimates put the percentage of food arriving on container ships as high as 90. Like many places, though, efforts are afoot to change that. And you can help.

Shop Local Farms and Markets

From Kauai to the Big Island, farmers' markets are cropping up, providing a place for growers to sell fresh fruits and vegetables. There is no reason to buy imported mangoes, papayas, avocadoes, and bananas at grocery stores, when the ones you'll find at farmers' markets are not only fresher but tastier, too. Some markets allow the sale of fresh-packaged foods—salsa, say, or smoothies—and the on-site preparation of food—like pork *laulau* (pork, beef, and fish or chicken with taro, or luau, leaves wrapped and steamed in *ti* leaves) or roasted corn on the cob—so you can make your run to the market a dining experience.

Not only is the locavore movement vibrantly alive at farmers' markets, but Hawaii's top chefs are sourcing more of their produce—and fish, beef, chicken, and cheese—from local providers as well. You'll notice this movement on restaurant menus, featuring Kilauea greens or Hamakua tomatoes or locally caught mahimahi.

And while most people are familiar with Kona coffee farm tours on Big Island, if you're interested in the growing slow-food movement in Hawaii, you'll be heartened to know many farmers are opening up their operations for tours—as well as sumptuous meals.

Support Hawaii's Merchants

Food isn't the only sustainable effort in Hawaii. Buying local goods like art and jewelry, Hawaiian heritage products, crafts, music, and apparel is another way to "green up" the local economy. The County of Kauai helps make it easy with a program called **Kauai Made** (⊕ *www.kauaimade.net*), which showcases products made on Kauai, by Kauai people, using Kauai materials. The Maui Chamber of Commerce does something similar with **Made in Maui** (⊕ *www.madeinmaui.com*). Think of both as the Good Housekeeping Seal of Approval for locally made goods.

Then there are the crafty entrepreneurs who are diverting items from the trash heap by repurposing garbage. Take Oahu's **Muumuu Heaven** (⊕ *www.muumuuheaven.com*). They got their start by reincarnating vintage aloha apparel into hip new fashions.

Choose Green Tour Operators

Conscious decisions when it comes to Island activities go a long way to protecting Hawaii's natural world. The **Hawaii Ecotourism Association** (⊕ *www.hawaiiecotourism.org*) recognizes tour operators for, among other things, their environmental stewardship. The **Hawaii Tourism Authority** (⊕ *www.hawaiitourismauthority.org*) recognizes outfitters for their cultural sensitivity. Winners of these awards are good choices when it comes to guided tours and activities.

HAWAIIAN PEOPLE AND THEIR CULTURE

By 2012, Hawaii's population was more than 1.3 million with the majority of residents living on Oahu. Ten percent are Hawaiian or other Pacific Islander, almost 40% are Asian American, 9% are Latino, and about 26% Caucasian. Nearly a fifth of the population list two or more races, making Hawaii the most diverse state in the United States.

Among individuals 18 and older, about 89% finished high school, half attained some college, and 29% completed a bachelor's degree or higher.

The Role of Tradition

The kingdom of Hawaii was ruled by a spiritual class system. Although the *alii*, or chief, was believed to be the direct descendent of a deity or god, high priests, known as *kahuna*, presided over every imaginable aspect of life and *kapu* (taboos) that strictly governed the commoners.

Each part of nature and ritual was connected to a deity—Kane was the highest of all deities, symbolizing sunlight and creation; Ku was the god of war; Lono represented fertility, rainfall, music, and peace; Kanaloa was the god of the underworld or darker spirits. Probably the most well known by outsiders is Pele, the goddess of fire.

The kapu not only provided social order, they also swayed the people to act with reverence for the environment. Any abuse was met with extreme punishment, often death, as it put the land and people's *mana*, or spiritual power, in peril.

Ancient deities play a huge role in Hawaiian life today—not just in daily rituals, but in the Hawaiians' reverence for their land. Gods and goddesses tend to be associated with particular parts of the land, and most of them are connected with

many places, thanks to the body of stories built up around each.

One of the most important ways the ancient Hawaiians showed respect for their gods and goddesses was through the hula. Various forms of the hula were performed as prayers to the gods and as praise to the chiefs. Performances were taken very seriously, as a mistake was thought to invalidate the prayer, or even to offend the god or chief in question. Hula is still performed both as entertainment and as prayer; it is not uncommon for a hula performance to be included in an official government ceremony.

Who Are the Hawaiians Today?

To define the Hawaiians in a page, let alone a paragraph, is nearly impossible. Those considered to be indigenous Hawaiians are descendants of the ancient Polynesians who crossed the vast ocean and settled Hawaii. According to the government, there are Native Hawaiians or native Hawaiians (note the change in capitalization), depending on a person's background.

Federal and state agencies apply different methods to determine Hawaiian lineage, from measuring blood percentage to mapping genealogy. This has caused turmoil within the community because it excludes many who claim Hawaiian heritage. It almost guarantees that, as races intermingle, even those considered Native Hawaiian now will eventually disappear on paper, displacing generations to come.

Modern Hawaiian Culture

Perfect weather aside, Hawaii might be the warmest place anyone can visit. The Hawaii experience begins and ends with *aloha*, a word that envelops love, affection, and mercy, and has become a salutation for hello and good-bye. Broken down, *alo* means "presence" and *ha* means "breath"—the presence of breath. It's to live with love and respect for self and others with every breath. Past the manicured resorts and tour buses, aloha is a moral compass that binds all of Hawaii's people.

Hawaii is blessed with some of the most unspoiled natural wonders, and aloha extends to the land, or *aina*. Hawaiians are raised outdoors and have strong ties to nature. They realize as children that the ocean and land are the delicate sources of all life. Even ancient gods were embodied by nature, and this reverence has been passed down to present generations who believe in *kuleana,* their privilege and responsibility.

Hawaii's diverse cultures unfold in a beautiful montage of customs and arts—from music, to dance, to food. Musical genres range from slack key to *Jawaiian* (Hawaiian reggae) to *hapa-haole* (Hawaiian music with English words). From George Kahumoku's Grammy-worthy laid-back strumming to the late Iz Kamakawiwoole's "Somewhere over the Rainbow" to Jack Johnson's more mainstream tunes, contemporary Hawaiian music has definitely carved its ever-evolving niche.

The Merrie Monarch Festival is celebrating more than 50 years of worldwide hula competition and education. The fine-dining culinary scene, especially in Honolulu, has a rich tapestry of ethnic influences and talent. But the real gems are the humble hole-in-the-wall eateries that serve authentic cuisines of many ethnic origins in one plate, a deliciously mixed plate indeed.

And perhaps, the most striking quality in today's Hawaiian culture is the sense of family, or *ohana*. Sooner or later, almost everyone you meet becomes an uncle or auntie, and it is not uncommon for near strangers to be welcomed into a home as a member of the family.

Until the last century, the practice of *hanai*, in which a family essentially adopts a child, usually a grandchild, without formalities, was still prevalent. While still practiced to a somewhat lesser degree, the *hanai*, which means to feed or nourish, still resonates within most families and communities.

How to Act Like a Local

Adopting local customs is a firsthand introduction to the Islands' unique culture. So live in T-shirts and shorts. Wear cheap rubber flip-flops, but call them slippers. Wave people into your lane on the highway, and, when someone lets you in, give them a wave of thanks in return. Never, ever blow your horn, even when the pickup truck in front of you is stopped for a long session of "talk story" right in the middle of the road.

Holoholo means to go out for the fun of it—an aimless stroll, ride, or drive. "Wheah you goin', braddah?" "Oh, holoholo." It's local speak for Sunday drive, no plan, it's not the destination but the journey. Try setting out without an itinerary. Learn to *shaka*: pinky and thumb extended, middle fingers curled in, waggle sideways. Eat white rice with everything. When someone says, "Aloha!" answer, "Aloha no!" ("And a real big aloha back to you"). And, as the locals say, "No make big body" ("Try not to act like you own the place").

ONLY IN HAWAII

Traveling to Hawaii is as close as an American can get to visiting another country while staying within the United States. There's much to learn and understand about the state's indigenous culture, the hundred years of immigration that resulted in today's blended society, and the tradition of aloha that has welcomed millions of visitors over the years.

Aloha Shirt

To go to Hawaii without taking an aloha shirt home is almost sacrilege. The first aloha shirts from the 1920s and 1930s—called "silkies"—were classic canvases of art and tailored for the tourists. Popular culture caught on in the 1950s, and they became a fashion craze. With the 1960s' more subdued designs, Aloha Friday was born, and the shirt became appropriate clothing for work, play, and formal occasions. Because of its soaring popularity, cheaper and mass-produced versions became available.

Hawaiian Quilt

Although ancient Hawaiians were already known to produce fine *kapa* (bark) cloth, the actual art of quilting originated from the missionaries. Hawaiians have created designs to reflect their own aesthetic, and bold patterns evolved over time. They can be pricey because the quilts are intricately made by hand and can take years to finish. These masterpieces are considered precious heirlooms that reflect the history and beauty of Hawaii.

Popular Souvenirs

Souvenir shopping can be intimidating. There's a sea of Islands-inspired and often kitschy merchandise, so we'd like to give you a breakdown of popular and fun gifts that you might encounter and consider bringing home. If authenticity is important to you, be sure to check labels and ask shopkeepers. Museum shops are good places for authentic, Hawaiian-made souvenirs.

Fabrics. Purchased by the yard or already made into everything from napkins to bedspreads, modern Hawaiian fabrics make wonderful keepsakes.

Home accessories. Deck out your kitchen or dining room in festive luau style with bottle openers, pineapple mugs, tiki glasses, shot glasses, slipper and surfboard magnets, and salt-and-pepper shakers.

Lei and shell necklaces. From silk or polyester flower lei to kukui or puka shell necklaces, lei have been traditionally used as a welcome offering to guests (although the artificial ones are more for fun, real flowers are always preferable).

Lauhala products. *Lauhala* weaving is a traditional Hawaiian art. The leaves come from the *hala*, or *pandanus*, tree and are handwoven to create lovely gift boxes, baskets, bags, and picture frames.

Spa products. Relive your spa treatment at home with Hawaiian bath and body products, many of them manufactured with ingredients found only on the Islands.

Vintage Hawaii. You can find vintage photos, reproductions of vintage postcards or paintings, heirloom jewelry, and vintage aloha wear in many specialty stores.

Traditional Canoe

Hawaii's ancestors voyaged across 2,500 miles from Polynesia on board a double-hulled canoe with the help of the stars, the ocean swells, and the flight patterns of birds. The creation of a canoe spanned months and involved many religious ceremonies by the *kahuna kalai waa*, or high priest canoe builder. In 1973, the Polynesian Voyaging Society was founded to rediscover and preserve this ancestral tradition. Since 1975, the group has built and launched the majestic *Hokulea* and *Hawaiiloa*, which regularly travel throughout the South Pacific. In 2014, Hokulea began an historic, three-year, around-the-world voyage.

Luau

The luau's origin, which was a celebratory feast, can be traced back to the earliest Hawaiian civilizations. In the traditional luau, the taboo or *kapu* laws were very strict, requiring men and women to eat separately. However, in 1819 King Kamehameha II broke the great taboo and shared a feast with women and commoners, ushering in the modern-era luau. Today, traditional luau usually commemorate a child's first birthday, graduation, wedding, or other family occasion. They also are a Hawaiian experience that most visitors enjoy, and resorts and other companies have incorporated the fire-knife dance and other Polynesian dances into their elaborate presentations.

Nose Flutes

The nose flute is an instrument used in ancient times to serenade a lover. For the Hawaiians, the nose is romantic, sacred, and pure. The Hawaiian word for kiss is *honi*. Similar to an Eskimo's kiss, the noses touch on each side, sharing one's spiritual energy or breath. The Hawaiian term, *ohe hano ihu*, simply translated to "bamboo," with which the instrument is made; "breathe," because one has to gently breathe through it to make soothing music; and "nose," as it is made for the nose and not the mouth.

Slack-Key Guitar and the Paniolo

Kihoalu, or slack-key music, evolved in the early 1800s when King Kamehameha III brought in Mexican and Spanish vaqueros to manage the overpopulated cattle that

had run wild on the Islands. The vaqueros brought their guitars and would play music around the campfire after work. When they left, supposedly leaving their guitars to their new friends, the Hawaiian *paniolo,* or cowboys, began to infuse what they learned from the vaqueros with their native music and chants, and so the art of slack-key music was born.

Today, the paniolo culture thrives where ranchers have settled.

Ukulele

The word *ukulele* literally translates to the "the jumping flea" and came to Hawaii in the 1880s by way of the Portuguese and Spanish. Once a fading art form, today it brings international kudos as a solo instrument, thanks to tireless musicians and teachers who have worked hard to keep it by our fingertips.

One such teacher is Roy Sakuma. Founder of four ukulele schools and a legend in his own right, Sakuma and his wife Kathy produced Oahu's first Ukulele Festival in 1971. Since then, they've brought the tradition to the Big Island, Kauai, and Maui. The free event annually draws thousands of artists and fans from all over the globe.

Hula

"Hula is the language of the heart, therefore the heartbeat of the Hawaiian people." —Kalakaua, the Merrie Monarch.

Thousands—from tots to seniors—devote hours each week to hula classes. All these dancers need some place to show off their stuff. The result is a network of hula competitions (generally free or very inexpensive) and free performances in malls and other public spaces. Many resorts offer hula instruction.

WEDDINGS AND HONEYMOONS

There's no question that Hawaii is one of the country's foremost honeymoon destinations. Romance is in the air here, and the white-sand beaches, turquoise water, swaying palm trees, balmy tropical breezes, and perpetual sunshine put people in the mood for love. It's easy to understand why Hawaii is fast becoming a popular wedding destination as well, especially as the cost of airfare is often discounted, new resorts and hotels entice visitors, and same-sex marriage is now legal in the state. A destination wedding is no longer exclusive to celebrities and the superrich. You can plan a traditional ceremony in a place of worship followed by a reception at an elegant resort, or you can go barefoot on the beach and celebrate at a luau. There are almost as many wedding planners in the Islands as real estate agents, which makes it oh-so-easy to wed in paradise, and then, once the knot is tied, stay and honeymoon as well.

The Big Day

Choosing the Perfect Place. When choosing a location, remember that you really have two choices to make: the ceremony location and where to have the reception, if you're having one. For the former, there are beaches, bluffs overlooking beaches, gardens, private residences, resort lawns, and, of course, places of worship. As for the reception, there are these same choices, as well as restaurants and even luau. If you decide to go outdoors, remember the seasons—yes, Hawaii has seasons. If you're planning a winter wedding outdoors, be sure you have a backup plan (such as a tent), in case it rains. Also, if you're planning an outdoor wedding at sunset—which is very popular—be sure you match the time of your ceremony to the time the sun sets at that time of year. If you choose an indoor spot, be sure to ask

for pictures of the location when you're planning. You don't want to plan a pink wedding, say, and wind up in a room that's predominantly red. Or maybe you do. The point is, it should be your choice.

Finding a Wedding Planner. If you're planning to invite more than an officiant and your loved one to your wedding ceremony, seriously consider an on-island wedding planner who can help select a location; help design the floral scheme and recommend a florist as well as a photographer; help plan the menu and choose a restaurant, caterer, or resort; and suggest Hawaiian traditions to incorporate into your ceremony. And more: Will you need tents, a cake, music? Maybe transportation and lodging? Many planners have relationships with vendors, providing packages—which mean savings.

If you're planning a resort wedding, most have on-site wedding coordinators; however, there are many independents around the Islands and even those who specialize in certain types of ceremonies—by locale, size, religious affiliation, and so on. A simple "Hawaii weddings" Google search will reveal dozens. What's important is that you feel comfortable with your coordinator. Ask for references and call them. Share your budget. Get a proposal—in writing. Ask how long they've been in business, how much they charge, how often you'll meet with them, and how they select vendors. Request a detailed list of the exact services they'll provide. If your idea of your wedding doesn't match their services, try someone else. If you can afford it, you might want to meet the planner in person.

Getting Your License. The good news about marrying in Hawaii is that there is no waiting period, no residency or citizenship requirement, and no blood test or shots are required. You can apply and pay the fee online; however, both the bride and groom must appear together in person before a marriage-license agent to receive the marriage license (the permit to get married). You'll need proof of age—the legal age to marry is 18. (If you're 19 or older, a valid driver's license will suffice; if you're 18, a certified birth certificate is required.) Upon approval, a marriage license is immediately issued and costs $60 (credit cards accepted online and in person; cash only accepted in-person). After the ceremony, your officiant will mail the marriage certificate (proof of marriage) to the state. Approximately four months later, you will receive a copy in the mail. (For $10 extra, you can expedite this process. Ask your marriage-license agent when you apply.) For more detailed information, visit ⊕ *marriage. ehawaii.gov.*

Also—this is important—the person performing your wedding must be licensed by the Hawaii Department of Health, even if he or she is a licensed officiant. Be sure to ask.

Wedding Attire. In Hawaii, basically anything goes, from long, formal dresses with trains to white bikinis. Floral sundresses are fine, too. For men, tuxedos are not the norm; a pair of solid-colored slacks with a nice aloha shirt is. In fact, tradition in Hawaii for the groom is a beautiful white aloha shirt (they do exist) with slacks or long shorts and a colored sash around the waist. If you're planning a wedding on the beach, barefoot is the way to go.

If you decide to marry in a formal dress and tuxedo, you're better off making your selections on the mainland and hand-carrying them aboard the plane. Yes, it can

be a pain, but ask your wedding-gown retailer to provide a special carrying bag. After all, you don't want to chance losing your wedding dress in a wayward piece of luggage.

Local Customs. The most obvious traditional Hawaiian wedding custom is the lei exchange in which the bride and groom take turns placing a lei around the neck of the other—with a kiss. Bridal lei are usually floral, whereas the groom's is typically made of *maile*, a green leafy garland that drapes around the neck and is open at the ends. Brides often also wear a *lei poo*—a circular floral headpiece. Other Hawaiian customs include the blowing of the conch shell, hula, chanting, and Hawaiian music.

The Honeymoon

Do you want champagne and strawberries delivered to your room each morning? A breathtaking swimming pool in which to float? A five-star restaurant in which to dine? Then a resort is the way to go. If, however, you prefer the comforts of a home, try a bed-and-breakfast. A small inn is also good if you're on a tight budget or don't plan to spend much time in your room. On the other hand, maybe you want your own private home in which to romp naked—or just laze around recovering from the wedding planning. Maybe you want your own kitchen so you can whip up a gourmet meal for your loved one. In that case, a private vacation-rental home is the answer. Or maybe a condominium resort. That's another beautiful thing about Hawaii: the lodging accommodations are almost as plentiful as the beaches, and there's one that will perfectly match your tastes and your budget.

TOP 10 HAWAIIAN FOODS TO TRY

Food in Hawaii is a reflection of the state's diverse cultural makeup and tropical location. Fresh seafood, organic fruits and vegetables, free-range beef, and locally grown products are the hallmarks of Hawaii regional cuisine. Its preparations are drawn from across the Pacific Rim, including Japan, the Philippines, Korea, and Thailand—and "local food" is a cuisine in its own right. Don't miss Hawaiian-grown coffee, either, whether it's smooth Kona from the Big Island or coffee grown on other islands.

Saimin

The ultimate hangover cure and the perfect comfort food during Hawaii's mild winters, *saimin* ranks at the top of the list of local favorites. In fact, it's one of the few dishes deemed truly local, having been highlighted in cookbooks since the 1930s. Saimin is an Asian-style noodle soup so ubiquitous, it's even on McDonald's menus statewide. In mom-and-pop shops, a large melamine bowl is filled with homemade *dashi*, or broth, and wheat-flour noodles and then topped off with strips of omelet, green onions, bright pink fish cake, and *char siu* (Chinese roast pork) or canned luncheon meat, such as SPAM. Add *shoyu* (the "local" name for soy sauce) and chili pepper water, lift your chopsticks, and slurp away.

SPAM

Speaking of SPAM, Hawaii's most prevalent grab-and-go snack is SPAM *musubi*. Often displayed next to cash registers at groceries and convenience stores, the glorified rice ball is rectangular, topped with a slice of fried SPAM and wrapped in *nori* (seaweed). Musubi is a bite-size meal in itself. But just like sushi, the rice part hardens when refrigerated. So it's best to gobble it up right after purchase.

Hormel Company's SPAM actually deserves its own recognition—way beyond as a mere musubi topping. About 5 million cans are sold per year in Hawaii, and the Aloha State even hosts a festival in its honor. It's inexpensive protein and goes a long way when mixed with rice, scrambled eggs, noodles or, well, anything. The spiced luncheon meat gained popularity in World War II days, when fish was rationed. Gourmets and those with aversions to salt, high cholesterol, or high blood pressure may cringe at the thought of eating it, but SPAM in Hawaii is here to stay.

Manapua

Another savory snack is *manapua*, fist-size dough balls fashioned after Chinese *bao* (a traditional Chinese bun) and stuffed with fillings such as *char siu* (Chinese roast pork) and then steamed. Many mom-and-pop stores sell them in commercial steamer display cases along with pork hash and other dim sum. Modern-day fillings include curry chicken.

Fresh Ahi or Tako Poke

There's nothing like fresh ahi or *tako* (octopus) *poke* to break the ice at a backyard party, except, of course, the cold beer handed to you from the cooler. The perfect *pupu*, poke (pronounced poh-kay) is basically raw seafood cut into bite-size chunks and mixed with everything from green onions to roasted and ground *kukui* nuts. Other variations include mixing the fish with chopped round onion, sesame oil, seaweed, and chili pepper water. Shoyu is the constant. These days, grocery stores sell a rainbow of varieties such as kimchi crab and anything goes, from adding mayonnaise to tobiko caviar. Fish lovers who want to take it to the next level order sashimi, the best cuts of ahi sliced and dipped in a mixture of shoyu and wasabi.

Tropical Fruits

Tropical fruits such as apple banana and strawberry papaya are plucked from trees in Island neighborhoods and eaten for breakfast—plain or with a squeeze of fresh lime. Give them a try; the banana tastes like an apple and the papaya's rosy flesh explains its name. Locals also love to add their own creative touches to exotic fruits. Green mangoes are pickled with Chinese five spice, and Maui Gold pineapples are topped with *li hing mui* powder (heck, even margarita glasses are rimmed with it). Green papaya is tossed in a Vietnamese salad with fish paste and fresh prawns.

Plate Lunch

It would be remiss not to mention the plate lunch as one of the most beloved dishes in Hawaii. It generally includes two scoops of sticky white rice, a scoop of macaroni or macaroni-potato salad, heavy on the mayo, and perhaps kimchi or *koko* (salted cabbage). There are countless choices of main protein such as chicken *katsu* (fried cutlet), fried mahimahi, and beef tomato. The king of all plate lunches is the Hawaiian plate. The main item is laulau or kalua pig and cabbage along with poi, *lomilomi* salmon, chicken long rice, and sticky white rice.

Bento Box

The bento box gained popularity back in the plantation days, when workers toiled in the sugarcane fields. No one brought sandwiches to work then. Instead it was a lunch box with the ever-present steamed white rice, pickled *ume* (plum) to preserve the rice, and main meats such as fried chicken or fish. Today, many stores sell prepackaged bentos or you may go to an

okazuya (Japanese deli) with a hot buffet counter and create your own.

Malasadas

The Portuguese have contributed much to Hawaii cuisine in the form of sausage, soup, and sweetbread. But their most revered food is *malasadas*, hot, deep-fried doughnuts rolled in sugar. Malasadas are crowd-pleasers. Buy them by the dozen, hot from the fryer, placed in brown paper bags to absorb the grease. Or bite into gourmet malasadas at restaurants, filled with vanilla or chocolate cream.

Shave Ice

Much more than just a snow cone, shave ice is what locals crave after a blazing day at the beach or a hot-as-Hades game of soccer. If you're lucky, you'll find a neighborhood store that hand-shaves the ice, but it's rare. Either way, the counter person will ask you first if you'd like ice cream and/or adzuki beans scooped into the bottom of the cone or cup. Then they shape the ice into a giant mound and add colorful fruit syrups. First-timers should order the Rainbow, of course.

Crack Seed

There are dozens of varieties of crack seed in dwindling specialty shops and at the drugstores. Chinese call the preserved fruits and nuts *see mui* but somehow the Pidgin English version is what Hawaiians prefer. Those who like hard candy and salty foods will love *li hing* mangoes and rock salt plums, and those with an itchy throat will feel relief from the lemon strips. Peruse large glass jars of crack seed sold in bulk or smaller hanging bags—the latter make good gifts to give to friends back home.

CRUISING THE ISLANDS

Cruising has become popular in Hawaii. They are a comparatively inexpensive way to see all of Hawaii, and you'll save travel time by not having to check in at hotels and airports on each Island. The limited amount of time in each port can be an argument against cruising, but you can make reservations for tours, activities, rental cars, and more aboard the cruise ship.

The larger cruise lines such as Carnival, Princess, and Holland America offer itineraries of 10–16 days departing from the West Coast of the United States, most with stops at all the major Hawaiian Islands. Some cruise lines, such as Crystal, Cunard, and Disney, include ports in Hawaii on around-the-world cruises. All have plenty on board to keep you busy during the four to five days that you are at sea between the U.S. mainland and Hawaii.

Cruise ships plying the Pacific from the continental United States to Hawaii are floating resorts complete with pools, spas, rock-climbing walls, restaurants, nightclubs, shops, casinos, children's programs, and much more. Most hold thousands of passengers with an average staff-to-passenger ratio of three to one.

Prices for cruises are based on accommodation type: interior (no window, in an inside corridor); outside (includes a window or porthole); balcony (allows you to go outside without using a public deck); and suite (larger cabin, more amenities and perks). Passages start at about $1,000 per person for the lowest class accommodation (interior) and include room, on-board entertainment, and food. Ocean-view, balcony, and suite accommodations can run up to $6,500 and beyond per person.

Cruising to Hawaii

Carnival Cruises is great for families, with plenty of kid-friendly activities. Departing from Los Angeles or Vancouver, Carnival's "fun ships" show your family a good time, both on board and on shore (☎ 888/227–6482 ⊕ www.carnival.com). The grand dame of cruise lines, Holland America has a reputation for service and elegance. Their 14-day Hawaii cruises leave from and return to San Diego, with a brief stop at Ensenada (☎ 877/932–4259 ⊕ www.hollandamerica.com). More affordable luxury is what Princess Cruises offers. While their prices seem a little higher, you get more bells and whistles on your trip (more affordable balcony rooms, more restaurants to chose from, personalized service) (☎ 800/774–6237 ⊕ www.princess.com).

Cruising within Hawaii

Norwegian Cruise Lines is the only major operator to begin and end cruises in Hawaii. *Pride of Hawaii* (vintage America theme, family focus with lots of connecting staterooms and suites) offers a seven-day itinerary that includes stops on Maui, Oahu, the Big Island, and Kauai. This is the only ship to cruise Hawaii that does not spend days at sea visiting a foreign port, allowing you more time to explore destinations (☎ 800/327–7030 ⊕ www.ncl.com). Ocean conditions in the channels between islands can be a consideration when booking an interisland cruise on a smaller vessel such as Un-Cruise Adventures—a stately yacht accommodating only 36 passengers. This yacht's small size allows it to dock at less frequented islands such as Molokai and Lanai. The cruise is billed as "all inclusive"—your passage includes shore excursions, water activities, and a massage (☎ 888/862–8881 ⊕ www.un-cruise.com).

EXPLORING
OAHU

Updated by
Anna Weaver

Oahu is one-stop Hawaii—all the allure of the Islands in a chop-suey mix that has you kayaking around offshore islets by day and sitting in a jazz club 'round midnight, all without ever having to take another flight or repack your suitcase. It offers both the buzz of modern living in jam-packed Honolulu (the state's capital) and the allure of slow-paced island life on its northern and eastern shores. It is, in many ways, the center of the Hawaiian universe.

There are more museums, staffed historic sites, and walking tours here than you'll find on any other island. And only here do a wealth of renovated buildings and well-preserved neighborhoods so clearly spin the story of Hawaii's history. It's the only place to experience island-style urbanity, since there are no other true cities in the state. And yet you can get as lost in the rural landscape and be as laid-back as you wish.

Oahu is home to Waikiki, the most famous Hawaiian beach, as well as some of the world's most famous surf on the North Shore and Hawaii's best known historical site—Pearl Harbor. If it's isolation, peace, and quiet you want, Oahu might not be for you, but if you'd like a bit of spice with your piece of paradise, this island provides it.

GEOLOGY

Encompassing 597 square miles, Oahu is the third-largest island in the Hawaiian chain. Scientists believe the island was formed about 4 million years ago by two volcanoes: Waianae and Koolau. Waianae, the older of the two, created the mountain range on the western side of the island, whereas Koolau shapes the eastern side. Central Oahu is an elevated plateau bordered by the two mountain ranges, with Pearl Harbor to the south. Several of Oahu's most famous natural landmarks, including Diamond Head and Hanauma Bay, are tuff rings and cinder cones formed during a renewed volcanic stage (roughly 1 million years ago).

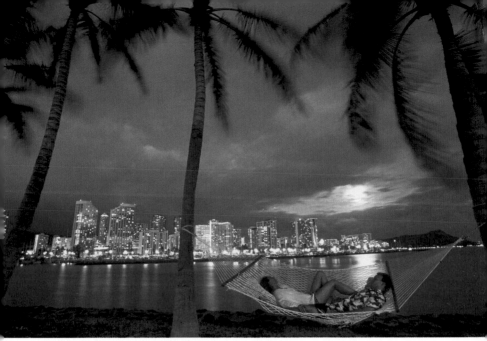
Kick back in a hammock and gaze off at Diamond Head in the distance.

FLORA AND FAUNA

The eastern (Koolau) side of Oahu is much cooler and wetter than the western side of the island, which tends to be dry and arid. The island's official flower, the little orange *ilima*, grows predominantly in the east, but lei throughout the island incorporate *ilima*. Numerous tropical fish call the reef at Hanauma Bay home, migrating humpback whales can be spotted off the coast past Waikiki and Diamond Head from December through April, spinner dolphins pop in and out of the island's bays, and dozens of islets off Oahu's eastern coast provide refuge for endangered seabirds.

HISTORY

Oahu is the most populated island because early tourism to Hawaii started here. Although Kilauea volcano on Hawaii was a tourist attraction in the late 1800s, it was the building of the Moana Hotel on Waikiki Beach in 1901 and subsequent advertising of Hawaii to wealthy San Franciscans that really fueled tourism in the Islands. Oahu was drawing tens of thousands of guests yearly when, on December 7, 1941, Japanese Zeros appeared at dawn to bomb Pearl Harbor. Though tourism understandably dipped during the war (Waikiki Beach was fenced with barbed wire), the subsequent memorial only seemed to attract more visitors, and Oahu remains hugely popular with tourists—especially the Japanese—to this day.

GUIDED TOURS

Guided tours are convenient; you don't have to worry about finding a parking spot or getting admission tickets. Most of the tour guides have taken special classes in Hawaiian history and lore, and many are certified by the state of Hawaii. On the other hand, you won't have the freedom to proceed at your own pace, nor will you have the ability to take a detour trip if something else catches your attention.

BUS AND VAN TOURS

Polynesian Adventure. This company leads tours of Pearl Harbor and other historic Honolulu sights and also offers a circle-island tour by motor coach, van, and minicoach. ☎ *808/833–3000* ⊕ *www. polyadhawaiitours.com/.*

Roberts Hawaii. Choose from a large selection of tours, including downtown Honolulu ghost tours, underwater submarine tours, and the more traditional Pearl Harbor excursions. Tours are conducted via everything from vans to president-worthy limousines. ☎ *808/539–9400* ⊕ *www. robertshawaii.com.*

THEME TOURS

Discover Hawaii Tours. In addition to circle-island and other Oahu-based itineraries on motor and minicoaches, this company can also get you from Waikiki to the lava flows of the Big Island or to Maui's Hana Highway and back in one day. ☎ *808/690–9050* ⊕ *www. discoverhawaiitours.com.*

E Noa Tours. This outfitter's certified tour guides conduct circle-island, Pearl Harbor, nature, and shopping tours. ☎ *808/591–2561* ⊕ *www. enoa.com.*

Home of the Brave Victory Tours. Perfect for military history buffs, these narrated tours visit Oahu's military bases and the National Memorial Cemetery of the Pacific. Tours also include a visit to the company's private "brewseum," which displays artifacts and memorabilia from World War II. Evening "Night at the Brewseum" tours also include stops in Honolulu and craft beer tastings. ☎ *808/396–8112* ⊕ *www. pearlharborhq.com.*

HONOLULU

Here is Hawaii's only true metropolis, its seat of government, center of commerce and shipping, entertainment and recreation mecca, a historic site, and an evolving urban area—conflicting roles that engender endless debate and controversy. For the visitor, Honolulu is an everyman's delight: hipsters and scholars, sightseers and foodies, nature lovers and culture vultures all can find their bliss.

Once there was the broad bay of Mamala and the narrow inlet of Kou, fronting a dusty plain occupied by a few thatched houses and the great Pakaka *heiau* (shrine). Nosing into the narrow passage in the early 1790s, British sea captain William Brown named the port Fair Haven. Later, Hawaiians would call it Honolulu, or "sheltered bay." As shipping traffic increased, the settlement grew into a Western-style town of streets and buildings, tightly clustered around the single freshwater source, Nuuanu Stream. Not until piped water became available in the early 1900s did Honolulu spread across the greening plain. Long before that, however, Honolulu gained importance when King Kamehameha I reluctantly abandoned his home on the Big Island to build a chiefly compound near the harbor in 1804 to better protect Hawaiian interests from the Western incursion.

Two hundred years later, the entire island is, in a sense, Honolulu—the City and County of Honolulu. The city has no official boundaries, extending across the flatlands from Pearl Harbor to Waikiki and high into the hills behind.

The main areas (Waikiki, Pearl Harbor, Downtown, Chinatown) have the lion's share of the sights, but greater Honolulu also has a lot to offer. One reason to venture farther afield is the chance to glimpse Honolulu's residential neighborhoods. Species of classic Hawaii homes include the tiny green-and-white plantation-era house with its corrugated tin roof, two windows flanking a central door and small porch; the breezy bungalow with its swooping Thai-style roofline and two wings flanking screened French doors through which breezes blow into the living room. Note the tangled "Grandma-style" gardens and many *ohana* houses—small homes in the backyard of a larger home or built as apartments perched over the garage, allowing extended families to live together. Carports, which rarely house cars, are the island's version of rec rooms, where parties are held and neighbors sit to "talk story." Sometimes you see gallon jars on the flat roofs of garages or carports: these are pickled lemons fermenting in the sun. Also in the neighborhoods, you find the folksy restaurants and takeout spots favored by the islanders.

WAIKIKI

Waikiki is approximately 3 miles east of downtown Honolulu.

A short drive from downtown Honolulu, Waikiki is Oahu's primary resort area. A mix of historic and modern hotels and condos front the sunny 2-mile stretch of beach, and many have clear views of Diamond Head. The area is home to much of the island's dining, nightlife, and shopping scene—from posh boutiques to hole-in-the-wall eateries to craft booths at the International Marketplace.

Waikiki was once a favorite retreat for Hawaiian royalty. In 1901 the Moana Hotel debuted, introducing Waikiki as an international travel destination. The region's fame continued to grow when Duke Kahanamoku helped popularize the sport of surfing, offering lessons to visitors at Waikiki. You can see Duke immortalized in a bronze statue, with a surfboard, on Kuhio Beach. Today, there is a decidedly "urban resort" vibe here; streets are clean, gardens are manicured, and the sand feels softer than at beaches farther down the coast. There isn't much of a local culture—it's mainly tourist crowds—but you'll still find the relaxed surf-y vibe that has drawn people here for more than a century.

Diamond Head Crater (*see ⇨ Diamond Head*) is perhaps Hawaii's most recognizable natural landmark. It got its name from sailors who thought

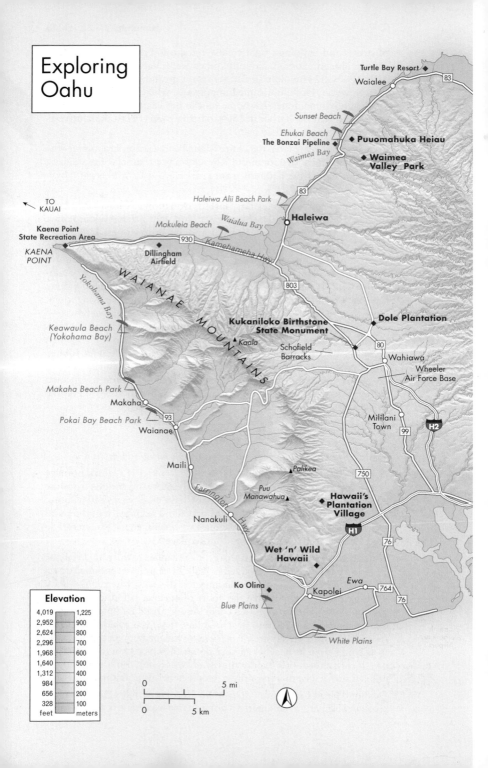

Exploring Oahu

TO
KAUAI

Turtle Bay Resort
Waialee

83

Sunset Beach

Ehukai Beach
The Bonzai Pipeline
Waimea Bay

Puuomahuka Heiau

Waimea
Valley Park

Haleiwa Alii Beach Park

83

Mokuleia Beach
Waialua Bay
Kamehameha Hwy

Haleiwa

Kaena Point
State Recreation Area

KAENA
POINT

930

Dillingham
Airfield

803

WAIANAE

Yokohama Bay

Keawaula Beach
(Yokohama Bay)

Kukaniloko Birthstone
State Monument

Kaala

Dole Plantation

80

MOUNTAINS

Schofield
Barracks

Wahiawa

Wheeler
Air Force Base

Makaha Beach Park

Makaha

Pokai Bay Beach Park

93

Waianae

Mililani
Town

99

H2

Maili

Palikea

Farrington Hwy

Puu
Manawahua

750

Hawaii's
Plantation
Village

Nanakuli

H1

76

Wet 'n' Wild
Hawaii

Ko Olina

Blue Plains

Ewa

Kapolei

764

76

White Plains

Elevation

feet	meters
4,019	1,225
2,952	900
2,624	800
2,296	700
1,968	600
1,640	500
1,312	400
984	300
656	200
328	100
feet	meters

0   5 mi

0   5 km

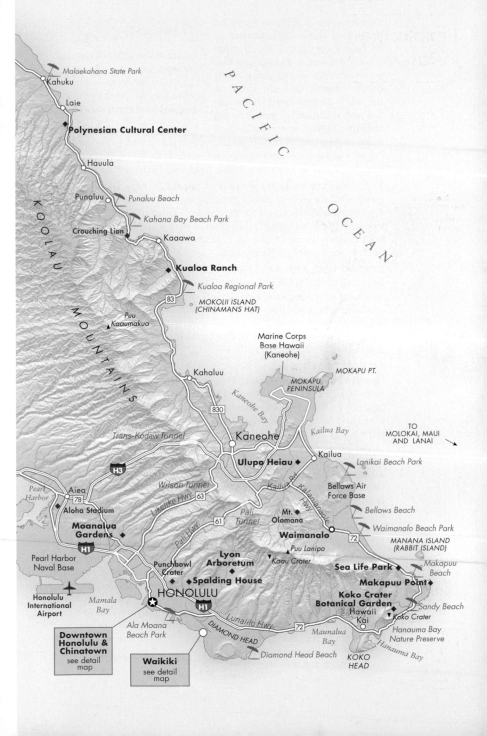

PACIFIC OCEAN

Malaekahana State Park
Kahuku

Laie

Polynesian Cultural Center

Hauula

Punaluu *Punaluu Beach*

Kahana Bay Beach Park

Crouching Lion
Kaaawa

Kualoa Ranch

Kualoa Regional Park

83

MOKOLII ISLAND
(CHINAMANS HAT)

*Puu
Kaaumakua*

Marine Corps
Base Hawaii
(Kaneohe)

Kahaluu

MOKAPU PT.

MOKAPU
PENINSULA

830

Kaneohe Bay

Trans-Koolau Tunnel

Kaneohe

Kailua Bay

TO
MOLOKAI, MAUI
AND LANAI

Ulupo Heiau
Kailua

Lanikai Beach Park

H3

Wilson Tunnel

Likelike Hwy.

63

Kailua Rd.

Kalanianaole Hwy.

Bellows Air
Force Base

Pearl
Harbor

Aiea

78

Aloha Stadium

61

*Pali
Tunnel*

Mt.
Olomana

Bellows Beach

**Moanalua
Gardens**

H1

Waimanalo

72

Waimanalo Beach Park

MANANA ISLAND
(RABBIT ISLAND)

Puu Lanipo

Pali Hwy.

Pearl Harbor
Naval Base

**Lyon
Arboretum**

Punchbowl
Crater

Kaau Crater

Sea Life Park

*Makapuu
Beach*

Honolulu
International
Airport

*Mamala
Bay*

Spalding House

HONOLULU

H1

Makapuu Point

**Koko Crater
Botanical Garden**

Hawaii
Kai

Koko Crater

Sandy Beach

**Downtown
Honolulu &
Chinatown**
see detail
map

*Ala Moana
Beach Park*

Lunalilo Hwy.

DIAMOND HEAD

72

*Maunalua
Bay*

*Hanauma Bay
Nature Preserve*

KOKO
HEAD

Waikiki
see detail
map

Diamond Head Beach

Hanauma Bay

KOOLAU MOUNTAINS

they had found precious gems on its slopes; these later proved to be calcite crystals, a much more common mineral. Hawaiians saw a resemblance in the sharp angle of the crater's seaward slope to the oddly shaped head of the ahi fish and so called it Leahi, though later they Hawaiianized the English name to Kaimana Hila. It is commemorated in a widely known hula— "*A ike i ka nani o Kaimana Hila, Kaimana Hila, kau mai i luna*" ("We saw the beauty of Diamond Head, Diamond Head set high above").

> ### CHEAP GAS
>
> For those with a Costco card, the cheapest gas on the island is at the Costco station on Arakawa Street between Dillingham Boulevard and Nimitz Highway.

Kapiolani Park lies in the shadow of the crater. King David Kalakaua established the park in 1887, named it after his queen, and dedicated it "to the use and enjoyment of the people." Kapiolani Park is a 500-acre expanse where you can play all sorts of field sports, enjoy a picnic, see wild animals at the Honolulu Zoo, or hear live music at the Waikiki Shell or the Kapiolani Bandstand.

GETTING HERE AND AROUND

Bounded by the Ala Wai Canal on the north and west, the beach on the south, and the Honolulu Zoo to the east, Waikiki is compact and easy to walk around. TheBus runs multiple routes here from the airport and downtown Honolulu. By car, finding Waikiki from H1 can be tricky; look for the Punahou exit for the west end of Waikiki, and the King Street exit for the eastern end.

TOP ATTRACTIONS

Hawaii Pirate Ship Adventures. The *Treasure Seeker*, an 83-foot black galleon, sailed from San Diego to Hawaii in 2013 to bring swashbuckling fun to Waikiki waters. Daytime Lost Treasure excursions include costumed actors leading kids of all ages in a pirate adventure complete with props. At night, the ship brightens up with flashing lights and music for an adults-only Evening Cruise, a BYOB party on the high seas. Check the website for the specific sailing times, and arrive at least 30 minutes prior to departure time. ■TIP➔ Time your evening cruise for a Friday night to get a great water view of the Hilton Hawaiian Village fireworks. ⊠ *Kewalo Basin Harbor, 1085 Ala Moana Blvd., Slip P for Pirate, Waikiki* ☎ *808/593–2469* ⊕ *www.hawaiipirateship.com* ⌨ *$42 daytime cruise, $50 evening cruise* ☉ *Actual sailing times vary by season.*

FAMILY **Honolulu Zoo.** There are bigger and better zoos, but this one, though showing signs of neglect due to budget constraints, is a lush garden and has some great programs. To get a glimpse of the endangered *nene*, the Hawaii state bird, check out the zoo's Kipuka Nene Sanctuary. Though many animals prefer to remain invisible, particularly the elusive big cats, the monkeys appear to enjoy being seen and are a hoot to watch. It's best to get to the zoo right when it opens, since the animals are livelier in the cool of the morning.

Exploring Waikiki

Ala Wai Golf Course

Ala Wai Field & Park

Ala Wai Canal

Ala Wai Yacht Harbor

Mamala Bay

Waianui Way
Ala Wai Blvd.
Puahani Wy.
Kapahulu Ave.
Kanekapolei St.
Kaiolu St.
Kalaimoku St.
Saratoga Rd.
Lewers St.
Kuhio Ave.
Lauula St.
Launiu St.
Aloha Drive
Manukai St.
Royal Hawaiian Ave.
Seaside Ave.
Nahua St.
Walina St.
Kaiulani Ave.
Liliuokalani Ave.
Prince Edward St.
Cleghorn St.
Tusitala St.
Olohana St.
Namahana St.
Keoniana St.
Nahua St.
Kuamoo St.
Pau St.
Niu St.
Kalakaua Ave.
Kaiulani Ave.
Uluniu Ave.
Koa Ave.
Kealohilani Ave.
Ohua Ave.
Paoakalani Ave.
Lemon Rd.
Cartwright Rd.
Kanekapolei St.
Kaiulani Ave.
Dukes La.
Kaiulani Ave.
Beach Walk
Helumoa Rd.
Kalia Rd.
Kalia Rd.
Ena Rd.
Ala Moana Blvd.
Ala Wai Blvd.
Kalakaua Ave.
Hobron La.
Hoonanea St.
McCully St.
Kapiolani Blvd.

King Kalakaua Plaza

International Market Place

Royal Hawaiian Shopping Center

The Royal Hawaiian

Moana Surfrider

Sheraton Waikiki

Halekulani

Waikiki Beach Marriott

Honolulu Zoo

Waikiki Shell

Kapiolani Bandstand

Waikiki Aquarium

Waikiki War Museum

Natatorium

Queen's Surf

TO DIAMOND HEAD

Kuhio Beach Park

Kuhaloa & Ulukou Beach

Gray's Beach

Fort DeRussy Beach

Fort DeRussy

Duke Kahanamoku Beach

TO DOWNTOWN HONOLULU

0   1/4 mile
0   1/4 km

The Wildest Show in Town is a 10-week summer concert series ($3 participation fee), and you can have a family sleepover inside the zoo during Snooze in the Zoo on Saturday nights between May and October. Or just head for the petting zoo, where kids can make friends with a llama or stand in the middle of a koi pond. There's an exceptionally good gift shop. On weekends, the Art on the Zoo Fence, on Monsarrat Avenue on the Diamond Head side outside the zoo, has affordable artwork by contemporary artists. Metered parking is available all along the *makai* (ocean) side of the park and

in the lot next to the zoo—but it can fill up early. TheBus makes stops here along the way to and from Ala Moana Center and Sea Life Park (Routes 8 and 22). ⊠ *151 Kapahulu Ave., Waikiki* ☎ *808/971–7171* ⊕ *honoluluzoo.org* 🎟 *$14* ☼ *Daily 9–4:30.*

Kapiolani Bandstand. The Victorian-style Kapiolani Bandstand, which was originally built in the late 1890s and was recently renovated, is Kapiolani Park's stage for community entertainment and concerts. The nation's only city-sponsored band, the Royal Hawaiian Band, performs free concerts at the bandstand as well as at Iolani Palace and the Moana Surfrider. Local newspapers list event information. ⊠ *2805 Monsarrat Ave., Waikiki* ☎ *808/922–5331.*

FAMILY **Waikiki Aquarium.** This amazing little attraction harbors more than 3,500 organisms and 500 species of Hawaiian and South Pacific marine life, endangered Hawaiian monk seals, sharks, and the only chambered nautilus living in captivity. The Edge of the Reef exhibit showcases five different types of reef environments found along Hawaii's shorelines. Check out the new endangered green sea turtle exhibit, the Northwestern Hawaiian Islands display that explains the formation of the island chain, the Ocean Drifters jellyfish exhibit, the outdoor touch pool, and the self-guided audio tour, which is included with admission. The aquarium offers activities of interest to adults and children alike, including the Aquarium After Dark program when visitors grab a flashlight and view fish going about their rarely observable nocturnal activities. ⊠ *2777 Kalakaua Ave., Waikiki* ☎ *808/923–9741* ⊕ *www.waquarium. org* 🎟 *$12* ☼ *Daily 9–5; last entrance 4:30.*

WORTH NOTING

Waikiki Shell. Grab one of the 6,000 "grass seats" (i.e., lawn seating) for music under the stars (there are actual seats, as well). An eclectic array of musical acts put on concerts at this landmark venue throughout the summer and occasionally during the winter, weather permitting. Check newspaper entertainment sections to see who is performing.

MOILILI

Ala Wai Co.
Golf Course

WAIKIKI

KAIMUKI

Honolulu Zoo ◆
Queens Surf Beach
Kapiolani Bandstand ◆
Waikiki Aquarium ◆
Waikiki War Memorial ◆
Natatorium

Monsarrat Av.

◆ Waikiki Shell

Diamond Head
State Monument
and Park
◆

Sans Souci Street
Recreation Area

Diamond Head
Beach

Diamond Head Rd.

Kaalawai
Beach

DIAMOND
HEAD

BLACK
POINT

0   1/2 mile
0   1/2 km

⊠ *2805 Monsarrat Ave., Waikiki* ☎ *808/768–5400* ⊕ *blaisdellcenter. com/venues/waikiki-shell*.

Waikiki War Memorial Natatorium. This Beaux-Arts-style, 1927 World War I monument, dedicated to the 102 Hawaiian servicemen who lost their lives in battle, stands proudly in Waikiki. The 100-meter saltwater swimming pool, the training spot for Olympians Johnny Weissmuller and Buster Crabbe and the U.S. Army during World War II, has been closed for decades as the pool needs repair. Plans are under study to tear down the natatorium, though a nonprofit group continues fighting to save the facility. The site is closed to visitors, but you can stop by and look at it from the outside. ⊠ *2777 Kalakaua Ave., Waikiki* ⊕ *www. natatorium.org*.

DIAMOND HEAD

Besides hiking Diamond Head, visitors will enjoy the eclectic shops and restaurants along Monsarrat Avenue like Diamond Head Market & Grill. Don't forget the amazing *poke* (seasoned raw fish) and other local goodies at Fort Ruger Market, and the Saturday farmers' market at Kapiolani Community College is arguably the best on the island.

TOP ATTRACTIONS

Diamond Head State Monument and Park. Panoramas from this 760-foot extinct volcanic peak, once used as a military fortification, extend from Waikiki and Honolulu in one direction and out to Koko Head in the other, with surfers and windsurfers scattered like confetti on the cresting waves below. This 360-degree perspective is a great orientation for first-time visitors. On a clear day, look east past Koko Head to glimpse the outlines of the islands of Maui and Molokai.

To enter the park from Waikiki, take Kalakaua Avenue east, turn left at Monsarrat Avenue, head a mile up the hill, and look for a sign on the right. Drive through the tunnel to the inside of the crater. The ¾-mile trail to the top begins at the parking lot. Be aware that the hike to the crater is an upward ascent with numerous stairs to climb; if you aren't in the habit of getting occasional exercise, this might not be for you. At the top, you'll find a somewhat awkward scramble through a tunnel and bunker out into the open air, but the view is worth it.

Take bottled water with you to stay hydrated under the tropical sun. ■TIP➜ To beat the heat and the crowds, rise early and make the hike before 8 am. As you walk, note the color of the vegetation; if the mountain is brown, Honolulu has been without significant rain for a while; but if the trees and undergrowth glow green, you'll know it's the wet season (winter) without looking at a calendar. This is when rare Hawaiian marsh plants revive on the floor of the crater. Keep an eye on your watch if you're here at day's end: the gates close promptly at 6. ⊠ *Diamond Head Rd. at 18th Ave., Diamond Head* ☎ *808/587–0300* ⊕ *www. hawaiistateparks.org/parks/oahu/?park_id=15* 🖃 *$1 per person, $5 per vehicle* ⊗ *Daily 6–6; last trail entry at 4:30.*

PEARL HARBOR

Pearl Harbor is approximately 9 miles west of downtown Honolulu, beyond Honolulu International Airport.

December 7, 1941. Every American then alive recalls exactly what he or she was doing when the news broke that the Japanese had bombed Pearl Harbor, the catalyst that brought the United States into World War II. More than 2,000 people died that day, and a dozen ships were sunk.

Here, in what is still a key Pacific naval base, the attack is remembered every day by thousands of visitors. In recent years, the memorial has been the site of reconciliation ceremonies involving Pearl Harbor veterans from both sides.

TOP ATTRACTIONS

Fodor's Choice ★ **Pearl Harbor Visitor Center.** The Pearl Harbor Visitor Center, reopened after a $58 million renovation, is now the gateway to the World War II Valor In the Pacific National Monument and the starting point for visitors to this historic site. Pearl Harbor is a must-see for many, but there are things to know before you go. Consider whether you want to see only the *Arizona* Memorial, or the USS *Bowfin* and USS *Missouri* as well (the latter two charge separate admission fees). Allow approximately an hour and 15 minutes for the USS *Arizona* tour. The majority

Continued on page 57

USS *West Virginia* (BB48), 7 December 1941

PEARL HARBOR

December 7, 1941. Every American then alive recalls exactly what he or she was doing when the news broke that the Japanese had bombed Pearl Harbor, the catalyst that brought the United States into World War II.

Although it was clear by late 1941 that war with Japan was inevitable, no one in authority seems to have expected the attack to come in just this way, at just this time. So when the Japanese bombers swept through a gap in Oahu's Koolau Mountains in the hazy light of morning, they found the bulk of America's Pacific fleet right where they hoped it would be: docked like giant stepping stones across the calm waters of the bay named for the pearl oysters that once prospered there. More than 2,000 people died that day, including 49 civilians. A dozen ships were sunk. And on the nearby air bases, virtually every American military aircraft was destroyed or damaged. The attack was a stunning success, but it lit a fire under America, which went to war with "Remember Pearl Harbor" as its battle cry. Here, in what is still a key Pacific naval base, the attack is remembered every day by thousands of visitors, including many curious Japanese, who for years heard little World War II history in their own country. In recent years, the memorial has been the site of reconciliation ceremonies involving Pearl Harbor veterans from both sides.

GETTING AROUND

Pearl Harbor is both a working military base and the most-visited Oahu attraction. Four distinct destinations share a parking lot and are linked by footpath, shuttle, and ferry.

The visitor center is accessible from the parking lot. The USS *Arizona* Memorial itself is in the middle of the harbor; get tickets for the ferry ride at the visitor center. The USS *Bowfin* is also reachable from the parking lot.

The USS *Missouri* is docked at Ford Island, a restricted area of the naval base. Vehicular access is prohibited.To get there, take a shuttle bus from the station near the *Bowfin*.

ARIZONA MEMORIAL

Snugged up tight in a row of seven battleships off Ford Island, the USS *Arizona* took a direct hit that December morning, exploded, and rests still on the shallow bottom where she settled.

The swooping, stark-white memorial, which straddles the wreck of the USS *Arizona*, was designed to represent both the depths of the low-spirited, early days of the war, and the uplift of victory.

A visit here begins at the Pearl Harbor Visitor Center, which recently underwent a $58 million renovation. High definition projectors and interactive exhibits were installed, and the building was modernized. From the visitor center, a ferry takes you to the memorial itself, and a new shuttle hub now gives access to sites that were previously inaccessible, like the USS *Utah* and USS *Oklahoma*.

A somber, contemplative mood descends upon visitors during the ferry ride to the *Arizona*; this is a place where 1,177

crewmen lost their lives. Gaze at the names of the dead carved into the wall of white marble. Scatter flowers (but no lei—the string is bad for the fish). Salute the flag. Remember Pearl Harbor.

☎ *808/422–0561*
⊕ *www.nps.gov/valr*

USS *MISSOURI* (BB63)

Together with the *Arizona* Memorial, the *Missouri's* presence in Pearl Harbor perfectly bookends America's WWII experience that began December 7, 1941, and ended on the "Mighty Mo's" starboard deck with the signing of the Terms of Surrender.

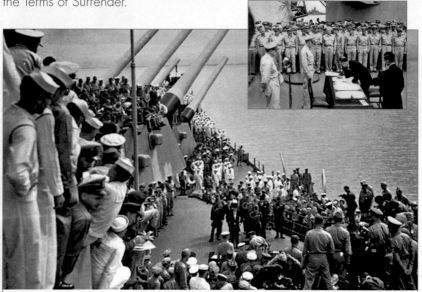

Surrender of Japan, USS *Missouri*, 2 September 1945

In the parking area behind the USS *Bowfin* Museum, board a shuttle for a breezy, eight-minute ride to Ford Island and the teak decks and towering superstructure of the *Missouri*, docked for good in the very harbor from which she first went to war on January 2, 1945. The last battleship ever built, the *Missouri* famously hosted the final act of WWII, the signing of the Terms of Surrender. The commission that governs this floating museum has surrounded her with buildings tricked out in WWII style—a canteen that serves as an orientation space for tours, a WACs and WAVEs lounge with a flight simulator the kids will love ($10 per person), Truman's Line restaurant serving Navy-style meals, and a Victory Store housing a souvenir shop and covered with period mottos ("Don't be a blabateur"). ■TIP→ Definitely hook up with a tour guide (additional charge) or audio tour—these add a great deal to the experience.

The *Missouri* is all about numbers: 209 feet tall, six 239,000-pound guns, capable of firing up to 23 mi away. Absorb these during the tour, then stop to take advantage of the view from the decks. The Mo is a work in progress, with only a handful of her hundreds of spaces open to view.

☎ 808/423–2263 or ☎ 888/877–6477
⊕ *www.ussmissouri.com*

USS *BOWFIN* (SS287)

SUBMARINE MUSEUM & PARK

Launched one year to the day after the Pearl Harbor attack, the USS *Bowfin* sank 44 enemy ships during WWII and now serves as the centerpiece of a museum honoring all submariners.

Although the *Bowfin* no less than the *Arizona* Memorial commemorates the lost, the mood here is lighter. Perhaps it's the childlike scale of the boat, a metal tube just 16 feet in diameter, packed with ladders, hatches, and other obstacles, like the naval version of a jungle gym. Perhaps it's the World War II-era music that plays in the covered patio. Or it might be the museum's touching displays—the penciled sailor's journal, the Vargas girlie posters. Aboard the boat nicknamed "Pearl Harbor Avenger," compartments are fitted out as though "Sparky" was away from the radio room just for a moment, and "Cooky" might be right back to his pots and pans. The museum includes many artifacts to spark family conversations, among them a vintage dive suit that looks too big for Shaquille

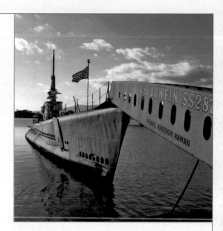

O'Neal. A caution: The *Bowfin* could be hazardous for very young children; no one under four allowed.

☎ *808/423–1341*
⊕ *www.bowfin.org*

THE PACIFIC AVIATION MUSEUM

This museum opened on December 7, 2006, as phase one of a four-phase tribute to the air wars of the Pacific. Located on Ford Island in Hangar 37, an actual seaplane hangar that survived the Pearl Harbor attack, the museum is made up of a theater where a short film on Pearl Harbor kicks off the tour, an education center, a shop, and a restaurant. Exhibits—many of which are interactive and involve sound effects—include an authentic Japanese Zero in a diorama setting a chance to don a flight suit and play the role of a World War II pilot using one of six flight simulators. Various aircrafts are employed to narrate the great battles: the Doolittle Raid on Japan, the Battle of Midway, Guadalcanal, and so on. The actual Stearman N2S-3 in which President George H. W. Bush soloed is another exhibit. ☎ *808/441–1000* ⊕ *www.pacificaviationmuseum.org* ✈ $25.

PLAN YOUR PEARL HARBOR DAY LIKE A MILITARY CAMPAIGN

DIRECTIONS

Take H–1 west from Waikiki to Exit 15A and follow signs. Or take The-Bus route 20 or 47 from Waikiki. Beware high-priced private shuttles. It's a 30-minute drive from Waikiki.

WHAT TO BRING

Picture ID is required during periods of high alert; bring it just in case.

You'll be standing, walking, and climbing all day. Wear something with lots of pockets and a pair of good walking shoes. Carry a light jacket, sunglasses, hat, and sunscreen.

No purses, packs, or bags are allowed. Take only what fits in your pockets. Cameras are okay but without the bags. A private bag storage booth is located in the parking lot near the visitors' center. Leave nothing in your car; theft is a problem despite bicycle security patrols.

HOURS

Hours are 7 AM to 5 PM for the visitor center, though the attractions open at 8 AM. The *Arizona* Memorial starts giving out tickets on a first-come, first-served basis at 7:30 AM; the last tickets are given out at 3 PM. Spring break, summer, and holidays are busiest, and tickets sometimes run out by noon or earlier.

TICKETS

Arizona: Free. Add $7.50 for museum audio tours.

Aviation: $25 adults, $15 children. Add $10 for aviator's guided tour.

Missouri: $25 adults, $13 children. Add $25 for in-depth, behind-the-scenes tours.

Bowfin: $12 adults, $5 children. Children under 4 may go into the museum but not aboard the *Bowfin.*

KIDS

This might be the day to enroll younger kids in the hotel children's program. Preschoolers chafe at long waits, and attractions involve some hazards for toddlers. Older kids enjoy the *Bowfin* and *Missouri,* especially.

MAKING THE MOST OF YOUR TIME

Expect to spend at least half a day; a whole day is better if you're a military history buff.

At the *Arizona* Memorial, you'll get a ticket, be given a tour time, and then have to wait anywhere from 15 minutes to 3 hours. You must pick up your own ticket so you can't hold places. If the wait is long, skip over to the *Bowfin* to fill the time.

SUGGESTED READING

Pearl Harbor and the USS Arizona Memorial, by Richard Wisniewski. $5.95. 64-page magazine-size quick history.

Bowfin, by Edwin P. Hoyt. $14.95. Dramatic story of undersea adventure.

The Last Battleship, by Scott C. S. Stone. $11.95. Story of the Mighty Mo.

If you're a snorkeler, head straight for Hanauma Bay, the best and most popular place to snorkel on Oahu.

of *Arizona* tickets are now given out at recreation.gov where you book a specific time slot. But if you didn't get a ticket online, arrive early for a limited number of same-day tickets and prepare to wait for your time slot. There are restrictions on what you can bring with you, including purses, backpacks, and camera cases (although cameras are allowed). Baggage lockers are available for a small fee. Also, don't forget ID. ⇨ *For much more detailed information, see the highlighted feature in this chapter.* ⊠ *World War II Valor in the Pacific National Monument, 1 Arizona Memorial Pl., Pearl Harbor* ☎ *808/422-3300* ⊕ *www.nps. gov/valr/* ✉ *Arizona admission is free with a $1.50 online reservation charge; separate fees for Bowfin, Missouri, Arizona audio tour; package deals available* ⊙ *Daily 7–5; Arizona Memorial tours daily 8–3* ☞ *Call 877/444–6777 or go to recreation.gov for timed reservations.*

DOWNTOWN HONOLULU

Honolulu's past and present play a delightful counterpoint throughout the downtown sector, which is approximately 6 miles east of Honolulu International Airport. Postmodern glass-and-steel office buildings look down on the Aloha Tower, built in 1926 and, until the early 1960s, the tallest structure in Honolulu. Hawaii's history is told in the architecture of these few blocks: the cut-stone turn-of-the-20th-century storefronts of Merchant Street, the gracious white-columned American-Georgian manor that was the home of the Islands' last queen, the jewel-box palace occupied by the monarchy before it was overthrown, the Spanish-inspired stucco and tile-roofed Territorial Era government buildings, and the 21st-century glass pyramid of the First Hawaiian Bank Building.

GETTING HERE AND AROUND

To reach downtown Honolulu from Waikiki by car, take Ala Moana Boulevard to Alakea Street and turn right; three blocks up on the right, between South King and Hotel, there's a municipal parking lot in Alii Place on the right. There are also public parking lots in buildings along Alakea, Smith, Beretania, and Bethel streets (Chinatown Gateway on Bethel Street is a good choice). The best parking downtown, however, is metered street parking along Punchbowl Street—when you can find it.

Another option is to take Route 20 or 42 of highly popular and convenient TheBus to the Aloha Tower Marketplace, or take a trolley from Waikiki.

WALKING TOURS

American Institute of Architects (AIA) Honolulu Walking Tour. Join an AIA tour to see downtown Honolulu from an architectural perspective, including the restored Hawaii Theatre, city seat Honolulu Hale, and the open-air state capitol. Advance reservations are required. Tours are offered only on Saturday mornings. ☎ *808/628–7243* ⊕ *www.aiahonolulu.org* ✉ *$10.*

Hawaii Geographic Society. The society offers three historic downtown Honolulu walking tours focusing on the monarchy era, architecture, and temples. Email the organization for more information. ☎ *808/538–3952* ✉ *hawaiigeographicsociety@gmail.com* ✉ *$15.*

TIMING

Plan a couple of hours for exploring downtown's historic buildings, more if you're taking a guided tour or walk. The best time to visit is in the cool and relative quiet of morning or on the weekends when downtown is all but deserted except for the historic sites.

TOP ATTRACTIONS

Fodor's Choice ★ **Iolani Palace.** America's only royal residence was built in 1882 on the site of an earlier palace. It contains the thrones of King Kalakaua and his successor (and sister) Queen Liliuokalani, who was imprisoned in her home after the 1893 overthrow. Bucking the stereotype of simple island life, the palace had electricity and telephone lines installed even before the White House. Downstairs galleries showcase the royal jewelry and a kitchen and offices restored to the glory of the monarchy. The palace is open for guided tours or self-guided audio tours, and reservations are recommended. ■TIP➜ If you're set on taking a guided tour, call for reservations a few days in advance. The main gift shop was formerly the Iolani Barracks, built to house the Royal Guard. ⊠ *King and Richards Sts., Downtown Honolulu* ☎ *808/522–0832* ⊕ *www.iolanipalace.org* ✉ *$21.75 guided tour, $14.75 audio tour, $7 downstairs galleries only* ☉ *Mon.–Sat. 9–4; guided tours every 15 mins Tues.–Sat. mornings.*

Kamehameha I Statue. Paying tribute to the Big Island chieftain who united all the warring Hawaiian Islands into one kingdom at the turn of the 18th century, this statue, which stands with one arm outstretched in welcome, is one of three originally cast in Paris, France, by American sculptor T. R. Gould. The original statue, lost at sea and replaced by this one, was eventually salvaged and is now in Kapaau, on the Big Island, near the king's birthplace. Each year on the king's birthday, June

Take a guided tour of Iolani Palace, said to be America's only royal residence, built in 1882.

11, the more famous copy is draped in fresh lei that reach lengths of 18 feet and longer. A parade proceeds past the statue, and Hawaiian civic clubs, women in hats and impressive long *holoku* dresses, and men in sashes and cummerbunds pay honor to the leader whose name means "The One Set Apart." ⊠ *417 S. King St., outside Aliiolani Hale, Downtown Honolulu.*

Kawaiahao Church. Fancifully called Hawaii's Westminster Abbey, this historic house of worship witnessed the coronations, weddings, and funerals of generations of Hawaiian royalty. Each of the building's 14,000 coral blocks was quarried from reefs offshore at depths of more than 20 feet and transported to this site. Interior woodwork was created from the forests of the Koolau Mountains. The upper gallery has an exhibit of paintings of the royal families. The graves of missionaries and of King Lunalilo are adjacent. Services in English and Hawaiian are held each Sunday, and the church members are exceptionally welcoming, greeting newcomers with lei; their affiliation is United Church of Christ. Although there are no guided tours, you can look around the church at no cost. ⊠ *957 Punchbowl St., at King St., Downtown Honolulu* ☏ *808/469–3000* ⊕ *www.kawaiahao.org* ✉ *Free* ☉ *Services Sun. at 9 am.*

WORTH NOTING

FAMILY **Aloha Tower Marketplace.** In two stories of shops and kiosks you can find island-inspired clothing, jewelry, art, and home furnishings. The Marketplace also has indoor and outdoor restaurants and live entertainment. For a bird's-eye view of this working harbor, take a free ride up to the observation deck of Aloha Tower. Cruise ships usually dock at

Downtown Honolulu

Kuan Yin Temple

Chinatown
see detail map

TheBus & police vehicles only

Oahu Marketplace

PUNCH-BOWL CRATER

River St.

Aala St.

Maunakea

Kukui St.

Nuuanu

Lunalilo Frwy.

Pali Hwy.

Iolani Ave.

61

H1

H1

N. Beretania

Pauahi

N. Hotel St.

King St.

Kekaulike

Maunakea

Smith

Fort St.

Bethel St.

Vineyard Blvd.

Queen Emma

Bishop St.

Alakea

Miller St.

Punchbowl St.

S. Beretania St.

Tamarind Park

Hotel St.

Richards St.

DOWNTOWN

Merchant St.

Queen St.

Fort St.

Mililani

S. King St.

South St.

Kapiolani Blvd.

Ala Moana Blvd.

Punchbowl St.

Pohukaina

Keaweohou

Queen St.

Ilaniwai

Halekauwila

Waimanu

Kawaiahao

Cooke

Honolulu Harbor

Auahi St.

Keawe

Coral

Cooke

One

Kamani

Ward Ave.

Auahi St.

Sand Island

92

2

3

5

6

4

7

8

9

10

1

11

Kewalo Basin

12

0 ————— 500 yards
0 ————— 500 meters

Piers 10 and 11 alongside the Marketplace, making it a prime visitor spot. ⊠ *1 Aloha Tower Dr., at Piers 10 and 11, Downtown Honolulu* ☎ *808/566–2337 entertainment info* ⊕ *www.alohatower.com* ◷ *Mon.– Sat. 9–9, Sun. 9–6; restaurants open later.*

✕ **Murphy's Bar & Grill.** In a vintage brick building at the corner of Nuuanu Street and Merchant, Murphy's Bar & Grill is an old-fashioned Irish pub, sports bar, and *kamaaina*-style family restaurant. Comfort food is the order of the day, and the friendly bartenders happily handle the weekend bar crowd. ⊠ *2 Merchant St., Downtown Honolulu* ☎ *808/531–0422* ⊕ *murphyshawaii.com.*

Hawaiian Mission Houses. The determined Hawaii missionaries arrived in 1820, gaining royal favor and influencing a wide array of island life. Their descendants became leaders in government and business. At Hawaiian Mission Houses Historic Site and Archives (previously Mission Houses Museum), you can learn about their influence and walk through their original dwellings, including Hawaii's oldest wooden structure, a white-frame house that was prefabricated in New England and shipped around the Horn. Certain areas of the museum may be seen only on a one-hour guided tour given every hour. Docents paint an excellent picture of what mission life was like. Rotating displays showcase such arts as Hawaiian quilting, portraits, even toys, and a rich archival library is also open to the public. ⊠ *553 S. King St., Downtown Honolulu* ☎ *808/447–3910* ⊕ *www.missionhouses.org* ⌑ *$10* ◷ *Tues.– Sat. 10–4; guided tours hourly 11–3.*

Hawaii State Art Museum. Hawaii was one of the first states in the nation to legislate that a portion of the taxes paid on commercial building projects be set aside for the purchase of artwork. The state purchased an ornate period-style building (that once was the Armed Services YMCA Building) and in 2002 opened a 12,000-square-foot museum on the second floor dedicated to the art of Hawaii in all its ethnic diversity. HiSAM, as it's nicknamed, has a **Diamond Head Gallery** featuring new acquisitions and thematic shows from the State Art Collection and the Hawaii State Foundation on Culture and the Arts. The **Ewa Gallery** houses more than 150 works documenting Hawaii's visual-arts history since becoming a state in 1959. Also included are a sculpture gallery, a gift shop, a café, and educational meeting rooms. Check for occasional evening events like on First Fridays in Chinatown. ⊠ *250 S. Hotel St., 2nd fl., Downtown Honolulu* ☎ *808/586–0300* ⊕ *www.hawaii.gov/sfca* ⌑ *Free* ◷ *Tues.–Sat. 10–4.*

Hawaii State Capitol. The capitol's architecture is richly symbolic: the columns resemble palm trees, the legislative chambers are shaped like volcanic cinder cones, and the central court is open to the sky, representing Hawaii's open society. Replicas of the Hawaii state seal, each weighing 7,500 pounds, hang above both its entrances. The building, which in 1969 replaced Iolani Palace as the seat of government, is surrounded by reflecting pools, just as the Islands are embraced by water. A pair of statues, often draped in lei, flank the building: one of the beloved queen Liliuokalani and the other of the sainted Father Damien de Veuster, famous for helping Molokai leprosy patients. Free guided and self-guided tours are available. ✉ *415 S. Beretania St., Downtown Honolulu* ☎ *808/586–0178, 808/586–0221* ⊕ *governor.hawaii.gov/about/capitol-tour-information* 📧*Free* ⊙ *Guided tours Tues.–Fri. at 1 pm; self-guided tours weekdays 9–3.*

Hawaii State Library. This beautifully renovated main library was built in 1913. Its Samuel M. Kamakau Reading Room, on the first floor in the Mauka (Hawaiian for "mountain") Courtyard, houses an extensive Hawaii and Pacific book collection and pays tribute to Kamakau, a missionary student whose 19th-century writings in English offer rare and vital insight into traditional Hawaiian culture. ✉ *478 S. King St., Downtown Honolulu* ☎ *808/586–3617* 📧 *Free* ⊙ *Mon. and Wed. 10–5; Tues., Fri., and Sat. 9–5; Thurs. 9–8.*

Honolulu Hale. This Mediterranean Renaissance–style building was constructed in 1929 and serves as the center of government for the City and County of Honolulu. Stroll through the shady, open-ceiling lobby with exhibits of local artists. During the winter holiday season, the Hale becomes the focal point for the annual Honolulu City Lights, a display of lighting and playful holiday scenes spread around the campus, including the famous, gigantic Shaka Santa and Tute Mele. The Mayor's Office of Culture and the Arts keeps a calendar of upcoming events. ✉ *530 S. King St., Downtown Honolulu* ☎ *808/768–6622 events, 808/768–4385 general city information* ⊕ *www1.honolulu.gov/moca/calendar.htm* 📧 *Free* ⊙ *Weekdays 7:45–4:30.*

Honolulu Museum of Art. Originally built around the collection of a Honolulu matron who donated much of her estate to the museum, the academy is housed in a maze of courtyards, cloistered walkways, and quiet, low-ceilinged spaces. There's an impressive permanent collection that includes Hiroshige's *ukiyo-e* Japanese prints, donated by James Michener; Italian Renaissance paintings; and American and European art. The newer Luce Pavilion complex, nicely incorporated into the more traditional architecture of the place, has a traveling-exhibit gallery, a Hawaiian gallery, an excellent café, and a gift shop. The Doris Duke Theatre screens art films. This is also the jumping-off point for tours of Doris Duke's estate, Shangri-La. Admission here includes same-day entry to Spalding House, formerly the Contemporary Museum. Call or check the website for special exhibits, concerts, and films. ✉ *900 S. Beretania St., Downtown Honolulu* ☎ *808/532–8700* ⊕ *www.honolulumuseum.org* 📧 *$10; free 1st Wed. and 3rd Sun. of month* ⊙ *Tues.–Sat. 10–4:30, Sun. 1–5.*

CHINATOWN

Chinatown's original business district was made up of dry-goods and produce merchants, tailors and dressmakers, barbers, herbalists, and dozens of restaurants. The meat, fish, and produce stalls remain, but the mix is heavier now on gift and curio stores, lei stands, jewelry shops, and bakeries, with a smattering of noodle makers, travel agents, Asian-language video stores, and dozens of restaurants.

CLOSE UP

Shangri La

The marriage of heiress Doris Duke, at age 23, to a much older man didn't last. But their around-the-world honeymoon did leave her with two lasting loves: Islamic art and architecture, which she first encountered on that journey; and Hawaii, where the honeymooners made an extended stay while Doris learned to surf and befriended Islanders unimpressed by her wealth.

Today visitors to her beloved Islands—where she spent most winters—can share both loves by touring her home. The sought-after tours, which are coordinated by and begin at the Honolulu Museum of Art in downtown Honolulu, start with a visit to the Arts of the Islamic World Gallery. A short van ride then takes small groups on to the house itself, on the far side of Diamond Head. *For more information, see the listing in Southeast Oahu.*

The name *Chinatown* here has always been a misnomer. Though three-quarters of Oahu's Chinese lived closely packed in these 25 acres in the late 1800s, even then the neighborhood was half Japanese. Today, you hear Vietnamese and Tagalog as often as Mandarin and Cantonese, and there are voices of Japan, Singapore, Malaysia, Korea, Thailand, Samoa, and the Marshall Islands, as well.

Perhaps a more accurate name is the one used by early Chinese: *Wah Fau* ("Chinese port"), signifying a landing and jumping-off place. Chinese laborers, as soon as they completed their plantation contracts, hurried into the city to start businesses here. It's a launching point for today's immigrants, too: Southeast Asian shops almost outnumber Chinese; stalls carry Filipino specialties like winged beans and goat meat; and in one tiny space, knife-wielding Samoans skin coconuts to order.

In the half century after the first Chinese laborers arrived in Hawaii in 1851, Chinatown was a link to home for the all-male cadre of workers who planned to return to China rich and respected. Merchants not only sold supplies, they held mail, loaned money, wrote letters, translated documents, sent remittances to families, served meals, offered rough bunkhouse accommodations, and were the center for news, gossip, and socializing.

Though much happened to Chinatown in the 20th century—beginning in January 1900, when almost the entire neighborhood was burned to the ground to halt the spread of bubonic plague—it remains a bustling, crowded, noisy, and odiferous place bent primarily on buying and selling, and sublimely oblivious to its status as a National Historic District or the encroaching gentrification on nearby Nuuanu Avenue.

GETTING HERE AND AROUND
Chinatown occupies 15 blocks immediately north of downtown Honolulu—it's flat, compact, and very walkable.

TIMING

This area is easily explored in half a day. The best time to visit is morning, when the *popos* (grandmas) shop—it's cool out, and you can enjoy a cheap dim-sum breakfast. Chinatown is a seven-days-a-week operation. Sundays are especially busy with families sharing dim sum in raucous dining hall–size restaurants.

If you're here between January 20 and February 20, check local newspapers for Chinese New Year activities. Bakeries stock special sweets, stores and homes sprout bright-red scrolls, and lion dancers cavort through the streets feeding on *li-see* (money envelopes). The Narcissus Queen is chosen, and an evening street fair draws crowds.

GUIDED TOURS

Hawaii Food Tours. Come hungry for food writer Matthew Gray's culinary "Hole-in-the-Wall Tour" through Honolulu, which includes discussion of Hawaiian culinary history and the diversity of the island's food culture, along with 15- to 20-plus samples of local favorites as you walk to a variety of ethnic restaurants, markets, and bakeries, including two hours in Chinatown. It's a great way to get a delicious taste of Hawaii's culture. The tour costs $99 per person. Gray also has a progressive dinner tour through Honolulu and a new North Shore Food Tour. ☏ *808/926–3663* ⊕ *www. hawaiifoodtours.com* ✑ *$99 for Hole-in-the-Wall Tour.*

TOP ATTRACTIONS

Chinatown Cultural Plaza. This sprawling multistory shopping square surrounds a courtyard with an incense-wreathed shrine and Moongate stage for holiday performances. The Chee Kung Tong Society has a beautifully decorated meeting hall here; a number of such *tongs* (meeting places) are hidden on upper floors in Chinatown. Outside, near the canal, local members of the community play cards and mah-jongg. ⊠ *100 N. Beretania St., Chinatown.*

Hawaiian Chinese Multicultural Museum & Archives. Within the Maunakea Marketplace, the small Hawaiian Chinese Multicultural Museum and Archives displays historic photographs and artifacts where you can learn about events like the Great Chinatown Fire of 1900 that burned down most of the neighborhood. ⊠ *Maunakea Marketplace, 1120 Maunakea St., 2nd fl., Chinatown* ☏ *808/524–3409* ✑ *$2* ⊙ *Mon.– Sat. 10–2.*

Izumo Taisha Shrine. From Chinatown Cultural Plaza, cross a stone bridge to the Izumo Taishakyo Mission of Hawaii to visit this shrine

BEST SNACKS IN CHINATOWN

A world of small, inexpensive restaurants exists within Chinatown, among them:

■ **Golden Palace:** $1.50 dim sum

■ **Lucky Belly:** Tasty ramen and late-night snacks

■ **Maunakea Marketplace:** Eclectic food court

■ **Char Hung Sut:** Manapua and dim sum

■ **Grand Café & Bakery:** Newly relocated in HiSAM

■ **Mabuhay:** Filipino standards

■ **Little Village Noodle House:** Diverse Chinese menu

established in 1906. It honors Okuninushi-no-Mikoto, a *kami* (god) who is believed in Shinto tradition to bring good fortune if properly courted (and thanked afterward). ✉ *215 N. Kukui St., at the canal, Chinatown* ☎ *808/538–7778.*

Kuan Yin Temple. A couple of blocks *mauka* (toward the mountains) from Chinatown is the oldest Buddhist temple in the Islands. Mistakenly called a goddess by some, Kuan Yin, also known as Kannon, is a *bodhisattva*—one who chose to remain on Earth doing good even after achieving enlightenment. Transformed from a male into a female figure centuries ago, she is credited with a particular sympathy for women. You will see representations of her all over the Islands: holding a lotus flower (beauty from the mud of human frailty), as at the temple; pouring out a pitcher of oil (like mercy flowing); or as a sort of Madonna with a child. Visitors are permitted but be aware this is a practicing place of worship. ✉ *170 N. Vineyard Blvd., Chinatown.*

Maunakea Marketplace. On the corner of Maunakea and Hotel streets is this busy plaza surrounded by shops, an indoor market, and a food court. It gets packed every year for the annual Chinese Lunar New Year. ■ **TIP➔ If you appreciate fine tea, visit the unpretentious tea counter in the Tea Hut, a curio shop filled with Chinese gifts and good-luck charms.** ✉ *1120 Maunakea St., Chinatown* ☎ *808/524–3409.*

DID YOU KNOW?

Just north of downtown Honolulu is Chinatown, where you can explore temples, eat authentic cuisine, and watch Chinese New Year festivities.

Oahu Market. In this market founded in 1904, you'll find a taste of old-style Chinatown, where you might be hustled aside as a whole pig (dead, of course) is wrestled through the crowd and where glassy-eyed fish of every size and hue lie stacked forlornly on ice. Try the bubble tea (juices and flavored teas with tapioca bubbles inside) or pick up a bizarre magenta dragonfruit for breakfast. ⊠ *N. King St. at Kekaulike St., Chinatown.*

WORTH NOTING

Foster Botanical Gardens. Some of the trees in this botanical garden, open since 1931, date back to 1853 when Queen Kalama allowed a young German doctor to lease a portion of her land. Over 150 years later, you can see these trees and countless others along with bromeliads, orchids, and other tropical plants, some of which are rare or endangered. Look out in particular for the cannonball tree and the redwood-size Quipo tree. A docent-led tour is available Monday through Saturday at 1 pm (call for reservations). ⊠ *50 N. Vineyard Blvd., Chinatown* ☎ *808/522–7066* ⊕ *www1.honolulu.gov/parks/hbg/fbg.htm* ☑ *$5* ⊙ *Daily 9–4.*

Hawaii Theatre. Opened in 1922, this theater earned rave reviews for its neoclassical design, with Corinthian columns, marble statues, and plush carpeting and drapery. Nicknamed the "Pride of the Pacific," the facility was rescued from demolition in the early 1980s and underwent a $30 million renovation. Listed on both the State and National Register of Historic Places, it has become the centerpiece of revitalization efforts of Honolulu's downtown area. The 1,400-seat venue hosts concerts, theatrical productions, dance performances, and film screenings. Guided tours of the theater (reservations required) end with a mini-concert on the historic orchestral pipe organ and can be booked through the box office. ⊠ *1130 Bethel St., Chinatown* ☎ *808/528–0506* ⊕ *www.hawaiitheatre.com* ☑ *$10* ⊙ *Tours Tues. at 11 am, subject to performances.*

Nuuanu Avenue. Here on Chinatown's main *mauka–makai* drag and on Bethel Street, which runs parallel, are clustered art galleries, restaurants, a wineshop, an antiques auctioneer, a dress shop or two, one small theater/exhibition space (the Arts at Mark's Garage), and one historic stage (the Hawaii Theatre). **First Friday** art nights, when galleries stay open until 9 pm, draw crowds. Many stay later and crowd Chinatown's bars. If you like art and people-watching and are fortunate enough to be on Oahu the first Friday of the month, this event shouldn't be missed. ⊠ *Nuuanu Ave., Chinatown.*

KAKAAKO

This 600-acre section of Honolulu between Ala Moana Center and downtown is in the first phase of a decade-long redevelopment plan. Now home to everything from ramshackle mechanic shops to the University of Hawaii's medical school, Kakaako's old warehouses and mom-and-pop storefronts are being replaced by gleaming luxury condos, shops, and restaurants. Experience a neighborhood in transition.

Kakaako Waterfront Park. Rolling hills carpeted in lush green grass greet the visitor to Kakaako park. Popular with local families and perfect for watching the sunset or the Friday evening sailboat races, it has a seaside promenade following a lava-rock wall. Though it has no beach access, the Diamond Head end of the promenade is a great spot to watch surfers and Friday evening fireworks off of Waikiki. ⊠ *677 Ala Moana Blvd., Kakaako* ☯ *Daily 7–7.*

ALA MOANA

Ala Moana abuts Waikiki to the east (stopping at the Ala Wai Canal) and King Street to the north. Kakaako, Kewalo Basin Harbor, and the Blaisdell Center complex roughly mark its western edge. Probably it's most notable attraction is the sprawling Ala Moana Center, jam-packed with almost any store you could wish for.

IWILEI

Before the arrival of Captain Cook, Iwilei was a network of fishponds. After his arrival it became home to a prison, railway depot, and houses of ill repute. (When the red-light district was shut down in 1916, one prostitute hopped a ship to Pago Pago. Also on the ship was Somerset Maugham, who immortalized her as Sadie Thompson in his short story *Rain.*) Today it is an industrial zone offering a few reasons to visit—the Dole Cannery complex of shops and a multiplex (home to the Hawaii International Film Festival each October) begin the primary one. The shopping center really was a pineapple cannery before its conversion; almost any local of a certain age has tales of summer jobs there.

MAKIKI HEIGHTS

Makiki includes the more unassuming neighborhood where President Barack Obama grew up. Other highlights include the exclusive Punahou School he attended and the notable Central Union Church, as well as the Tantalus area overlook.

TOP ATTRACTIONS

Spalding House. In the exclusive Makiki Heights neighborhood, just minutes from downtown Honolulu, the Spalding House features an array of artwork with a large contemporary art collection. A new, school curriculum–themed gallery rotates every six months with topics like art, math, science, and music, making it accessible for kids and interesting for adults. Situated in the 3½-acre Alice Cooke Spalding home and estate (built in 1925), the museum boasts ever-changing exhibitions as well as a peaceful sculpture garden with breathtaking views of Diamond Head and Waikiki and a gift shop. Previously known as the Contemporary Museum, Spalding House became part of the Honolulu Museum of Art organization, so a single admission gets you into both museums on the same day. ⊠ *2411 Makiki Heights Dr., Makiki Heights* ☎ *808/526–1322* ⊕ *honolulumuseum.org/11981-contemporary_ museum_spalding_house* ⊠ *$10, includes entry to Honolulu Museum of Art* ☯ *Tues.–Sat. 10–4, Sun. noon–4.*

WORTH NOTING

Tantalus and Round Top Scenic Drive. A few minutes and a world away from Waikiki and Honolulu, this scenic drive shaded by vine-draped trees has frequent pullouts with views of Diamond Head and the Ewa side of Honolulu. It's a nice change of pace from urban life below. At Puu Ualakaa Park, stop to see the sweeping view from Manoa Valley to Honolulu. To start the drive, go to Punchbowl Memorial Cemetery and follow Tantalus Drive as it climbs uphill. ⊠ *3200 Round Top Dr., Makiki.*

KALIHI

North of downtown Honolulu, just off H1, is the tightly packed neighborhood of Kalihi. It's home to large industrial pockets but also the stellar Bishop Museum, Lion Coffee headquarters, and great local eateries like Young's Fish Market, Helena's Hawaiian Food, Mitsu-Ken (plus Liliha Bakery in neighboring Liliha that's not to be missed due to its ono coco puffs).

TOP ATTRACTIONS

Fodors Choice
★

Bishop Museum. Founded in 1889 by Charles R. Bishop as a memorial to his wife, Princess Bernice Pauahi Bishop, the museum began as a repository for the royal possessions of this last direct descendant of King Kamehameha the Great. Today it's the state's designated history and cultural museum. Its five exhibit halls house almost 25 million items that tell the history of the Hawaiian Islands and their Pacific neighbors. The latest addition to the complex is a 16,500 square-foot natural-science wing with a three-story simulated volcano at its center, where twice-daily "lava melt" shows take place much to the enjoyment of younger museum patrons. Newly renovated Pacific Hall (formerly Polynesian Hall) now focuses on the history of the entire Pacific region.

The Hawaiian Hall, with state-of-the-art and often interactive displays, teaches about the Hawaiian culture. Spectacular Hawaiian artifacts—lustrous feather capes, bone fish hooks, the skeleton of a giant sperm whale, photography and crafts displays, and an authentic, well-preserved grass house—are displayed inside a three-story 19th-century Victorian-style gallery. The building alone, with its huge Victorian turrets and immense stone walls, is worth seeing. Also check out the planetarium, daily tours, hula and science demonstrations, special exhibits, and the Shop Pacifica. ⊠ *1525 Bernice St., Kalihi* ☎ *808/847–3511* ⊕ *www.bishopmuseum.org* ⊡ *$19.95* ☉ *Wed.–Mon. 9–5.*

NUUANU

Immediately *mauka* of Kalihi, off Pali Highway, are a renowned resting place and a carefully preserved home where royal families retreated during the doldrums of summer. Nuuanu Pali was the sight of a famous battle that was key to King Kamehameha I's success in uniting all of the Hawaiian Islands under his rule and becoming the Islands' first monarch. Nuuanu Valley is known for its lush, quiet beauty and has several notable cemeteries, churches, and embassies.

Greater
Honolulu

Honolulu Watershed
Forest Reserve

Lyon
Arboretum ◆

MANOA

PALOLO

Tantalus
Drive ◆

MAKIKI
HEIGHTS

Round Top
Drive ◆

Spalding
House ◆

Nehoa St.

Manoa Rd.

Hwy. O.

Wilder
Ave.

ST. LOUIS
HEIGHTS

WILHELMINA
RISE

University Ave.

Lunalilo Fwy.

H1

Beretania St.

King St.

University
of Hawaii
(Manoa Capus)

Chaminade
University
of Honolulu

St. Louis

Paloto Ave.

8th Ave.

10th Ave.

Wilhelmina

16th Ave.

MOILIILI

Kapiolani Blvd.

Hawaii
Convention
Center ◆

Ala Wai Canal

KAPAHULU

Waialae Ave.

Lunalilo Fwy.

Pahoa

Kalakaua Ave.

Ala Wai Blvd.

Date St.

Ala Wai
Golf Course

KAIMUKI

Kilauea Ave.

KAHALA

Fort
DeRussy

Ala Wai
Yacht
Harbor

Waikiki Beach ☂

WAIKIKI

Kapahulu

Alohea Ave.

12th Ave.

Makapuu

Kapiolani
Community College

Honolulu
Zoo ◆

Monsarrat Ave.

Diamond Head Rd.

Kahala
Ave.

Kapiolani
Park

Waikiki Aquarium ◆

Diamond Head
State Monument
and Park

Diamond
Head ▲

Kaalawai Beach ☂

Waikiki and
Diamond Head
see detail map

Diamond Head Rd.

Diamond Head Rd.

Diamond
Head Beach ☂

2

TOP ATTRACTIONS

Queen Emma Summer Palace. Queen Emma, King Kamehameha IV's wife, used this stately white home, built in 1848, as a retreat from the rigors of court life in hot and dusty Honolulu during the mid-1800s. It has an eclectic mix of European, Victorian, and Hawaiian furnishings and has excellent examples of Hawaiian quilts and koa-wood furniture. ✉ *2913 Pali Hwy., Nuuanu* ☎ *808/595–3167* ⊕ *www. queenemmasummerpalace.org* ➲ *$10 guided tours, $8 self-guided tours* ⊙ *Daily 9–4 (last tour at 3).*

WORTH NOTING

National Memorial Cemetery of the Pacific. Nestled in the bowl of Puowaina, or Punchbowl Crater, this 112-acre cemetery is the final resting place for more than 50,000 U.S. war veterans and family members and is a solemn reminder of their sacrifice. Among those buried here is Ernie Pyle, the famed World War II correspondent who was killed by a Japanese sniper on Ie Shima, an island off the northwest coast of Okinawa. There are intricate stone maps providing a visual history military history lesson. Puowaina, formed 75,000–100,000 years ago during a period of secondary volcanic activity, translates as "Hill of Sacrifice." Historians believe this site once served as an altar where ancient Hawaiians offered sacrifices to their gods. ■**TIP→ The entrance to the cemetery has unfettered views of Waikiki and Honolulu—perhaps the finest on Oahu.** ✉ *2177 Puowaina Dr., Nuuanu* ☎ *808/532–3720* ⊕ *www.cem. va.gov/cem/cems/nchp/nmcp.asp* ➲ *Free* ⊙ *Mar.–Sept., daily 8–6:30; Oct.–Feb., daily 8–5:30.*

MOILIILI

Packed into the neighborhood of Moiliili are flower and lei shops, restaurants (Spices, Fukuya Delicatessen, Sweet Home Café), and little stores such as Kuni Island Fabrics, a great source for Hawaiian quilting and other crafting materials; Siam Imports, for goodies from Thailand; and Revolution Books, Honolulu's only leftist bookshop. Most places of interest are along King Street, between Isenberg and Waialae avenues.

KAPAHULU

Walk just a few minutes from the eastern end of Waikiki, and you'll find yourself in this very local main drag of restaurants, antiques shops (Bailey's Antiques and Aloha Shirts, ✉ *517 Kapahulu Ave.*, is the place for rare, $5,000 wearable collectibles), and sports rental outfits (kayaking, surfing, diving, biking).

KAIMUKI

Ten minutes beyond Kapahulu is this commercial thoroughfare that runs through an old neighborhood filled with cool old craftsman bungalows (that are slowly being knocked down to make room for tickytacky boxes). It may have the highest and most diverse concentration of eateries on the island, from a Jamaican restaurant and a shabu-shabu house to a chic, contemporary bistro and a nougat manufacturer.

Waikiki and Honolulu, looking west to Diamond Head, as seen from above

MANOA

Manoa is probably best known as the home to the University of Hawaii's main campus. The surrounding area is chock-full of interesting coffee shops, restaurants, and stores fed by the collegiate and professorial crowd. History and beauty linger around verdant Manoa Valley at places like the Manoa Chinese Cemetery, Lyon Arboretum, and Waioli Tea Room. Manoa Valley Theatre puts on top-notch community theater productions year-round.

WORTH NOTING

Lyon Arboretum. Tucked all the way back in Manoa Valley, this is a gem of an arboretum operated by the University of Hawaii. Hike to a waterfall or sit and enjoy beautiful views of the valley. You'll also see an ethnobotanical garden, a Hawaiian hale and garden, and one of the largest palm collections anywhere—all within a parklike setting. Its educational mission means there are regular talks and walks with university faculty. Docents give 60-minute tours weekdays at 10 am (call ahead to reserve a spot). There are also self-guided tours. ✉ *3860 Manoa Rd., Manoa* ☎ *808/988-0456* ⊕ *www.hawaii.edu/lyonarboretum* ✉ *Tours $5* ⊙ *Weekdays 8–4, Sat. 9–3.*

KAHALA

Oahu's wealthiest neighborhood has streets lined with multimillion-dollar homes. At intervals along tree-lined Kahala Avenue are narrow lanes that provide public access to Kahala's quiet, narrow coastal beaches offering views of Koko Head. Kahala Mall is one of the island's largest indoor shopping centers and includes restaurants, a movie theater, and a Whole Foods grocery store. Kahala is also the home of the private Waialae Country Club and golf course, site of the annual Sony Open PGA golf tournament in January.

WORTH NOTING

FAMILY **Dolphin Quest at The Kahala.** This worldwide dolphin-encounter group has an Oahu location in the Kahala. Trained Atlantic bottlenose dolphins hold court in an enclosed lagoon at the center of the hotel. The Kid's Aquatic Adventure is a 90-minute, in-the-water session of feeding and interacting with stingrays and dolphins. For the adults, there is more variety, starting with a 15-minute encounter and going up to the 5½-hour "Trainer for a Day" experience. ⊠ *The Kahala, 5000 Kahala Ave., Kahala* ☎ *808/739–8918* ⊕ *www.dolphinquest.com* ✉ *From $125 for a 15-min encounter.*

MAPUNAPUNA

Mapunapuna is an area filled with factories and offices surrounding the airport. Tucked amid car dealerships, a Kaiser Permanente medical center, and the island's Harley Davidson outlet are fast-food joints, a Chinese restaurant, local plate-lunch places, and Mitch's, a somewhat undiscovered gem of a sushi spot.

KAPALAMA

This sliver of land that runs from ocean to mountain (known as an *ahupuaa* in Hawaiian), is presided over by famed Kamehameha Schools, which from its hillside perch looks down on this warren of modest homes and shops—and the Bishop Museum.

SALT LAKE

There's no longer a lake, salty or not, in this suburb of Honolulu. Instead, you'll find a largely residential neighborhood with a commercial core at Salt Lake Shopping Center plus the oasis of Moanalua Gardens.

WORTH NOTING

Moanalua Gardens. This lovely park is a great place to bring a picnic, spread out a blanket, and take a snooze, fly a kite, or simply idle an afternoon away. It's also the location of the internationally acclaimed Prince Lot Hula Festival on the third weekend in July. You'll often see Japanese visitors taking pictures by a sprawling monkeypod tree nicknamed the Hitachi Tree and famous for advertising the Hitachi brand in Japan. Call the Moanalua Gardens Foundation to see about park booklets and occasional hikes. To reach Moanalua Gardens, take the Moanalua Freeway westbound (78). Take the Tripler exit, then take a right on Mahiole Street. Pineapple Place is just after Moanalua Elementary School. ⊠ *1352 Pineapple Pl., Salt Lake* ☎ *808/839–5334* ⊕ *www. moanaluagardens.com* ✉ *Free* ⊙ *Daily 8–5.*

SOUTHEAST OAHU

Approximately 10 miles southeast of Waikiki.

Driving southeast from Waikiki on busy four-lane Kalanianaole Highway, you'll pass a dozen bedroom communities tucked into the valleys at the foot of the Koolau Range, with fleeting glimpses of the ocean from a couple of pocket parks. Suddenly, civilization falls away, the road narrows to two lanes, and you enter the rugged coastline of Koko Head and Ka Iwi.

This is a cruel coastline: dry, windswept, and rocky shores, with untamed waves that are notoriously treacherous. While walking its beaches, do not turn your back on the ocean, don't venture close to wet areas where high waves occasionally reach, and be sure to heed warning signs.

At this point, you're passing through Koko Head Regional Park. On your right is the bulging remnant of a pair of volcanic craters that the Hawaiians called Kawaihoa, known today as Koko Head. To the left is Koko Crater and an area of the park that includes a hiking trail, a dryland botanical garden, a firing range, and a riding stable. Ahead is a sinuous shoreline with scenic pullouts and beaches to explore. Named the Ka Iwi Coast (*iwi,* "ee-vee," are bones—sacred to Hawaiians and full of symbolism) for the channel just offshore, this area was once home to a ranch and small fishing enclave that were destroyed by a tidal wave in the 1940s.

TOP ATTRACTIONS

QUICK BITES

Kokonuts Shave Ice and Snacks. Stop for shave ice on the South Shore. President Barack Obama did while visiting the island after the 2008 election. Kokonuts Shave Ice and Snacks in Koko Marina Center serves, arguably, the best shave ice this side of Haleiwa. ⊠ *7192 Kalanianaole Hwy., Hawaii Kai* ☎ *808/396–8809* ☉ *Sun.–Thurs. 10:30–7:30, Fri. and Sat. 10:30–9.*

Halona Blowhole. Below a scenic turnout along the Koko Head shoreline, this oft-photographed lava tube sucks the ocean in and spits it out. Don't get too close, as conditions can get dangerous. ■**TIP**➔ Look to your right to see the tiny beach below that was used to film the wave-washed love scene in *From Here to Eternity.* In winter this is a good spot to watch whales at play. Offshore, the islands of Molokai and Lanai call like distant sirens, and every once in a while Maui is visible in blue silhouette. Take your valuables with you and lock your car, because this scenic location is overrun with tourists and therefore a hot spot for petty thieves. ⊠ *Kalanianaole Hwy., 1 mile east of Hanauma Bay, Hawaii Kai.*

Koko Crater Botanical Gardens. If you've visited any of Oahu's other botanical gardens, this one will be in stark contrast. Inside the tallest tuff cone on Oahu, in one of the hottest and driest areas on the island, Koko Crater Botanical Garden allows visitors the opportunity to see dryland species of plants including baobab trees, cacti, plumeria, and bougainvillea. Guided group tours are available by appointment.

Southeast Oahu

Southeast Oahu map showing TO KAILUA, Mt. Olomana, Bellows Beach, Waimanalo, Waimanalo Beach Park, Puu Lanipo, Kaau Crater, KOOLAU RANGE, Kalanianaole Hwy, MANANA ISLAND (RABBIT ISLAND), KAOHIKAIPU ISLAND, Makapuu Beach, Makapuu Point, MAKAPUU HEAD, Koko Crater Botanical Garden, Koko Crater, Sandy Beach, TO HONOLULU, Kalanianaole Hwy, PAIKO PENINSULA, Hawaii Kai, Halona Blowhole, Lanai Lookout, Maunalua Bay, Hanauma Bay, KOKO HEAD, Kaiwi Channel, 0 3 mi, 0 3 km

✉ *Entrance at end of Kokonani St., near Hawaii Kai Dr., Hawaii Kai* ☎ *808/522–7066* ⊕ *www1.honolulu.gov/parks/hbg/kcbg.htm* 🏷 <u>Free</u> ⊙ *Daily sunrise–sunset.*

Lanai Lookout. A little over a half-mile past Hanauma Bay as you head toward Makapuu Point, you'll see a turnout on the ocean side with some fine views of the coastline. In winter, you'll have an opportunity to see storm-generated waves crashing against lava cliffs. This is also a popular place for <u>winter whale-watching</u> so bring your binoculars, some sunscreen, and a picnic lunch and join the small crowd scanning for telltale white spouts of water only a few hundred yards away. On clear days, you should be able to see the islands of Molokai and Lanai off in the distance, hence the name. ✉ *Kalanianaole Hwy., just past Hanauma Bay, Hawaii Kai.*

Makapuu Point. This spot has breathtaking views of the ocean, mountains, and the windward Islands. The point of land jutting out in the distance is **Mokapu Peninsula,** site of a U.S. Marine base. The spired mountain peak is **Mt. Olomana.** On the long pier is part of the **Makai Undersea Test Range,** a research facility that's closed to the public. Offshore is **Manana Island (Rabbit Island),** a picturesque cay said to resemble a swimming bunny with its ears pulled back. Ironically enough, Manana Island was once overrun with rabbits, thanks to a rancher who let a few hares run wild on the land. They were eradicated in 1994 by biologists who grew concerned that the rabbits were destroying the island's native plants.

Nestled in the cliff face is the **Makapuu Lighthouse,** which became operational in 1909 and has the largest lighthouse lens in America. The lighthouse is closed to the public, but near the Makapuu Point turnout you can find the start of a mile-long paved road (closed to vehicular traffic). Hike up to the top of the 647-foot bluff for a closer view of the lighthouse and, in winter, a great whale-watching vantage point. For the more adventurous, at the whale-watching sign on the main path, head down a switchback trail to the **Makapuu tidepools** below. ⊠ *Ka Iwi State Scenic Shoreline, Kalanianaole Hwy., at Makapuu Beach, Kaneohe* ⊕ *www.hawaiistateparks.org.*

Shangri La. In 1936, heiress Doris Duke bought 5 acres at Black Point, down the coast from Waikiki, and began to build and furnish the first home that would be all her own. She called it Shangri La. For more than 50 years, the home was a work in progress as Duke traveled the world, buying art and furnishings, picking up ideas for her Mughul garden, for the Playhouse in the style of a 17th-century Irani pavilion, and for the water terraces and tropical gardens. When she died in 1993, Duke left instructions that her home was to become a public center for the study of Islamic art.

To walk through the house and its gardens—which have remained much as Duke left them with only some minor conservation-oriented changes—is to experience the personal style of someone who saw everything as raw material for her art.

With her trusted houseman, Jin de Silva, she helped build the elaborate Turkish Room, trimming tiles and painted panels to retrofit the existing space (including raising the ceiling and lowering the floor) and building a fountain of her own design. Among many aspects of the home inspired by the Muslim tradition is the entry: an anonymous gate, a blank white wall, and a wooden door that bids you "Enter herein in peace and security" in Arabic characters. Inside, tiles glow, fountains tinkle, and shafts of light illuminate artworks through arches and high windows. This was her private world, entered only by trusted friends.

The house is open by guided tour only and reservations are highly recommended. Tours take 2½ hours including transportation from the Honolulu Museum of Art. Children under 12 are not admitted. All tours begin at the museum, 900 South Beretania, in Downtown Honolulu. ⊠ *Hawaii Kai* ☎ *808/532–3853 Honolulu Museum of Art* ⊕ *www. shangrilahawaii.org or honolulumuseum.org/385-about_shangri_la* 💷 *Tour $25; $1.50 fee for online reservations; $2 for phone reservations* ⊙ *Wed.–Sat. at 9, 10:30, and 1:30 by reservation only.*

WINDWARD OAHU

Approximately 15 miles northeast of downtown Honolulu (20–25 minutes by car), approximately 25 miles southeast of downtown Honolulu via Ka Iwi and Waimanalo (35–45 minutes by car).

Looking at Honolulu's topsy-turvy urban sprawl, you would never suspect the windward side existed. It's a secret Oahuans like to keep, so they can watch the awe on the faces of their guests when the car emerges from the tunnels through the mountains and they gaze for the first time on the panorama of turquoise bays and emerald valleys watched over by the knife-edged Koolau ridges. Jaws literally drop. Every time. And this just a 15-minute drive from downtown.

It's on this side of the island where many Native Hawaiians live. Evidence of traditional lifestyles is abundant in crumbling fishponds, rock platforms that once were altars, taro patches still being worked, and throw-net fishermen posed stock-still above the water (though today, they're invariably wearing polarized sunglasses, the better to spot the fish).

Here, the pace is slower, more oriented toward nature. Beach-going, hiking, diving, surfing, and boating are the draws, along with a visit to the Polynesian Cultural Center, and poking through little shops and wayside stores.

GETTING HERE AND AROUND

For a driving experience you won't soon forget, take the H3 freeway over to the windward side. As you pass through the tunnels, be prepared for one of the most breathtaking stretches of road anywhere. Flip a coin before you leave to see who will drive and who will gape.

TIMING

You can easily spend an entire day exploring Windward Oahu, or you can just breeze on through, nodding at the sights on your way to the North Shore. Waikiki to Windward is a drive of less than half an hour; to the North Shore via Kamehameha Highway along the Windward Coast is one hour, minimum.

TOP ATTRACTIONS

Byodo-In Temple. Tucked away in the back of the Valley of the Temples cemetery is a replica of the 11th-century Temple at Uji in Japan. A 2-ton carved wooden statue of the Buddha presides inside the main temple building. Next to the temple building are a meditation pavilion and gardens set dramatically against the sheer, green cliffs of the Koolau Mountains. You can ring the 5-foot, 3-ton brass bell for good luck and feed some of the hundreds of carp, ducks, and swans that inhabit the garden's 2-acre pond. Or, you can enjoy the peaceful surroundings and just relax. ⊠ *47-200 Kahekili Hwy., Kaneohe* ☎ *808/239–8811* ⊕ *www.byodo-in.com* ⊠ *$3* ☉ *Daily 9–5.*

NEED A BREAK?

Kalapawai Market. Generations of children have purchased their beach snacks and sodas at Kalapawai Market, near Kailua Beach. A Windward Oahu landmark since 1932, the green-and-white market has distinctive charm. You'll see slipper-clad locals sitting in front, enjoying a cup of

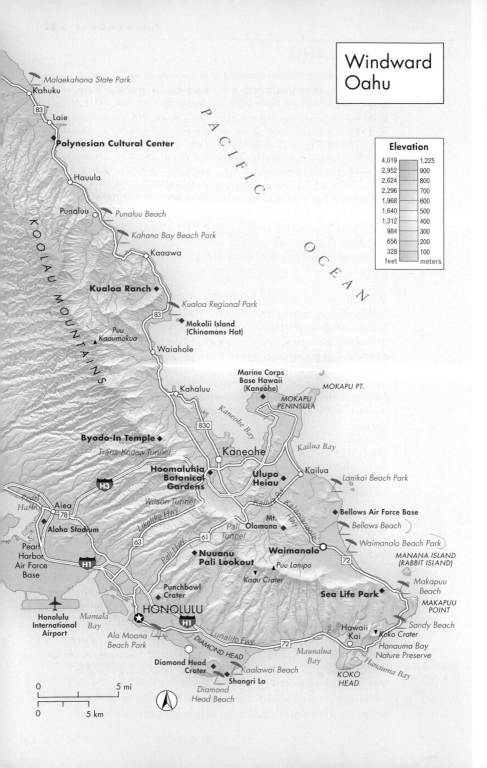

Windward Oahu

Elevation

feet	meters
4,019	1,225
2,952	900
2,624	800
2,296	700
1,968	600
1,640	500
1,312	400
984	300
656	200
328	100
feet	meters

PACIFIC OCEAN

Malaekahana State Park
Kahuku
83
Laie
Polynesian Cultural Center
Hauula
Punaluu
Punaluu Beach
Kahana Bay Beach Park
Kaaawa
Kualoa Ranch
Kualoa Regional Park
83
Mokolii Island
(Chinamans Hat)
Puu
Kaaumakua
Waiahole

KOOLAU MOUNTAINS

Kahaluu
830
Marine Corps
Base Hawaii
(Kaneohe)
MOKAPU PT.
MOKAPU
PENINSULA
Byodo-In Temple
Trans-Kodaw Tunnel
Kaneohe Bay
Kaneohe
Kailua Bay
**Hoomaluhia
Botanical
Gardens**
**Ulupo
Heiau**
Kailua
Lanikai Beach Park
H3
Wilson Tunnel
Aiea
78
Kailua Rd.
Kalanianaole Hwy.
Bellows Air Force Base
Aloha Stadium
Likelike Hwy.
Pali Hwy.
63
Pali
Tunnel
61
Mt.
Olomana
Bellows Beach
Pearl
Harbor
Air Force
Base
H1
Waimanalo Beach Park
Waimanalo
72
MANANA ISLAND
(RABBIT ISLAND)
**Nuuanu
Pali Lookout**
Puu Lanipo
Kaou Crater
Makapuu
Beach
Punchbowl
Crater
Sea Life Park
MAKAPUU
POINT
HONOLULU
H1
Hawaii
Kai
Koko Crater
Sandy Beach
Honolulu
International
Airport
Mamala
Bay
Ala Moana
Beach Park
Lunalilo Fwy.
DIAMOND HEAD
72
Maunalua
Bay
Hanauma Bay
Nature Preserve
KOKO
HEAD
Hanauma Bay
**Diamond Head
Crater**
Kaalawai Beach
Shangri La
Diamond
Head Beach

Pearl
Harbor

0   5 mi

0   5 km

CLOSE UP

Windward Oahu Villlages

Tiny villages—generally consisting of a sign, store, a beach park, possibly a post office, and not much more—are strung along Kamehameha Highway on the windward side. Each has something to offer. In **Waiahole**, look for fruit stands and an ancient grocery store. In **Kaaawa**, there's a lunch spot and convenience store–gas station. In **Punaluu**, stop at the gallery of fanciful landscape artist Lance Fairly, get a plate lunch at Keneke's, or visit venerable Ching General Store or the Shrimp Shack. Kim Taylor Reece's photo studio, featuring haunting portraits of hula dancers, is between Punaluu and Hauula. **Hauula** has Hauula Gift Shop & Art Gallery, formerly yet another Ching Store, now a clothing shop where sarongs wave like banners, and, at Hauula Kai Shopping Center, Tamura's Market, with excellent seafood and the last liquor before Mormon-dominated Laie.

coffee and talking story at picnic tables or in front of the market. It's a good source for your carryout lunch, since there's no concession stand at the beach. With one of the better selections of wine on the island, the market is also a great place to pick up a bottle. There's a sister Kalapawai Cafe with a sit-down menu closer to the entrance to Kailua. ✉ *306 S. Kalaheo Ave., Kailua* ☎ *808/262–4359* ⊕ *www.kalapawaimarket.com* ⊙ *Daily 6 am–9 pm; deli 6:30 am–7 pm.*

Nuuanu Pali Lookout. This panoramic perch looks out to expansive views of Windward Oahu. It was in this region that King Kamehameha I drove defending forces over the edges of the 1,000-foot-high cliffs, thus winning the decisive battle for control of Oahu. ■TIP→ From here you can see views that stretch from Kaneohe Bay to Mokolii ("little lizard"), a small island off the coast, and beyond. Temperatures at the summit are several degrees cooler than in warm Waikiki, so bring a jacket along. Hang on tight to any loose possessions and consider wearing pants; it gets extremely windy at the lookout, which is part of the fun. Lock your car in the pay-to-park lot; break-ins have occurred here (this wayside is in the most trafficked state park in Hawaii). ✉ *Top of Pali Hwy., Kaneohe* ⊕ *www.hawaiistateparks.org/parks/oahu/nuuanu.cfm* ⊙ *Daily during daylight hours.*

NEED A BREAK?

Island Snow. Long a favorite of Windward Oahu residents for its shave ice counter within the clothing store, Island Snow has more recently become known as the place where President Obama and his daughters have gone to for the sweet treat when they vacation in Hawaii. Extra fluffy shave ice topped off with local syrup flavors and a milky "snow cap" make this one of the best shave ice stops on the island. ✉ *130 Kailua Rd., separate entrance from clothing shop, Kailua* ☎ *808/263-6339* ⊕ *www.islandsnow.com* ⊙ *Mon.–Thurs. 10–6, Fri.–Sun. 10–7.*

You can catch a great sunrise over Manana Island, otherwise known as Rabbit Island, located on the windward side of Oahu.

EN ROUTE

Mokolii. As you drive the Windward and North shores along Kamehameha Highway, you'll note a number of interesting geological features. At Kualoa look to the ocean and gaze at the uniquely shaped little island of Mokolii (little lizard), a 206-foot-high sea stack also known as Chinaman's Hat. According to Hawaiian legend, the goddess Hiiaka, sister of Pele, slew the dragon Mokolii and flung its tail into the sea, forming the distinct islet. Other dragon body parts—in the form of rocks, of course—were scattered along the base of nearby Kualoa Ridge. ■TIP➡ In Laie, if you turn right on Anemoku Street, and right again on Naupaka, you come to a scenic lookout where you can see a group of islets, dramatically washed by the waves. ✉ 49-479 *Kamehameha Hwy., Kaneohe* ⊕ *www1.honolulu.gov/parks/programs/beach/kualoa.htm.*

FAMILY **Polynesian Cultural Center.** Re-created individual villages showcase the lifestyles and traditions of Hawaii, Tahiti, Samoa, Fiji, the Marquesas Islands, New Zealand, and Tonga. Focusing on individual islands within its 42-acre center, 35 miles from Waikiki, the Polynesian Cultural Center was founded in 1963 by the Church of Jesus Christ of Latter-day Saints. It houses restaurants, hosts luaus, and demonstrates cultural traditions such as tribal tattooing, fire dancing, and ancient customs and ceremonies. The expansive open-air shopping village carries Polynesian handicrafts. ■TIP➡ If you're staying in Honolulu, see the center as part of a van tour so you won't have to drive home late at night after the two-hour evening show. There are multiple packages available, from basic admission to an all-inclusive deal. Every May, the PCC hosts the World Fireknife Dance Competition, an event that draws the top fire-knife dance performers from around the world. Get tickets for that event in advance. ⊠ *55-370 Kamehameha Hwy., Laie* ☎ *808/293–3333, 800/367–7060* ⊕ *www.polynesia.com* ⊠ *From $50; $8 parking fee* ⊙ *Mon.–Sat. noon–9:15 (villages noon–6).*

WORTH NOTING

Ahupuaa O Kahana State Park. This park offers the true Hawaiian experience: a beautiful windward bay sits a short walk away from the Huilua Fishpond, a national historic landmark. There are rain-forest hikes chock-full of local fruit trees, a hunting area for pigs, and a coconut grove for picnicking. The water is suitable for swimming and bodysurfing, though it's a little cloudy for snorkeling. ⊠ *51–222 Kamehameha Hwy., near Kahana Bay, Kaaawa.*

Hoomaluhia Botanical Gardens. The name, which means "to make a place of peace and tranquillity," describes the serenity and feeling of endless space you find in this verdant garden framed by the stunning Koolau mountain range. Inside its 400 acres are plant collections from such tropical areas as the Americas, Africa, Melanesia, the Philippines, and Hawaii. Guided nature tours are offered by reservation on Saturday at 10 and Sunday at 1. Not just for the botanist, Hoomaluhia also has a 32-acre lake and open lawns ideal for picnicking and camping by permit. ⊠ *45-680 Luluku Rd., Kaneohe* ☎ *808/233–7323* ⊕ *www1. honolulu.gov/parks/hbg/hmbg.htm* ⊠ *Free* ⊙ *Daily 9–4.*

Kualoa Ranch. Encompassing 4,000 acres, about 45 minutes by car from Waikiki, this working ranch offers a wide range of activities—from ATV and horseback tours to hula lessons or jungle expeditions in six-wheel-drive vehicles. The mountains, which serve as the backdrop of this scenic ranch, may seem familiar as the ranch has served as the set for movies such as *Jurassic Park* and *Wind Talkers,* and TV shows like *Magnum PI* and *Lost* (and you can take a movie sites tour). From the grounds, you'll have a wonderful view of the ocean and Chinaman's Hat. You can drop by the visitor center anytime, but it's best to book activities and tours two or three days in advance. ⊠ *49-560 Kamehameha Hwy., Kaaawa* ☎ *808/237–7321* ⊕ *www.kualoa.com* ⊠ *From $26* ⊙ *Daily 7:30–5:30.*

FAMILY **Sea Life Park.** Dolphins leap and spin and penguins frolic at this marine-life attraction 15 miles from Waikiki at scenic Makapuu Point. The park has a 300,000-gallon Hawaiian reef aquarium, a breeding sanctuary for Hawaii's endangered *honu* sea turtle, a penguin habitat, and many more marine attractions. Sign up for a dolphin, seal, stingray, or shark encounter and get up close and personal in the water with these sea creatures (don't worry, the rays' stingers have been removed, and you'll be behind a wire mesh with the sharks). ⊠ *41-202 Kalanianaole Hwy., Waimanalo* ☎ *808/259–2500* ⊕ *www.sealifeparkhawaii.com* ⊠ *$30* ⊙ *Daily 10:30–5.*

Ulupo Heiau. Though they may look like piles of rocks to the uninitiated, *heiau* are sacred stone platforms for the worship of the gods and date from ancient times. Ulupo means "night inspiration," referring to the legendary *Menehune,* a mythical race of diminutive people who are said to have built the heiau under the cloak of darkness. Find this spot, with

Stroll along Kailua Beach, which many consider to be Oahu's best beach, as well as the hottest place to windsurf on the island.

signs near the heiau also explaining Kailua's early history, tucked next to the Kailua YMCA. ⊠ *Kalanianaole Hwy. and Kailua Rd., behind the YMCA, Kailua* ⊕ *www.hawaiistateparks.org/parks/oahu/ulupo.cfm.*

Waimanalo. This modest little seaside town flanked by chiseled cliffs is worth a visit. Home to more Native Hawaiian families than Kailua to the north or Hawaii Kai to the south, Waimanalo's biggest draws are its beautiful beaches, offering glorious views to the Windward side. **Bellows Beach** is great for swimming, bodysurfing, and camping, and **Waimanalo Beach Park** is also safe for swimming. Down the side roads, as you head *mauka* (toward the mountains), are little farms that grow a variety of fruits and flowers. Toward the back of the valley are small ranches with grazing horses. ■TIP→ If you see any trucks selling corn and you're staying at a place where you can cook it, be sure to get some in Waimanalo. It may be the sweetest you'll ever eat, and the price is the lowest on Oahu. ⊠ *Kalanianaole Hwy., Waimanalo.*

THE NORTH SHORE

Approximately 35 miles (one hour by car) north of downtown Honolulu, approximately 25 miles (one hour by car) from Kualoa Regional Park (Chinaman's Hat) in Windward Oahu.

An hour from town and a world away in atmosphere, Oahu's North Shore, roughly from Kahuku Point to Kaena Point, is about small farms and big waves, tourist traps, and otherworldly landscapes. Parks and beaches, roadside fruit stands and shrimp shacks, a bird sanctuary, and

Continued on page 90

Imagine picking your seat for free at the Super Bowl or wandering the grounds of Augusta National at no cost during The Masters, and you glimpse the opportunity you have when attending the Vans Triple Crown of Surfing on the North Shore.

NORTH SHORE SURFING & THE TRIPLE CROWN

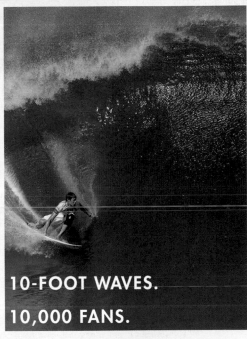

10-FOOT WAVES.
10,000 FANS.
TOP 50 SURFERS.

Long considered the best stretch of surf breaks on Earth, the North Shore surf area encompasses 6 miles of coastline on the northwestern tip of Oahu from Haleiwa to Sunset Beach. There are over 20 major breaks within these 6 miles. Winter storms in the North Pacific send huge swells southward which don't break for thousands of miles until they hit the shallow reef of Oahu's remote North Shore. This creates optimum surfing all winter long and was the inspiration for having surf competitions here each holiday season.

Every November and December the top 50 surfers in world rankings descend on "The Country" to decide who is the best all-around surfer in the world. Each of the three invitation-only contests that make up the Triple Crown has its own winner; competitors also win points based on the final standings. The surfer who excels in all three contests, racking up the most points overall, wins the Vans Triple Crown title. The first contest is held at **Haleiwa Beach,** the second at **Sunset Beach.** The season reaches its crescendo at the most famous surf break in the world, the **Banzai Pipeline.**

The best part is the cost to attend the events—nothing; your seat for the show—wherever you set down your beach towel. Just park your car, grab your stuff, and watch the best surfers in the world tame the best waves in the world.

The only surfing I understand involves the TV.

The contests were created not only to name an overall champion, but to attract the casual fan to the sport. Announcers explain each ride over the loudspeakers, discussing the nuances and values being weighed by the judges. A scoreboard displays points and standings during the four days of each event.

If this still seems incomprehensible to you, the action on the beach can also be exciting as some of the most beautiful people in the world are attracted to these contests.

For more information, see www.triplecrownofsurfing.com.

What should I bring?

Pack for a day at the Triple Crown the way you would for any day at the beach—sun block, beach towel, bottled water, and if you want something other than snacks, food.

These contests are held in rural neighborhoods (read: few stores), so pack anything you might need during the day. Also, binoculars are suggested, especially for the contest at Sunset. The pros will be riding huge outside ocean swells, and it can be hard to follow from the beach without binoculars. Haleiwa's breaks and Pipeline are considerably closer to shore, but binoculars will let you see the intensity on the contestants' faces.

Haleiwa Alii Beach Park
Vans Triple Crown Contest #1: Reef Pro Hawaii

The Triple Crown gets underway with high-performance waves (and the know-how to ride them) at Haleiwa. Though lesser known than the other two breaks of the Triple Crown, it is the perfect wave for showing off: the contest here is full of sharp cutbacks (twisting the board dramatically off the top or bottom of the wave), occasional barrel rides, and a crescendo of floaters (balancing the board on the top of the cresting wave) before the wave is destroyed on the shallow tabletop reef called the Toilet Bowl. The rider who can pull off the most tricks will win this leg, evening the playing field for the other two contests, where knowledge of the break is the key. Also, the beach park is walking distance from historic Haleiwa town, a mecca to surfers worldwide who make their pilgrimage here every winter to ride the waves. Even if you are not a fan, immersing yourself in their culture will make you one by nightfall.

Sunset Beach
Vans Triple Crown Contest #2: Vans World Cup of Surfing

At Sunset, the most guts and bravado win the day. The competition is held when the swell is at 8 to 12 feet and from the northwest. Sunset gets the heaviest surf because it is the exposed point on the northern tip of Oahu. Surfers describe the waves here as "moving mountains." The choice of waves is the key to this contest as only the perfect one will give the competitor a ride through the jigsaw-puzzle outer reef, which can kill a perfect wave instantly, all the way into the inner reef. Big bottom turns (riding all the way down the face of the wave before turning dramatically back onto the wave) and slipping into a super thick tube (slowing down to let the wave catch you and riding inside its vortex) are considered necessary to carry the day.

Banzai Pipeline
Vans Triple Crown Contest #3: Billabong Pipeline Masters

Surfing competitions are generally judged on the top three waves ridden by the competitors. In the Pipeline Masters, however, instead of accruing points through tricks and jumps, the surfers score high by dropping in the deepest and staying inside the tube the longest. The best trick at Pipeline is surviving this incredibly hollow and heavy wave, no other artistry is necessary.

How does the wave become hollow in the first place? When the deep ocean floor ascends steeply to the shore, the waves that meet it will pitch over themselves sharply, rather than rolling. This pitching causes a tube to form, and in most places in the world that tube is a mere couple of feet in diameter. In the case of Pipeline, however, its unique, extremely shallow reef causes the swells to open into 10-foot-high moving hallways that surfers can pass through. Only problem: a single slip puts them right into the raggedly sharp coral heads that caused the wave to pitch in the first place. Broken arms and boards are the rule rather than the exception for those who dare to ride and fail.

■TIP→ The Banzai Pipeline is a surf break, not a beach. The best place to catch a glimpse of the break is from Ehukai Beach.

When Are the Contests?

The first contests at Haleiwa begin the second week of November, and the Triple Crown finishes up right before Christmas.

Surfing, more so than any other sport, relies on Mother Nature to allow competition. Each contest in the Triple Crown requires only four days of competition, but each is given a window of twelve days. Contest officials decide by 7 AM of each day whether the contest will be held or not, and they release the information to radio stations and via a hotline (the number changes each year, unfortunately). By 7:15, you will know if it is on or not. Consult the local paper's sports section for the hotline number or listen to the radio announcement. The contests run from 8:30 to 4:30, featuring half-hour heats with four to six surfers each.

If big crowds bother you, go early on in the contests, within the first two days of each one. While the finale of the Pipeline Masters may draw about 10,000 fans, the earlier days have the same world-class surfers with fewer than a thousand fans.

How Do I Get There?

If you hate dealing with parking and traffic, take TheBus. It will transport you from Waikiki to the contest sites in an hour for two bucks and no hassle.

If you must drive, watch the news the night before. If they are expecting big waves that night, there is a very good chance the contest will be on in the morning. Leave by 6 AM to beat the crowd. When everybody else gets the news at 7:15 AM that the show is on, you will be parking your car and taking a snooze on the beach waiting for the surfing to commence.

Parking is limited so be prepared to park alongside Kamehameha Highway and trek it in.

But I'm not coming until Valentine's Day.

There doesn't need to be a contest underway for you to enjoy these spots from a spectator's perspective. The North Shore surf season begins in October and concludes at the end of March. Only the best can survive the wave at Pipeline. You may not be watching 11-time world champ Kelly Slater ripping, but, if the waves are up, you will still see surfing that will blow your mind. Also, there are surf contests year-round on all shores of Oahu, so check the papers to see what is going on during your stay. A few other events to be on the lookout for:

Buffalo's Annual Big Board Surfing Classic

Generally held in March at legendary waterman "Buffalo" Keaulana's home beach of Makaha, this is the Harlem Globetrotters of surfing contests. You'll see tandem riding, headstands, and outrigger canoe surfing. The contest is more about making the crowds cheer than beating your competitors, which makes it very accessible for the casual fan.

Converse Hawaiian Open

During the summer months, the waves switch to the south shore, where there are surf contests of one type or another each week. The Open is one of the biggest and is a part of the US Professional Longboard Surfing Championships. The best shoot it out every August on the waves Duke Kahanamoku made famous at Queen's Beach in Waikiki.

Quiksilver in Memory of Eddie Aikau Big Wave Invitational

The granddaddy of them all is a one-day, winner-take-all contest in 25-foot surf at Waimea Bay. Because of the need for huge waves, it can be held only when there's a perfect storm. That could be at any time in the winter months, and there have been many years when it didn't happen at all. When Mother Nature does comply, however, it is not to be missed. You can hear the waves from the road, even before you can see the beach or the break.

BOARD SHAPES

Longboard: Lengthier (about 2.5–3 m/9–10.5 feet), wider, thicker, and more buoyant than the often-miniscule shortboards. Offers more flotation and speedier paddling, which makes it easier to get into waves. Great for beginners and those with relaxed surf styles. Skill level: Beginner to Intermediate.

Funboard: A little shorter than the longboard with a slightly more acute nose and blunt tail, the Funboard combines the best attributes of the longboards with some similar characteristics of the shorter boards. Good for beginners or surfers looking for a board more maneuverable and faster than a longboard. Skill level: Beginner to Intermediate.

Fishboard: A stumpy, blunt-nosed, twin-finned board that features a "V" tail (giving it a "fish" like look, hence the name) and is fast and maneuverable. Good for catching small, steep, slow waves and pulling tricks. At one point this was the world's best-selling surfboard. Skill level: Intermediate to Expert.

Shortboard: Shortboards came on the scene in 1967-70 when the average board length dropped from 9'6" to 6'6" (2.9m to 2m) and changed the wave riding styles in the surf world forever. This board is a short, light, high-performance stick that is designed for carving the wave with a high amount of maneuverability. These boards need a fast steep wave, completely different than a longboard break, which tends to be slower with shallower wave faces. Skill level: Expert.

Beginner   Expert

Funboards

Fishboards

Longboards

Shortboards

Shallow wave faces, easiest surfing   Steeper wave faces, difficult surfing a valley preserve offer a dozen reasons to stop between the onetime plantation town of Kahuku and the surf mecca of Haleiwa.

Haleiwa has had many lives, from resort getaway in the 1900s to plantation town through the 20th century to its life today as a surf and tourist magnet. Beyond Haleiwa is the tiny village of Waialua, a string of beach parks, an airfield where gliders, hang gliders, and parachutists play, and, at the end of the road, Kaena Point State Recreation Area, which offers a brisk hike, striking views, and whale-watching in season.

Pack wisely for a day's North Shore excursion: swim and snorkel gear, light jacket and hat (the weather is mercurial, especially in winter), sunscreen and sunglasses, bottled water and snacks, towels and a picnic blanket, and both sandals and closed-toe shoes for hiking. A small cooler is nice; you may want to pick up some fruit or fresh corn. As always, leave valuables in the hotel safe and lock the car whenever you park.

GETTING HERE AND AROUND

From Waikiki, the quickest route to the North Shore is H1 east to H2 north, and then the Kamehameha Highway past Wahiawa; you'll hit Haleiwa in less than an hour. The windward route (H1 east, H3, Likelike or Pali Highway, through the mountains, or Kamehameha Highway north) takes at least 90 minutes to Haleiwa, but the drive is far prettier.

TIMING

It's best to dedicate an entire day for an excursion to the North Shore, as it's about an hour from downtown Honolulu, depending on traffic. Start your trip in Kailua and drive up the Windward coast for the full scenic experience.

TOP ATTRACTIONS

Haleiwa. Today Haleiwa is a fun mix of old and new, with charming general stores and contemporary boutiques, galleries, and eateries. During the 1920s this seaside hamlet boasted a posh hotel at the end of a railroad line (both long gone), while the 1960s saw hippies gathered here, followed by surfers from around the world. Be sure to stop in at **Liliuokalani Protestant Church,** founded by missionaries in the 1830s. It's fronted by a large, stone archway built in 1910 and covered with night-blooming cereus. ✉ *Haleiwa ✛ Follow H1 west from Honolulu to H2 north, exit at Wahiawa, follow Kamehameha Hwy. 6 miles, turn left at signaled intersection, then right into Haleiwa.*

NEED A BREAK?

Matsumoto's. For a real slice of Haleiwa life, stop at Matsumoto's, a family-run business in a building dating from 1910, for shave ice in every flavor imaginable. For something different, order a shave ice with adzuki beans—the red beans are boiled until soft, mixed with sugar, and then placed in the cone with the ice on top. ✉ *66-087 Kamehameha Hwy., Haleiwa* ☎ *808/637–4827* ⊕ *www.matsumotoshaveice.com* ◷ *Daily 9–6.*

Kaena Point State Recreation Area. The name means "the heat" and, indeed, this windy barren coast lacks both shade and fresh water (or any man-made amenities). Pack water, wear sturdy closed-toe shoes, don sunscreen and a hat, and lock the car. The hike is along a rutted dirt road, mostly flat and 3 miles long, ending in a rocky, sandy headland. It is here that Hawaiians believed the souls of the dead met with their family gods, and, if judged worthy to enter the afterlife, leapt off into eternal darkness at Leinaakauane, just south of the point. In summer and at low tide, the small coves offer bountiful shelling; in winter,

WORD OF MOUTH

"[Waimea Valley Park] was very nice. It has paved trails through beautiful gardens; there are also some other trails. It was very peaceful! Peacocks run around the property." —Kerry392

don't venture near the water. Rare native plants dot the landscape. If you're lucky, you might spot seals sunbathing on the rocks. From November through March, watch for humpbacks, spouting and breaching. Binoculars and a camera are highly recommended. ⊠ 69-385 Farrington Hwy., Makua ⊕ www.hawaiistateparks.org/parks/oahu.

FAMILY
Fodor's Choice
★

Waimea Valley Park. Waimea may get lots of press for the giant winter waves in the bay, but the valley itself is a newsmaker and an ecological treasure in its own right. The Office of Hawaiian Affairs is working to conserve and restore the natural habitat. Follow the Kamananui Stream up the valley through the 1,800 acres of gardens. The botanical collections here include more than 5,000 species of tropical flora, including a superb gathering of Polynesian plants. It's the best place on the island to see native species, such as the endangered Hawaiian moorhen. You can also see the remains of the Hale O Lono *heiau* (temple) along with other ancient archaeological sites; evidence suggests that the area was an important spiritual center. Daily activities include hula lessons, native plant walks, and traditional Hawaiian games, depending on how many staff members are working on a given day. At the back of the valley, **Waihi Falls** plunges 45 feet into a swimming pond. ■TIP→ Bring your board shorts—a swim is the perfect way to end your hike. Be sure to bring mosquito repellent, too; it can get buggy. ⊠ 59-864 Kamehameha Hwy., Haleiwa ☎ 808/638–7766 ⊕ www.waimeavalley.net ☞ $15 ⊙ Daily 9–5.

QUICK
BITES

Ted's Bakery. The chocolate *haupia* (coconut pudding) pie at Ted's Bakery is legendary. Stop in for a takeout pie or for a quick plate lunch or sandwich. ⊠ 59-024 Kamehameha Hwy., near Sunset Beach, Haleiwa ☎ 808/638–8207 ⊕ www.tedsbakery.com ⊙ Daily 7 am–8 pm.

WORTH NOTING

Puuomahuka Heiau. Worth a stop for its spectacular views from a bluff high above the ocean overlooking Waimea Bay, this sacred spot was once the site of human sacrifices. It's now on the National Register of Historic Places. Turn up the road at the Haleiwa Foodland, and follow the road up to the heiau. ⊠ Pupukea Rd., ½ mile north of Waimea Bay, Haleiwa ⊹ From Rte. 83, turn right on Pupukea Rd. and drive 1 mile uphill.

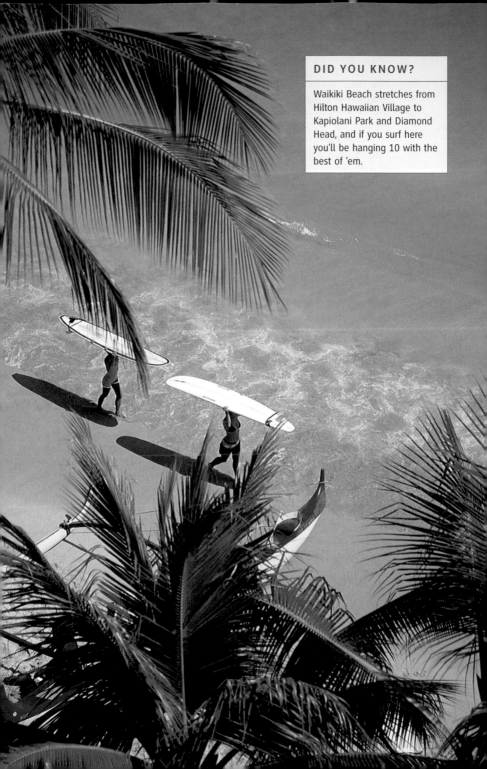

DID YOU KNOW?

Waikiki Beach stretches from Hilton Hawaiian Village to Kapiolani Park and Diamond Head, and if you surf here you'll be hanging 10 with the best of 'em.

CENTRAL OAHU

2

Wahiawa is approximately 20 miles (30–35 minutes by car) north of downtown Honolulu, 15 miles (20–30 minutes by car) south of the North Shore.

Oahu's central plain is a patchwork of old towns and new residential developments, military bases, farms, ranches, and shopping malls, with a few visit-worthy attractions and historic sites scattered about. Central Oahu encompasses the Moanalua Valley, residential Pearl City and Mililani, and the old plantation town of Wahiawa, on the uplands halfway to the North Shore.

GETTING HERE AND AROUND

For Central Oahu, all sights are most easily reached by either the H1 or H2 freeway.

TIMING

In Central Oahu, check out the Dole Plantation for all things pineapple. This area is about 35 minutes' drive from downtown Honolulu and might make a good stop on the drive to the North Shore or after a morning at Pearl Harbor, but the area is probably not worth a separate visit, particularly if you're short on time.

TOP ATTRACTIONS

Dole Plantation. Pineapple plantation days are nearly defunct in Hawaii, but you can still celebrate Hawaii's famous golden fruit at this promotional center with exhibits, a huge gift shop, a snack concession, educational displays, and the world's largest maze. Take the self-guided Garden Tour, plant your own pineapple, or hop aboard the *Pineapple Express* for a 20-minute train tour to learn a bit about life on a pineapple plantation. Kids love the more than 3-acre Pineapple Garden Maze, made up of 14,000 tropical plants and trees. If you do nothing else, stop by the cafeteria in the back for a delicious pineapple soft-serve Dole Whip. This is about a 40-minute drive from Waikiki, a suitable stop on the way to or from the North Shore. ✉ *64-1550 Kamehameha Hwy., Wahiawa* ☎ *808/621–8408* ⊕ *www.dole-plantation.com* ☞ *Pavilion free,* <u>*maze $6, train $8.50, garden tour $5*</u> ⊗ *Daily 9:30–5:30; train, maze, and garden 9:30–5.*

Kukaniloko Birthstone State Monument. In the cool uplands of Wahiawa is haunting Kukaniloko, where noble chieftesses went to give birth to high-ranking children. One of the most significant cultural sites on the island, the lava-rock stones here were believed to possess the power to ease the labor pains of childbirth. The site is marked by approximately 180 stones covering about a half acre. It's about a 40- to 45-minute drive from Waikiki. ✉ *Kamehameha Hwy. and Whitmore Ave., north side of Wahiawa town, Wahiawa* ⊕ *www.hawaiistateparks.org/parks/oahu/index.cfm?park_id=24.*

WEST (LEEWARD) OAHU

Kapolei is approximately 20 miles (30 minutes by car) west of downtown Honolulu, and 12 miles (20 minutes by car) from Mililani; traffic can add significantly to driving time.

West (or Leeward) Oahu has the island's fledgling "second city"—the planned community of Kapolei, where the government hopes to attract enough jobs to lighten inbound traffic to downtown Honolulu—then continues on past a far-flung resort to the Hawaiian communities of Nanakuli and Waianae, to the beach and the end of the road at Keaweula, aka Yokohama Bay.

A couple of cautions as you head to the leeward side: Highway 93 is a narrow, winding, two-lane road notorious for accidents. There's an abrupt transition from freeway to highway at Kapolei, and by the time you reach Nanakuli, it's a country road, so *slow down*. ⚠ Car break-ins and beach thefts are common here.

GETTING HERE AND AROUND

West Oahu begins at folksy Waipahu and continues past Makakilo and Kapolei on H1 and Highway 93, Farrington Highway.

TIMING

If you've got to leave one part of this island for the next trip, this is the part to skip. It's a longish drive to West Oahu by island standards—45 minutes to Kapolei from Waikiki and 90 minutes to Waianae—and Central Oahu has little to offer. The Waianae Coast is naturally beautiful, but the area doesn't have the tourist amenities you'll find elsewhere on the island. The attraction most worth the trek to West Oahu is Hawaii's Plantation Village in Waipahu, about a half hour out of town; it's a living-history museum built from actual homes of turn-of-the-20th-century plantation workers.

TOP ATTRACTIONS

Hawaii's Plantation Village. Starting in the 1800s, immigrants seeking work on the sugar plantations came to these Islands like so many waves against the shore. At this living museum 30 minutes from downtown Honolulu, visit authentically furnished buildings, original and replicated, that re-create and pay tribute to the plantation era. See a Chinese social hall; a Japanese shrine, sumo ring, and saimin stand; a dental office; and historic homes. The village is open for guided tours only. ✉ *Waipahu Cultural Gardens Park, 94-695 Waipahu St., Waipahu* ☎ *808/677–0110* ⊕ *www.hawaiiplantationvillage.org* 🎟 *$13* ⏱ *Tours on the hr, Mon.–Sat. 10–2.*

FAMILY   **Wet'n'Wild Hawaii.** This 25-acre family attraction has waterslides, water cannons, and waterfalls. ✉ *400 Farrington Hwy., off H1 at Exit 1, Kapolei* ☎ *808/674–9283* ⊕ *www.wetnwildhawaii.com* 🎟 *$47* ⏱ *June–Aug., daily 10:30–3:30 or 4 or 5; Sept.–May, Thurs.–Mon. 10:30–3:30 or 4.*

BEACHES

Updated by
Trina Kudlacek

Tropical sun mixed with cooling trade winds and pristine waters make Oahu's shores a literal heaven on Earth. But contrary to many assumptions, the island is not one big beach. There are miles and miles of coastline without a grain of sand, so you need to know where you're going to fully enjoy the Hawaiian experience.

Much of the island's southern and eastern coast is protected by inner reefs. The reefs provide still coastline water but not much as far as sand is concerned. However, where there are beaches on the south and east shores, they are mind-blowing. In West Oahu and on the North Shore you can find the wide expanses of sand you would expect for enjoying the sunset. Sandy bottoms and protective reefs make the water an adventure in the winter months. Most visitors assume the seasons don't change a bit in the Islands, and they would be mostly right—except for the waves, which are big on the South Shore in summer and placid in winter. It's exactly the opposite on the north side, where winter storms bring in huge waves, but the ocean becomes glasslike come May and June.

HONOLULU

WAIKIKI

The 2-mile strand called Waikiki Beach extends from Hilton Hawaiian Village on one end to Kapiolani Park and Diamond Head on the other. Although it's one contiguous piece of beach, it's as varied as the people that inhabit the Islands. Whether you're an old-timer looking to enjoy the action from the shade or a sports nut wanting to do it all, you can find every beach activity here without ever jumping in the rental car.

■TIP→ If you're staying outside the area, our best advice is to park at either end of the beach and walk in. Plenty of parking exists on the west end at the Ala Wai Marina, where you can park in metered stalls around the harbor for $1 an hour. For parking on the east end, Kapiolani Park

Oahu
Beaches

PACIFIC

OCEAN

North Shore

Windward

Southeast

KOOLAU MOUNTAINS

WAIANAE MOUNTAINS

KOKO HEAD

DIAMOND HEAD

MOKAPU PENINSULA

MOKAPU PT.

KAENA POINT

HONOLULU

Waikiki

Kaneohe

Kailua

Wahiawa

Mililani Town

Kapolei

Ewa

Nanakuli

Maili

Waianae

Makaha

Haleiwa

Waialee

Kahuku

Laie

Hauula

Punaluu

Kahaluu

Kaaawa

Aiea

Waimanalo

Hawaii Kai

Maunalua Bay

Kaohinani

Kaala

Puu Manawahua

Puu

Palikea

Puu Kaaumakua

Puu Lanipo

Mt. Olomana

Kaau Crater

Punchbowl Crater

Koko Crater

Koko Head

Diamond Head Beach

Ala Moana Beach Park

Honolulu International Airport

Pearl Harbor Naval Base

Pearl Harbor

Kaneohe Bay Marine Corps Base

Kaneohe Bay

Bellows Air Force Base

Kailua Bay

Kaneohe Bay

Turtle Bay

Sunset Beach

Ehukai Beach Park (The Banzai Pipeline)

Waimea Bay

Haleiwa Alii Beach Park

Waialua Bay

Mokuleia Beach

Yokohama Bay

Makaha Beach Park

Papaoneone Beach

Pokai Bay Beach Park

Ko Olina

White Plains

Mamala Bay

Malaekahana State Recreation Area

Punaluu Beach Park

Kahana Bay Beach Park

Kualoa Park

Kailua Beach Park

Kanikai Beach Park

Bellows Beach

Waimanalo Beach Park

Makapuu Beach

Sandy Beach

Halona Cove

Hanauma Bay

Kaalawi Beach

Kaaawa

Kahaluu

Kahuku

Waimanalo

Puu Lanipo

H1

H2

H3

H1

83

83

83

83

80

930

803

99

750

76

76

93

93

72

72

61

63

78

830

5 mi

5 km

0

0

and the Honolulu Zoo also have metered parking for $1 an hour—more affordable than the $10 per hour the resorts want.

FAMILY **Duke Kahanamoku Beach.** Named for Hawaii's famous Olympic swimming champion, Duke Kahanamoku, this is a hard-packed beach with the only shade trees on the sand in Waikiki. It's great for families with young children because it has both shade and the calmest waters in Waikiki, thanks to a rock wall that creates a semiprotected cove. The ocean clarity here is not as brilliant as most of Waikiki because of the stillness of the surf, but it's a small price to pay for peace of mind about youngsters. The beach fronts the Hilton Hawaiian Village Beach Resort and Spa. **Amenities:** food and drink; showers; toilets. **Best for:** sunset; walking. ⊠ *2005 Kalia Rd.*

FAMILY **Fort DeRussy Beach Park.** This is one of the finest beaches on the south side of Oahu. A wide, soft, ultrawhite beachfront with gently lapping waves makes it a family favorite for running-jumping-frolicking fun (this also happens to be where the NFL holds its rookie sand football game when Hawaii hosts the Pro Bowl). The new, heavily shaded grass grilling area, sand volleyball courts, and aquatic rentals make this a must for the active visitor. The beach fronts Hale Koa Hotel as well as Fort DeRussy. **Amenities:** food and drink; lifeguards; showers; toilets; water sports. **Best for:** swimming; walking. ⊠ *2161 Kalia Rd.*

Gray's Beach. A little guesthouse called Gray's-by-the-Sea stood here in the 1920s; now it's a gathering place for eclectic beach types from sailing pioneers like George Parsons to the "bird men" of Waikiki: stop and watch the show as up to six parrots are placed on the heads, shoulders, and arms of squealing tourists waiting impatiently for their photos to be taken. The tides often put sand space at a premium, but if you want a look back into old Waikiki, have a mai tai at the Shorebird and check out a time gone by. The Halekulani Hotel and Outrigger Reef hotel are on this beach. **Amenities:** food and drink; lifeguards; parking (fee); showers; toilets. **Best for:** partiers; walking. ⊠ *2199 Kalia Rd.*

Kahaloa and Ulukou Beaches. The beach widens back out here, creating the "it" spot for the bikini crowd. Beautiful bodies abound. This is where you find most of the catamaran charters for a spectacular sail out to Diamond Head, or surfboard and outrigger canoe rentals for a ride on the rolling waves of the Canoe surf break. Great music and outdoor dancing beckon the sand-bound visitor to Duke's Canoe Club, where shirt and shoes not only aren't required, they're discouraged. The Royal Hawaiian Hotel and the Moana Surfrider are both on this

OUTRIGGER CANOES

Outrigger canoes are a simple, cheap, but often-overlooked way to have fun in Waikiki. Everyone clamors to be on the water near Waikiki, and most people go for pricey sailing trips or surf lessons.

The long, funny-looking boats in front of Duke's Canoe Club allow you to get out on the water for much less money. At $10 for three rides, the price hasn't changed in a

decade, and the thrill hasn't changed in centuries. You can get a paddle, but no one expects you to use it—the beach boys negotiate you in and out of the break as they have been doing all their lives.

If you think taking off on a wave on a 10-foot board is a rush, wait until your whole family takes off on one in a 30-foot boat!

3

beach. **Amenities:** food and drink; lifeguards; parking (fee); showers; toilets; water sports. **Best for:** partiers; surfing. ⊠ *2259 Kalakaua Ave.*

FAMILY **Kuhio Beach Park.** This beach has experienced a renaissance after a recent face-lift. Now bordered by a landscaped boardwalk, it's great for romantic walks any time of day. Check out the Kuhio Beach hula mound Tuesday to Sunday at 6:30 for free hula and Hawaiian-music performances and a torch-lighting ceremony at sunset. Surf lessons for beginners are available from the beach center every half hour. **Amenities:** food and drink; lifeguards; showers; toilets; water sports. **Best for:** surfing; walking. ⊠ *2461 Kalakaua Ave.* ✛ *Go past the Moana Surfrider Hotel to the Kapahulu Ave. pier.*

FAMILY **Queen's Surf Beach.** So named as it was once the site of Queen Liliuokalani's beach house, this beach draws a mix of families and gay couples—and it seems as if someone is always playing a steel drum. Many weekends, movie screens are set up on the sand, and major motion pictures are shown after the sun sets (⊕ *www.sunsetonthebeach.net*). In the daytime, there are banyan trees for shade and volleyball nets for pros and amateurs alike. The water fronting Queen's Surf is an aquatic preserve, providing the best snorkeling in Waikiki. **Amenities:** lifeguards; showers; toilets. **Best for:** snorkeling; swimming; walking. ⊠ *2598 Kalakaua Ave., across from the entrance to Honolulu Zoo.*

FAMILY **Sans Souci State Recreational Park.** Nicknamed Dig-Me Beach because of its outlandish display of skimpy bathing suits, this small rectangle of sand is nonetheless a good sunning spot for all ages. Children enjoy its shallow, safe waters, which are protected (for now) by the walls of the historic natatorium, an Olympic-size saltwater swimming arena that's been closed for decades. Serious swimmers and triathletes also swim in the channel here, beyond the reef. Sans Souci is favored by locals wanting to avoid the crowds while still enjoying the convenience of Waikiki. The New Otani Kaimana Beach Hotel is next door. **Amenities:** lifeguards; parking (fee and no fee); showers; toilets. **Best for:** swimming; walking. ⊠ *2776 Kalakaua Ave., across from Kapiolani Park, between the New Otani Kaimana Beach Hotel and the Waikiki War Memorial Natatorium.*

If you've never been on a surfboard before, Oahu is the place to give it a try, just like these students on Waikiki Beach.

ALA MOANA

Honolulu proper only has one beach, Ala Moana. Popular with locals, it hosts everything from Dragon Boat competitions to the Aloha State Games.

FAMILY **Ala Moana Beach Park.** A protective reef makes Ala Moana essentially a ½-mile-wide saltwater swimming pool. Very smooth sand and no waves create a haven for families and stand-up paddle surfers. After Waikiki, this is the most popular beach among visitors, and the free parking area can fill up quickly on sunny weekend days. On the Waikiki side is a peninsula called Magic Island, with shady trees and paved sidewalks ideal for jogging. Ala Moana also has playing fields, tennis courts, and a couple of small ponds for sailing toy boats. This beach is for everyone, but only in the daytime. It's a high-crime area, with lots of homeless people, after dark. **Amenities:** food and drink; lifeguards; parking (no fee); showers; toilets. **Best for:** swimming; walking. ⊠ *1201 Ala Moana Blvd., Ala Moana ⊕ From Waikiki take Bus 8 to Ala Moana Shopping Center and cross Ala Moana Blvd.*

DIAMOND HEAD

Diamond Head Beach. You have to like a little hiking to like Diamond Head Beach. This beautiful, remote spot is at the base of Diamond Head crater. The beach is just a small strip of sand with lots of coral in the water. This said, the views looking out from the point are breathtaking, and it's amazing to watch the windsurfers skimming along, driven by the gusts off the point. From the parking area, look for an opening in the wall where an unpaved trail leads down to the beach. Even for the unadventurous, a stop at the lookout point is well worth the time. **Amenities:** parking (free); showers. **Best for:** solitude; surfing; windsurfing. ⊠ *At base of Diamond Head, 3500 Diamond Head Rd., Diamond Head* ✢ *Park at the crest of Diamond Head Rd. and walk down.*

SOUTHEAST OAHU

Much of Southeast Oahu is surrounded by reef, making most of the coast uninviting to swimmers, but the spots where the reef opens up are true gems. The drive along this side of the island is amazing, with its sheer lava-rock walls on one side and deep-blue ocean on the other. There are plenty of restaurants in the suburb of Hawaii Kai, so you can make a day of it, knowing that food isn't far away.

Halona Cove. Also known as *From Here to Eternity Beach* and "Pounders," this little beauty is never crowded due to the short, treacherous climb down to the sand. But for the intrepid, what a treat this spot can be. It's in a break in the ocean cliffs, with the surrounding crags providing protection from the wind. Open-ocean waves roll up onto the beach (thus the second nickname), but unlike at Sandy Beach, a gently sloping sand bottom takes much of the punch out of them before they hit the shore. Turtles frequent the small cove, seeking respite from the otherwise blustery coast. It's great for packing a lunch and holing up for the day. ⚠ The current is mellow inside the cove but dangerous once you get outside it. **Amenities:** parking (no fee). **Best for:** solitude; sunrise. ⊠ *8699 Kalanianaole Hwy., below the Halona Blow Hole Lookout parking lot, Hawaii Kai.*

FAMILY **Hanauma Bay Nature Preserve.** Picture this as the world's biggest open-air aquarium. You go here to see fish, and fish you'll see. Due to their exposure to thousands of visitors every week, these fish are more like family pets than the skittish marine life you might expect. An old volcanic crater has created a haven from the waves where the coral has thrived. There's an educational center where you must watch a nine-minute video about the nature preserve before being allowed down to the bay. ■TIP→ The bay is best early in the morning (around 7), before the crowds arrive; it can be difficult to park later in the day.

Snorkel equipment and lockers are available for rent, and there's an entry fee for nonresidents. Smoking is not allowed, and the beach is closed on Tuesday. Wednesday to Monday, the beach is open from 6

BEACH SAFETY ON OAHU

Hawaii's world-renowned, beautiful beaches can be dangerous at times due to large waves and strong currents—so much so that the state rates wave hazards using three signs: a yellow square (caution), a red stop sign (high hazard), and a black diamond (extreme hazard). Signs are posted and updated three times daily or as conditions change.

Visiting beaches with lifeguards is strongly recommended, and you should swim only when there's a normal caution rating. Never swim alone or dive into unknown water or shallow breaking waves. If you're unable to swim out of a rip current, don't fight the pull but instead tread water and wave your arms in the air to signal for help.

Even in calm conditions, there are other dangerous things in the water to be aware of, including razor-sharp coral, jellyfish, eels, and sharks.

Jellyfish cause the most ocean injuries, and signs are posted along beaches when they're present. Reactions to a sting are usually mild (burning sensation, redness, welts); however, in some cases they can be severe (breathing difficulties). If you're stung, pick off the tentacles, rinse the affected area with water, and apply ice.

The chances of getting bitten by a shark in Hawaiian waters are very low; sharks attack swimmers or surfers fewer than three or four times per year. Of the 40 species of sharks found near Hawaii, tiger sharks are considered the most dangerous because of their size and indiscriminate feeding behavior. They're easily recognized by their blunt snouts and vertical bars on their sides. Here are a few tips to reduce your shark-attack risk:

■ Swim, surf, or dive with others at beaches patrolled by lifeguards.

■ Avoid swimming at dawn, dusk, and night, when some shark species may move inshore to feed.

■ Don't enter the water if you have open wounds or are bleeding.

■ Avoid murky waters, harbor entrances, areas near stream mouths (especially after heavy rains), channels or steep drop-offs.

■ Don't wear high-contrast swimwear or shiny jewelry.

■ Don't swim near dolphins, which are often prey for large sharks.

■ If you spot a shark, leave the water quickly and calmly; never provoke or harass a shark, no matter how small.

The website ⊕ *oceansafety.soest. hawaii.edu* provides statewide beach-hazard maps as well as weather and surf advisories, listings of closed beaches, and safety tips.

am to 6 pm. There's a tram from the parking lot to the beach, or you can walk the short distance on foot. Need transportation? Hanauma Bay Dive Tours runs snorkeling, snuba, and scuba tours to Hanauma Bay with transportation from Waikiki hotels on Monday, Wednesday, Thursday, and Friday only. ⇨ *See Scuba Diving in Chapter 4, Water Sports and Tours.* **Amenities:** food and drink; lifeguards; parking (fee); showers; toilets. **Best for:** snorkeling; swimming. ⊠ *7455 Kalanianaole Hwy., Hawaii Kai* ☎ *808/396–4229* ✉ *Nonresident fee $7.50; parking*

Not a water baby? Come to Sandy Beach—otherwise known as Break-Neck Beach—to watch the massive ocean swells and awesome pounding surf.

$1; mask, snorkel, and fins rental $12; tram from parking lot to beach $1.75 round-trip ⊗ *Wed.–Mon. 6–6.*

Fodor's Choice **Sandy Beach.** Probably the most popular beach with locals on this side ★ of Oahu, the broad, sloping beach is covered with sunbathers there to watch the "Show" and soak up rays. The Show is a shore break that's like no other in the Islands. Monster ocean swells rolling into the beach combined with the sudden rise in the ocean floor causes waves to jack up and crash magnificently on the shore. Expert surfers and body boarders young and old brave this danger to get some of the biggest barrels you can find for bodysurfing. ⚠ **But keep in mind that the beach is nicknamed "Break-Neck Beach" for a reason: many neck and back injuries are sustained here each year. Use extreme caution when swimming here, or just kick back and watch the drama unfold from the comfort of your beach chair. Amenities:** lifeguards; parking (no fee); showers; toilets. **Best for:** surfing; walking. ⊠ *7850 Kalanianaole Hwy., makai (toward the ocean) of Kalanianaole Hwy., 2 miles east of Hanauma Bay., Hawaii Kai.*

WINDWARD OAHU

The Windward side lives up to its name, with ideal spots for windsurfing and kiteboarding, or for the more intrepid, hang gliding. For the most part the waves are mellow, and the bottoms are all sand—making for nice spots to visit with younger kids. The only drawback is that this side does tend to get more rain. But the vistas are so beautiful that a little sprinkling of "pineapple juice" shouldn't dampen your experience; plus, it benefits the waterfalls that cascade down the Koolaus.

Bellows Beach. Bellows is the same beach as Waimanalo, but it's under the auspices of the military, making it more friendly for visitors—though that also limits public beach access to weekends. The park area is excellent for camping, and ironwood trees provide plenty of shade. ■TIP➔ The beach is best before 2 pm. After 2, the trade winds bring clouds that get hung up on steep mountains nearby, causing overcast skies until midafternoon. There are no food concessions, but McDonald's and other takeout fare, including *huli huli* (rotisserie) chicken on weekends, are right outside the entrance gate. **Amenities:** lifeguards; parking (no fee); showers; toilets. **Best for:** solitude; swimming. ⊠ *520 Tinker Rd., Waimanalo* ⊕ *Entrance on Kalanianaole Hwy. near Waimanalo town center.*

FAMILY **Kahana Bay Beach Park.** Local parents often bring their children here to wade in safety in the very shallow, protected waters. This pretty beach cove, surrounded by mountains, has a long arc of sand that is great for walking and a cool, shady grove of tall ironwood and pandanus trees that is ideal for a picnic. An ancient Hawaiian fishpond, which was in use until the 1920s, is visible nearby. The water here is not generally a clear blue due to the runoff from heavy rains in the valley. **Amenities:** lifeguards; parking (no fee); showers; toilets. **Best for:** swimming; walking. ⊠ *52-201 Kamehameha Hwy., north of Kualoa Park, Kaneohe.*

FAMILY **Kailua Beach Park.** A cobalt-blue sea and a wide continuous arc of pow-
Fodor's Choice dery sand make Kailua Beach Park one of the island's best beaches,
★ illustrated by the crowds of local families who spend their weekend days here. This is like a big Lanikai Beach, but a little windier and a little wider, and a better spot for spending a full day. Kailua Beach has calm water, a line of palms and ironwoods that provide shade on the sand, and a huge park with picnic pavilions where you can escape the heat. This is the "it" spot if you're looking to try your hand at windsurfing or kiteboarding. You can rent kayaks nearby at Kailua Sailboards and Kayaks (⊠ *130 Kailua Rd.*) and take them to the Mokulua Islands for the day. Two-seaters cost $69 for four hours or $79 for a full day. ⇨ *See Windsurfing and Kiteboarding in Chapter 4.* **Amenities:** lifeguards; parking (no fee); showers; toilets; water sports. **Best for:** walking; windsurfing. ⊠ *437 Kawailoa Rd., Kailua* ⊕ *Near Kailua town, turn right on Kailua Rd. At market, cross bridge, then turn left into beach parking lot.*

Kailua Beach is an ideal place for a picnic, as nearby pavilions and palm trees provide a break from the strong Hawaiian sun.

Kualoa Park. Grassy expanses border a long, narrow stretch of beach with spectacular views of Kaneohe Bay and the Koolau Mountains, making Kualoa one of the island's most beautiful picnic, camping, and beach areas. Dominating the view is an islet called Mokolii, better known as Chinaman's Hat, which rises 206 feet above the water. You can swim in the shallow areas year-round. The one drawback is that it's usually windy here, but the wide-open spaces are ideal for kite flying. **Amenities:** lifeguards; showers; toilets. **Best for:** solitude; swimming. ⊠ *49-479 Kamehameha Hwy., north of Waiahole, Kaaawa.*

Fodor's Choice
★ **Lanikai Beach Park.** Think of the beaches you see in commercials: peaceful jade-green waters, powder-soft white sand, families and dogs frolicking mindlessly, offshore islands in the distance. It's an ideal spot for camping out with a book. Though the beach hides behind multimillion-dollar houses, by state law there is public access every 400 yards. You'll find street parking on Mokulua Drive for the various public-access points to the beach. ■TIP→ **Look for walled or fenced pathways every 400 yards, leading to the beach. Be sure not to park in the marked bike/jogging lane.** There are no shower or bathroom facilities here—they are a two-minute drive away at Kailua Beach Park. **Amenities:** none. **Best for:** swimming; walking. ⊠ *974 Mokulua Dr., past Kailua Beach Park, Kailua.*

Fodor's Choice
★ **Makapuu Beach.** A magnificent beach protected by Makapuu Point welcomes you to the Windward side. Hang gliders circle above the beach, and the water is filled with body boarders. Just off the coast you can see Bird Island, a sanctuary for aquatic fowl, jutting out of the blue. The currents can be heavy, so check with a lifeguard if you're unsure

of safety. Before you leave, take the prettiest (and coldest) outdoor shower available on the island. Being surrounded by tropical flowers and foliage while you rinse off that sand will be a memory you will cherish from this side of the rock. **Amenities:** lifeguards; parking (no fee); showers; toilets. **Best for:** swimming; walking. ⊠ *41-095 Kalanianaole Hwy., across from Sea Life Park, 2 miles south of Waimanalo, Waimanalo.*

Malaekahana State Recreation Area. The big attraction here is tiny Goat Island, a bird sanctuary just offshore. At low tide the water is shallow enough—never more than waist-high—so that you can wade out to it. Wear sneakers or aqua socks so you don't cut yourself on the coral. The beach itself is fairly narrow but long enough for a 20-minute stroll, one-way. The waves are never too big, and sometimes they're just right for the beginning bodysurfer. The entrance gates, which close at 6:45 pm, are easy to miss, and you can't see the beach from the road. Families love to camp in the groves of ironwood trees at Malaekahana State Park. Cabins are also available here, making a perfect rural getaway. **Amenities:** parking (no fee); showers; toilets. **Best for:** swimming; walking. ⊠ *56-207 Kamehameha Hwy., Kahuku ✛ Entrance gates are ½ mile north of Laiie on Kamehameha Hwy.*

Punaluu Beach Park. If you're making a circle of the island, this is a great stopping point to jump out of your car and stretch your legs and get your toes wet. It's easy, because the sand literally comes up to your parked car, and nice, because there is a sandy bottom and mostly calm conditions. Plus there are full facilities and lots of shade trees. Often overlooked, and often overcast, Punaluu can afford you a moment of fresh air before you get back to your sightseeing. **Amenities:** parking (no fee); showers; toilets. **Best for:** solitude; swimming. ⊠ *53-400 Kamehameha Hwy., Hauula.*

FAMILY **Waimanalo Beach Park.** One of the most beautiful beaches on the island, Waimanalo is a local pick, busy with picnicking families and active sports fields. Expect a wide stretch of sand; turquoise, emerald, and deep blue seas; and gentle shore-breaking waves that are fun for all ages. Theft is an occasional problem, so lock your car. **Amenities:** lifeguards; parking (no fee); showers; toilets. **Best for:** sunrise; swimming; walking. ⊠ *41-849 Kalanianaole Hwy., south of Waimanalo town center, Waimanalo.*

NORTH SHORE

"North Shore, where the waves are mean, just like a washing machine," sing the Kaau Crater Boys about this legendary side of the island. And in winter they are absolutely right. At times the waves overtake the road, stranding tourists and locals alike. When the surf is up, there are

signs on the beach telling you how far to stay back so that you aren't swept out to sea. The most prestigious big-wave contest in the world, the Eddie Aikau, is held at Waimea Bay on waves the size of a five- or six-story building. The Triple Crown of Surfing roams across three North Shore beaches in the winter months.

All this changes come summer when this tiger turns into a kitten, with water smooth enough to water-ski on and ideal for snorkeling. The fierce Banzai Pipeline surf break becomes a great dive area, allowing you to explore the coral heads that, in winter, have claimed so many lives on the ultra-shallow but big, hollow tubes created here. Even with the monster surf subsided, this is still a time for caution: lifeguards are scarce, and currents don't subside just because the waves do.

That said, it's a place like no other on Earth, and must be explored. From the turtles at Mokuleia to the tunnels at Shark's Cove, you could spend your whole trip on this side and not be disappointed.

Ehukai Beach Park. What sets Ehukai apart is the view of the famous Banzai Pipeline. Here the winter waves curl into magnificent tubes, making it an experienced wave-rider's dream. It's also an inexperienced swimmer's nightmare, though spring and summer waves are more accommodating to the average person, and there's good snorkeling. Except when the surf contests are going on, there's no reason to stay on the central strip. Travel in either direction from the center, and the conditions remain the same but the population thins out, leaving you with a magnificent stretch of sand all to yourself. **Amenities:** lifeguards; parking (no fee); showers; toilets. **Best for:** snorkeling; surfing. ⊠ *59-406 Kamehameha Hwy., 1 mile north of Foodland at Pupukea, Haleiwa.*

FAMILY **Haleiwa Alii Beach Park.** The winter waves are impressive here, but in summer the ocean is like a lake, ideal for family swimming. The beach itself is big and often full of locals. Its broad lawn off the highway invites volleyball and Frisbee games and groups of barbecuers. This is also the opening break for the Triple Crown of Surfing, and the grass is often filled with art festivals or carnivals. **Amenities:** lifeguards; parking (no fee); showers; toilets. **Best for:** surfing; swimming. ⊠ *66-162 Haleiwa Rd., north of Haleiwa town center and past harbor, Haleiwa.*

Mokuleia Beach Park. There is a reason why the producers of the TV show *Lost* chose this beach for their set. On the remote northwest point of the island, it is about 10 miles from the closest store or public restroom; you could spend a day here and not see another living soul. And that is precisely its beauty—all the joy of being stranded on a deserted island

SUN SAFETY ON OAHU

Hawaii's weather—seemingly never-ending warm, sunny days with gentle trade winds—can be enjoyed year-round with good sun sense. Because of Hawaii's subtropical location, the length of daylight here changes little throughout the year. The sun is particularly strong, with a daily UV average of 14. Visitors should take extra precaution to avoid sunburns and long-term cancer risks due to sun exposure.

The Hawaii Dermatological Society recommends these sun safety tips:

■ Plan your beach, golf, hiking, and other outdoor activities for the early morning or late afternoon, avoiding the sun between 10 am and 4 pm, when it's the strongest.

■ Apply a broad-spectrum sunscreen with a sun protection factor (SPF) of at least 15. Hawaii lifeguards use sunscreens with an SPF of 30. Cover areas that are most prone to burning, like your nose, shoulders, tops of feet, and ears. And don't forget to use sun-protection products on your lips.

■ Apply sunscreen at least 30 minutes before you plan to be outdoors and reapply every two hours, even on cloudy days. Clouds scatter sunlight so you can still burn on an overcast day.

■ Wear light, protective clothing, such as a long-sleeve shirt and pants, broad-brimmed hat, and sunglasses.

■ Stay in the shade whenever possible—especially on the beach—by using an umbrella. Remember that sand and water can reflect up to 85% of the sun's damaging rays.

■ Children need extra protection from the sun. Apply sunscreen frequently and liberally on children over six months of age and minimize their time in the sun. Sunscreen is not recommended for children under six months.

without the trauma of the plane crash. The beach is wide and white, the waters bright blue (but a little choppy) and full of sea turtles and other marine life. Mokuleia is a great secret find; just remember to pack supplies and use caution, as there are no lifeguards. **Amenities:** parking (no fee). **Best for:** solitude. ⊠ *68-67 Farrington Hwy., west of Haleiwa town center, across from Dillingham Airfield, Haleiwa.*

Sunset Beach. The beach is broad, the sand is soft, the summer waves are gentle, making for good snorkeling, and the winter surf is crashing. Many love searching this shore for the puka shells that adorn the necklaces you see everywhere. Food trucks selling shave ice, plate lunches, and sodas usually line the adjacent highway. **Amenities:** food and drink; lifeguards; parking (no fee); showers; toilets. **Best for:** snorkeling; sunset; surfing. ⊠ *59 Kamehameha Hwy., 1 mile north of Ehukai Beach Park, Haleiwa.*

Turtle Bay. Now known more for its resort (the Turtle Bay Resort) than its magnificent beach, Turtle Bay is mostly passed over on the way to the better-known beaches of Sunset and Waimea. But for the average visitor with average swimming capabilities, this is a good place to be on the North Shore. The crescent-shaped beach is protected by a huge sea

Sunset Beach on Oahu's North Shore is known for its ample supply of puka shells, which are a staple of Hawaiian jewelry.

wall. You can see and hear the fury of the northern swell while blissfully floating in cool, calm waters. The convenience of this spot is also hard to pass up—there is a concession selling sandwiches and sunblock right on the beach. The resort has free parking for beach guests. **Amenities:** food and drink; parking (no fee); showers; toilets. **Best for:** sunset; swimming. ⊠ *57-20 Kuilima Dr., 4 miles north of Kahuku, Kahuku* ✢ *Turn into Turtle Bay Resort, and let guard know where you are going.*

Fodor'sChoice
★
Waimea Bay. Made popular in that old Beach Boys song "Surfin' U.S.A.," Waimea Bay is a slice of big-wave heaven, home to king-size 25- to 30-foot winter waves. Summer is the time to swim and snorkel in the calm waters. The shore break is great for novice bodysurfers. Due to its popularity, the postage-stamp parking lot is quickly filled, but it's also possible to park along the side of the road and walk in. **Amenities:** lifeguards; parking (no fee); showers; toilets. **Best for:** snorkeling (in summer); surfing (in winter); swimming (in summer). ⊠ *61-31 Kamehameha Hwy., across from Waimea Valley, 3 miles north of Haleiwa, Haleiwa.*

WEST (LEEWARD) OAHU

The North Shore may be known as "Country," but the west side is truly the rural area on Oahu. There are commuters from this side to Honolulu, but many are born, live, and die on this side with scarcely a trip to town. For the most part, there's little hostility toward outsiders, but occasional problems have flared up, mostly due to drug abuse that has ravaged the fringes of the island. The problems have generally

been car break-ins, not violence. So, in short, lock your car, don't bring valuables, and enjoy the amazing beaches.

The beaches on the west side are expansive and empty. Most Oahu residents and tourists don't make it to this side simply because of the drive; in traffic it can take almost 90 minutes to make it to Kaena Point from downtown Honolulu. But you'll be hard-pressed to find a better sunset anywhere.

Electric Beach. Directly across from the electricity plant—hence the name—Electric Beach (also known as Kahe Point) is a haven for tropical fish, making it a great snorkeling spot. The expulsion of hot water from the plant raises the temperature of the ocean, attracting Hawaiian green sea turtles, spotted moray eels, and spinner dolphins. Although the visibility is not always the best, the crowds are often small, but growing, and the fish are guaranteed. It's best to wear reef shoes here because of the sharp rocks. Unfortunately, there can be a strong current here, so it's not very kid-friendly. This is a great place to stop for a picnic and admire the views. **Amenities:** parking (no fee); showers; toilets. **Best for:** snorkeling; sunset; walking. ⊠ *Farrington Hwy., 1 mile west of Ko Olina Resort, Kapolei.*

FAMILY **Ko Olina.** This is the best spot on the island if you have small kids. The resort area commissioned a series of four man-made lagoons, but, as it has to provide public beach access, you are the winner. Huge rock walls protect the lagoons, making them into perfect spots for kids to get their first taste of the ocean without getting bowled over. The large expanses of seashore grass and hala trees that surround the semicircle beaches are made-to-order for naptime. A 1½-mile jogging track connects the lagoons. Due to its appeal for *keiki* (children), Ko Olina is popular, and the parking lot fills up quickly when school is out and on weekends, so try to get here before 10 am. The biggest parking lot is at the farthest lagoon from the entrance. There are actually three resorts here: Aulani (the Disney resort), the J.W. Marriott Ihilani Resort & Spa, and the Ko Olina Beach Villas Resort (which has a time-share section as well). **Amenities:** food and drink; parking (no fee); showers; toilet. **Best for:** sunset; swimming; walking. ⊠ *92 Aliinui Dr., 23 miles west of Honolulu, Kapolei* ⊹ *Take Ko Olina exit off H1 West and proceed to guard shack.*

Makaha Beach Park. This beach provides a slice of local life most visitors don't see. Families string up tarps for the day, fire up hibachis, set up lawn chairs, get out the fishing gear, and strum ukulele while they "talk story" (chat). Legendary waterman Buffalo Keaulana can be found in the shade of the palms playing with his grandkids and spinning yarns of yesteryear. In these waters Buffalo not only invented some of the most outrageous methods of surfing, but also raised his world-champion son Rusty. He also made Makaha the home of the world's first international surf meet in 1954 and still hosts his Big Board Surfing Classic. With its long, slow-building waves, it's a great spot to try out longboarding. The swimming is generally decent in summer, but avoid the big winter waves. The only parking is along the highway, but it's free. **Amenities:** lifeguards; showers; toilets. **Best for:** surfing; swimming. ⊠ *84-450*

Farrington Hwy., Waianae ✣ *Go 32 miles west of Honolulu on the H1, then exit onto Farrington Hwy. The beach will be on your left.*

Papaoneone Beach. You may have to do a little exploring to find Papaoneone Beach, which is tucked away behind three condos. Duck through a wide, easy-to-spot hole in the fence, and you find an extremely wide, sloping beach that always seems to be empty. You'll have to park on the street. The waters are that eerie blue found only on the west side. The waves can get high here (it faces the same direction as the famed Makaha Beach), but, for the most part, the shore break makes for great easy rides on your body board or belly. The only downside is that, with the exception of a shower, all the facilities are for the condos at the adjacent Beach Lovers Hawaii, so it's just you and the big blue. **Amenities:** showers. **Best for:** solitude; swimming (carefully). ⊠ *84-946 Farrington Hwy., in Makaha, across from Jade St., Waianae.*

Pokai Bay Beach Park. This gorgeous swimming and snorkeling beach is protected by a long breakwater left over from a now-defunct boat harbor. The beach's entire length is sand, and a reef creates smallish waves perfect for novice surfers. **Amenities:** parking (no fee); toilets. **Best for:** snorkeling, surfing; swimming. ⊠ *85-027 Waianae Valley Rd., off Farrington Hwy., Waianae.*

FAMILY
Fodor'sChoice
★
White Plains. Concealed from the public eye for many years as part of the former Barbers Point Naval Air Station, this beach is reminiscent of Waikiki but without the condos and the crowds. It is a long, sloping beach with numerous surf breaks, but it is also mild enough at shore for older children to play freely. It has views of Pearl Harbor and, over that, Diamond Head. Although the sand lives up to its name, the real joy of this beach comes from its history as part of a military property for the better part of a century. Expansive parking, great restroom facilities, and numerous tree-covered barbecue areas make it a great day-trip spot. As a bonus, a Hawaiian monk seal takes up residence here several months out of the year (seals are rare in the Islands). **Amenities:** lifeguards; parking (no fee); showers; toilets. **Best for:** surfing; swimming. ⊠ *Essex Rd. and Tripoli Rd., off H1 W., Kapolei* ✣ *Take the Makakilo exit off H1 West, then turn left. Follow it into base gates, make a left. Blue signs lead to beach.*

Yokohama Bay. You'll be one of the few outsiders at this Waianae Coast beach at the very end of the road. If it weren't for the little strip of paved road, it would feel like a deserted isle: no stores, no houses, just a huge sloping stretch of beach and some of the darkest-blue water off the island. Locals come here to fish and swim in waters that are calm enough for children in summer. Early morning brings with it spinner dolphins by the dozens just offshore. Though Makua Beach up the road is the best spot to see these animals, it's not nearly as beautiful or sandy as "Yokes." **Amenities:** parking (no fee); showers; toilets. **Best for:** solitude; sunset; swimming. ⊠ *81-780 Farrington Hwy., about 7 miles north of Makaha, Waianae.*

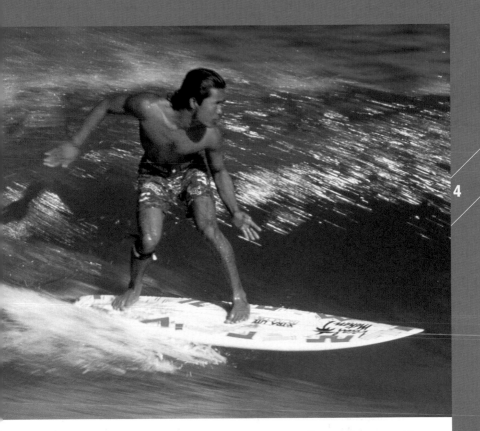

WATER SPORTS AND TOURS

Updated by
Trina Kudlacek

From snorkeling on the North Shore to kayaking to small islands off Kailua Beach to stand-up paddleboarding in Waikiki—when you're on Oahu, there's always a reason to get wet. You can swim with native fish in a protected bay, surf waves in an outrigger canoe, take to the skies in a parasail above Diamond Head, or enjoy panoramic views of Waikiki aboard a 45-foot catamaran. Diving into the ocean—whether in a boat, on a board, or with your own finned feet—is a great way to experience Oahu.

But, as with any physical activity, heed the warnings. The ocean is unpredictable and unforgiving, and it can be as dangerous as it can be awe-inspiring. But if you respect it, it can offer you the kind of memories that last well after your vacation.

ANIMAL ENCOUNTERS

Pods of dolphins surround the Islands, and spotting them can be as easy as just getting yourself out in the ocean. They are wild animals, of course, and do not follow a schedule, but a catamaran sail off Waikiki will usually net you a spotting. Dolphins also generally make appearances shortly after sunrise on the West Shore and can be clearly observed from beaches like Makua and Makaha. And while they won't have the peppy music of Sea World in the background, their jumping and spinning is even more awe-inspiring when you realize they are just doing it as a natural part of their lives rather than for a reward.

Some tour operators offer opportunities to swim with dolphins, but keep in mind that these are federally protected marine mammals, so you should always follow the instructions given by the tour operator if you attend one of these trips. The National Oceanographic and Atmospheric Administration (NOAA), provides specific guidelines for tour operators encountering dolphins through their Dolphin Safe program.

The cost for dolphin encounters can be pricey and range from $120 for a chance to swim with wild dolphins on a snorkel cruise to getting in a pool with them as a trainer for a day for $700. *Both Sea Life Park in Waimanolo and Dolphin Quest at The Kahala offer opportunities to view and interact with captive dolphins; for more information, see Chapter 2, Exploring Oahu.*

Similarly, you can also swim with sharks, though you do so in a protective cage.

Dolphin Quest at The Kahala. This worldwide dolphin-encounter group has an Oahu location in the Kahala. Trained Atlantic bottlenose dolphins hold court in an enclosed lagoon at the center of the hotel. The Kid's Aquatic Adventure is a 90-minute, in-the-water session of feeding and interacting with stingrays and dolphins. For the adults, there is more variety, starting with a 15-minute encounter and going up to the 5½-hour "Trainer for a Day" experience. ⊠ *The Kahala, 5000 Kahala Ave., Kahala, Honolulu* ☎ *808/739–8918* ⊕ *www.dolphinquest.com* ⬚ *From $125 for a 15-min encounter.*

Hanauma Bay Dive Tours. For those who are a little timid about entering these waters, this outfitter provides a tour with a guide to help alleviate your fears. The company's three-hour Dolphin Adventure departs from Waianae Boat Harbor and includes transportation to/from Waikiki. The company also offers cheaper guided snorkeling tours (⇨ *see Snorkeling*). ⊠ *Waianae Boat Harbor, 85-491 Farrington Hwy., Waianae* ☎ *808/256–8956* ⊕ *www.hanaumabaydivetours.com* ⬚ *From $120.*

North Shore Shark Adventures. "You go in the cage, cage goes in the water, you go in the water, shark's in the water." You remember this line from *Jaws*, and now you get to play the role of Richard Dreyfus, as North Shore Shark Adventures provides you with an interactive experience out of your worst nightmare. The tour allows you to swim and snorkel in a cage as dozens of sharks lurk just feet from you in the open ocean off the North Shore, and all for just $120. They'll provide transportation from Waikiki for an additional charge. ■TIP➡ If you go, go early: it's the shark's natural feeding time and they are a lot more aggressive. ⊠ *Haleiwa Small Boat Harbor, 66-105 Haleiwa Rd., Boat Slip #40, Haleiwa* ☎ *808/228–5900* ⊕ *sharktourshawaii.com.*

BOAT TOURS AND CHARTERS

Being on the water can be the best way to enjoy the Islands. Whether you want to see the fish in action or experience how they taste, there is a tour for you.

For a sailing experience in Oahu, you need go no farther than the beach in front of your hotel in Waikiki. Strung along the sand are several beach catamarans that will provide you with one-hour rides during the day and 90-minute sunset sails. Look for $23 to $25 for day sails and $30 to $34 for sunset rides. ■TIP➡ Feel free to haggle, especially with the smaller boats. Some provide drinks for free, some charge for them, and some let you pack your own, so keep that in mind when pricing the ride. Or choose to go the ultra-luxe route and charter a boat for a

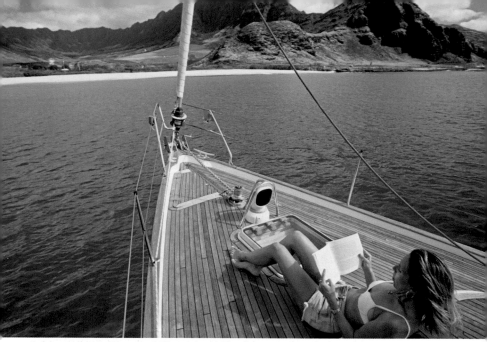
Sail around the island to spot wildlife and deserted beaches.

day or week. These run from less than $100 per person per day to over $1,000. *Sashimi Fun Fishing also offers a variety of boat trips as well as deep-sea fishing trips (⇨ see Deep-Sea Fishing).*

FAMILY **Hawaii Duck Tours.** Offering three itineraries, these unique tours in WWII-era amphibious assault vehicles take advantage of the ducks' dual means of travel by navigating the streets of Oahu and then gliding into the water in sheltered bays. The Honolulu City Tour takes you through Waikiki to downtown Honolulu and Chinatown, passing historic landmarks along the way. The Pearl Harbor tours give you the option of visiting the WWII Valor in the Pacific National Monument (aka The *Arizona* Memorial) for $89 or, for $10 more, you can visit the USS *Missiouri*. Both spend some time on the water at Keehi Lagoon. For $69, the Maunalua Bay Tour takes you east out of Waikiki past Diamond Head toward Hawaii Kai for some time on the water off the coast of Koko Head Crater. All tours offer pick up at central locations in Waikiki. ✉ *Ala Wai Boat Harbor, Waikiki, Honolulu* ☎ *808/988–3825* ⊕ *www.hawaiiducktours.com* ✆ *From $49.*

Hawaii Nautical. With one location in Waikiki and one on the Waianae Coast, this outfit offers a wide variety of cruise options including guaranteed dolphin sightings, gourmet dinners, lunches, snorkeling, scuba diving, or sunset viewing. Three-hour cruises, including lunch and two drinks, depart from the Hilton in Waikiki.

For those interested in leaving from the Waianae Coast, three-hour morning and two-hour afternoon snorkel tours are available from the Waianae Boat Harbor on Farrington Hwy. (✉ *91-607 Malakole St.* ☎ *808/234–7245*). Prices include all gear, food, and two alcoholic beverages. The dock in the Waianae Boat Harbor is a little more out of the way, but this is a much more luxurious option than what is offered in Waikiki. Three-hour morning and two-hour afternoon tours of the west side of Oahu include stops for observing dolphins from the boat and a snorkel spot well populated with fish. All gear, snacks, sandwiches, and two alcoholic beverages make for a more complete experience. Pickup in Ko Olina is free, but the company will also pick you up and take you back Waikiki for an additional fee. ⊠ *Hilton Pier at Hilton Hawaiian Village, 2005 Kalia Rd., Waikiki, Honolulu* ☎ *808/234–7245* ⊕ *www.hawaiinautical.com* ⌖ *From $109.*

Honolulu Sailing Company. With a small fleet of mono- and multi-hull sail and powerboats, the Honolulu Sailing Company combines boat charters with sailing instruction opportunities. Itineraries may include chartered, private day-sails or powerboating around Oahu as well as multiday interisland cruises. ⊠ *Kewalo Basin Harbor, 1125 Ala Moana Blvd., Honolulu* ☎ *808/239–3900* ⊕ *www.honsail.com.*

Maitai **Catamaran.** Taking off from the stretch of sand between the Sheraton Waikiki and the Halekulani Hotel, this 44-foot cat is the fastest and sleekest on the beach. There are a variety of tours to choose from, including a sunset sail and a snorkel excursion. If you have a need for speed and enjoy a little more upscale experience, this is the boat for you. ⊠ *Waikiki Beach, between the Sheraton Waikiki and the Halekulani Hotel, Waikiki, Honolulu* ☎ *808/922–5665, 800/462–7975* ⊕ *www.maitaicatamaran.net* ⌖ *From $28.*

Makani Catamaran. This 65-foot *Makani* is the top catamaran in Hawaii for luxury, from its Bose stereo system to its LCD TVs to its freshwater bathrooms. It sails out of Kewalo Basin three times daily, offering breakfast, "city lights" dinner cruises, and Friday-night "fireworks" cruises. ⊠ *Kewalo Basin Harbor, 1125 Ala Moana Blvd., Ala Moana, Honolulu* ☎ *808/591–9000* ⊕ *www.sailmakani.com* ⌖ *From $49.*

Na Hoku II **Catamaran.** Features a variety music and free booze in its $30 price tag. The 45-foot catamaran is tied up near the Westin Moana Surfrider hotel and sails four times daily. ■TIP→ Make reservations in advance for the sunset sail as the boat fills up quickly. ⊠ *Waikiki Beach, between the Moana Surfrider Hotel and Duke's Barefoot Bar, Waikiki, Honolulu* ☎ *808/554–5990* ⊕ *www.waikikicat.com* ⌖ *From $30.*

Star of Honolulu Cruises. Founded in 1957, this company recently expanded its fleet to include the 65-foot *Dolfin Star,* docked on Oahu's west coast. It offers everything from snorkeling cruises in the pristine waters off the Waianae coast to gourmet-dinner cruises with live entertainment to seasonal whale-watching sails on one of two vessels. Popular cruises teach you how to string lei and dance hula. Two-hour whale-watching-excursion rates begin at $33 per person, while dinner cruises start at $84 and go up to $184. The company has a second location at 85-491 Farrington Highway in Waianae. ⊠ *Aloha Tower Marketplace, 1 Aloha Tower Dr., Downtown Honolulu, Honolulu* ☎ *808/983–7827*⊕ *www.starofhonolulu.com.*

Tradewind Charters. This company's half-day private excursions can include sailing, snorkeling, reef fishing, and whale-watching. Traveling on these luxury yachts not only gets you away from the crowds, but also gives you the opportunity to "take the helm" if you wish. The cruises may include snorkeling at an exclusive anchorage, as well as hands-on snorkeling and sailing instruction. Base charter prices cover up to six passengers. ⊠ *Kewalo Basin Harbor, 1125 Ala Moana Blvd., Ala Moana, Honolulu* ☎ *808/227–4956* ⊕ *tradewindvacationshawaii. com* ⤳ *From $495.*

BODY BOARDING AND BODYSURFING

Body boarding (or sponging) has long been a popular alternative to surfing for a couple of reasons. First, the start-up cost is much less—a usable board can be purchased for $30 to $40 or can be rented on the beach for $5 an hour. Second, it's a whole lot easier to ride a body board than to tame a surfboard. All you have to do is paddle out to the waves, then turn toward the beach as the wave approaches and kick like crazy.

Most grocery and convenience stores sell body boards. Though these boards don't compare to what the pros use, beginners won't notice a difference in their handling on smaller waves.

Though they are not absolutely necessary for body boarding, fins do give you a tremendous advantage when you're paddling. If you plan to go out into bigger surf, we would also suggest getting a leash, which reduces the chance you'll lose your board. The smaller, sturdier versions of dive fins used for body boarding sell for $25 to $60 at surf and dive stores, and sporting-goods stores. Most beach stands don't rent fins with the boards, so if you want them you'll probably need to buy them.

Bodysurfing requires far less equipment—just a pair of swim fins with heel straps—but it can be a lot more challenging to master. Typically, surf breaks that are good for body boarding are good for bodysurfing.

If the direction of the current or dangers of the break are not readily apparent to you, don't hesitate to ask a lifeguard for advice.

BEST SPOTS

Body boarding and bodysurfing can be done anywhere there are waves, but due to the paddling advantage surfers have over spongers, it's usually more fun to go to surf breaks exclusively for body boarding. *For more information on Oahu beaches, see Chapter 3, Beaches.*

Bellows Beach. On Oahu's windward side, Bellows Field Beach has shallow waters and a consistent break that makes it an ideal spot for body boarders and bodysurfers. (Surfing isn't allowed between the two lifeguard towers.) But take note: the Portuguese man-o-war, a blue jellyfish-like invertebrate that delivers painful and powerful stings, is often seen here. ⊠ *41-043 Kalanianaole Hwy., Waimanalo.*

Kuhio Beach Park. This beach is an easy spot for first-timers to check out the action. The Wall, a break near the large pedestrian walkway called Kapahulu Groin, is the quintessential body-boarding spot. The soft, rolling waves make it perfect for beginners. Even during summer's south swells, it's relatively tame because of the outer reefs. ⊠ *Waikiki*

The windward side has many good spots for body boarding.

Beach, between the Sheraton Moana Surfrider Hotel and the Kapahulu Groin, Honolulu.

Makapuu Beach. With its extended waves, Makapuu Beach is a sponger's dream. If you're a little more timid, go to the far end of the beach to **Keiki's,** where the waves are mellowed by Makapuu Point. Although the main break at Makapuu is much less dangerous than Sandy's, check out the ocean floor—the sands are always shifting, sometimes exposing coral heads and rocks. Always check (or ask lifeguards about) the currents, which can get pretty strong. ⊠ *41-095 Kalanianaole Hwy., across from Sea Life Park.*

Sandy Beach. The best spot—and arguably one of the most dangerous—on the island for advanced body boarding is Sandy Beach, located on Oahu's eastern shore. Dubbed one of the most treacherous shore breaks in the nation, the break can be extremely dangerous even when it's small. As lifeguards will attest, there are more neck injuries suffered here than at any other surf break in the United States. It's awesome for the advanced, but know its danger before paddling out. ⊠ *8800 Kalanianaole Hwy., 2 miles east of Hanauma Bay, Honolulu.*

FAMILY **Waimanalo Beach Park.** With the longest sand beach on Oahu's windward side, Waimanalo Bay has a shallow sandbar at the water's edge that provides good waves for body boarding and bodysurfing. It's an ideal break for novices because of its soft waves. Like Walls in Waikiki, this area is protected by an outer reef. And like Bellows, it's favored by the dangerous Portuguese man-o-war. ⊠ *Aloiloi St., Waimanalo.*

EQUIPMENT

There are more than 30 rental spots along Waikiki Beach, all offering basically the same prices. But if you plan to body board for more than just an hour, we would suggest buying an inexpensive board for $20 to $40 at an ABC Store—there are more than 30 in the Waikiki area—and giving it to a kid at the end of your vacation. It will be more cost-effective for you, and you'll be passing along some aloha spirit in the process.

DEEP-SEA FISHING

Fishing isn't just a sport in Hawaii, it's a way of life. A number of charter boats with experienced crews can take you on a sportfishing adventure throughout the year. Sure, the bigger yellowfin tuna (ahi) are generally caught in summer, and the coveted spearfish are more frequent in winter, but you can still hook them any day of the year. You can also find dolphinfish (mahimahi), wahoo (ono), skipjacks, and the king—Pacific blue marlin—ripe for the picking on any given day. The largest marlin ever caught, weighing in at 1,805 pounds, was reeled in along Oahu's coast.

When choosing a fishing boat in the Islands, keep in mind the immensity of the surrounding ocean. Look for veteran captains who have decades of experience. Better yet, find those who care about Hawaii's fragile marine environment. Many captains now tag and release their catches to preserve the state's fishing grounds.

The general rule for the catch is an even split with the crew. Unfortunately, there are no "freeze-and-ship" providers in the state, so unless you plan to eat the fish while you're here, you'll probably want to leave it with the boat. Most boats do offer mounting services for trophy fish; ask your captain.

Prices vary greatly, but expect to pay from around $75 per person for a spot on a boat with more than 20 people to $2,000 for an overnight trip for up to 6 people. Besides the gift of fish, a gratuity of 10% to 20% is standard, but use your own discretion depending on how you feel about the overall experience.

BOATS AND CHARTERS

Hawaii Fishing Charters. Based out of Ko Olina resort, Captain Jim and his crew try to bring the full Hawaiian experience to their fishing trips. While most fishing boats head straight out to the open ocean, Captain Jim trolls along the leeward coast, giving visitors a nice sense of the island while stalking the fish. Your cheapest option will be a shared charter, and prices increase from there. The company also offers a private overnighter to Molokai's Penguin Banks, reputed to be some of Hawaii's best fishing grounds, for up to four people. ⊠ *Ko Olina Resort and Marina, 92 Aliinui Dr., Kapolei* ☎ *808/208–2512* ⊕ *www. hawaiifishingcharters.net* ☎ *From $375.*

Maggie Joe Sport Fishing. The oldest sportfishing company on Oahu boasts landing one of the largest marlins every caught out of Kewalo Basin. With a fleet of three boats including the 53-foot custom *Maggie Joe* (which can hold up to 15 anglers and has air-conditioned cabins, hot showers, and cutting-edge fishing equipment) they can offer a variety of off-shore fishing packages including night shark fishing. A marine taxidermist can mount the monster you reel in. Half-day exclusive on the 41-foot *Sea Hawk* or the 38-foot *Ruckus* can accommodate up to six people and are the cheapest option. Charters on the larger *Maggie Joe* can start at ¾ day or a full day (but not a half day). ⊠ *Kewalo Basin, 1025 Ala Moana Blvd., Ala Moana, Honolulu* ☎ *808/591–8888, 877/806–3474* ⊕ *www.maggiejoe.com* ☐ *Half-day charters from $850.*

Magic Sportfishing. This 50-foot Pacifica fishing yacht, aptly named *Magic*, boasts a slew of sportfishing records, including some of largest marlins caught in local tournaments and the most mahimahi hooked during a one-day charter. This yacht is very comfortable, with twin diesel engines that provide a smooth ride, air-conditioning, and a cozy seating area. The boat can accommodate up to six passengers and offers both shared and full charters. ⊠ *Kewalo Basin Harbor, 1025 Ala Moana Blvd., Ala Moana, Honolulu* ☎ *808/596–2998, 808/286–2998* ⊕ *www. magicsportfishing.com* ☐ *From $200 per person for shared charter; from $975 for a private charter.*

Sashimi Fun Fishing. With a glass-bottomed boat, speedboat, and two 65-foot fishing vessels, Sashimi Fun Fishing offers a variety of water activities. Choose a shark hunt, rock and roll blues cruise, or traditional deep-sea fishing. Or, for those who aren't quite ready to troll for big game in the open-ocean swells, you can take a trip that combines a dinner cruise with fishing and music. The boat keeps close enough to shore so that while you're hooking reef fish, you can still see Oahu. The cruise includes a local barbecue dinner or you can cook what you catch. Rates can include hotel transportation. ⊠ *Kewalo Basin Harbor, 1125 Ala Moana Blvd., Ala Moana, Honolulu* ☎ *808/955–3474* ⊕ *www.808955fish.com* ☐ *From $63 per person for shared trips.*

JET SKIING AND WATERSKIING

Aloha Jet Ski. Skip across the surface of the immense Keehi Lagoon as planes from Honolulu International Airport soar above you. After an instructional safety course, you can try your hand at navigating the buoyed course. The company provides free pick-up and drop-off from Waikiki hotels. Waverunners can either be operated tandem or solo. ⊠ *Keehi Lagoon, Sand Island Access Rd., Honolulu* ☎ *808/721–1754* ⊕ *www.alohajetski.com* ☐ *From $49 per person for a tandem trip from $78 for a solo trip.*

FAMILY **Hawaii Water Sports Center.** This company transforms Maunalua Bay into a water park with activities for all ages. You can bounce around in a bumper tube, zoom around on Jet Skis, wake board, scuba dive, or ride the six-person banana boats. Jet Ski rentals can be as short as 30 minutes. ⊠ *Koko Marina Center, 7192 Kalanianaole Hwy., Honolulu* ☎ *808/395–3773* ⊕ *www.hawaiiwatersportscenter.com* ☐ *From $49.*

H2O Sports Hawaii. Parasailing, banana boats, bumper boats, snorkeling, and scuba diving: this company offers a wide variety of tours and activities on the water. But the Jet Pack is H2O's most famous program.

OAHU'S TOP WATER ACTIVITIES

Tour Company/ Outfitter	Length	AM/ PM	Departure Point	Adult/Kid Price	Ages	Snack vs. Meal	Alcoholic Beverages	Boat Type	Worth Noting
Sailing									
Hawaii Nautical	3 hrs	AM/ PM	West Side	$109	All ages	Snack	Yes	50-foot cat	Leaves from Ko Olina resort, lots of whales in the wintertime
Makani Catamaran	2 hrs	AM/ PM	South Shore	$49	All ages	Snack	Yes	64-foot catamaran	Offers all variety of sails, from sunset to snorkel sails
Maitai Catamaran	2 hrs– Full day	AM/ PM	South Shore	$28	All ages	Lunch	Yes	44-ft catamaran	Fast sail on upscale cat
Na Hoku II Catamaran	90 minutes	AM/ PM	South Shore	$30	All ages	N/A	Yes	45-ft catamaran	Sunset sail is a top ticket
Star of Honolulu Cruises	2–3 hrs	AM/ PM	South Shore/ West Side	$33–$184	All ages	Dinner	Yes	Variety of Vessels	Does seasonal AM whale watching; other cruises in PM
Tradewind Charters	Half day	AM/ PM	South Shore	$495 for 6 people	All Ages	Upon request	Yes	Variety of vessels	Great for weddings or private parties
Deep Sea Fishing									
Maggie Joe Sport Fishing	3/4 day	AM	South Side	$850 for 6 people	N/A	N/A	BYOB	53-foot deep-sea fishing boat	Oldest running sports-fishing company on Oahu
Magic Sportfishing	Full day	AM	South Side	$200 per person	N/A	N/A	BYOB	50-foot fishing yacht	Boat is built for comfort

Deep Sea Fishing cont'd.

Sashimi Fun Fishing	4 hrs	PM	South Side	$63 a person	N/A	Meal	BYOB	50-foot fishing boat	Reef fishing for those not ready for the open ocean
Hawaii Fishing Charters	6 hrs	AM/PM	West Side	$375	N/A	N/A	BYOB	44-foot luxury boat	Sails out of Ko Olina Resort
Diving									
Captain Bruce's Hawaii	2 hrs	AM/PM	West/East Shore	$150	N/A	N/A	N/A	Pro 42 Jet Boat	Hot showers on board
Hanauma Bay Dive Tours	3 hrs	AM/PM	West Side/South Side	$120	N/A	N/A	N/A	Variety of Vessels	Can take you to a wide range of dive spots
Surf-N-Sea	2 hrs	AM/PM	North Shore	$100	N/A	N/A	N/A	Variety of Vessels	Cameraman available to shoot your dive
Snorkeling									
Hanauma Bay Snorkeling Excursions	5½ hrs	AM/PM	South Side	$22	All ages	N/A	N/A	Variety of Vessels	Includes pick-up in Waikiki. Park admission ($7.50) is extra.
Whale Watching									
Wild Side Specialty Tours	2½–3½ hrs	AM/PM	West Side	$175	All ages	Lunch	Yes	42- and 34-foot catamaran	Year-round dolphin and whale watching

DID YOU KNOW?

Inexperienced kayakers should stick to Windward Oahu, where calmer waters allow you to relax and check out what's down below.

Pumping 1,000 gallons of sea water per minute through the pack gets you airborne like a character in a sci-fi film. With a 90% success rate for first-time flyers, this safety-conscious outfitter allows you to rocket into the air or walk on water. Launches for first-timers last 15 minutes and depart from a floating platform in Maunalua Bay near Hawaii Kai, but you can add additional time if you can't bear to stop. ■**TIP➜ Make your reservations early as flights book up more than two weeks in advance, and note that the company is only open weekdays.** ⊠ *Hawaii Kai Shopping Center, 377 Keahole St., near Long's Drugs, Hawaii Kai* ☎ *808/396-0100* ⊕ *www.h2osportshawaii.com* ⏎ *From $199.*

KAYAKING

Kayaking is an easy way to explore the ocean—and Oahu's natural beauty—without much effort or skill. It offers a vantage point not afforded by swimming or surfing, and a workout you won't get lounging on a catamaran. Even novices can get in a kayak and enjoy the island's scenery.

The ability to travel long distances can also get you into trouble. ⚠ **Experts agree that rookies should stay on the windward side.** Their reasoning is simple: if you get tired, break or lose an oar, or just plain pass out, the onshore winds will eventually blow you back to the beach. The same cannot be said for the offshore breezes of the North Shore and West Oahu.

Kayaks are specialized: some are better suited for riding waves while others are designed for traveling long distances. Your outfitter can address your needs depending on your skill level. Sharing your plans with your outfitter can lead to a more enjoyable—and safer—experience. Expect to pay from $45 for a half-day single rental to $125 for a guided kayak tour with lunch. Some kayaking outfitters also rent stand-up paddleboards (*see Stand-Up Paddleboarding*).

BEST SPOTS

If you want to try your hand at surfing kayaks, **Bellows Field Beach** (near Waimanalo Town Center, entrance on Kalanianaole Highway) on the windward side and **Mokuleia Beach** (across from Dillingham Airfield) on the North Shore are two great spots. Hard-to-reach breaks, the ones that surfers exhaust themselves trying to reach, are easily accessed by kayak. The buoyancy of the kayak also allows you to catch the wave earlier and get out in front of the white wash. One reminder on these spots: if you're a little green, stick to Bellows Field Beach with those onshore winds. Generally speaking, you don't want to be catching waves where surfers are; in Waikiki, however, pretty much anything goes.

The perennial favorite of kayakers is **Lanikai Beach**, on the island's windward side. Tucked away in an upscale residential area, this award-winning beach has become a popular spot for amateur kayakers because of its calm waters and onshore winds. More adventurous paddlers can head to the Mokulua Islands, two islets less than 1 mile from the beach. You can land on Moku Nui, which has surf breaks and small beaches great for picnicking. Take a dip in Queen's Bath, a small saltwater swimming hole.

For something a little different, try the Kahana River on the island's windward side, which empties into the ocean at **Kahana Bay Beach Park**. The river may not have the blue water of the ocean, but the majestic Koolau Mountains, with waterfalls during rainy months, make for a picturesque backdrop. It's a short jaunt, about 2 miles round-trip from the beach, but it's tranquil and packed with rain-forest foliage. Bring mosquito repellent. ⇨ *For more information on this and other beaches in Oahu, see Chapter 3.*

EQUIPMENT, LESSONS, AND TOURS

Go Bananas. Staffers make sure that you rent the appropriate kayak for your abilities, and can also outfit your rental car with soft racks to transport your boat to the beach. (The racks are included in the rental fee.) The store also carries clothing and kayaking accessories and rents stand-up paddleboards. Full-day rates begin at $30 for single kayaks, $45 for doubles, and $30 for stand-up paddleboards. ⊠ *799 Kapahulu Ave., Kapahulu, Honolulu* ☎ *808/737–9514* ⊕ *www.gobananaskayaks.com.*

Kailua Sailboards and Kayaks. One of the best places for beginners to rent kayaks is Kailua Beach, and Kailua Sailboards and Kayaks has an ideal location just across the street. Guided kayak tours start at $130 for four hours or, for the more adventurous, rent a kayak and venture to the Mokulua Islands off Lanikai. They also rent snorkeling equipment, stand-up paddleboards, kiteboarding gear, and bikes. Kayak rentals start at $69 for a half day in a double kayak, $59 for single. ⊠ *Kailua Beach Shopping Center, 130 Kailua Rd., Kailua* ☎ *808/262–2555* ⊕ *www.kailuasailboards.com.*

Surf 'N Sea. This outfitter is located in a rustic wooden building on the beach, so in minutes you can start paddling. Full-day rates begin at $60 for single kayaks, $75 for doubles ■**TIP→ Keep in mind that these plastic boats are great from spring to fall, but winter weather can be hazardous for even veteran kayakers.** This company offers just about any surf-related activity you can imagine on the North Shore in addition to kayaking. ⊠ *62-595 Kamehameha Hwy., Haleiwa* ☎ *800/899–7873* ⊕ *www.surfnsea.com.*

Twogood Kayaks Hawaii. The outfitter offers kayak rentals, lessons, and guided tours. Guides are trained in the history, geology, and birds of the area. Full-day rental rates begin at $45 for single kayaks, $55 for doubles. Fully guided kayak excursions are $125, including lunch, snorkeling gear, and transportation to and from Waikiki. ⊠ *134B Hamakua Dr., Kailua* ☎ *808/262–5656* ⊕ *www.twogoodkayaks.com.*

SCUBA DIVING

Not all of Hawaii's beauty is above water. What lurks below can be just as magnificent.

While snorkeling provides adequate access to this underwater world, nothing gives you the freedom—or depth, quite literally—as scuba.

The diving on Oahu is comparable with any you might do in the tropics, but its uniqueness comes from the isolated environment of the Islands. There are literally hundreds of species of fish and marine life that you can find only in this chain. In fact, about 25% of Hawaii's marine life can be seen here only—nowhere else in the world. Adding to the singularity of diving off Oahu is the human history of the region. Military activities and tragedies of the 20th century filled the waters surrounding Oahu with wreckage that the ocean creatures have since turned into their homes.

Although instructors certified to license you in scuba are plentiful in the Islands, we suggest that you get your PADI certification before coming, as a week of classes may be a bit of a commitment on a short vacation. Expect to pay around $100 for a two-tank boat dive (provided that you are certified). ■TIP→ **You can go on short, shallow introductory dives without the certification, but the best dives require it and cost a bit more.**

> ### KAYAKING TO THE MOKES
>
> The Mokulua Islands—commonly referred to as "The Mokes"—are two islets off Lanikai Beach. The larger of the islands, Moku Niu, is a perfect kayaking destination and a popular place for picnics. The islands are state-protected bird sanctuaries, and sometimes you can catch a glimpse of one of the 11 different kinds of seabirds that nest there. Some outfitters offer guided tours. But since the water between the islets and Lanikai is typically calm and as it would be impossible to miss them, spend your money on sunscreen and snacks instead and enjoy the paddle.

BEST SPOTS

Hanauma Bay Nature Preserve. On Oahu's southeast shore, Hanauma Bay Nature Preserve is home to more than 250 different species of fish, of which a quarter can be found nowhere else in the world. This has made this volcanic crater bay one of the most popular dive sites in the state. It's a long walk from the parking lot to the beach—even longer lugging equipment—so consider hooking up with a licensed dive-tour operator. Preservation efforts have aided the bay's delicate ecosystem, so expect to see various butterfly fish, surgeonfish, tangs, parrot fish, and endangered Hawaiian sea turtles. ⊠ *7455 Kalanianaole Hwy., Honolulu* ☎ *808/396–4229.*

Hundred Foot Hole. Once an ancient Hawaiian fishing ground reserved for royalty, the Hundred Foot Hole is a cluster of volcanic boulders that have created ledges, caves, and a large open-ended cavern perfect for diving. Accessible from shore, this spot near Diamond Head attracts octopus, manta rays, and the occasional white-tip shark. ⊠ *Honolulu.*

Mahi Waianae. Hawaii's waters are littered with shipwrecks, but one of the most intact and accessible is the *Mahi Waianae*, a 165-foot minesweeper that was sunk in 1982 off the Waianae Coast. It lays upright in about 90 feet of calm and clear water, encrusted in coral and patrolled by white spotted eagle rays and millet seed butterfly fish. The wreck serves as an artificial reef for such Hawaii aquatic residents as blue-striped snappers, puffer fish, lionfish, moray eels, and octopus. Visibility averages about 100 feet, making this one of the most popular dives on the island. ⊠ *Waianae.*

Maunalua Bay. The bay stretches about 7 miles, from Portlock Point to Black Point on Oahu's southeastern shore. Teeming with marine life, this spot has several accessible dive sites of varying difficulty. The shallow-water Turtle Canyon is home to endangered Hawaiian green sea turtles. Fantasy Reef is another shallow dive with three plateaus of volcanic rock lined with coral that is home to fish, eels, and sea turtles. In about 85 feet of water, *Baby Barge* is an easy-to-penetrate sunken vessel encrusted in coral. An advanced dive, the wreck of a Vought F4U Corsair gives you a close-up look at garden eels and stingrays. ⊠ *Honolulu.*

Fodor's Choice **Shark's Cove.** Oahu's best shore dive is accessible only during the summer
★ months. Shark's Cove, on Oahu's North Shore, churns with monster surf during the winter, making this popular snorkeling and diving spot extremely dangerous. In summer, the cavernous lava tubes and tunnels are great for both novices and experienced divers. Some dive-tour companies offer round-trip transportation from Waikiki. ⊠ *Haleiwa.*

Three Tables. A short walk from Shark's Cove is Three Tables, named for a trio of flat rocks running perpendicular to shore. There are lava tubes to the right of these rocks that break the surface and then extend out about 50 feet. While this area isn't as active as Shark's Cove, you can still spot octopus, moray eels, parrot fish, green sea turtles, and the occasional shark. ⊠ *Haleiwa.*

EQUIPMENT, LESSONS, AND TOURS

Captain Bruce's Hawaii. Focusing on the island's western shore, this full-service company offers refresher and introductory dives as well as more advanced drift and night dives. Everything is provided, including transportation to and from Waikiki. Most importantly, the boat has hot showers. The company is based in the Waianae Boat Harbor. ⊠ *Waianae Boat Harbor, 85-491 Farrington Hwy., Waianae* ☎ *808/234–7245* ⊕ *www.captainbruce.com* ✉ *From $150 for 2-tank dives.*

Hanauma Bay Dive Tours. You can guess the specialty here. This company offers introductory courses in the federally protected reserve for divers ages 12 and above. ⊠ *460 Ena Rd., Honolulu* ☎ *808/256–8956, 800/505–8956* ⊕ *www.hanaumabaydivetours.com* ✉ *From $120 (1-tank dive).*

Surf 'N Sea. The North Shore headquarters for all things water-elated is also great for diving. An interesting perk—a cameraman can shoot a video of you diving. It's hard to see facial expressions under the water, but it still might be fun for those who want to prove that they took the plunge. Two-tank shore dives are the most economical choice (prices for noncertified divers are higher), but the company also offers night dives, and in the summer, night dives are available for only slightly more. ⊠ *62-595 Kamehameha Hwy., Haleiwa* ☎ *800/899–7873* ⊕ *www. surfnsea.com* ✉ *From $100 (2-tank shore dives).*

4

Here in the warm waters off the coast of Oahu, there's a good chance you'll find yourself swimming alongside a green sea turtle.

SNORKELING

If you can swim, you can snorkel. And you don't need any formal training, either.

Snorkeling is a favorite pastime for both visitors and residents and can be done anywhere there's enough water to stick your face in. You can pick up a mask and snorkel at a corner ABC store for around $35, including fins, and get going on your own or pay up to $175 for a luxurious snorkel cruise including lunch and drinks. Each spot will have its great days depending on the weather and time of year, so consult with the purveyor of your gear for tips on where the best viewing is that day. Keep in mind that the North Shore should be attempted only when the waves are calm, namely in the summertime.

Make sure you put plenty of sunscreen on your back (or better yet, wear a T-shirt) because once you start gazing below, your head may not come back up for hours.

BEST SPOTS

Electric Beach. Directly across from the electricity plant—hence the name—Electric Beach is a haven for tropical fish, making it a great snorkeling spot. The expulsion of hot water from the plant raises the temperature of the ocean, attracting Hawaiian green sea turtles, spotted moray eels, and spinner dolphins. Although the visibility is not always the best, the crowds are small and the fish are guaranteed. ⊠ *Farrington Hwy., 1 mile west of Ko Olina Resort, Kapolei.*

Continued on page 138

SNORKELING IN HAWAII

The waters surrounding the Hawaiian Islands are filled with life—from giant manta rays cruising off the Big Island's Kona Coast to humpback whales giving birth in the warm waters surrounding Maui. Dip your head beneath the surface to experience a spectacularly colorful world: pairs of milletseed butterflyfish dart back and forth, redlipped parrotfish snack on coral algae, and spotted eagle rays flap past like silent spaceships. Sea turtles bask at the surface while tiny wrasses give them the equivalent of a shave and a haircut. The water quality is typically outstanding; many sites afford 30-foot-plus visibility. On snorkel cruises, you can often stare from the boat rail right down to the bottom.

Certainly few destinations are as accommodating to every level of snorkeler as Hawaii. Beginners can tromp in from sandy beaches while more advanced divers descend to shipwrecks, reefs, craters, and sea arches just offshore. Because of Hawaii's extreme isolation, the island chain has fewer fish species than Fiji or the Caribbean—but many of the fish that are here exist nowhere else. The Hawaiian waters are home to the highest percentage of endemic fish in the world.

The key to enjoying the underwater world is slowing down. Look carefully. Listen. You might hear the strange crackling sound of shrimp tunneling through coral, or you may hear whales singing to one another during winter. A shy octopus may drift along the ocean's floor beneath you. If you're hooked, pick up a waterproof fishkey from Long's Drugs. You can brag later that you've looked the Hawaiian turkeyfish in the eye.

Picasso Triggerfish	Milletseed Butterflyfish*	Yellow Tang
Moorish Idol	Hawaiian Whitespotted Toby*	Saddleback Wrasse*
Redlip Parrotfish	Hawaiian Turkeyfish*	Zebra Moray Eel
Stocky Hawkfish	Green Sea Turtle (Honu)	Spotted Eagle Ray

*endemic to Hawaii

POLYNESIA'S FIRST CELESTIAL NAVIGATORS: HONU

Honu is the Hawaiian name for two native sea turtles, the hawksbill and the green sea turtle. Little is known about these dinosaur-age marine reptiles, though snorkelers regularly see them foraging for *limu* (seaweed) and the occasional jellyfish in Hawaiian waters. Most female honu nest in the uninhabited Northwestern Hawaiian Islands, but a few sociable ladies nest on Maui and Big Island beaches. Scientists suspect that they navigate the seas via magnetism—sensing the earth's poles. Amazingly, they will journey up to 800 miles to nest—it's believed that they return to their own birth sites. After about 60 days of incubation, nestlings emerge from the sand at night and find their way back to the sea by the light of the stars.

SNORKELING

Many of Hawaii's reefs are accessible from shore.

The basics: Sure, you can take a deep breath, hold your nose, squint your eyes, and stick your face in the water in an attempt to view submerged habitats . . . but why not protect your eyes, retain your ability to breathe, and keep your hands free to paddle about when exploring underwater? That's what snorkeling is all about.

Equipment needed: A mask, snorkel (the tube attached to the mask), and fins. In deeper waters (any depth over your head), life jackets are advised.

Steps to success: If you've never snorkeled before, it's natural to feel a bit awkward at first, so don't sweat it. Breathing through a mask and tube, and wearing a pair of fins take getting used to. Like any activity, you build confidence and comfort through practice.

If you're new to snorkeling, begin by submerging your face in shallow water or a swimming pool and breathing calmly through the snorkel while gazing through the mask.

Next you need to learn how to clear water out of your mask and snorkel, an essential skill since splashes can send water into tube openings and masks can leak. Some snorkels have built-in drainage valves, but if a tube clogs, you can force water up and out by exhaling through your mouth. Clearing a mask is similar: lift your head from water while pulling forward on mask to drain. Some masks have built-in purge valves, but those without can be cleared underwater by pressing the top to the forehead and blowing out your nose (charming, isn't it?), allowing air to bubble into the mask, pushing water out the bottom. If it sounds hard, it really isn't. Just try it a few times and you'll soon feel like a pro.

Now your goal is to get friendly with fins—you want them to be snug but not too tight—and learn how to propel yourself with them. Fins won't help you float, but they will give you a leg up, so to speak, on smoothly moving through the water or treading water (even when upright) with less effort.

Flutter stroking is the most efficient underwater kick, and the farther your foot bends forward the more leg power you'll be able to transfer to the water and the farther you'll travel with each stroke. Flutter kicking movements involve alternately separating the legs and then drawing them back together. When your legs separate, the leg surface encounters drag from the water, slowing you down. When your legs are drawn back together, they produce a force pushing you forward. If your kick creates more forward force than it causes drag, you'll move ahead.

Submerge your fins to avoid fatigue rather than having them flailing above the water when you kick, and keep your arms at your side to reduce drag. You are in the water—stretched out, face down, and snorkeling happily away—but that doesn't mean you can't hold your breath and go deeper in the water for a closer look at some fish or whatever catches your attention. Just remember that when you do this, your snorkel will be submerged, too, so you won't be breathing (you'll be holding your breath). You can dive head-first, but going feet-first is easier and less scary for most folks, taking less momentum. Before full immersion, take several long, deep breaths to clear carbon dioxide from your lungs.

If your legs tire, flip onto your back and tread water with inverted fin motions while resting. If your mask fogs, wash condensation from lens and clear water from mask.

TIPS FOR SAFE SNORKELING

■ Snorkel with a buddy and stay together.

■ Plan your entry and exit points prior to getting in the water.

■ Swim into the current on entering and then ride the current back to your exit point.

■ Carry your flippers into the water and then put them on, as it's difficult to walk in them.

■ Make sure your mask fits properly and is not too loose.

■ Pop your head above the water periodically to ensure you aren't drifting too far out, or too close to rocks.

■ Think of the water as someone else's home—don't take anything that doesn't belong to you, or leave any trash behind.

■ Don't touch any sea creatures; they may sting.

■ Wear a T-shirt over your swimsuit to help protect you from being fried by the sun.

■ When in doubt, don't go without a snorkeling professional; try a guided tour.

Green sea turtle (Honu)

Hanauma Bay Nature Preserve. What Waimea Bay is to surfing, Hanauma Bay in Southeast Oahu is to snorkeling. Easily the most popular snorkeling spot on the island, it's home to more more than 250 different species of marine life. Due to the protection of the narrow mouth of the cove and the prodigious reef, you will be hard-pressed to find a place you will feel safer while snorkeling. ✉ *7455 Kalanianaole Hwy., Honolulu* ☎ *808/396-4229.*

Queen's Surf Beach. On the edge of Waikiki, Queen's Surf is a marine reserve located between Kapahulu Groin and the Waikiki Aquarium. It's not as chock-full of fish as Hanauma Bay, but it has its share of colorful reef fish and the occasional Hawaiian green sea turtle. Just yards from shore, it's a great spot for an escape if you're stuck in Waikiki and have grown weary of watching the surfers. ✉ *Kalakaua Ave., Honolulu.*

Fodor'sChoice
★
Shark's Cove. Great shallows protected by a huge reef make Shark's Cove on the North Shore a prime spot for snorkelers, even young ones, in the summer. You'll find a plethora of critters, from crabs to octopus, in water that's no more than waist deep. When the winter swells come, this area can turn treacherous. ✉ *Kamehameha Hwy., across from Foodland, Haleiwa.*

EQUIPMENT AND TOURS

Hanauma Bay Rental Stand. You can get masks, fins, and snorkels right at the park. ✉ *Hanauma Bay Nature Preserve, 7455 Kalanianaole Hwy., Hawaii Kai.*

Hanauma Bay Snorkeling Excursions. If you're going to Hanauma Bay, you have three options: take a chance with limited parking spaces at the park, take TheBus, or contact Hanauma Bay Snorkeling Excursions. They provide transportation to and from Waikiki hotels, equipment, and instruction on how to use the equipment for a reasonable price that does not include the park entrance fee. Guided snorkeling tours are more expensive. ☎ *808/306-3393* ⊕ *www.hanaumabaysnorkel.com* ✉ *From $22.*

Snorkel Bob's. This place has all the stuff you'll need—and more—to make your water adventures more enjoyable. Bob makes his own gear and is active in protecting reef fish species. Feel free to ask the staff about good snorkeling spots, as the best ones can vary with weather and the seasons. ✉ *700 Kapahulu Ave., Kapahulu, Honolulu* ☎ *808/735-7944* ⊕ *www.snorkelbob.com.*

SUBMARINE TOURS

Atlantis Submarines. This is the underwater adventure for the unadventurous. Not fond of swimming, but want to see what you've been missing? Board this 64-passenger vessel for a ride past shipwrecks, turtle breeding grounds, and coral reefs. The tours, which depart from the pier at the Hilton Hawaiian Village, are available in several languages. A smaller 48-passenger boat with underwater viewing windows is a bit cheaper than the submarine trip. ✉ *Hilton Hawaiian Village Beach Resort and Spa, 2005 Kalia Rd., Honolulu* ☎ *808/973-1296, 800/548-6262* ⊕ *www.atlantisadventures.com* ✉ *From $119.*

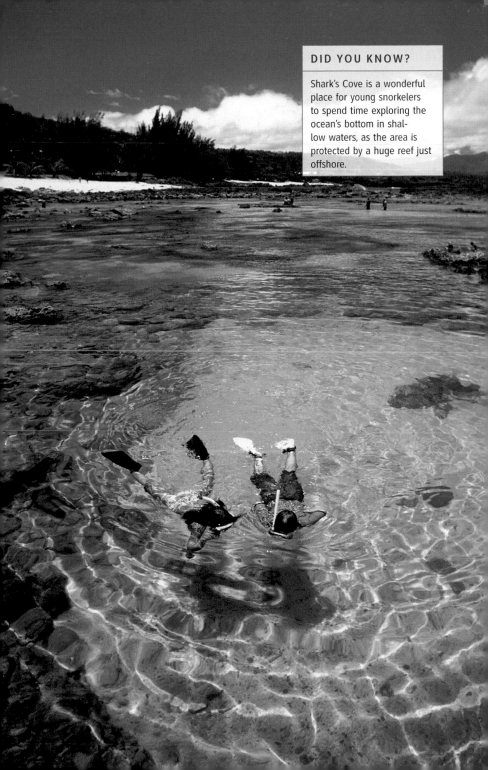

STAND-UP PADDLEBOARDING

From the lakes of Wisconsin to the coast of Lima, Peru, stand-up paddleboarding (or SUP, for short) is taking the sport of surfing to the most unexpected places. Still, the sport remains firmly rooted in the Hawaiian Islands.

Back in the 1960s, Waikiki beach boys would paddle out on their longboards using a modified canoe paddle. It was longer than a traditional paddle, enabling them to stand up and stroke. It was easier this way to survey the ocean and snap photos of tourists learning how to surf. Eventually it became a sport unto itself, with professional contests at world-class surf breaks and long-distance races across treacherous waters.

Stand-up paddleboarding is easy to learn—though riding waves takes some practice—and most outfitters on Oahu offer lessons for all skill levels starting at $50. It's also a great workout; you can burn off yesterday's dinner buffet, strengthen your core, and experience the natural beauty of the island's coastlines all at once. Once you're ready to head out on your own, half-day rentals start at $40.

If you're looking to learn, go where there's already an SUP presence. Avoid popular surf breaks, unless you're an experienced stand-up paddle surfer, and be wary of ocean and wind conditions. You'll want to find a spot with calm waters, easy access in and out of the ocean, and a friendly crowd that doesn't mind the occasional stand-up paddleboarder.

BEST SPOTS

Ala Moana Beach Park. About a mile west of Waikiki, Ala Moana is the most SUP-friendly spot on the island. In fact, the state installed a series of buoys in the flat-water lagoon to separate stand-up paddlers and swimmers. There are no waves here, making it a great spot to learn, but beware of strong trade winds, which can push you into the reef.

Anahulu Stream. Outfitters on the North Shore like to take SUP beginners to Anahulu Stream, which empties into Waialua Bay near the Haleiwa Boat Harbor. This area is calm and protected from winds, plus there's parking at the harbor, and surf shops nearby rent boards.

Waikiki. There are a number of outfitters on Oahu's South Shore that take beginners into the waters off Waikiki. **Canoes,** the surf break fronting the Duke Kahanamoku statute, and the channels between breaks are often suitable for people learning how to maneuver their boards in not-so-flat conditions. But south swells here can be deceptively menacing, and ocean conditions can change quickly. Check with lifeguards before paddling out and be mindful of other surfers in the water.

White Plains. If you've got a car with racks, you might want to venture to White Plains, a fairly uncrowded beach about 27 miles west of Waikiki. It's a long, sandy beach with lots of breaks, and plenty of room for everyone. There are lifeguards, restrooms, and lots of parking, making this a great spot for beginners and those just getting comfortable in small waves.

EQUIPMENT AND LESSONS

Hans Hedemann Surf School. Get professional instruction in stand-up paddleboarding right in Waikiki, where the sport originated. This school offers group lessons, semiprivate lessons, and private training. Lessons are also offered through locations at the Halekulani hotel in Waikiki, Turtle Bay Resort in Kahuku, and at the Kahala Hotel. ⊠ *Park Shore Waikiki, 2586 Kalakaua Ave., Honolulu* ☎ *808/924–7778, 808/447–6755* ⊕ *www.hhsurf.com* ◻ *From $75.*

Hawaiian Watersports. Paddle in the picturesque Kailua Bay or in the waters off Waikiki with Hawaiian Watersports. Two-hour lessons are offered in groups or in one-on-one sessions. Look for deals on the website. Half-day rentals are also available. There's also a branch in Kailua. ⊠ *415 Kapahulu Ave., Waikiki, Honolulu* ☎ *808/262–5483, 808/739–5483* ⊕ *www.hawaiianwatersports.com* ◻ *Rentals from $49, lessons from $99.*

Paddle Core Fitness. Paddling is a way of life for Reid Inouye, who now shares his passion for the sport with students. (He's also the publisher of *Standup Paddle Magazine*.) His company offers introductory classes as well as fitness programs for serious paddlers. Lessons are held in the flat waters of Ala Moana Beach, where there's a designated area for paddling, and you can have either group or private lessons. ⊠ *Ala Moana Beach Park, Ala Moana Blvd., Ala Moana, Honolulu* ☎ *808/385–0717* ⊕ *www.paddlecorefitness.com* ◻ *Lessons from $50.*

Rainbow Watersports Adventures. When you spot this company's colorful "Rainbow Water Sports Van" at the bay near Haleiwa Beach Park, you'll know you're in the right place. You can get a two-hour group lesson on Oahu's North Shore, semiprivate lessons—two paddlers, one instructor— or one-on-one lessons. All lessons are held in spots popular with the resident green sea turtles. A three- to four-hour coastal-eco adventure trip including snorkeling and lunch is also offered. ⊠ *Haleiwa Beach Park, Kamehameha Hwy., Haleiwa* ☎ *800/470–4964, 808/372–9304* ⊕ *www.rainbowwatersports.com* ◻ *Lessons from $69.*

Surf 'N Sea. With stand-up paddleboarding lessons for every skill level, Surf 'N Sea is a great place to start. Beginners can take the introductory lesson to learn proper paddling technique. A two-hour session focuses on honing your skills. More-advanced paddlers can book surf trips that take you out to several North Shore breaks. ⊠ *62-595 Kamehameha Hwy., Haleiwa* ☎ *808/637–3008, 800/899–7873* ⊕ *www.surfnsea.com* ◻ *Lessons from $55.*

SURFING

Perhaps no word is more associated with Hawaii than surfing. Every year the best of the best gather on Oahu's North Shore to compete in their version of the Super Bowl: the prestigious Vans Triple Crown of Surfing. The pros dominate the waves for a month, but the rest of the year belongs to folks just trying to have fun.

Oahu is unique because it has so many famous spots: Banzai Pipeline, Waimea Bay, Kaiser Bowls, and Sunset Beach. These spots, however, require experience. However, with most dependable sets and access to lessons, Waikiki is still a great place for beginners to learn or for novice surfers to catch predictable waves. Group lessons on Waikiki Beach start at $30, but if you really want to fine-tune your skills, you can pay up to $500 for a daylong private outing with a former pro.

The island also has miles of coastline with surf spots that are perfect for everyday surfers. But remember this surfer's credo: when in doubt, don't go out. If you're unsure about conditions, stay on the beach and, talk to locals to get more info about surf breaks before trying yourself.

If you don't want to run the risk of a confrontation with local surfers, who can be very territorial about their favorite breaks, try some of the alternate spots listed below. They may not have the name recognition, but the waves can be just as great.

BEST SPOTS

Makaha Beach Park. If you like to ride waves, try Makaha Beach on Oahu's west side. It has legendary, interminable rights that allow riders to perform all manner of stunts: from six-man canoes with everyone doing headstands to bully boards (oversize body boards) with whole families along for the ride. Mainly known as a longboarding spot, it's predominantly local but respectful to outsiders. Use caution in the winter, as the surf can get huge. It's not called Makaha—which means "fierce"—for nothing. ⊠ *84-369 Farrington Hwy., Waianae.*

Sunset Beach. If you want to impress your surfing buddies back home, catch a wave at the famous Sunset Beach on Oahu's North Shore. Two of the more manageable breaks are **Kammie Land** (or Kammie's) and **Sunset Point.** For the daring, Sunset is part of the Vans Triple Crown of Surfing for a reason. Thick waves and long rides await, but you're going to want to have a thick board and a thicker skull. Surf etiquette here is a must, as it's mostly local. ⊠ *59-104 Kamehameha Hwy., 1 mile north of Ehukai Beach Park, Haleiwa.*

Ulukou Beach. In Waikiki you can paddle out to **Populars,** a break at Ulukou Beach. Nice and easy, Populars—or Pops—never breaks too hard and is friendly to both newbies and veterans. It's one of the best places to surf during pumping south swells, as this thick wave breaks in open ocean, making it more rideable. The only downside is the long paddle out to the break from Kuhio Beach, but that keeps the crowds manageable. ⊠ *Waikiki Beach, in front of the Sheraton Waikiki hotel, Honolulu.*

White Plains Beach. Known among locals as "mini Waikiki," the surf at White Plains breaks in numerous spots, preventing the logjams that are inevitable at many of Oahu's more popular spots. It's a great break for novice to intermediate surfers, though you do have to keep a lookout for wayward boards. From the H1, take the Makakilo exit. ⊠ *Off H1, Kapolei.*

EQUIPMENT AND LESSONS

Aloha Beach Services. It may sound like a cliché, but there's no better way to learn to surf than from a beach boy in Waikiki. And there's no one better than Harry "Didi" Robello, a second-generation beach

This surfer is doing a stellar job of surfing the infamous Banzai Pipeline on Oahu's North Shore.

boy and owner of Aloha Beach Services. Learn to surf in an hour-long group lesson, a semiprivate lesson, or with just you and an instructor. You can also rent a board here. ✉ *2365 Kalakaua Ave., on the beach near the Moana Surfrider, Waikiki, Honolulu* ☎ *808/922–3111* ⊕ *www.alohabeachservices.com* ✆ *Lessons from $40, board rentals from $15.*

Faith Surf School. Professional surfer Tony Moniz started his own surf school in 2000, and since then he and his wife Tammy have helped thousands of people catch their first waves in Waikiki. The 90-minute group lessons include all equipment and are the cheapest option. You can pay more (sometimes a lot more) for semiprivate lessons with up to three people or private lessons. You can also book an all-day surf tour with Moniz, riding waves with him at his favorite breaks. ✉ *Sheraton Waikiki, 2255 Kalakaua Ave., Waikiki, Honolulu* ☎ *808/931–6262* ⊕ *www.faithsurfschool.com* ✆ *From $50.*

Hans Hedemann Surf School. Hans Hedemann spent 17 years on the professional surfer circuit. He and his staff offer surfing, bodysurfing, and stand-up paddleboard instruction; four-day intensive surf camps; and fine-tuning courses with Hedemann himself. One-hour group lessons are the cheapest option, but private lessons are also available. There are also locations at Turtle Bay Resort in Kahuku, the Kahala Hotel and the Halekulani in Waikiki. ✉ *Park Shore Waiki, 2586 Kalakaua Ave., Waikiki, Honolulu* ☎ *808/924–7778, 808/447–6755* ⊕ *www.hhsurf.com* ✆ *From $50.*

FAMILY **Hawaiian Fire.** Learn how to surf from some of Hawaii's most knowledgeable water-safety experts at this school, owned and operated by Honolulu firefighters. Lessons include 45 minutes of ocean safety

SURF SMART

A few things to remember when surfing in Oahu:

■ The waves switch with the seasons—they're big in the south in summer and loom large in the north in winter. If you're not experienced, it's best to go where the waves are small. There will be smaller crowds, and your chances of injury will dramatically decrease.

■ Always wear a leash. It may not look the coolest, but when your board gets swept away from you and you're swimming a half mile after it, you'll remember this advice.

■ Watch where you're going. Take a few minutes and scan the surf from the shore. Observe how big it is, where it's breaking, and how quickly the sets are coming. This will allow you to get in and out more easily and to spend more time riding waves and less time paddling.

■ Ask a local before going out: they're the best bet for specifics about surf breaks.

instruction and 75 minutes in the water at a secluded beach near Barbers Point. Transportation is available to and from the Ko Olina area only. Both cheaper group lessons and private lessons are offered. A great option for kids ages seven and up. ⊠ *Ko Olina Resorts, 92-1047 Olani St., Suite 1-109, Kapolei* ☎ *808/737–3473* ⊕ *www.hawaiianfire. com* ⊠ *From $119.*

Surf 'N Sea. This is a one-stop shop for surfers (and other water-sports enthusiasts) on the North Shore. Rent a shortboard by the hour or for a full day. Three-hour group lessons are offered, as well as surf safaris for experienced surfers, which can last from four to five hours. ⊠ *62-595 Kamehameha Hwy., Haleiwa* ☎ *800/899–7873, 808/637-9887* ⊕ *www. surfnsea.com* ⊠ *Lessons from $85; rentals from $5 per hr.*

WHALE-WATCHING

December is marked by the arrival of snow in much of America, but in Hawaii it marks the return of the humpback whale. These migrating behemoths move south from their North Pacific homes during the winter months for courtship and calving, and they put on quite a show. Watching males and females alike throwing themselves out of the ocean and into the sunset awes even the saltiest of sailors. Newborn calves riding gently next to their 2-ton mothers will stir you to your core. These gentle giants can be seen from the shore as they make a splash, but there is nothing like having your boat rocking beneath you in the wake of a whale's breach.

FAMILY **Atlantis Navatek Cruises.** Offering the only cruise on Oahu to guarantee a whale sighting, the 140-foot catamaran *Navatek 1* bills itself as the smoothest whale-watching tour on Oahu. Because of the boat's size, you can choose from indoor or outdoor viewing while listening to Hawaiian music and an onboard naturalist who provides information as you search for the leviathans. Included among the offerings are two-hour morning cruises as well as lunch cruises. Departures are from the

historic Aloha Tower Market Place at Pier 6. ■TIP➜ Check-in begins 30 minutes before departure. Arrive early to get a table near a window for the best views while you dine. ⊠ *Aloha Tower Market Place, 1 Aloha Tower Dr., Pier 6, Downtown Honolulu, Honolulu* ☏ *800/548–6262* ⊕ *www.atlantisadventures.com* ✉ *From $44.*

Wild Side Specialty Tours. Boasting a marine-biologist crew, this company takes you to undisturbed snorkeling areas. Along the way you may see dolphins and turtles. The company promises a sighting of migrating whales year-round on some itineraries. Tours may depart as early as 8 am from Waianae, so it's important to plan ahead. The three-hour deluxe wildlife tour is the most popular option. ⊠ *Waianae Boat Harbor, 87-1286 Farrington Hwy., Waianae* ☏ *808/306–7273* ⊕ *www.sailhawaii.com* ✉ *From $175.*

WINDSURFING AND KITEBOARDING

Those who call windsurfing and kiteboarding cheating because they require no paddling have never tried hanging on to a sail or kite. It will turn your arms to spaghetti quicker than paddling ever could, and the speeds you generate earn these sports the label of "extreme."

Windsurfing was born here in the Islands. For amateurs, the windward side is best because the onshore breezes will bring you back to land even if you're not a pro. The newer sport of kiteboarding is tougher but more exhilarating, as the kite will sometimes take you in the air for hundreds of feet. ■TIP➜ Recent changes to local laws prohibit lessons on the beach, so renting equipment is your only option on Oahu, leaving these sports as options only for those who know what they're doing.

EQUIPMENT RENTAL

Kailua Sailboards and Kayaks. Within walking distance of Kailua Beach, this outfitter offers everything you'll need for a day on the water including kayak and stand-up paddleboarding lessons, rentals, and guided tours. Kayak rentals start at $59 for a single for a half day or $69 for 24 hours. Double kayaks run $10 more. Guided kayak tours start at $129. ⊠ *Kailua Beach Center, 130 Kailua Rd., Kailua* ☏ *808/262–2555* ⊕ *www.kailuasailboards.com.*

Naish Hawaii. While they are prohibited by law from providing instruction, Naish Hawaii continues as the sole provider of equipment rentals for those who are already proficient. You can rent windsurfing equipment and kiteboards for a half day or for 24 hours. The company also rents stand-up paddleboards by the half day or for 24 hours. ⊠ *155A Hamakua Dr., Kailua* ☏ *808/262–6068* ⊕ *www.naish.com* ✉ *Windsurfers from $50; kiteboards from $25.*

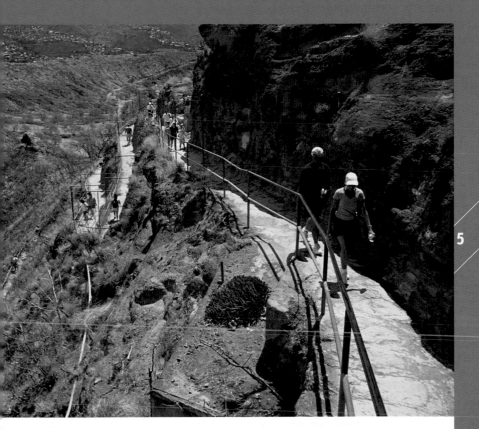

GOLF, HIKING, AND OUTDOOR ACTIVITIES

Updated by
Trina Kudlacek

Although much is written about the water surrounding this little rock known as Oahu, there is as much to be said for the rock itself. It's a wonder of nature, thrust from the ocean floor thousands of millennia ago by a volcanic hot spot that is still spitting out islands today. Hawaii is the most remote island chain on Earth, and there are creatures and plants that can be seen here and nowhere else. And there are dozens of ways for you to check them all out.

From the air you can peer down into nooks and crannies in the mountains—where cars cannot reach and hikers don't dare. Whether flitting here and there amid a helicopter's rush and roar, or sailing by in the silence of a glider's reverie, you glimpse sights that few have experienced. Or, if you would rather, take a step back in time and take off from the waters of Keehi Lagoon in a World War II–era seaplane. Follow the flight path flown by the Japanese Zeros as they attempted to destroy Pearl Harbor and the American spirit.

Would you prefer the ground tour, where you and gravity are no longer at odds? Oahu is covered in hiking trails that vary from tropical rain forest to arid desert. Even when in the bustling city of Honolulu, you are but minutes from hidden waterfalls and bamboo forests. Out west you can wander a dusty path that has long since given up its ability to accommodate cars but is perfect for hikers. You can splash in tidal pools, admire sea arches, and gape at caves opened by the rock slides that closed the road. You can camp out for free on many of these treks and beaches.

If somewhat less rugged and less vigorous exploration is more your style, how about letting horses do your dirty work? You can ride them on the beaches and in the valleys, checking out ancient holy sites, movie sets, and brilliant vistas.

Finally, there is the ancient sport of Scotland. Why merely hike into the rain forest when you can slice a 280-yard drive through it and

Take a helicopter tour for a unique perspective of the island.

then hunt for your Titleist in the bushy leaves instead? Almost 40 courses cover this tiny expanse, ranging from the target jungle golf of the Royal Hawaiian Golf Club to the pro-style links of Turtle Bay. There is no off-season in the tropics, and no one here knows your real handicap.

AERIAL TOURS

Taking an aerial tour of the Islands opens up a world of perspective. Look down from the sky at the outline of the USS *Arizona* where it lies in its final resting place below the waters of Pearl Harbor, or get a glimpse of the vast carved expanse of a volcanic crater—here are views only seen by an "eye in the sky." Don't forget your camera.

Blue Hawaiian Helicopters. This company stakes its claim as Hawaii's largest copter company, with tours on all the major islands and more than two dozen choppers in its fleet. The 45-minute Oahu tour seats up to 12 passengers and includes narration from your friendly pilot along with sweeping views of Waikiki, the beautiful windward coast, and the North Shore. If you like to see the world from above or are just pinched for time and want to get a quick overview of the whole island without renting a car, this is the way to go. ⊠ *99 Kaulele Pl., Honolulu* ☎ *808/831–8800* ⊕ *www.bluehawaiian.com* ✉ *From $233.*

Island Seaplane Service. Harking back to the days of the earliest air visitors to Hawaii, the seaplane has always had a special spot in island lore. The only seaplane service still operating in Hawaii takes off from Keehi Lagoon. Flight options are either a half hour south and eastern Oahu shoreline tour or an hour-long island circle tour. The *Pan Am Clipper* may be gone, but you can revisit the experience with this company. ✉ *85 Lagoon Dr., Honolulu* ☎ *808/836–6273* ⊕ *www.islandseaplane. com* 🖅 *From $169.*

Makani Kai Helicopters. This may be the best way to see the beautiful Sacred Falls on the windward side of the island, as the park around the falls was closed to hikers after a deadly 1999 rock slide. Makani Kai dips the helicopter down to show you one of Hawaii's former favorite trails and the pristine waterfall it leads to. Tours can last either a half or full hour. Customized private charters are available for up to six passengers. ✉ *130 Iolana Pl., Honolulu* ☎ *808/834–5813* ⊕ *www. makanikai.com* 🖅 *From $170.*

The Original Glider Rides. "Mr. Bill" has been offering piloted glider (sailplane) rides over the northwest end of Oahu's North Shore since 1970. Choose from piloted scenic rides for one or two passengers in sleek, bubble-top, motorless aircraft with aerial views of mountains, shoreline, coral pools, windsurfing sails, and, in winter, humpback whales. Seeking more thrills? You can also take a more acrobatic ride or take control yourself in a "mini lesson." Flights range from 15 to 60 minutes long and depart continuously from 10 to 5 daily. ✉ *Dillingham Airfield, 69-132 Farrington Hwy., Waialua* ☎ *808/677–3404* ⊕ *www. honolulusoaring.com* 🖅 *From $79.*

BIKING

Oahu's coastal roads are flat, well paved, and unfortunately, awash in vehicular traffic. Frankly, biking is no fun in either Waikiki or Honolulu, but things are a bit better outside the city. Your best bet is to cycle early in the morning or get off the road and check out the island's bike trails.

BEST SPOTS

Kaena Point Trail. If going up a mountain is not your idea of mountain biking, then perhaps Kaena Point Trail is better suited to your needs. A longer ride (10 miles) but much flatter, this trail takes you ocean side around the westernmost point on the island. You pass sea arches and a mini-blowhole, then finish up with some motocross jumps right before you turn around. There's no drinking water available on this ride, but at least at the end you have the Yokohama beach showers to cool you off. ✉ *69–385 Farrington Hwy., Waialua.*

Waimanalo Demonstration Trail. Locals favor biking this 10-mile trail that has breathtaking views as you descend into Waimanalo. There are many flat portions but also some uneven ground to negotiate unless you're willing to carry your bike for small stretches. The trailhead is at the Pali Lookout on the blacktop of Old Pali Road. ✉ *Nuuanu Pali Dr., at Pali Lookout, Honolulu.*

West Kaunala Trail. Biking the North Shore may sound like a great idea, but the two-lane road is narrow and traffic-heavy. We suggest you try the West Kaunala Trail. It's a little tricky at times, but with the rain-forest surroundings and beautiful ocean vistas you'll hardly

Ka'ena Point in the northwestern corner of the island is windy and dry, and is where rare, native Hawaiian plants grow.

notice your legs burning on the steep ascent at the end. It's about 5½ mile round-trip. Bring water because there's none on the trail unless it comes from the sky. ⊠ *59-777 Pupukea Rd., at the end of Pupukea Rd., Haleiwa ⊕ Pupukea Rd. is next to Foodland, the only grocery store on North Shore.*

EQUIPMENT AND TOURS

Bike Hawaii. Whether it's road tours of the North Shore or muddy off-road adventures in Kaaawa Valley, this is the company to get you there. There are combination packages that pair cycling with kayaking, snorkeling, sailing, or hiking. They also offer guided hikes combined with sailing and snorkeling. The company offers both three-hour road tours and a six-hour mountain-biking foray. Tours include equipment, transportation, water, and lunch. The company will pick you up at your hotel. A highlight is the Urban Cultural Bike Tour, which includes visits to Iolani Palace and historic downtown Honolulu. ☎ *877/682–7433* ⊕ *www.bikehawaii.com* ✉ *From $60.*

Hawaii Bicycling League. Don't want to go cycling by yourself? Visit this shop online, and you can get connected with rides and contests. ☎ *808/735–5756* ⊕ *www.hbl.org.*

GOLF

Unlike on the other Hawaiian Islands, the majority of Oahu's golf courses are not associated with hotels and resorts. In fact, of the island's three dozen–plus courses, only five are tied to lodging and none of them is in the tourist hub of Waikiki.

Municipal courses are a good choice for budget-conscious golfers but are more crowded and are not always maintained to the same standard as the private courses. Your best bet is to call the day you want to play and inquire about walk-on availability. Greens fees are standard at city courses: walking rate, $55 for visitors; riding cart, $20 for 18 holes; pull carts, $4.

Greens fees listed here are the highest course rates per round on week-days and weekends for U.S. residents. (Some courses charge non–U.S. residents higher prices.) Discounts are often available for resort guests and for those who book tee times online. Twilight fees are usually offered; call individual courses for information.

HONOLULU

There is only one spot to golf near Waikiki and it is the busiest course in America. While not a very imaginative layout, the price is right and the advantage of walking from your hotel to the course is not to be overlooked. Just make sure you bring a newspaper because it will be a little while before you tee off.

Ala Wai Municipal Golf Course. Just across the Ala Wai Canal from Waikiki, this municipal golf course is said to host more rounds than any other U.S. course—up to 500 per day. Not that it's a great course, just really convenient. Although residents can obtain a city golf card that allows automated tee-time reservation over the phone, the best bet for a visitor is to show up and expect to wait at least an hour. The course itself is flat. Robin Nelson did some redesign work in the 1990s, adding mounding, trees, and a lake. The Ala Wai Canal comes into play on several holes on the back nine, including the treacherous 18th. There's also an on-site restaurant and bar. ⊠ *404 Kapahulu Ave., Waikiki* ☎ *808/733–7387 starter's office, 808/738–4652 golf shop* ⊕ *www1.honolulu.gov/des/golf/alawai.htm* ⊡ *$55* 🏌 *18 holes, 5861 yards, par 70.*

Moanalua Golf Club. Said to be (but not without dispute) the oldest golf club west of the Rockies, this 9-holer is private but allows public play except on weekend and holiday mornings. Near Pearl Harbor and nestled in the hardwoods, this course will remind you more of golf in Pennsylvania than the tropics, but it offers the cheapest green fees in the area, and by the time you get here, you'll probably be over the whole palm tree theme anyway. The course is a bit quirky, but the final two holes, a par-3 off a cliff to a smallish tree-rimmed green and a par-4 with an approach to a green set snugly between stream and jungle, are classic. ⊠ *1250 Ala Aolani St., Salt Lake* ☎ *808/839–2411* ⊡ *$45, including cart; $60 unlimited play (weekdays only)* 🏌 *9 holes, 2972 yards, par 36.*

SOUTHEAST OAHU

Prepare to keep your ball down on this windy corner of Oahu. You'll get beautiful ocean vistas, but you may need them to soothe you once your perfect drive gets blown 40 yards off course by a gusting trade wind.

Continued on page 156

HAWAII'S PLANTS 101

Hawaii is a bounty of rainbow-colored flowers and plants. The evening air is scented with their fragrance. Just look at the front yard of almost any home, travel any road, or visit any local park and you'll see a spectacular array of colored blossoms and leaves. What most visitors don't know is that many of the plants they are seeing are not native to Hawaii; rather, they were introduced during the last two centuries as ornamental plants, or for timber, shade, or fruit.

Hawaii boasts nearly every climate on the planet, excluding the two most extreme: arctic tundra and arid desert. The Islands have wine-growing regions, cactus-speckled ranchlands, icy mountaintops, and the rainiest forests on earth.

Plants introduced from around the world thrive here. The lush lowland valleys along the windward coasts are predominantly populated by non-native trees including yellow- and red-fruited **guava**, silvery-leafed **kukui**, and orange-flowered **tulip trees.**

The colorful **plumeria flower**, very fragrant and commonly used in lei making, and

the giant multicolored **hibiscus flower** are both used by many women as hair adornments, and are two of the most common plants found around homes and hotels. The umbrella-like **monkeypod tree** from Central America provides shade in many of Hawaii's parks including Kapiolani Park in Honolulu. Hawaii's largest tree, found in Lahaina, Maui, is a giant **banyan tree.** Its canopy and massive support roots cover about two-thirds of an acre. The native **ohia tree,** with its brilliant red brush-like flowers, and the **hapuu,** a giant tree fern, are common in Hawaii's forests and are also used ornamentally in gardens.

Bougainvillea	Guava	Monkeypod
Banyan	Ohia Lehua*	Tulip Tree
Plumeria	Pandanus	Hibiscus
Anthurium	Kukui	Hapuu

*endemic to Hawaii

DID YOU KNOW?

More than 2,200 plant species are found in the Hawaiian Islands, but only about 1,000 are native. Of these, 320 are so rare, they are endangered. Hawaii's endemic plants evolved from ancestral seeds arriving in the Islands over thousands of years as baggage with birds, floating on ocean currents, or drifting on winds from continents thousands of miles away. Once here, these plants evolved in isolation, creating many new species known nowhere else in the world.

CLOSE UP

Camping in Oahu

If you are looking for a more rugged escape from the resorts of Waikiki, consider pitching a tent on the beach or in the mountains, where you have easy access to hiking trails and the island's natural features.

■ **TIP**→ Camping here is not as highly organized as it is on the mainland: expect few marked sites, scarce electrical outlets, and nary a ranger station. What you find instead are unblemished spots in the woods and on the beach. Both the Division of Forestry and Wildlife and the State Park Service offer recreation areas at which you can camp, both in the mountains and on the beach. All state park and Division of Forestry and Wildlife campsites can now be

reserved up to a year in advance online at ⊕ *www.hawaiistateparks.org*. The fee is $18 a night per campsite for up to six people. As for the county spots, there are 17 currently available and all require a permit. The good news is that the permits are only $10 per night and are easy to obtain, as long as you're not trying to go on a holiday weekend. Visit ⊕ *www1.hono-lulu.gov/parks* for more information.

If tent camping sounds a little too rugged, consider cabin camping on the beach. These spots do not offer the amenities of the island's hotels and resorts, but they do provide oceanfront rooms for those on smaller budgets.

Hawaii Kai Golf Course. The Championship Golf Course (William F. Bell, 1973) winds through a Honolulu suburb at the foot of Koko Crater. Homes (and the liability of a broken window) come into play on many holes, but they are offset by views of the nearby Pacific and a crafty routing of holes. With several lakes, lots of trees, and bunkers in all the wrong places, Hawaii Kai really is a "championship" golf course, especially when the trade winds howl. The Executive Course (1962), a par-55 track, is the first of only three courses in Hawaii built by Robert Trent Jones Sr. Although a few changes have been made to his original design, you can find the usual Jones attributes, including raised greens and lots of risk-reward options. Greens fees include cart. ⊠ *8902 Kalanianaole Hwy., Hawaii Kai* 🕾 *808/395–2358* ⊕ *www. hawaiikaigolf.com* 🖃 *$110 for Championship Course; $39 for Executive Course* 🏌 *Championship Course: 18 holes, 6222 yards, par 72; Executive Course: 18 holes, 2223 yards, par 54.*

WINDWARD OAHU

Windward Oahu is what you expect when you think of golfing in the Islands. Lush, tropical foliage will surround you, with towering mountains framing one shot and the crystal blue Pacific framing the next. While it's a bit more expensive to golf on this side, and a good deal wetter, the memories and pictures you take on these courses will last a lifetime.

Koolau Golf Club. Koolau Golf Club is marketed as the toughest golf course in Hawaii and one of the most challenging in the country. Dick Nugent and Jack Tuthill (1992) routed 10 holes over jungle ravines

TIPS FOR THE GREEN

Before you head out to the first tee, there are a few things you should know about golf in Hawaii:

■ All resort courses and many daily-fee courses provide rental clubs. In many cases, they're the latest lines from Titleist, Ping, Callaway, and the like. This is true for both men and women, as well as left-handers, which means you don't have to schlep clubs across the Pacific.

■ Most courses offer deals varying from twilight deep-discount rates to frequent-visitor discounts, even for tourists. Ask questions when calling pro shops, and don't just accept the first quote—deals abound if you persist.

■ Pro shops at most courses are well stocked with balls, tees, and other accoutrements, so even if you bring your own bag, it needn't weigh a ton.

■ Come spikeless—very few Hawaii courses still permit metal spikes.

■ Sunscreen. Buy it, apply it (minimum 30 SPF). The subtropical rays of the sun are intense, even in December.

■ Resort courses, in particular, offer more than the usual three sets of tees, sometimes four or five. So bite off as much or little challenge as you can chew. Tee it up from the tips and you'll end up playing a few 600-yard par-5s and see a few 250-yard forced carries.

■ In theory, you can play golf in Hawaii 365 days a year. But there's a reason the Hawaiian Islands are so green. Better to bring an umbrella and light jacket and not use them than not to bring them and get soaked.

■ Unless you play a muni or certain daily-fee courses, plan on taking a cart. Riding carts are mandatory at most courses and are included in the greens fees.

that require at least a 110-yard carry. The par-4 18th may be the most difficult closing hole in golf. The tee shot from the regular tees must carry 200 yards of ravine, 250 from the blue tees. The approach shot is back across the ravine, 200 yards to a well-bunkered green. Set at the Windward base of the Koolau Mountains, the course is as much beauty as beast. Kaneohe Bay is visible from most holes, orchids and yellow ginger bloom, the shama thrush (Hawaii's best singer since Don Ho) chirps, and waterfalls flute down the sheer, green mountains above. Greens fee includes cart. ✉ 45-550 Kionaole Rd., Kaneohe ☎ 808/236–4653 ⊕ www.koolaugolfclub.com 💲 $145 ⚑ 18 holes, 6406 yards, par 72.

Olomana Golf Links. Bob and Robert L. Baldock are the architects of record for this layout, but so much has changed since it opened in 1969 that they would recognize little of it. A turf specialist was brought in to improve fairways and greens, tees were rebuilt, new bunkers added, and mangroves cut back to make better use of natural wetlands. But what really puts Olomana on the map is that this is where wunderkind Michelle Wie learned the game. ✉ 41-1801 Kalanianaole Hwy., Waimanalo ☎ 808/259–7926 ⊕ www.olomanagolflinks.com 💲 $59 *for 9 holes, $95 for 18 holes 🏌 18 holes, 5896 yards, par 72.*

Fodor's Choice
★

Royal Hawaiian Golf Club. In the cool, lush Maunawili Valley, Pete and Perry Dye created what can only be called target jungle golf. In other words, the rough is usually dense jungle, and you may not hit a driver on three of the four par-5s, or several par-4s, including the perilous 18th that plays off a cliff to a narrow green protected by a creek. Mt. Olomana's twin peaks tower over the course. ■**TIP→** The back nine wanders deep into the valley, and includes an island green (par-3 11th) and perhaps the loveliest inland hole in Hawaii (par-4 12th). ✉ *770 Auloa Rd., at Luana Hills Rd., Kailua* ☎ *808/262–2139* ⊕ *www.royalhawaiiangolfclub.com* 🗊 *$155* 🏌 *18 holes, 6609 yards, par 72.*

WORD OF MOUTH

"The best Oahu golf courses are the Koolau Golf Course, the Waikele Country Club, the Coral Creek Golf Course, and the Pearl Country Club. Give your hotel concierge a call to have your tee times all set up when you arrive."
—bobludlow

NORTH SHORE

The North Shore has both the cheapest and most expensive courses on the island. You can play nine holes in your bare feet, and you can chunk up the course played by both the LPGA and Champions Tour here, too. Don't try to go the barefoot route on the LPGA course, or the only course you may be allowed on in the Islands will be the Kahuku muni.

Kahuku Municipal Golf Course. The only true links course in Hawaii, this 9-hole municipal course is not for everyone. Maintenance is an ongoing issue, and in summer it can look a bit like the Serengeti. It's walking-only (a few pull-carts are available for rent); there's no pro shop, just a starter who sells lost-and-found balls; and the 19th hole is a soda machine and a covered picnic bench. And yet the course stretches out along the blue Pacific where surf crashes on the shore, the turf underfoot is spongy, sea mist drifts across the links, and wildflowers bloom in the rough. ✉ *56-501 Kamehameha Hwy., Kahuku* ☎ *808/293–5842* ⊕ *www1.honolulu.gov/des/golf/kahuku.htm* 🗊 *$27.50* 🏌 *9 holes, 2,699 yards, par 35.*

Turtle Bay Resort & Spa. When the Lazarus of golf courses, the **Fazio Course** at Turtle Bay (George Fazio, 1971), rose from the dead in 2002, Turtle Bay on Oahu's rugged North Shore became a premier golf destination. Two holes had been plowed under when the **Palmer Course** at Turtle Bay (Arnold Palmer and Ed Seay, 1992) was built, while the other seven lay fallow, and the front nine remained open. Then new owners came along and re-created holes 13 and 14 using Fazio's original plans, and the Fazio became whole again. It's a terrific track with 90 bunkers. The gem at Turtle Bay, though, is the Palmer Course. The front nine is mostly open as it skirts Punahoolapa Marsh, a nature sanctuary, while the back nine plunges into the wetlands and winds along the coast. The short par-4 17th runs along the rocky shore, with a diabolical string of bunkers cutting diagonally across the fairway from tee to green. ✉ 57-049 *Kuilima Dr., Kahuku* ☎ *808/293–8574* ⊕ *www.turtlebaygolf.com* ⛳ *Fazio Course, $115 for 18 holes, $75 for 9 holes; Palmer Course, $185* 🏌 *Fazio Course: 18 holes, 6769 yards, par 72; Palmer Course: 18 holes, 6795 yards, par 72.*

CENTRAL OAHU

Golf courses are densest here in Central Oahu, where plantations morphed into tract housing and golf courses were added to anchor communities. The vegetation is much sparser, but some of the best greens around can be found here. Play early to avoid the hot afternoons, but if you can handle the heat, note that most courses offer substantial discounts for twilight hours.

Hawaii Country Club. Also known as Kunia—but not to be confused with Royal Kunia a few miles away—this course is in the middle of sugarcane fields and dates to plantation times. Several par-4s are drivable, including the 9th and 18th holes. This is a fun course, but it's a bit rough around the edges. ✉ *94-1211 Kunia Rd., Waipahu* ☎ *808/621–5654* ⊕ *www.hawaiicc.com* ⛳ *$70* 🏌 *18 holes, 5910 yards, par 71.*

Mililani Golf Course. Located on Oahu's central plain, Mililani is usually a few degrees cooler than downtown, 25 minutes away. The eucalyptus trees through which the course plays add to the cool factor, and stands of Norfolk pines give Mililani a "mainland course" feel. Bob and Robert L. Baldock (1966) make good use of an old irrigation ditch reminiscent of a Scottish burn. ✉ *95-176 Kuahelani Ave., Mililani* ☎ *808/623–2222* ⊕ *www.mililanigolf.com* ⛳ *$99* 🏌 *18 holes, 6274 yards, par 72.*

Pearl Country Club. Carved in the hillside high above Pearl Harbor, the 18 holes here are really two courses. The front nine rambles out along gently sloping terrain, while the back nine zigzags up and down a steeper portion of the slope as it rises into the Koolau Mountains. ■TIP→ The views of Pearl Harbor are breathtaking. ✉ *98-535 Kaonohi St., Aiea* ☎ *808/487–3802* ⊕ *www.pearlcc.com* ⛳ *$140* 🏌 *18 holes, 6232 yards, par 72.*

Royal Kunia Country Club. At one time the PGA Tour considered buying Royal Kunia Country Club and hosting the Sony Open there. It's that good. ■TIP→ Every hole offers fabulous views from Diamond Head to Pearl Harbor to the nearby Waianae Mountains. Robin Nelson's eye for natural sight lines and dexterity with water features adds to the visual pleasure. ✉ *94-1509 Anonui St., Waipahu* ☎ *808/688–9222* ⊕ *www.royalkuniacc.com* ⛳ *$150* 🏌 *18 holes, 6507 yards, par 72.*

Waikele Country Club. Outlet stores are not the only bargain at Waikele. The adjacent golf course is a daily-fee course that offers a private club-like atmosphere and a terrific Ted Robinson (1992) layout. The target off the tee is Diamond Head, with Pearl Harbor to the right. Robinson's water features are less distinctive here but define the short par-4 fourth hole, with a lake running down the left side of the fairway and guarding the green; and the par-3 17th, which plays across a lake. The

par-4 18th is a terrific closing hole, with a lake lurking on the right side of the green. ⊠ *94-200 Paioa Pl., Waipahu* ☎ *808/676–9000* ⊕ *www. golfwaikele.com* ▣ *$130* ⚑ *18 holes, 6261 yards, par 72.*

WEST (LEEWARD) OAHU

On the leeward side of the mountains, shielded from the rains that drench the Kaneohe side, West Oahu is arid and sunny and has a unique kind of beauty. The Ewa area is dotted with golf courses and new development, so you'll have your pick of a number of different options—golfers generally choose courses in Ewa and Kapolei because they provide a totally different landscape from Waikiki or the North Shore. The resort courses on the west side are a long drive from town, but the beaches are magnificent, and you can find deals if you're combining a room with a round or two on the greens.

Coral Creek Golf Course. On the Ewa Plain, 4 miles inland, Coral Creek is cut from ancient coral—left from when this area was still underwater. Robin Nelson (1999) does some of his best work in making use of the coral, and of some dynamite, blasting out portions to create dramatic lakes and tee and green sites. They could just as easily call it Coral Cliffs, because of the 30- to 40-foot cliffs Nelson created. They include the par-3 10th green's grotto and waterfall, and the vertical drop-off on the right side of the par-4 18th green. An ancient creek meanders across the course, but there's not much water, just enough to be a babbling nuisance. ⊠ *91-1111 Geiger Rd., Ewa Beach* ☎ *808/441–4653* ⊕ *www.coralcreekgolfhawaii.com* ▣ *$140* ⚑ *18 holes, 6810 yards, par 72.*

Ewa Beach Golf Club. A private course open to the public, Ewa is one of the delightful products of the too-brief collaboration of Robin Nelson and Rodney Wright (1992). Trees are very much part of the character here, but there are also elements of links golf, such as a double green shared by the 2nd and 16th holes. ⊠ *91-050 Fort Weaver Rd., Ewa Beach* ☎ *808/689–6565* ⊕ *www.ewabeachgc.com* ▣ *$160* ⚑ *18 holes, 5861 yards, par 72.*

Hawaii Prince Golf Course. Affiliated with the Hawaii Prince Hotel in Waikiki, the Hawaii Prince Golf Course (not to be confused with the Prince Course at Princeville, Kauai) has a links feel to it, and it is popular with local charity fund-raiser golf tournaments. Arnold Palmer and Ed Seay (1991) took what had been flat, featureless sugarcane fields and sculpted 27 challenging, varied holes. Mounding breaks up the landscape, as do 10 lakes. Water comes into play on six holes of the A course, three of B, and seven of C. The most difficult combination is A and C (A and B from the forward tees). ⊠ *91-1200 Fort Weaver Rd., Ewa Beach* ☎ *808/944–4567* ⊕ *www.princeresortshawaii.com* ▣ *$77 for 9 holes, $160 for 18 holes* ⚑ *A Course: 9 holes, 3138 yards, par 36; B Course: 9 holes, 3099 yards, par 36; C Course: 9 holes, 3076 yards, par 36.*

Kapolei Golf Course. This is a Ted Robinson water wonderland with waterfalls and four lakes—three so big they have names—coming into play on 10 holes. Set on rolling terrain, Kapolei is a serious golf course, especially when the wind blows. ✉ *91-701 Farrington Hwy., Kapolei* ☎ *808/674–2227* ⊕ *www.kapoleigolfcourse.com* ✎ *$185* 🏌 *18 holes, 6136 yards, par 72.*

Ko Olina Golf Club. Hawaii's golden age of golf-course architecture came to Oahu when Ko Olina Golf Club opened in 1989. Ted Robinson, king of the water features, went splash-happy here, creating nine lakes that come into play on eight holes, including the par-3 12th, where you reach the tee by driving behind a Disney-like waterfall. Tactically, though, the most dramatic is the par-4 18th, where the approach is a minimum 120 yards across a lake to a two-tiered green guarded on the left by a cascading waterfall. Today, Ko Olina, affiliated with the adjacent Ihilani Resort and Spa (guests receive discounted rates), has matured into one of Hawaii's top courses. You can niggle about routing issues—the first three holes play into the trade winds (and the morning sun), and two consecutive par-5s on the back nine play into the trades—but Robinson does enough solid design to make those of passing concern. ■**TIP➜** The course provides free transportation from Waikiki hotels. ✉ *92-1220 Aliinui Dr., Kapolei* ☎ *808/676–5300* ⊕ *www.koolinagolf.com* ✎ *$89 for 9 holes; $189 for 18 holes* 🏌 *18 holes, 6432 yards, par 72.*

Makaha Valley Country Club. This course (William F. Bell, 1968), known locally as Makaha East, is indeed a valley course, taking great advantage of the steep valley walls and natural terrain. It's shorter than the nearby West course, but offers plenty of challenge from the back tees. The double-dogleg, downhill-uphill, par-5 18th is a doozy of a closer. ✉ *84-627 Makaha Valley Rd., Waianae* ☎ *808/695–7111* ⊕ *www.makahavalleycc.com* ✎ *$65 for 18 holes, $40 for 9 holes* 🏌 *18 holes, 6260 yards, par 71.*

West Loch Municipal Golf Course. The best of Honolulu's municipal courses, this Robin Nelson (1991) design plays along Pearl Harbor's West Loch. In the process of building the course, wetlands were actually expanded, increasing bird habitat. ✉ *91-1126 Okupe St., Ewa Beach* ☎ *808/675–6076* ⊕ *www1.honolulu.gov/des/golf/westloch.htm* ✎ *$55* 🏌 *18 holes, 6,335 yards, par 72.*

HIKING

The trails of Oahu cover a full spectrum of environments: desert walks through cactus, slippery paths through bamboo-filled rain forest, and scrambling rock climbs up ancient volcanic calderas. The only thing you won't find is an overnighter, as even the longest of hikes won't take you more than half a day. In addition to being short in length, many of the prime hikes are within 10 minutes of downtown Waikiki, meaning that you won't have to spend your whole day getting back to nature.

Hawaii State Department of Land and Natural Resources. Go to this website for information on all major hiking trails on Oahu. You can also obtain camping permits for state parks here. ✉ *1151 Punchbowl St., Room 130, Honolulu* ☎ *808/587–0300* ⊕ *www.hawaiistateparks.org.*

Na Ala Hele Trails and Access. Contact the Na Ala Hele ("Trails To Go On") folks for a free hiking-safety guide and trail information. The interactive website has maps and information about the current status of trails on all of the Islands. You can also stop in their office for free printed maps and information. ✉ *1151 Punchbowl St., Room 325, Downtown Honolulu, Honolulu* ☎ *808/587–0166* ⊕ *www.hawaiitrails.org.*

BEST SPOTS

Diamond Head Crater. Every vacation has requirements that must be fulfilled so that when your neighbors ask, you can say, "Yeah, did it." Climbing Diamond Head is high on that list of things to do on Oahu. It's a moderately easy hike if you're in good physical condition, but be prepared to climb many stairs along the way. Be sure to bring a water bottle because it's hot and dry. Only a mile up, a clearly marked trail with handrails scales the inside of this extinct volcano. At the top, the fabled final 99 steps take you up to the pillbox overlooking the Pacific Ocean and Honolulu. It's a breathtaking view and a lot cheaper than taking a helicopter ride for the same photo op. Last entry for hikers is 4:30 pm. ✉ *Diamond Head Rd. at 18th Ave., Honolulu* ⊕ *Enter on the east side of the crater; there's limited parking inside, so most park on street and walk in* ⊕ *www.hawaiistateparks.org/hiking/oahu* ✉ *$1 per person; $5 to park* ☉ *Daily 6–6.*

Fodor's Choice ★   **Kaena Point Trail.** This hike is a little longer (a 5-mile round-trip) and both hotter and more exposed than the Makapuu Lighthouse Trail *(see below)*, but it is right next to the beach, and there are spots where you can get in and cool off. Sea-carved cliffs give way to lava-rock beaches and sea arches. Halfway to the point, there is a double blow-hole, which is a good indicator of sea conditions. If it is blowing good, stay out of the water. Though the area is hot and dry, there is still much wildlife here, as it is the only nesting ground for many rare sea birds. ■TIP➔ Keep a lookout for the Laysan albatrosses; these enormous birds have recently returned to the area. Don't be surprised if they come in for a closer look at you, too. There has been a cave-in of an old lava tube, so be careful when crossing it, but enjoy the view in its enormous mouth. ✉ *81-780 Farrington Hwy., Waianae* ⊕ *Take Farrington Hwy. to its end at Yokohamas. Hike in on the old 4WD trail.*

Makapuu Lighthouse Trail. For the less adventurous hiker and anyone looking for a great view, this paved trail that runs up the side of Makapuu Point in Southeast Oahu fits the bill. Early on, the trail is surrounded by lava rock but, as you ascend, foliage—the tiny white *koa haole* flower and the cream-tinged spikes of the *kiawe*—begins taking over the barren rock. At the easternmost tip of Oahu, where the island divides the sea, this trail gives you a spectacular view of the cobalt ocean meeting the land in a cacophony of whitecaps. To the south are several tide pools and the lighthouse, while the eastern view looks down upon Rabbit and Kaohikaipu islands, two bird sanctuaries just off the coast. The 2-mile round-trip hike is a great break on a circle-island trip. ■TIP➔ Be sure not to leave valuables in your car as break-ins are common. ✉ *Makapuu Lighthouse Rd., Honolulu* ⊕ *Take Kalanianaole Hwy. to base of Makapuu Point. Look for asphalt strip snaking up mountain.*

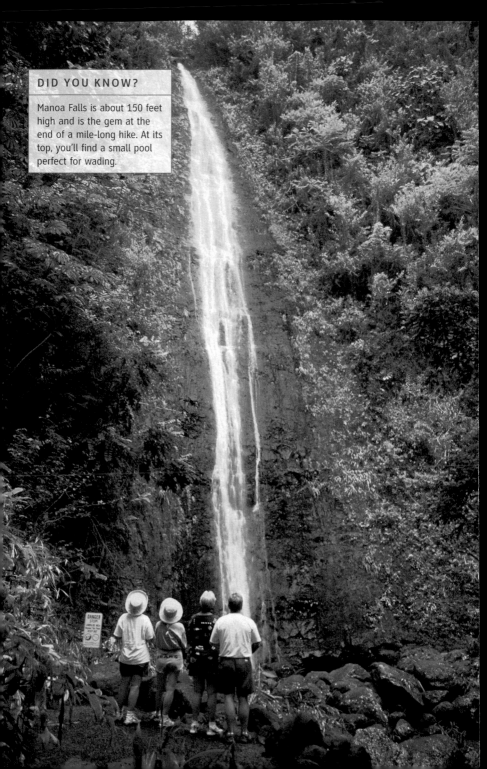

DID YOU KNOW?

Manoa Falls is about 150 feet high and is the gem at the end of a mile-long hike. At its top, you'll find a small pool perfect for wading.

TIPS FOR THE TRAIL

■ When hiking the waterfall and rain-forest trails, use insect repellent. The dampness draws huge swarms of bloodsuckers that can ruin a walk in the woods.

■ Volcanic rock is very porous and therefore likely to be loose. Rock climbing is strongly discouraged, as you never know which little ledge is going to go.

■ Avoid hiking after heavy rains and check for flash flood warnings. Keep in mind that those large boulders in the idyllic pools beneath the waterfalls were carried by torrential flows high up in the mountains.

■ Always let someone know where you're going and never hike alone. The foliage gets very dense, and, small as the island is, hikers have been known to get lost for a week or longer.

5

Fodor's Choice
★
Manoa Falls Trail. Travel up into the valley beyond Honolulu to make the Manoa Falls hike. Though only a mile long, this well-trafficked path—visited by an estimated 100,000 hikers a year—passes through so many different ecosystems that you feel as if you're in an arboretum—and you're not far off. (The beautiful Lyon Arboretum is right near the trailhead, if you want to make another stop.) Walk among the elephant ear ape plants, ruddy fir trees, and a bamboo forest straight out of China. At the top is a 150-foot waterfall, which can be an impressive cascade, or, if rain has been sparse, the falls can be little more than a trickle. This hike is more about the journey than the destination; make sure you bring some mosquito repellent because they grow em big up here. ⊠ *3998 Manoa Rd., Manoa, Honolulu ✥ West Manoa Rd. is behind Manoa Valley in Paradise Park. Take West Manoa Rd. to end, park on side of road or in the parking lot for a small fee, and follow trail signs in.*

Maunawili Falls. Want to find a waterfall that you can actually swim in? Then Maunawili Falls is your trip. In fact, even if you don't want to get wet, you're going to have to cross Maunawili Stream several times to get to the falls. Along the 1½-mile trek enjoy the ginger, vines, and heliconia before greeting fern-shrouded falls that are made for swimming. The water is not the clearest, but it's cool and refreshing after battling the bugs to get here. ■**TIP**➜ Be sure to bring mosquito repellant. ⊠ *1221 Kelewina St., Kailua ✥ Take Pali Hwy. (Rte. 61) from Honolulu through the tunnels, then take the 3rd right onto Auloa Rd., then take the left fork immediately. At the dead end, climb over the vehicle gate to find the trailhead.*

Trails at Turtle Bay Resort. When on the North Shore, check out the Turtle Bay Resort, which has more than 12 miles of trails and ocean-side pathways. You can pick up a map of the resort property that includes trail and coastal jogging paths. ⊠ *57-091 Kamehameha Hwy., Kahuku* ☎ *808/293–8811* ⊕ *www.turtlebayresort.com.*

GOING WITH A GUIDE

FAMILY **Hawaii Nature Center.** A good choice for families, the center in upper Makiki Valley conducts a number of programs for both adults and children. There are guided hikes into tropical settings that reveal hidden waterfalls and protected forest reserves. They don't run tours every day so it's a good idea to get advance reservations. ⊠ *2131 Makiki Heights Dr., Makiki Heights, Honolulu* ☎ *808/955–0100* ⊕ *www. hawaiinaturecenter.org.*

Oahu Nature Tours. Guides explain the native flora and fauna and history that are your companions on their Manoa Waterfall, Mountain Rainforest, and Diamond Head walking tours. Tours include pick-up at centralized Waikiki locations. ☎ *808/924–2473* ⊕ *www.oahunaturetours. com.*

HORSEBACK RIDING

A great way to see the island is atop a horse, leaving the direction to the pack while you drink in the views of mountains or the ocean. It may seem like a cliché, but there really is nothing like riding a horse with spectacular ocean views to put you in a romantic state of mind.

FAMILY **Happy Trails Hawaii.** Take a guided horseback ride above the North Shore's Waimea Bay along trails that offer panoramic views from Kaena Point to the famous surfing spots. Specializing in families, they have groups of no more than 10 and provide instruction. Children six and older are welcome. You can take either a 90-minute or two-hour ride. Reservations are required. ⊠ *59-231 Pupukea Rd., Pupukea* ✛ *Go 1 mile mauka (toward the mountain) up Pupakea Rd. The office is on the right* ☎ *808/638–7433* ⊕ *happytrailshawaii.com* 🎟 *From $80.*

FAMILY **Kualoa Ranch.** This ranch across from Kualoa Beach Park on the Windward side leads trail rides in the Kaaawa Valley. The most basic offering is a one-hour trail ride. Kualoa has other activities such as bus and jeep tours, all-terrain-vehicle trail rides, and children's activities, which may be combined for half- or full-day package rates. ⊠ *49-560 Kamehameha Hwy., Kaneohe* ☎ *800/231–7321* ⊕ *www.kualoa.com* 🎟 *From $69.*

Turtle Bay Stables. Trail rides follow the coast line and even step out onto sandy beaches. The stables here are part of the North Shore resort but can be utilized by nonguests. The sunset ride is a definite must if you are a friend of our four-legged friends. A basic trail ride lasts 45 minutes. ⊠ *Turtle Bay Resort, 57-091 Kamehameha Hwy., Kahuku* ☎ *808/293–6024* ⊕ *www.turtlebayresort.com/experiences/outdoor_ activities/horseback_riding/* 🎟 *From $70.*

JOGGING

In Honolulu, the most popular places to jog are the two parks, **Kapiolani** and **Ala Moana**, at either end of Waikiki. In both cases, the loop around the park is just under 2 miles. You can run a 4-mile ring around **Diamond Head crater,** past scenic views, luxurious homes, and herds of other joggers.

Hawaii State Department of Health Community Resources Section. This department provides a free "Honolulu Walking Map" and "The Fitness Fun Map," which list more than two dozen walking and jogging routes and suggested itineraries. ⊠ *1250 Punchbowl St., Room 422, Honolulu* ☎ *808/586–4488* ⊕ *www.healthyhawaii.com/.*

Honolulu Marathon. The Honolulu Marathon is a thrilling event to watch as well as to participate in. Join the throngs who cheer at the finish line at Kapiolani Park as internationally famous and local runners tackle the 26.2-mile challenge. It's held on the second Sunday in December and is sponsored by the Honolulu Marathon Association. ☎ *808/734–7200* ⊕ *www.honolulumarathon.org.*

Running Room. Once you leave Honolulu, it gets trickier to find places to jog that are scenic as well as safe. It's best to stick to the well-traveled routes, or ask the experienced folks at this store for advice. Their website includes information about local races as well as a list of jogging routes complete with maps. ⊠ *819 Kapahulu Ave., Kapahulu, Honolulu* ☎ *808/737–2422* ⊕ *www.runningroomhawaii.com.*

TENNIS

While tennis has given way to golf as the biggest resort attraction, and many of the hotel courts have closed, there are still locations in Waikiki to get your tennis match on. Both sides of Waikiki are framed by tennis complexes, with Ala Moana Park containing a 12-court spread, and two different sets at Kapiolani Park. Play is free at public courts, which are readily available during the day—but they tend to fill up after the sun goes down and the asphalt cools off.

Ala Moana Park Tennis Courts. With 10 public courts, those located in Ala Moana Park are the closest to the *ewa* (west) end of Waikiki. ⊠ *Ala Moana Park, 1141 Ala Moana Blvd., Ala Moana, Honolulu* ☎ *808/592–2288.*

Diamond Head Tennis Center. Across the street from Kapiolani Park, this center has 10 courts open to the public. ⊠ *3908 Paki Ave., Waikiki, Honolulu* ☎ *808/768-4626.*

Kapiolani Tennis Courts. There are four courts for play here. ⊠ *2765 Kalakaua Ave., Waikiki, Honolulu* ☎ *808/768–4626.*

Waikiki Tennis Club. On the rooftop of the Pacific Beach Hotel you can play on the only synthetic clay court in the Hawaiian Islands which is open to the public. Hotel guests play for free but courts are also open to nonguests. ■ **TIP→** Make reservations via the tennis club's website. ⊠ *Pacific Beach Hotel, 2490 Kalakaua Ave., Waikiki, Honolulu* ☎ *808/206–6735* ⊕ *www.thewaikikitennisclub.com.*

5

VOLLEYBALL

With no shortage of sand, beach volleyball is an extremely popular sport on the Islands.

BEST SPOTS

There are sand-volleyball courts in Waikiki near **Fort DeRussy**. These are open to the public, so talent levels vary. However, the winner-plays-on policy here guarantees a higher level of play as the day progresses. For more advanced play, go to **Queen's Beach**, where you must bring your own net (which can lead to court possessiveness). This is the area where college kids and pros come when they're in town.

6

SHOPS AND SPAS

Updated by
Chris Oliver

Eastern and Western traditions meet on Oahu, where savvy shoppers find luxury goods at high-end malls and scout tiny boutiques and galleries filled with pottery, blown glass, woodwork, and Hawaiian-print clothing by local artists. This blend of cultures is pervasive in the wide selection of spas as well. Hawaiian *lomilomi* and hot-stone massages are as omnipresent as the orchid and plumeria flowers decorating every treatment room.

Exploring downtown Honolulu, Kailua on the windward side, and the North Shore often yields the most original merchandise. Some of the small stores carry imported clothes and gifts from around the world—a reminder that, on this island halfway between Asia and the United States, shopping is a multicultural experience.

If you're getting a massage at a spa, there's a spiritual element to the *lomilomi* that calms the soul while the muscles release tension. During a hot-stone massage, smooth rocks, taken from the earth with permission from Pele, the goddess of volcanoes, are heated and placed at focal points on the body. Others are covered in oil and rubbed over tired limbs, feeling like powerful fingers. For an alternative, refresh skin with mango scrubs so fragrant they seem edible. Savor the unusual sensation of bamboo tapped against the arches of the feet. Indulge in a scalp massage that makes the entire body tingle. Day spas provide additional options to the self-indulgent services offered in almost every major hotel on the island.

HONOLULU

There are two distinct types of shopping experiences for visitors: vast malls with the customary department stores, and tiny boutiques with specialty items. Three malls in Honolulu provide a combination of the standard department stores and interesting shops showcasing original paintings and woodwork from local artists and craftsmen. Shoppers who know where to look in Honolulu will find everything from designer merchandise to unusual Asian imports.

Possibilities are endless, but a bit of scouting is usually required to get past the items you'll find in your own hometown. Industrious bargain hunters can detect the perfect gift in the sale bin of a slightly hidden store at every mall.

You'll find that shops stay open fairly late in Waikiki. Stores open at around 9 am and many don't close until 10 or even 11 pm.

WAIKIKI

Most hotels and shops are clustered along a relatively short strip in Waikiki, which can be convenient or overwhelming, depending on your sensibilities. Clothing, jewelry, and handbags from Europe's top designers sit across the street from the International Marketplace, a conglomeration of booths reminiscent of New York City's Canal Street—with a tropical flair. It's possible to find interesting items at reasonable prices in Waikiki, but shoppers have to be willing to search beyond the $4,000 purses and the tacky wooden tikis to find innovation and quality.

SHOPPING CENTERS

DFS Galleria Waikiki. Hermès, Cartier, Michael Kors, and Marc Jacobs are among the shops on the Waikiki Luxury Walk in this enclosed mall, as well as Hawaii's largest beauty and cosmetic store. The third floor caters to duty-free shoppers only and features an exclusive Watch Shop. The Kalia Grill and Starbucks offer a respite for weary shoppers. ⊠ *330 Royal Hawaiian Ave., Waikiki, Honolulu* ☏ *808/931–2700* ⊕ *www. dfsgalleria.com.*

King's Village. This shopping center looks like a Hollywood stage set of monarchy-era Honolulu, complete with a changing-of-the-guard ceremony every evening at 6:15; shops include The Jade Tree Jewelry, Honolulu Surf & Sport, and Solid Stone. ⊠ *131 Kaiulani Ave., Waikiki, Honolulu* ☏ *808/695–4325* ⊕ *www.kings-village.com.*

Royal Hawaiian Center. An open and inviting facade has made this three-block-long shopping center a garden of Hawaiian shops. There are more than 100 stores and restaurants, including local gems such as Aloha Aina Boutique, Honolulu Home Collection, and Koi Boutique. Check out tropical Panama hats at Hawaiian Island Arts, or offerings at Island Soap & Candleworks while Bob's Ukulele may inspire musicians to learn a new instrument. Nine restaurants round out the dining options, along with the Paina Lanai Food Court, the Five-O Bar & Lounge, plus a theater and nightly outdoor entertainment. ⊠ *2201 Kalakaua Ave., Waikiki, Honolulu* ☏ *808/922–0588* ⊕ *www.royalhawaiiancenter.com.*

6

2100 Kalakaua. Tenants of this elegant, town house–style center known as "Luxury Row" include Chanel, Coach, Tiffany & Co., Yves Saint Laurent, Bottega Veneta, Gucci, Hugo Boss, and Tod's. ⊠ *2100 Kalakaua Ave., Waikiki, Honolulu* ⊕ *www.2100kalakaua.com.*

Waikiki Beach Walk. This open-air shopping center greets visitors at the west end of Waikiki's Kalakaua Avenue with 70 locally owned stores and restaurants. Get reasonably priced, fashionable resort wear for yourself at Mahina; find unique pieces by local artists at Under the Koa Tree; or buy local treats from Coco Cove. Or you can browse Koa and sandalwood gifts at Martin & MacArthur in the nearby Outrigger Reef hotel. The mall also features free local entertainment on the outdoor fountain stage at least once a week. ⊠ *226 Lewers St., Waikiki, Honolulu* ☎ *808/931–3591* ⊕ *www.waikikibeachwalk.com.*

Waikiki Shopping Plaza. This five-floor shopping center is across the street from the Royal Hawaiian Shopping Center. Sephora, Armani Exchange, Guess, Alter Ego, and Tanaka of Tokyo Restaurant are some of its 50 shops and eateries. The Big Kahuna marketplace on the third floor has a bazaar-type feel to it with great, cheap souvenirs. The Visitor Aloha Society/Travelers Aid of Honolulu is also located here if you run into trouble while on vacation. ⊠ *2250 Kalakaua Ave., Waikiki, Honolulu* ☎ *808/923–1191* ⊕ *waikikishoppingplaza.com.*

CLOTHING

Blue Ginger. Look inside this little shop across from The Yardhouse for beach-casual clothing, bags, jewelry and accessories in soft rayon aloha prints for adults and children. ⊠ *227 Lewers St., Waikiki, Honolulu* ☎ *808/942–2829* ⊕ *www.blueginger.com.*

Newt at the Royal. Newt is known for high-quality, handwoven Panama hats and tropical sportswear for men and women. ⊠ *The Royal Hawaiian Hotel, 2259 Kalakaua Ave., Waikiki, Honolulu* ☎ *808/949–4321* ⊕ *www.newtattheroyal.com.*

GALLERIES

Na Hoku Gallery. This is a smaller version of the designer and island-lifestyle jewelry store whose original is located in the Ala Moana Shopping Center. ⊠ *Outrigger Waikiki, 2335 Kalakaua Ave., Waikiki, Honolulu* ☎ *808/922–0556* ⊕ *www.NaHoku.com.*

GIFTS

Sand People. This little shop stocks beach-inspired, easy-to-carry gifts, such as fish-shaped Christmas ornaments, Hawaiian-style notepads, frames, charms in the shape of flip-flops (known locally as "slippahs"), soaps, kitchen accessories, and ceramic clocks. There's another branch in Kailua as well as three each on Kauai and Maui. ⊠ *Moana Surfrider, 2369 Kalakaua, Waikiki, Honolulu* ☎ *808/924–6773* ⊕ *www.sandpeople.com.*

JEWELRY

Philip Rickard. The heirloom design collection of this famed jeweler features custom Hawaiian jewelry, particularly its Wedding Collection often sought by various celebrities. Visitors to the factory and showroom in Ala Moana may watch jewelers and craftsmen designing, engraving, and polishing their work. ⊠ *Ala Moana Shopping Center, 1450 Ala Moana Blvd., Ala Moana, Honolulu* ☎ *808/946–6720* ⊕ *www.philiprickard.com.*

SPAS

Abhasa Spa. Natural organic skin and body treatments highlight this spa tucked away in the Royal Hawaiian Hotel's coconut grove. Vegetarian-lifestyle spa therapies, color-light therapy, a facial fusing invigorating *lomilomi* technique with hot *pohaku* stones are all available. You can choose to have your treatment in any of Abhasa's eight indoor rooms or in one of its three garden cabanas. ⊠ *Royal Hawaiian Hotel, 2259 Kalakaua Ave., Waikiki, Honolulu* ☎ *808/922–8200* ⊕ *www.abhasa. com* ☞ *50-min massages from $145.*

Mandara Spa at the Hilton Hawaiian Village Beach Resort & Spa. From its perch in the Kalia Tower, Mandara Spa, an outpost of the chain that originated in Bali, overlooks the mountains, ocean, and downtown Honolulu. Fresh Hawaiian ingredients and traditional techniques headline an array of treatments. Try an exotic upgrade, such as reflexology or a Balinese body polish. Or relieve achy muscles with a traditional Thai poultice massage. The delicately scented, candlelit foyer can fill up quickly with robe-clad conventioneers, so be sure to make a reservation. There are spa suites for couples, a private infinity pool, and a boutique. ⊠ *Hilton Hawaiian Village Beach Resort and Spa, 2005 Kalia Rd., Waikiki, Honolulu* ☎ *808/945–7721* ⊕ *www.mandaraspa. com* ☞ *50-min massages from $135.*

Na Hoola Spa at the Hyatt Regency Waikiki Resort & Spa. Na Hoola is the premier resort spa in Waikiki, with 16 treatment rooms sprawling across 10,000 square feet and two floors of the Hyatt on Kalakaua Avenue. Arrive early for your treatment to enjoy the postcard views of Waikiki Beach. Four packages identified by Hawaii's native healing plants—noni, kukui, awa, and kalo—combine various body, face, and hair treatments; the spa also has luxurious packages that last three to six hours. The Kele Kele body wrap employs a self-heating mud wrap to release tension and stress. The small exercise room is for use by hotel guests only. ⊠ *Hyatt Regency Waikiki Resort and Spa, 2424 Kalakaua Ave., Waikiki, Honolulu* ☎ *808/923–1234, 808/237–6330 Reservations* ⊕ *www.waikiki.hyatt.com/hyatt/pure/spas* ☞ *50-min massages from $155.*

Paul Brown's Spa Olakino at the Waikiki Beach Marriott Resort & Spa. Paul Brown has created a spa facing Waikiki Beach. Linger with a cup of tea between treatments and gaze through 75-foot-high windows at the activity outside. Lush Hawaiian foliage, sleek Balinese teak furnishings, and a mist of ylang-ylang and nutmeg in the air inspire relaxation. Treatments incorporate Brown's Hapuna line of essential oils, as well as a thermal masking system using volcanic ash. The couples' experience lasts four hours and includes massage, massage instruction, and chocolate-covered strawberries at sunset. ⊠ *Waikiki Beach Marriott Resort & Spa, 2552 Kalakaua Ave., Waikiki, Honolulu* ☎ *808/924–2121* ⊕ *www. spaolakino.com* ☞ *50-min massages from $120.*

6

Serenity Spa Hawaii. Only steps off the beach, this renovated Aveda Concept spa provides aromatherapy treatments, massages, and facials. Each room is extra spacious not just to give therapists area to move, but to accommodate handicapped guests as well. Signature massages include a stress-fix body massage that relieves jet lag and stiffness from traveling and a massage using *lomilomi* techniques and hot stones. ■TIP→ Book the last appointment of the day—usually 4, 5, or 6 pm—so you can watch the sunset as you're finishing your massage treatment. ✉ *Outrigger Reef on the Beach, 2169 Kalia Rd., Waikiki, Honolulu* ☎ *808/926–2882, 866/926–2882* ⊕ *www.serenityspahawaii.com* ☞ *50-min massages from $110.*

The Spa at Trump Waikiki. One of the newest in Waikiki, The Spa at Trump offers private changing and showering areas for each room, creating an environment of uninterrupted relaxation. No matter what treatment you choose, it is inspired by "personal intention," such as purify, balance, heal, revitalize, or calm, to elevate the senses throughout your time there. Don't miss the signature gemstone treatments, which feature products by Shiffa; or treat yourself to a Kate Somerville facial to emerge with younger-looking skin. The Hawaiian pineapple lime exfoliation massage is the most popular, as it is exclusive to this spa. ✉ *Trump International Hotel Waikiki, 223 Saratoga Rd., Waikiki, Honolulu* ☎ *808/683–7466* ⊕ *www.trumpwaikikihotel.com* ☞ *80-min massages from $165.*

Fodor'sChoice
★　**SpaHalekulani.** SpaHalekulani mines the traditions and cultures of the Pacific Islands with massages, body, and facial therapies. Try the Samoan Nonu, which uses warm stones and healing noni gel to relieve muscle tension. The exclusive line of bath and body products is scented by maile, lavender orchid, or coconut passion. Facilities specific to treatment but may include Japanese furo bath or steam shower. ✉ *Halekulani Hotel, 2199 Kalia Rd., Waikiki, Honolulu* ☎ *808/931–5322* ⊕ *www.halekulani.com/living/spahalekulani* ☞ *55-min massages from $180.*

Waikiki Plantation Spa. Located in the Outrigger Waikiki, this two-story spa, which sprawls over 5,000 square feet, is the only penthouse spa in Hawaii and offers unparalleled views of the beach and ocean. Try the spa's Healing Body Cocoon, an 80-minute treatment that starts with a full-body dry brushing with algae oil and ends with an anti-aging body balm. ✉ *Outrigger Waikiki, 2335 Kalakaua Ave., #17, Waikiki, Honolulu* ☎ *808/926–2880, 866/926–2889* ⊕ *www.waikikiplantationspa.com* ☞ *50-min massages from $125.*

DOWNTOWN HONOLULU

Downtown shopping is an entirely different, constantly changing experience from what you'll find elsewhere in Honolulu. Focus on the small galleries—which are earning the area a strong reputation for its arts and culture renaissance—and the burgeoning array of hip, home-decor stores tucked between ethnic restaurants. ■TIP→ Don't miss the festive atmosphere on the first Friday of every month, when stores, restaurants, and galleries stay open from 5 pm to 9 pm for the "Downtown Gallery Walk."

SHOPPING CENTERS

Aloha Tower Marketplace. Billing itself as a festival marketplace, Aloha Tower cozies up to Honolulu Harbor. Along with restaurants and entertainment venues, it has about two dozen shops and kiosks selling mostly visitor-oriented merchandise, from sunglasses to apparel to souvenir refrigerator magnets. To get there from Waikiki take the E-Transit Bus, which goes along TheBus routes every 15 minutes. ⊠ *1 Aloha Tower Dr., at Piers 8, 9, and 10, Downtown Honolulu, Honolulu* ☎ *808/566–2337* ⊕ *www.alohatower.com.*

BUYING TROPICAL FLOWERS AND FRUIT

You can bring home fresh pineapple, papaya, or coconut to share with friends and family. Orchids also will brighten your home and remind you of your trip to the Islands. By law, all fresh fruit and plant products must be inspected by the Department of Agriculture before export. Ask at the shop about Department of Agriculture rules so a surprise confiscation doesn't spoil your departure. Shipping to your home usually is best.

HOME DECOR

Robyn Buntin Galleries. Chinese antiques, Japanese art, Buddhist sculptures, and important works by Hawaiian artists are among the international pieces sold here as well as jewelry and an extensive selection of prints. The gallery has more than 7,000 items available online. ⊠ *Robyn Buntin Gallery, 848 S. Beretania St., Downtown Honolulu, Honolulu* ☎ *808/523–5913* ⊕ *www.robynbuntin.com.*

6

CHINATOWN

Chinatown offers the typical mix of the tacky and unique, depending on individual taste, but it is an experience not to be missed. The vital, bright colors of fresh fruits and vegetables blend with the distinct scent of recently killed pigs and poultry. Tucked in between are authentic shops with Asian silk clothing at reasonable prices. The bustling, ethnic atmosphere adds to the excitement. If you're hungry for a local experience you should at least walk through the area, even if you don't plan to purchase the mysterious herbs in the glass jars lining the shelves.

GALLERIES

Louis Pohl Gallery. Stop in this gallery to browse modern works from some of Hawaii's finest artists. In addition to pieces by resident artists, there are monthly exhibitions by local and visiting artists. ⊠ *1142 Bethel St., Chinatown, Honolulu* ☎ *808/521–1812* ⊕ *www.louispohlgallery.com.*

HOME DECOR

Place. This design studio/workshop is known for its sophisticated assemblage of carefully chosen home items in all price ranges. You'll find a global collection of fine lighting, fabrics, kitchenware, garden accessories, and clothing, as well as art by local artists and artisans. Hands-on workshops give shoppers a glimpse of how owner and interior designer Mary Philpotts McGrath creates a Hawaiian sense of place. ⊠ *40 S. School St., Chinatown, Honolulu* ☎ *808/275–3075* ⊕ *www.placehawaii.com.*

KAKAAKO

CLOTHING

Anne Namba Designs. This designer combines the beauty of classic kimonos with contemporary styles to make unique pieces for career and evening. In addition to women's apparel, she designs a men's line and a wedding couture line. ✉ *324 Kamani St., Kakaako, Honolulu* ☎ *808/589–1135* ⊕ *www.annenamba.com.*

HOME DECOR

Fishcake. A place to find unusual art, Fishcake is a gallery for designers that hosts changing exhibitions by favorite artists near and far. Plus, you'll find a unique collection of small and large home items you won't find anywhere else in Honolulu. ✉ *307c Kamani St., Kakaako, Honolulu* ☎ *808/593–1231* ⊕ *www.fishcake.us.*

SPORTING GOODS

Boca Hawaii. This triathlon shop near the Bike Factory offers training gear and bike rentals ($40 per day with a two-day minimum, $175 per week), aerial yoga and capoeira classes, and nutritional products. ■**TIP→** Inquire directly about the latest schedule of classes at the store, which is owned and operated by top athletes. ✉ *330 Cooke St., Kakaako, Honolulu* ☎ *808/591–9839* ⊕ *www.bocahawaii.com.*

ALA MOANA

Getting to the Ala Moana shopping centers from Waikiki is quick and inexpensive thanks to TheBus and the Waikiki Trolley.

SHOPPING CENTERS

Ala Moana Shopping Center. The world's largest open-air shopping mall is five minutes from Waikiki by bus. More than 240 stores and 60 restaurants make up this 50-acre complex, which is a unique mix of national and international chains as well as smaller, locally owned shops and eateries—and everything in between. Thirty-five luxury boutiques in residence include Gucci, Louis Vuitton, Christian Dior, and Emporio Armani. All of Hawai'i's major department stores are here, including the state's only Neiman Marcus and Nordstrom, plus Macy's. To get to the mall from Waikiki, catch TheBus line 8, 19, 20, 23, 24 or 42; a one-way ride is $2.50. Or hop aboard the Waikiki Trolley's Pink Line for $2 each way, which comes through the area every 10 minutes. ✉ *1450 Ala Moana Blvd., Ala Moana, Honolulu* ☎ *808/955–9517* ⊕ *www.alamoanacenter.com.*

Ward Centers. Heading west from Waikiki toward downtown Honolulu, you'll run into a section of town with five distinct shopping-complex areas; there are more than 80 specialty shops and 40 eateries here. The Ward Entertainment Center features 16 movie theaters, including a state-of-the-art, 3-D, big-screen auditorium. For distinctive Hawaiian gifts, such as locally made muumuu, koa-wood products, and Niihau shell necklaces, visit Nohea Gallery, Martin & MacArthur, and Native Books/Na Mea Hawaii. Island Soap and Candle Works makes all of its candles and soaps on-site with Hawaiian flower scents. Take TheBus routes 19, 20, and 42; fare is $2.50 one way. Or hop on the

Continued on page 180

ALL ABOUT LEI

Lei brighten every occasion in Hawaii, from birthdays to bar mitzvahs to baptisms. Creative artisans weave nature's bounty—flowers, ferns, vines, and seeds—into gorgeous creations that convey an array of heartfelt messages: "Welcome," "Congratulations," "Good luck," "Farewell," "Thank you," "I love you." When it's difficult to find the right words, a lei expresses exactly the right sentiment.

WHERE TO BUY THE BEST LEI

In Honolulu's Chinatown, you'll encounter numerous lei "stands" that offer grand arrays of gorgeous garlands. Every florist shop in the Islands sells lei; you can also treat yourself to a lei while shopping for provisions at any supermarket or box store. And you'll always find lei sellers at crafts fairs and outdoor festivals.

LEI ETIQUETTE

■ To wear a closed lei, drape it over your shoulders, half in front and half in back. Open lei are worn around the neck, with the ends draped over the front in equal lengths.

■ Pikake, ginger, and other sweet, delicate blossoms are "feminine" lei. Men opt for cigar, crown flower, and ti leaf, which are sturdier and don't emit as much fragrance.

■ Lei are always presented with a kiss, a custom that supposedly dates back to World War II when a hula dancer fancied an officer at a U.S.O. show. Taking a dare from members of her troupe, she took off her lei, placed it around his neck, and kissed him on the cheek.

■ You shouldn't wear a lei before you give it to someone else. Hawaiians believe the lei absorbs your *mana* (spirit); if you give your lei away, you'll be giving away part of your essence.

ORCHID

Growing wild on every continent except Antarctica, orchids—which range in color from yellow to green to purple—comprise the largest family of plants in the world. There are more than 20,000 species of orchids, but only three are native to Hawaii—and they are very rare. The pretty lavender vanda you see hanging by the dozens at local lei stands has probably been imported from Thailand.

MAILE

Maile, an endemic twining vine with a heady aroma, is sacred to Laka, goddess of the hula. In ancient times, dancers wore maile and decorated hula altars with it to honor Laka. Today, "open" maile lei usually are given to men. Instead of ribbon, interwoven lengths of maile are used at dedications of new businesses. The maile is untied, never snipped, for doing so would symbolically "cut" the company's success.

ILIMA

Designated by Hawaii's Territorial Legislature in 1923 as the official flower of the island of Oahu, the golden ilima is so delicate it lasts for just a day. Five to seven hundred blossoms are needed to make one garland. Queen Emma, wife of King Kamehameha IV, preferred ilima over all other lei, which may have led to the incorrect belief that they were reserved only for royalty.

PLUMERIA

This ubiquitous flower is named after Charles Plumier, the noted French botanist who discovered it in Central America in the late 1600s. Plumeria ranks among the most popular lei in Hawaii because it's fragrant, hardy, plentiful, inexpensive, and requires very little care. Although yellow is the most common color, you'll also find plumeria lei in shades of pink, red, orange, and "rainbow" blends.

PIKAKE

Favored for its fragile beauty and sweet scent, pikake was introduced from India. In lieu of pearls, many brides in Hawaii adorn themselves with long, multiple strands of white pikake. Princess Kaiulani enjoyed showing guests her beloved pikake and peacocks at Ainahau, her Waikiki home. Interestingly, pikake is the Hawaiian word for both the bird and the blossom.

KUKUI

The kukui (candlenut) is Hawaii's state tree. Early Hawaiians strung kukui nuts (which are quite oily) together and burned them for light; mixed burned nuts with oil to make an indelible dye; and mashed roasted nuts to consume as a laxative. Kukui nut lei may not have been made until after Western contact, when the Hawaiians saw black beads from Europe and wanted to imitate them.

Waikiki Trolley Red Line, which comes through the area every 40 minutes. There also is free parking nearby and a valet service. ✉ *1050–1200 Ala Moana Blvd., Ala Moana, Honolulu* ☎ *808/591– 8411* ⊕ *www.wardcenters.com.*

BOOKS

Native Books/Na Mea Hawaii. In addition to island-style clothing for adults and children, Hawaian cultural items, and unusual artwork such as Niihau shell necklaces, this boutique's book selection covers Hawaiian history and language, and offers children's books set in the Islands. ✉ *Ward Warehouse, 1050 Ala Moana Blvd., Ala Moana, Honolulu* ☎ *808/597–8967* ⊕ *www. nativebookshawaii.com.*

CLOTHING

Reyn Spooner. This clothing store is a good place to buy the aloha-print fashions residents wear. Look for the limited-edition Christmas shirt, a collector's item manufactured each holiday season. Reyn Spooner has eight locations statewide and offers styles for both men and children. ✉ *Ala Moana Shopping Center, 1450 Ala Moana Blvd., Ala Moana, Honolulu* ☎ *808/949–5929* ⊕ *www.reynspooner.com.*

FOOD

Honolulu Chocolate Company. To really impress those back home, pick up a box of gourmet chocolates here. Choose from dozens of flavors of Hawaii, from Kona coffee to macadamia nuts, dipped in fine chocolate. ✉ *Ward Centers, 1200 Ala Moana Blvd., Ala Moana, Honolulu* ☎ *808/591–2997* ⊕ *www.honoluluchocolate.com.*

Honolulu Cookie Co. Hugely popular with Islands residents and visitors, these pineapple-shaped shortbread cookies half-dipped in milk or dark chocolate come in an assortment of flavors from macadamia nut to mango and lilikoi. Made locally in Kalihi, these gourmet cookies come in boxes and tins of varying sizes at 11 locations in Ala Moana and Waikiki. ✉ *Ala Moana Shopping Center, 1450 Ala Moana Blvd., Ala Moana, Honolulu* ☎ *808/947–2805* ⊕ *www.honolulucookie.com.*

Longs Drugs. For gift items in bulk, try one of the many outposts of Longs, the perfect place to stock up on chocolate-covered macadamia nuts—at reasonable prices—to carry home. ✉ *Ala Moana Shopping Center, 1450 Ala Moana Blvd., 2nd level, Ala Moana, Honolulu* ☎ *808/941–4433* ⊕ *www.alamoana.com/Stores/Longs-Drugs.*

GALLERIES

Nohea Gallery. This shop is really a gallery representing more than 450 artisans who specialize in koa furniture, bowls, and boxes, as well as art glass and ceramics. Original paintings and prints—all with an island theme—add to the selection. They also carry unique handmade Hawaiian jewelry with ti leaf, maile, and coconut-weave designs. ■TIP➔ The koa photo albums in these stores are easy to carry home and make

INEXPENSIVE LOCAL SOUVENIRS

Hawaii can be an expensive place. If you are looking to bring someone a gift, consider the following, which can be found all over the island.

Try the coconut peanut butter from **North Shore Goodies**. Just when you thought peanut butter couldn't get any better, someone added coconut to it and made it even more delicious.

If you are a fan of plate lunches, **Rainbow Drive In** has T-shirts with regular orders—"All rice," "Gravy all over," "Boneless"—printed on them. They come packed in an iconic plate lunch box.

Relive your memories of tea on The Veranda by purchasing Island Essence Tea, created by the **Moana Surfrider**.

Harvested from a salt farm on Molokai, **Hawaii Traditional Salts** come in a variety of flavors, including black lava, cabernet, balsamic, and classic. They're colored to match their flavor, so they are beautiful as well as tasty.

Foodland makes insulated cooler bags that are decorated with uniquely local designs that go beyond tropical flowers and coconuts. Look for the pidgin or poke designs.

Made with all-natural, local ingredients, like kukui nut oil, local flowers, herbs, even seaweed indigenous bar soap is available online or in stores, like **Blue Hawaii Lifestyle**.

wonderful gifts. ⊠ *Ward Warehouse, 1050 Ala Moana Blvd., Ala Moana, Honolulu* ☎ *808/596–0074* ⊕ *www.noheagallery.com.*

GIFTS

Blue Hawaii Lifestyle. The Ala Moana store carries a large selection of locally made products, including soaps, honey, tea, salt, chocolates, art, and CDs. Every item, in fact, is carefully selected from various Hawaii companies, artisans, and farms, from the salt fields of Molokai to the lavender farms on Maui to the single-estate chocolate on Oahu's North Shore. ⊠ *Ala Moana Shopping Center, 1450 Ala Moana Blvd., Ala Moana, Honolulu* ☎ *808/949–0808* ⊕ *www.bluehawaiilifestyle.com.*

HAWAIIAN ARTS AND CRAFTS

Hawaiian Quilt Collection. Traditional island comforters, wall hangings, pillows, bags, and other Hawaiian-print quilt accessories are the specialty here. There are also three locations in Waikiki hotels. ⊠ *Ala Moana Shopping Center, 1450 Ala Moana Blvd., Ala Moana, Honolulu* ☎ *808/946–2233* ⊕ *www.hawaiian-quilts.com.*

Na Hoku. If you look at the wrists of *kamaaina* (local) women, you might see Hawaiian heirloom bracelets fashioned in either gold or silver and engraved in a number of Islands-inspired designs. Na Hoku sells traditional and modern jewelry in designs that capture the heart of the Hawaiian lifestyle in all its elegant diversity. ⊠ *Ala Moana Center, 1450 Ala Moana Blvd., Ala Moana, Honolulu* ☎ *808/946–2100* ⊕ *www.nahoku.com.*

SPAS
Hoala Salon and Spa. This Aveda concept spa has everything from Vichy showers to hydrotherapy rooms to customized aromatherapy. Ladies, they'll even touch up your makeup for free before you leave. ⊠ *Ala Moana Shopping Center, 3rd fl., 1450 Ala Moana Blvd., Ala Moana, Honolulu* ☎ *808/947–6141* ⊕ *www.hoalasalonspa.com* ☞ *75-min massages from $155.*

MOILIILI

This neighborhood, while considered separate from the University of Hawaii's Manoa campus, has a distinct college-town feel. About 3 miles from Waikiki, the area is extremely tired in some sections and needs updating. However, a look past the exterior reveals a haven for excellent family-owned restaurants, health food stores, and shops that have a loyal following in the residential community.

JEWELRY
Maui Divers Design Center. For a look into the harvesting and design of coral and black pearl jewelry, visit this shop and its adjacent factory near the Ala Moana Shopping Center. ⊠ *1520 Liona St., Moiliili, Honolulu* ☎ *808/946–7979* ⊕ *www.mauidivers.com/tour.*

IWILEI

CLOTHING
Hilo Hattie. Busloads of visitors pour in through the front doors of the world's largest manufacturer of Hawaiian and tropical aloha wear. Once shunned by Honolulu residents for its three-shades-too-bright tourist wear, it has become a favorite source for island gifts, jewelry, macadamia nut and chocolate packages, and clothing for elegant island functions. Free shuttle service is available from Waikiki hotels. ⊠ *700 N. Nimitz Hwy., Iwilei, Honolulu* ☎ *808/535–6500* ⊕ *www.hilohattie.com.*

GIFTS
Indich Collection. Bring home some aloha you can sink your bare feet into. Designs from this exclusive Hawaiian rug collection depict Hawaiian petroglyphs, banana leafs, heliconia, and other tropical plants or scenery. ⊠ *Gentry Pacific Design Center, 560 N. Nimitz Hwy., Iwilei, Honolulu* ☎ *808/524–7769* ⊕ *indichcollectionhawaii.com.*

KAPAHULU

Kapahulu, like many older neighborhoods, should not be judged at first glance. It begins at the Diamond Head end of Waikiki and continues up to the H1 freeway and is full of variety; shops and restaurants are located primarily on Kapahulu Avenue.

CLOTHING
Bailey's Antiques & Aloha Shirts. Vintage aloha shirts are the specialty at this kitschy store. Prices range from $3.99 to $8,000 for the 15,000 shirts in stock; thousands of them are used while others come from top designers. The tight space and musty smell are part of the thrift-shop

atmosphere. ■**TIP→** Antiques hunters can also buy old-fashioned postcards, authentic military clothing, funky hats, and denim jeans from the 1950s. ✉ *517 Kapahulu Ave., Kapahulu, Honolulu* ☎ *808/734–7628* ⊕ *alohashirts.com.*

SURF SHOPS AND SPORTING GOODS

Island Paddler. Fashionable beach footwear, clothing, bathing suits, fun beach bags, and rash guards supplement a huge selection of canoe paddles and paddling accessories. A second store at 350 Hahani Street in Kailua (☎ *808/262–4866*), where paddling out to offshore islands is a popular activity, serves the windward side of the island. ■**TIP→** Check out the wooden steering paddles: they become works of art when mounted on the wall at home. ✉ *716 Kapahulu Ave., Kapahulu, Honolulu* ☎ *808/737–4854* ⊕ *islandpaddlerhawaii.com.*

Island Triathlon & Bike. Another source for bikes, sports bathing suits, water bottles, and active clothing. The store also rents bicycles and organizes group bike rides around Honolulu. ✉ *569 Kapahulu Ave., Kapahulu, Honolulu* ☎ *808/732–7227* ⊕ *www.itbhawaii.com.*

Snorkel Bob's. This is a good place to seek advice about the best snorkeling beaches and conditions, which vary considerably with the season. The company, popular throughout the Islands, sells or rents necessary gear, including fins, snorkels, wet suits, and beach chairs, and schedules ocean activities with other suppliers. ✉ *700 Kapahulu Ave., Kapahulu, Honolulu* ☎ *808/735–7944* ⊕ *www.snorkelbob.com.*

KAIMUKI

FLOWERS AND PLANTS

Kawamoto Orchid Nursery. Kawamoto grows all flowers on its 3-acre orchid farm near downtown Honolulu. Their specialty is the Cattleya, a favorite for Mother's Day, but they also grow hundreds of hybrids. The nursery now does the bulk of its business online and they have decades of experience shipping temperamental orchids to the mainland. ✉ *Kawamoto Orchid Nursery, 2630 Waiomao Rd., Kaimuki, Honolulu* ☎ *808/732–5808* ⊕ *www.kawamotoorchids.com.*

TAKE IT HOME WITH YOU

You don't necessarily have to buy a whole pineapple to enjoy Hawaii's fruit flavors back home. Jams are easy to pack and don't spoil. They come in flavors such as poha, passion fruit, and guava. Coffee is another option. Kona- and Oahu-grown Waialua coffee beans have an international following. There are also dried-food products such as saimin, haupia, and teriyaki barbecue sauce. All kinds of cookies are available, as well as exotic teas, drink mixes, and pancake syrups. And don't forget the macadamia nuts, from plain to chocolate covered and brittled.

6

SURF SHOPS AND SPORTING GOODS

Downing Hawaii. Look for old-style Birdwell surf trunks here, along with popular labels such as Quiksilver, Roxy, DaKine, and Billabong, which supplement Downing's own line of surf wear and surfboards. ⊠ *3021 Waialae Ave., Kaimuki, Honolulu* ☎ *808/737-9696* ⊕ *www. downingsurf.com.*

KAHALA

The upscale residential neighborhood of Kahala, near the slopes of Diamond Head, is 10 minutes by car from Waikiki and has a shopping mall and some gift stores.

SHOPPING CENTERS

Kahala Mall. The upscale residential neighborhood of Kahala, near the slopes of Diamond Head, is 10 minutes by car from Waikiki. The only shopping of note in the area is located at the indoor mall, which has more than 100 stores and restaurants, including Macy's, Reyn Spooner, an Apple store, Island Sole footwear, and T&C Surf. Shops include local and national retailers. Don't miss fashionable boutiques such as **Ohelo Road** (☎ *808/735-5525*), where contemporary clothing for all occasions fills the racks. You can also browse local foods and products at Whole Foods. Eight movie theaters provide post-shopping entertainment. ⊠ *4211 Waialae Ave., Kahala, Honolulu* ☎ *808/732-7736* ⊕ *www.kahalamallcenter.com.*

SPAS

The Kahala Spa. Escape the hustle and bustle of metro Honolulu at the elegant yet homey Kahala property favored by celebrities and U.S. presidents. The two-story spa suites feature wooden floors, handmade Hawaiian quilts, Kohler infinity-edged whirlpool tubs, private vanity areas, and private gardens where clients can relax with a green tea extract infused with various fruit. Custom-designed treatments merge Hawaiian, Asian, and traditional therapies. "Romance packages" are also available. ⊠ *The Kahala Hotel & Resort, 5000 Kahala Ave., Kahala, Honolulu* ☎ *808/739-8938* ⊕ *www.kahalaresort.com* ☞ *60-min massages from $170.*

SOUTHEAST OAHU

GIFTS

Island Treasures at the Marina. Popular with local residents, who shop here for gifts that are both unique and within reach of almost every budget, this store's range of goods runs the gamut, from cards costing $1 to a koa table costing $18,000. Next to Zippy's and overlooking the ocean, it carries handmade items including koa-wood furniture, ceramics, handbags, toys, jewelry, home accessories, soaps and lotions, and locally made original artwork. It's certainly the most interesting shop in Hawaii Kai's suburban-mall atmosphere. ⊠ *Koko Marina Center, 7192 Kalanianaole Hwy., Hawaii Kai* ☎ *808/396-8827.*

WINDWARD OAHU

Shopping on the windward side is one of Oahu's best-kept secrets. The trip here takes a half hour by car or about an hour on TheBus. At Windward Mall in Kaneohe, stop by the Lomi Shop for authentic Tahitian oils and a 10-minute foot massage in the entrance built to resemble a voyaging canoe. The real treats, however, lie in the small boutiques and galleries in the heart of Kailua—the perfect place to gather unique gifts. After shopping, enjoy the outdoors in one of the most beautiful beach towns in the world. Kailua is the best place to rent kayaks and paddle out to the Mokulua Islands with a guide, take a windsurfing lesson, or watch the expert kiteboarders sailing across the bay. ■TIP➔ Stop by Kalapawai Market at Kailua Beach near the entrance to Lanikai—for sandwiches and cold drinks and souvenirs, and finish the day relaxing on a sparsely populated white-sand beach. The surf here is minimal, making it a perfect picnic spot with the kids, but not the place to learn to ride waves. Save that for Waikiki.

BOOKS

Fodor's Choice
★ **Bookends.** The perfect place to shop for gifts, or just take a break with the family, this independent bookstore feels more like a small-town library, welcoming browsers to linger for hours. The large children's section is filled with toys and books to read. ✉ *600 Kailua Rd., Kailua* ☎ *808/261–1996.*

CLOTHING

Fodor's Choice
★ **Global Village.** Tucked into a tiny strip mall near Maui Tacos, this boutique features jewelry, clothing, and housewares made by local artists, as well as Hawaiian-style children's clothing and unusual gifts from all over the world. Look for wooden beach signs, placemats made from lauhala and other natural fibers, and accessories you won't find anywhere else. ✉ *Kailua Village Shops, 539 Kailua Rd., #104, Kailua* ☎ *808/262–8183* ⊕ *www.globalvillagehawaii.com.*

HEALTH AND BEAUTY PRODUCTS

Lanikai Bath and Body. Take home the fragrances of the Islands with these organic body lotions, hand creams, soaps, sprays, bath salts, and scrubs. Botanical extracts such as papaya, mango, sea kelp, and calendula are combined with essential oils including macadamia and kukui nut to produce fine bath and body products. Try *Naupaka*, a blend of coconut, lime, and verbena that suits both men and women. ✉ *600 Kailua Rd., Kailua* ☎ *808/262–3260* ⊕ *www.lanikaibathandbody.com.*

HOME DECOR

Jeff Chang Pottery & Fine Crafts. Jeff Chang has become synonymous with excellent craftsmanship and originality in Raku pottery, blown glass, and koa wood. Gift ideas include petroglyph stoneware coasters, ceramic and glass jewelry, blown-glass penholders and business card holders, and Japanese Aeto chimes. The store also carries work from local and national artists. ✉ *Windward Mall, 46-56 Kamehameha Hwy., Kaneohe* ☎ *808/235–5150* ⊕ *www.windwardmall.com/store/jeff-chang-pottery.*

6

Fodor's Choice
★ **Under a Hula Moon.** Exclusive tabletop items and Pacific home decor, such as shell wreaths, shell night-lights, Hawaiian quilts, frames, and unique one-of-a-kind gifts with an island influence define this eclectic shop. ⊠ *Kailua Shopping Center, 600 Kailua Rd., Kailua* ☎ *808/261–4252* ⊕ *www.hulamoonhawaii.com.*

THE NORTH SHORE

A drive to the North Shore takes about one hour from Waikiki, but allot a full day to explore the beaches and Haleiwa, a burgeoning attraction that has managed to retain its surf-town charm. The occasional makeshift stand selling delicious fruit or shrimp beside the road adds character to the beach, farm, and artist-colony atmosphere. Eclectic shops are the best place to find skin-care products made on the North Shore, Hawaiian music CDs, sea glass and shell mobiles, coffee grown in the Islands, and clothing items unavailable anywhere else. Be sure to chat with the owners in each shop. North Shore residents are an animated, friendly bunch with multiple talents. Stop in for coffee and the shop's owner might reveal a little about his or her passion for creating distinguished pieces of artwork.

SHOPPING CENTERS
North Shore Marketplace. While playing on the North Shore, check out this open-air plaza that includes art galleries, clothing stores, and a surf museum as well as Jungle Gems, where almost all of the precious and semiprecious gemstone jewelry is made on the premises. And don't miss the Silver Moon Emporium for eclectic island fashions. People drive out of their way for The Coffee Gallery, or for happy hour at Cholo's Homestyle Mexican Restaurant. ⊠ *66-250 Kamehameha Hwy., Haleiwa* ☎ *808/637–4416* ⊕ *www.northshoremarketplacehawaii.com.*

CLOTHING
The Growing Keiki. Frequent visitors return to this store year after year for a fresh supply of original, hand-picked, Hawaiian-style clothing for youngsters. ⊠ *66-051 Kamehameha Hwy., Haleiwa* ☎ *808/637–4544* ⊕ *www.thegrowingkeiki.com.*

Fodor's Choice
★ **Silver Moon Emporium.** The small boutique carries everything from Brighton jewelry and designer wear to fashionable T-shirts, shoes, and handbags. Shoppers get attentive yet casual and personalized service. The stock changes frequently, and there's always something wonderful on sale. No matter what your taste, you'll find something for everyday wear or special occasions. ⊠ *North Shore Marketplace, 66-250 Kamehameha Hwy., Haleiwa* ☎ *808/637–7710* ⊕ *www.silvermoonhawaii.blogspot.com.*

FOOD
Tropical Fruits Distributors of Hawaii. Avoid the hassle of airport inspections. This company specializes in packing inspected pineapple and papaya; they will deliver to your hotel and to the airport check-in counter, or ship to the mainland United States and Canada. Think about ordering on the Web. ⊠ *Dole Plantation, 64-1550 Kamehameha Hwy., Haleiwa* ☎ *808/621–8408* ⊕ *www.dolefruithawaii.com.*

GIFTS

Global Creations Interiors. Look for Hawaiian bath products, pikake perfume, locally made jewelry, island bedding, and a carefully chosen selection of Hawaiian music CDs. Popular gifts include Hawaiian sarongs and island-inspired kitchen items. ✉ *66-079 Kamehameha Hwy., Haleiwa* ☎ *808/637–1780* ⊕ *www.globalcreationsinteriors.com.*

Island X Hawaii. This is a surprising, yet charming store in a section of the old Waialua Sugar Mill. Island X carries gifts, clothes, and local food items—especially coffee and chocolate that is grown in Waialua. Visitors get a short unofficial tour of the coffee and chocolate trees and the roasting area just outside. ✉ *Waialua Sugar Mill, 67-106 Kealohanui St., Waialua* ☎ *808/637–2624* ⊕ *www.islandxhawaii.com.*

North Shore Soap Factory. Housed in a converted silo in the historic Waialua Sugar Mill, this is a working factory where you can watch the soap as it's made. The soaps are all natural and use as many local ingredients as possible. The factory also sells gift sets and T-shirts. ✉ *Waialua Sugar Mill, 67-106 Kealohanui St., Waialua* ☎ *808/637–8400* ⊕ *www. hawaiianbathbody.com.*

SPAS

Nalu Kinetic Spa at Turtle Bay Resort. Luxuriate at the ocean's edge in this renovated spa on Oahu's North Shore. Try one of the spa's body wraps, including the lilikoi citrus polish using Hawaiian cane sugar and organic lehua honey in its Vichy shower treatment room. Or book an ashiatsu massage, which utilizes foot pressure to release soft tissue constrictions and improve circulation. There are private spa suites, an outdoor treatment cabana that overlooks the surf, an outdoor exercise studio, and a lounge area and juice bar. ✉ *Turtle Bay Resort, 57-091 Kamehameha Hwy., Kahuku* ☎ *808/447–6868* ⊕ *www.turtlebayresort.com/oahu–spa* ☞ *50-min massages from $150.*

SURF SHOPS AND SPORTING GOODS

Surf 'N Sea. A North Shore water-sports store with everything you need for an active vacation under one roof. Purchase rash guards, swimwear, T-shirts, footwear, hats, and shorts. Rent kayaks, snorkeling or scuba gear, spears for free diving, windsurfing equipment, surfboards, stand-up paddleboards, and body boards. Experienced surfing instructors will take beginners to the small breaks on the notoriously huge (winter) or flat (summer) North Shore beaches. Warning to fishing enthusiasts: a fishing pole is the one ocean apparatus they don't carry. ✉ *62-595 Kamehameha Hwy., Haleiwa* ☎ *808/637–9887* ⊕ *www.surfnsea.com.*

WEST (LEEWARD) OAHU

Shopping on this part of the island is at two extremes—an outdoor market that literally sells everything under the sun, and a high-end shopping outlet with many of the big designer names.

SHOPPING CENTERS

Aloha Stadium Swap Meet. This thrice-weekly outdoor bazaar attracts hundreds of vendors and even more bargain hunters. Every Hawaiian souvenir imaginable can be found here, from coral-shell necklaces to bikinis, as well as a variety of ethnic wares, from Chinese brocade dresses to Japanese pottery. There are also ethnic foods, silk flowers, and luggage in aloha floral prints. Shoppers must wade through the typical sprinkling of used and stolen goods to find value. Wear comfortable shoes, use sunscreen, and bring bottled water. The flea market takes place in the Aloha Stadium parking lot Wednesday and Saturday from 8 to 3; Sunday from 6:30 to 3. Admission is $1 per person ages 12 and up.

Several shuttle companies serve Aloha Stadium for the swap meet, including VIP Shuttle (☎ 808/839–0911), Reliable Shuttle (☎ 808/924–9292), and Hawaii Supertransit (☎ 808/841–2928). The average cost is $12 per person, round-trip. For a cheaper but slower ride, take TheBus (⊕ www.thebus.org). ⊠ Aloha Stadium, 99-500 Salt Lake Blvd., Aiea ☎ 808/486–6704 ⊕ www.alohastadiumswapmeet.net.

Waikele Premium Outlets. AIX Armani Exchange, Calvin Klein, Coach Luggage, and Saks Fifth Avenue Outlet anchor this discount destination of around 50 stores. You can take a shuttle from Waikiki for the 30-minute ride to the outlets for $15 round-trip, but the companies do change frequently. Reservations are recommended. ⊠ 94-790 Lumiaina St., Waipahu, Waikele ☎ 808/676–5656 ⊕ www.premiumoutlets.com.

SPAS

JW Marriott Ihilani Resort & Spa. Soak in warm seawater among velvety orchid blossoms at this unique Hawaiian hydrotherapy spa. Thalassotherapy treatments combine underwater jet massage with color therapy and essential oils. Specially designed treatment rooms have a hydrotherapy tub, a Vichy-style shower, and a needle shower with 12 heads. The spa's Ohia Ai Mountain Apple line of natural aromatherapy products uses the essence of the mountain apple fruit in lotions, bath salts, shampoos and conditioners. ⊠ JW Marriott Ihilani Resort, 92-1001 Olani St., Ko Olina ☎ 808/679–3321 ⊕ www.ihilanispa.com ⌒ 50-min massages from $145.

Laniwai Spa at Aulani, A Disney Resort & Spa. Every staff member at this spa, or "cast member," as they call themselves, is extensively trained in Hawaiian culture and history to ensure they are projecting the right mana, or energy, in their work. To begin each treatment, you select a special pohaku (rock) with words of intent, then cast it into a reflective pool. Choose from about 150 spa therapies, and indulge in Kulu Wai, the only outdoor hydrotherapy garden on Oahu—with private vitality pools, co-ed mineral baths, six different "rain" showers, whirlpool jet spas, and more. ⊠ Aulani, A Disney Resort & Spa, 92-1185 Aliinui Dr., Ko Olina, Kapolei ☎ 714/520–7001 ⊕ resorts.disney.go.com/aulani-hawaii-resort ⌒ 50-min massages from $165.

SURF SHOPS AND SPORTING GOODS

Hawaiian Fire. Some of the best-looking firefighters in Honolulu teach private and group surf lessons on the southwest side of Oahu; they also transport beginners from Waikiki to the less crowded southwest beaches and provide boards, reef shoes, rash guards, shade tents, and chairs. Their store sells T-shirts, backpacks, and accessories. ⊠ 92-1047 Olani St., 1-109, Ko Olina, Kapolei ☎ 808/737–3473 ⊕ www.hawaiianfire.com.

7

ENTERTAINMENT AND NIGHTLIFE

Visit Fodors.com for advice, updates, and bookings

Updated by
James Cave

Gone are the days when there was nothing to do in Honolulu at night. Any guidebook that tells you Honolulu isn't for the night owl is outdated. Most nights, it's hard to pick which DJ to see at which nightclub, or which art show opening to attend. In fact, many people who arrive in Oahu expecting to find white-sand beaches and nothing else are surprised at such a vibrant nightlife. Bask in the shade of the swaying palm trees, watch the sunset over Waikiki, and put on your nice clothes because more and more clubs in Honolulu enforce a dress code.

Posh bars are found in many of the larger hotels, but venture outside of the strip and into places such as Chinatown (which virtually explodes with events on the first Friday of each month) and surrounding neighborhoods, and you'll discover comfortable local watering holes. Every night of the week you can find musicians in venues from Kailua to Ko Olina—and everywhere in between. Or you can simply walk down Kalakaua Avenue to be entertained by Waikiki's street performers.

And if all-night dancing isn't for you, Oahu also has a thriving arts and culture scene, with community-theater productions, stand-up comedy, outdoor concerts, film festivals, and chamber-music performances. Major Broadway shows, dance companies, rock stars, and comedians come through the Islands, too. Check local newspapers—the *Honolulu Star-Advertiser* or *Midweek*—for the latest events. Websites like ⊕ *www.nonstophonolulu.com,* ⊕ *www.honolulupulse.com, and* ⊕ *www.theoffsetter.com* also have great information.

Whether you stay out all night or get up early to catch the morning surf, there's something for everyone on Oahu.

ENTERTAINMENT

DANCE

Ballet Hawaii. Established in 1976, Ballet Hawaii is a local company active during the holiday season. Its annual production of *The Nutcracker* is usually held at the nearby **Blaisdell Concert Hall** (✉ *777 Ward Ave., Honolulu*) Christmas week and is a local holiday tradition. Other performances can be seen at the Hawaii Theatre (✉ *1130 Bethel St.*) in Chinatown. ☎ *808/521–8600* ⊕ *www.ballethawaii.org.*

DINNER CRUISES AND SHOWS

Dinner cruises depart either from the piers adjacent to the Aloha Tower Marketplace in downtown Honolulu or from Kewalo Basin, near Ala Moana Beach Park, and head along the coast toward Diamond Head. There's usually a buffet-style dinner with a local flavor, dancing, drinks, and a sensational sunset. Except as noted, dinner cruises cost approximately $40 to $110, cocktail cruises $25 to $40. Some cruises offer discounts for online reservations. Most major credit cards are accepted. In all cases, reservations are essential. Check the websites for savings of up to 15%.

Alii Kai **Catamaran.** Patterned after an ancient Polynesian vessel, this 170-foot catamaran casts off from Aloha Tower with 1,000 passengers. The deluxe dinner cruise has two bars, a huge dinner, and an authentic Polynesian show with dancers, drummers, and chanters. The menu is varied, and the after-dinner show is loud and fun. Cost is around $80. Vegetarian meals are available. ✉ *Aloha Tower Marketplace, 1 Aloha Tower Dr., Honolulu* ☎ *808/954–8652, 866/898–2519* ⊕ *www.aliikaicatamaran.com.*

Atlantis Cruises. The sleekly high-tech *Navatek,* designed to sail smoothly in rough waters, powers farther along Waikiki's coastline than its competitors, sailing past Diamond Head. Enjoy sunset dinners or moonlight cruises aboard the 300-passenger boat, feasting on tenderloin or whole Maine lobster. Rates begin at $96 for a bountiful buffet; five-course dinners start at $128. ✉ *Aloha Tower Marketplace, 1 Aloha Tower Rd., Pier 6, Honolulu* ☎ *808/973–1311, 800/548–6262* ⊕ *www.atlantisadventures.com.*

Creation: A Polynesian Journey. A daring Samoan fire-knife dancer is the highlight of this show that traces Hawaii's culture and history from its origins of discovery to statehood. The buffet dinner is priced at $110; a sit-down dinner with steak and lobster is $160. You can also choose to see the show without dinner for $65. ✉ *Ainahau Showroom, Sheraton Princess Kaiulani Hotel, 120 Kaiulani Ave., Honolulu* ☎ *808/931–4660* ⊕ *www.creationshow.com* ☉ *Tues. and Thurs.–Sun. at 7:15 pm.*

Magic of Polynesia. Hawaii's top illusionist, John Hirokawa, displays mystifying sleight of hand in this highly entertaining show, which incorporates contemporary hula and Islands music into its acts. It's held in the Holiday Inn Waikiki's $7.5 million showroom. Reservations are required for dinner and the show; a teriyaki short-rib dinner starts at $80, while a deluxe steak and lobster dinner is $144. Walk-ups are permitted if you just want the entertainment for $55. ✉ *Holiday Inn*

Waikiki Beachcomber Hotel, 2300 Kalakaua Ave., Waikiki, Honolulu ☎ *808/971–4321, 866/898–2519* ⊕ *www.magicofpolynesia.com* ☾ *Nightly at 8.*

FAMILY **Polynesian Cultural Center.** Easily one of the best on the Islands, this Polynesia tradition–themed park takes guests throughout the various regions of the South Pacific, including Aotearoa, Fiji, Hawaii, Tonga, and an "erupting volcano." It's a long drive—about an hour and a half from Waikiki—but you can take part in the popular Alii Luau or stay for the heralded "Ha: Breath of Life" show. General admission starts at $39.95. ⊠ *55-370 Kamehameha Hwy., Laie* ☎ *808/293–3333, 800/367–7060* ⊕ *www.polynesia.com* ☾ *Mon.–Sat. 11:45 am–9:15 pm.*

Star of Honolulu Cruises. The award-winning 1,500-passenger *Star of Honolulu* boasts four sunset dinner-cruise packages, from a roast beef buffet and Polynesian show for $84 to a romantic seven-course fine-dining excursion with live jazz for $184. The company also runs whale- and dolphin-watching lunch cruises. ⊠ *Aloha Tower Marketplace, 1 Aloha Tower Dr., Pier 8, Downtown Honolulu, Honolulu* ☎ *808/983– 7827* ⊕ *www.starofhonolulu.com.*

FILM

Doris Duke Theatre–Honolulu Museum of Arts. Art, international, classic, and silent films are screened at the intimate 280-seat Doris Duke Theatre, which doubles as a concert venue. Many short film festivals are scheduled throughout the year on regional and global themes, as well as profession, such as the "Let's Film All The Lawyers" festival of movies about law. Although small, the theater is still classy and comfortable. It is known for its great sound system. ⊠ *Doris Duke Theatre, 900 S. Beretania St., Downtown Honolulu, Honolulu* ☎ *808/532–8768* ⊕ *www.honolulumuseum.org.*

Hawaii International Film Festival. One of the biggest film events in the state, the festival in the middle of October showcases top films from all over the world, as well as some by local filmmakers (many are Hawaii premieres; a few are world premieres) screened day and night to packed crowds. It's a must-see for film adventurers. A majority of films are screened at the Regal Dole Cannery Theaters, but recently festival organizers have branched out to other venues as well. Check the official HIFF website for updated locations. ⊠ *Regal Dole Cannery Theaters, 680 Iwilei Rd., Honolulu* ☎ *808/792–1577* ⊕ *www.hiff.org.*

Sunset on the Beach. It's like watching a movie at the drive-in, minus the car and the speaker box. Bring a blanket and find a spot on the sand to enjoy live entertainment, food from top local restaurants, and a movie on a 30-foot screen. Held six to seven times each year on Queen's Surf Beach across from the Honolulu Zoo, Sunset on the Beach is a favorite event for both locals and visitors. Additionally, season premiers of some current television shows are celebrated at Sunset on the Beach. Get there early if you want a good spot to view the film. If the weather is blustery, beware of flying sand. ⊠ *Queen's Surf Beach, Kalakaua Ave., Waikiki, Honolulu* ☎ *808/923–1094* ⊕ *www.waikikiimprovement.com.*

LUAU

The luau is an experience that everyone, both local and tourist, should have. Today's luau still offer traditional foods and entertainment, but there's often a fun, contemporary flair. With many, you can watch the roasted pig being carried out of its *imu*, a hole in the ground used for cooking meat with heated stones.

Luau average around $100 per person—some are cheaper, others twice that amount—and are held around the island, not just in Waikiki. Reservations—and a camera—are a must.

Fia Fia Luau. Just after sunset at the Marriott Ko Olina Beach Club, the charismatic Chief Sielu Avea leads the Samoan-based Fia Fia, an entertaining show that takes guests on the journey through the South Pacific. Every show is different and unscripted, but always a good look at Polynesian culture. It's the only recurring show with eight fire-knife dancers in a blazing finale. Admission costs $95 and includes a buffet. ⊠ *92-161 Waipahe Pl., Kapolei* ☎ *808/679–4700, 888/236–2427* ⊙ *Tues. at 4:30.*

Germaine's Luau. More than 3 million visitors have come to this luau, held about 45 minutes west of Waikiki in light traffic. Widely considered one of the most folksy and laid back, Germaine's offers a tasty, multicourse, all-you-can-eat buffet. Admission for adults is $78 and includes a buffet, three drinks, and shuttle transport from Waikiki. ⊠ *91-119 Olai St., Kapolei* ☎ *808/949–6626, 800/367–5655* ⊕ *www. germainesluau.com* ⊙ *Tues.–Sun. at 6 pm.*

Paradise Cove Luau. One of the largest shows on Oahu, the lively Paradise Cove Luau is held in the Ko Olina resort area, about 45 minutes from Waikiki. Drink in hand, you can stroll through the authentic village, learn traditional arts and crafts, and play local games. The stage show includes a fire-knife dancer, singing emcee, and both traditional and contemporary hula and other Polynesian dances. A finale dance features participation from the audience. Admission includes the buffet, activities, and the show, as well as shuttle transport from Waikiki. You pay extra for table service and box seating. The stunning sunsets are free. ⊠ *92-1089 Alii Nui Dr., Kapolei* ☎ *808/842–5911, 800/775–2683* ⊕ *www.paradisecove.com* 🖃 *$88–$153* ⊙ *Daily at 5.*

Fodor's Choice ★ **Polynesian Cultural Center Alii Luau.** While this elaborate luau has the sharpest production values, there is no booze allowed (it's a Mormon-owned facility in the heart of Laie—Mormon country). It's held amid the seven re-created villages at the Polynesian Cultural Center in the North Shore town of Laie, about an hour-and-a-half's drive from Honolulu. The luau—considered one of the most authentic on the island—includes the "Ha: Breath of Life" show that has long been popular with both residents and visitors. Rates start at $95 and go up depending on activities and amenities (personalized tours, reserved seats, or table service, for example). Waikiki transport is available. ⊠ *Polynesian*

Cultural Center, 55-370 Kamehameha Hwy., Laie ☎ *808/293–3333, 800/367–7060* ⊕ *www.polynesia.com* ☉ *Mon.–Sat. at 5.*

Waikiki Starlight Luau. Waikiki's only luau is done spectacularly on the rooftop of the Hilton Hawaiian Village. There isn't an *imu* ceremony (roasting of the pig), but the live entertainment is top-notch and the views are unparalleled. Prices range from $49.50 to $125, depending on your age and where you want to sit. The event includes traditional activities, such as hula lessons and conch blowing, but don't miss the fun of the pineapple-tossing contest. ⊠ *Hilton Hawaiian Village, 2005 Kalia Rd., Waikiki, Honolulu* ☎ *808/949–4321, 808/951–5458* ⊕ *www.hiltonhawaiianvillage.com/luau* ☉ *Sun.–Thurs. at 5:15 pm.*

MUSIC

Chamber Music Hawaii. This group, consisting of four ensembles, has been around for decades and performs about 25 concerts a year at the **Honolulu Museum of Arts's Doris Duke Theatre** (⊠ *900 S. Beretania St., Honolulu*), the **Paliku Theatre at Windward Community College** (⊠ *45-720 Keaahala Rd., Kaneohe*), and other locations around the island. Seasons run from fall through spring. ☎ *808/489–5038* ⊕ *www.chambermusichawaii.com.*

First Friday. Rain or shine, on the first Friday of every month, the downtown Honolulu and Chinatown districts come alive. The more family-friendly late afternoon art tours evolve into an adults-only club atmosphere with a lively street party. Art galleries and restaurants stay open late, and local musicians and DJs provide the sound track for the evening. ⊠ *Downtown Honolulu, Honolulu* ☎ *808/739–9797* ⊕ *www.hcadhawaii.org* ⊒ *Free entrance to galleries, cover for nightclubs.*

Hawaii Opera Theatre. Locals refer to it as "HOT," probably because the Hawaii Opera Theatre has been turning the opera-challenged into opera lovers since 1960. All operas are sung in their original language with a projected English translation. Tickets range from $34 to $125. ⊠ *Neal S. Blaisdell Center Concert Hall, 777 Ward Ave., Honolulu* ☎ *808/596–7372, 800/836–7372* ⊕ *www.hawaiiopera.org.*

Hawaii Symphony Orchestra. The Hawaii Symphony Orchestra is the latest incarnation of the now-defunct century-old Honolulu Symphony, with the mission to bring international talent to a Hawaii audience of any age. The orchestra performs at the Neil Blaisdell Concert Hall under the advisement of the internationally acclaimed conductor JoAnn Falletta, and features guest conductors and soloists. Ticket prices vary. ☎ *808/380–7784* ⊕ *www.hawaiisymphonyorchestra.org.*

Honolulu Zoo Concerts. Since the early 1980s the Honolulu Zoo Society has sponsored hour-long evening concerts branded the "Wildest Show in Town." They're held at 6 pm on Wednesday from June to August. Listen to local legends play everything from Hawaiian to jazz to Latin music. ■TIP➔ **At just $3 admission, this is one of the best deals in town.** Take a brisk walk through the zoo, or join in the family activities. This is an alcohol-free event, and there's a food for those who haven't brought their own picnic supplies. ⊠ *Honolulu Zoo, 151 Kapahulu Ave., Waikiki, Honolulu* ☎ *808/971–7171* ⊕ *www.honoluluzoo.org* ⊒ *$3* ☉ *Gates open at 4:30.*

Continued on page 200

HULA: MORE THAN A FOLK DANCE

Hula has been called "the heartbeat of the Hawaiian people" and also "the world's best-known, most misunderstood dance." Both are true. Hula isn't just dance. It is storytelling.

Chanter Edith McKinzie calls it "an extension of a piece of poetry." In its adornments, implements, and customs, hula integrates every important Hawaiian cultural practice: poetry, history, genealogy, craft, plant cultivation, martial arts, religion, protocol. So when 19th century Christian missionaries sought to eradicate a practice they considered depraved, they threatened more than just a folk dance.

With public performance outlawed and private hula practice discouraged, hula went underground for a generation. The fragile verbal link by which culture was transmitted from teacher to student hung by a thread. Even increasing literacy did not help because hula's practitioners were a secretive and protected circle.

As if that weren't bad enough, vaudeville, Broadway, and Hollywood got hold of the hula, giving it the glitz treatment in

an unbroken line from "Oh, How She Could Wicky Wacky Woo" to "Rock-A-Hula Baby." Hula became shorthand for paradise: fragrant flowers, lazy hours. Ironically, this development assured that hundreds of Hawaiians could make a living performing and teaching hula. Many danced *auana* (modern form) in performance; but taught *kahiko* (traditional), quietly, at home or in hula schools.

Today, 30 years after the cultural revival known as the Hawaiian Renaissance, language immersion programs have assured a new generation of proficient—and even eloquent—chanters, songwriters, and translators. Visitors can see more, and more authentic, traditional hula than at any other time in the last 200 years.

Like the culture of which it is the beating heart, hula has survived.

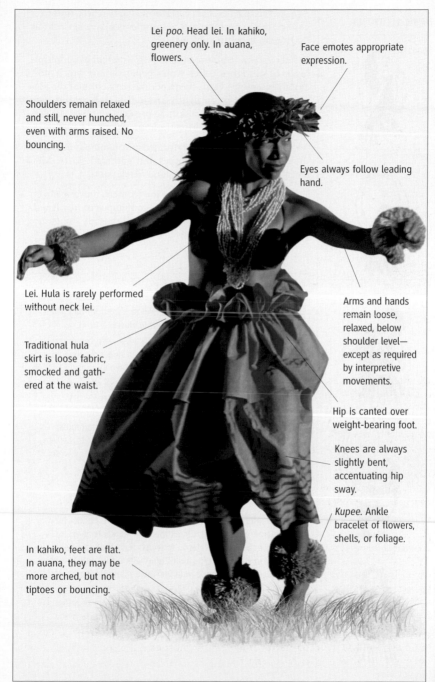

Lei *poo*. Head lei. In kahiko, greenery only. In auana, flowers.

Face emotes appropriate expression.

Shoulders remain relaxed and still, never hunched, even with arms raised. No bouncing.

Eyes always follow leading hand.

Lei. Hula is rarely performed without neck lei.

Traditional hula skirt is loose fabric, smocked and gathered at the waist.

Arms and hands remain loose, relaxed, below shoulder level— except as required by interpretive movements.

Hip is canted over weight-bearing foot.

Knees are always slightly bent, accentuating hip sway.

Kupee. Ankle bracelet of flowers, shells, or foliage.

In kahiko, feet are flat. In auana, they may be more arched, but not tiptoes or bouncing.

BASIC MOTIONS

Speak or Sing

Moon or Sun

Grass Shack or House

Mountains or Heights

Love or Caress

At backyard parties, hula is performed in bare feet and street clothes, but in performance, adornments play a key role, as do rhythm-keeping implements.

In hula *kahiko* (traditional style), the usual dress is multiple layers of stiff fabric (often with a pellom lining, which most closely resembles *kapa*, the paperlike bark cloth of the Hawaiians). These wrap tightly around the bosom but flare below the waist to form a skirt. In pre-contact times, dancers wore only kapa skirts. Men traditionally wear loincloths.

Monarchy-period hula is performed in voluminous muumuu or high-necked muslin blouses and gathered skirts. Men wear white or gingham shirts and black pants.

In hula *auana* (modern), dress for women can range from grass skirts and strapless tops to contemporary tea-length dresses. Men generally wear aloha shirts, but sometimes grass skirts over pants or even everyday gear.

SURPRISING HULA FACTS

■ Grass skirts are not traditional; workers from Kiribati (the Gilbert Islands) brought this custom to Hawaii.

■ In olden-day Hawaii, *mele* (songs) for hula were composed for every occasion—name songs for babies, dirges for funerals, welcome songs for visitors, celebrations of favorite pursuits.

■ Hula *mai* is a traditional hula form in praise of a noble's genitals; the power of the *alii* (royalty) to procreate gave *mana* (spiritual power) to the entire culture.

■ Hula students in old Hawaii adhered to high standards: scrupulous cleanliness, no sex, daily cleansing rituals, certain food prohibitions, and no contact with the dead. They were fined if they broke the rules.

WHERE TO WATCH

If you're interested in "the real thing," there are annual hula festivals on each island. Check the individual island visitors' bureaus websites. The Merrie Monarch Hula Festival—held annually in Hilo (the Big Island) the week after Easter—is the best place to experience hula. Advance planning is required (⊕ www.merriemonarch.com).

If you can't make it to a festival, there are plenty of other hula shows—at most resorts, many lounges, and even at certain shopping centers. Ask your hotel concierge for performance information.

Ke Kani O Ke Kai. Every other Thursday evening in June and July, the Waikiki Aquarium holds an ocean-side concert series called "Ke Kani O Ke Kai." You can listen to top performers while enjoying food from local restaurants. The aquarium stays open throughout the night, so you can see the marine life in a new light. Bring your own beach chairs. Proceeds support the aquarium, the third oldest in the United States. ✉ *Waikiki Aquarium, 2777 Kalakaua Ave., Waikiki, Honolulu* ☎ *808/923–9741* ⊕ *www.waquarium.org* ✉ *$30.*

THEATER

Hawaii can be an expensive gig for touring shows and music artists that depend on major theatrical sets. Not many manage to stop here, and those who do sell out fast. Oahu has developed several excellent local theater companies, which present first-rate entertainment all year long. Anyone who attends is always surprised to learn that the Honolulu Theatre for Youth is the only professional troupe in the city. Community support for these groups is strong.

Diamond Head Theatre. The repertoire of the third-oldest community theater in the United States includes a little of everything: musicals, dramas, and experimental productions. ✉ *520 Makapuu Ave., Diamond Head, Honolulu* ☎ *808/733–0274* ⊕ *www.diamondheadtheater.com.*

Hawaii Theatre Center. This beautifully restored theater, built in the 1920s in a Beaux-Arts style, hosts a wide variety of events, including international theatrical productions and touring acts, festivals, and films. It's easily the loveliest theater in Hawaii. Tours cost $10 and are offered Tuesday at 11 am. Admission for performances varies. ✉ *1130 Bethel St., Downtown Honolulu, Honolulu* ☎ *808/528–0506* ⊕ *www. hawaiitheatre.com.*

FAMILY **Honolulu Theatre for Youth.** This group stages delightful productions from September through May. Founded in 1955, it's one of the oldest children's theaters in the country (it's the only professional theater in Honolulu), serving more than 5 million people through school and family performances and drama-education programs. ✉ *Tenney Theatre, 229 Queen Emma Sq., Downtown Honolulu, Honolulu* ☎ *808/839–9885* ⊕ *www.htyweb.org.*

Kennedy Theatre. Eclectic programs—everything from musical theater to Kabuki to Chinese opera—are offered at this space at the Manoa campus of the University of Hawaii. The theater, which opened in 1963, was designed by internationally renowned architect I.M. Pei. ✉ *1770 East-West Rd., Manoa, Honolulu* ☎ *808/956–7655* ⊕ *www.hawaii. edu/kennedy.*

Kumu Kahua Theatre. This troupe sticks to producing only plays written by local playwrights. It stages five or six productions a year in a 100-seat auditorium that's perfect for getting up close and personal with the cast. ✉ *46 Merchant St., Downtown Honolulu, Honolulu* ☎ *808/536–4441* ⊕ *www.kumukahua.org.*

Manoa Valley Theatre. From September through July, wonderful performances grace this intimate community theater in lush Manoa Valley. ✉ *2833 E. Manoa Rd., Manoa, Honolulu* ☎ *808/988–6131* ⊕ *www. manoavalleytheater.com.*

Paliku Theatre. On the campus of Windward Community College, the 300-seat Paliku Theatre features everything from dramatic productions to chamber music concerts to hula and dance performances. The sound system is exceptional. ✉ *45-720 Keaahala Rd., Kaneohe* ☎ *808/235–7310* ⊕ *windward.hawaii.edu/Paliku.*

NIGHTLIFE

Oahu is the best of all the Islands for nightlife. The locals call it *pau hana*, but you might call it happy hour (the literal translation of the Hawaiian phrase means "done with work"). On weeknights, it's likely that you'll find the working crowd, still in their casual-business attire, downing chilled beers even before the sun goes down. Those who don't have to wake up in the early morning should change into a fresh outfit and start the evening closer to 10 pm.

On the weekends, it's typical to have dinner at a restaurant before hitting the clubs around 9:30. Some bar-hoppers start as early as 7, but partygoers typically don't patronize more than two establishments a night. That's because getting from one Oahu nightspot to the next usually requires packing your friends into the car and driving. Cab services are aplenty, and newcomer Uber, which offers the ambience of a private driver, gives Honolulu a San Francisco feel.

You can find a bar in just about any area on Oahu. Most of the clubs, however, are in Waikiki, near Ala Moana, and in Chinatown, near downtown Honolulu. The drinking age is 21 on Oahu and throughout Hawaii. Many bars will admit younger people but will not serve them alcohol. By law, all establishments that serve alcoholic beverages must close by 2 am, although you might get lucky and stumble into a secret all-night party. The only exceptions are those with a cabaret license, which can stay open until 4 am. ■**TIP→** Most places have a cover charge of $5 to $10, but with some establishments, getting there early means you don't have to pay.

HONOLULU

WAIKIKI
BARS
Duke's Waikiki. Making the most of its spot on Waikiki Beach, Duke's presents live music every Friday, Saturday, and Sunday. Contemporary Hawaiian musicians like Henry Kapono and Maunalua have performed here, as have nationally known musicians like Jimmy Buffett. Solo Hawaiian musicians take the stage nightly, and it's not unusual for surfers to leave their boards outside to step in for a casual drink after a long day on the waves. The bar and grill's surf theme pays homage to Duke Kahanamoku, who popularized the sport in the early 1900s. ✉ *Outrigger Waikiki, 2335 Kalakaua Ave., Suite 116* ☎ *808/922–2268* ⊕ *www.dukeswaikiki.com.*

Genius Lounge Sake Bar & Grill. Removed from the tourist traps along Kalakaua Avenue, the Genius Lounge is tucked away on the third floor of a former apartment building on Lewers Street. The extensive drink menu offers beer and wine, cocktails, house-made sangria, and, of course, sake. Japanese-inspired dishes are also available. Though small, the space, furnished with dark woods and lighted by candles, makes an intimate setting for small gatherings and Friday-night dates. The crowd is mostly Asian visitors and transplants, but the daily happy hour from 6 to 8 pm lures the office workers and pre-club prowlers. ⊠ *347 Lewers St., 3rd fl.* ☎ *808/626–5362* ⊕ *www.geniusloungehawaii.com.*

Lewers Lounge. A great spot for predinner drinks or post-sunset cocktails, Lewers Lounge offers a relaxed but chic atmosphere in the middle of Waikiki. There are classic and contemporary cocktails; the bar is helmed by Colin Field, known as one of the best bartenders in the industry; he has created several digestifs exclusively for Halekulani. He's also ditched the soda guns and mixes and brought back the craft of cocktails, using fresh and natural ingredients. Some standouts include the ginger lychee caipirissima and the blackberry julep. Enjoy your libation with live jazz and tempting desserts, such as the hotel's famous coconut cake. Or just sit back and relax in the grand setting of the luxurious lounge, which is decked in dramatic drapes and cozy banquettes. ⊠ *Halekulani Hotel, 2199 Kalia Rd.* ☎ *808/923–2311* ⊕ *www.halekulani.com.*

Lulu's Waikiki. Even if you're not a surfer, you'll love this place's retro vibe and the unobstructed second-floor view of Waikiki Beach. The open-air setting, casual dining menu, and tropical drinks are all you need to help you settle into your vacation. The venue transforms from a nice spot for lunch or dinner to a bustling, high-energy club with live music lasting into the wee hours. ⊠ *Park Shore Waikiki Hotel, 2586 Kalakaua Ave.* ☎ *808/926–5222* ⊕ *www.luluswaikiki.com.*

Mai Tai Bar at the Royal Hawaiian. The bartenders here sure know how to mix up a killer mai tai. This is, after all, the establishment that first concocted the famous drink. The umbrella-shaded tables at the outdoor bar are front-row seating for sunsets and also have an unobstructed view of Diamond Head. Contemporary Hawaiian musicians hold jam sessions onstage. ⊠ *Royal Hawaiian Hotel, 2259 Kalakaua Ave.* ☎ *808/923–7311* ⊕ *www.royal-hawaiian.com.*

Fodor's Choice
★

Moana Terrace. Three floors up from Waikiki Beach, this casual, open-air terrace where the Keawe Ohana, a family comprised of some of Hawaii's finest musicians, plays on Thursday evenings. Order a drink served in a fresh pineapple and watch the sun dip into the Pacific Ocean. ⊠ *Waikiki Beach Marriott Resort, 2552 Kalakaua Ave.* ☎ *808/922–6611.*

Moose McGillycuddy's Pub and Cafe. Loud bands play for the beach-and-beer gang in a blue jeans-and-T-shirt setting. Live bands play hits from the 1980s and 90s, and happy hour extends until 7 pm every night. Major sporting events are broadcast on the bar's flat-screen TVs. ⊠ *310 Lewers St.* ☎ *808/923–0751* ⊕ *www.moosemcgillycuddys.com.*

RumFire. Locals and visitors head here for the convivial atmosphere, trendy decor, and the million-dollar view of Waikiki Beach and Diamond Head. Come early to get a seat for happy hour, which is from 4 to 6 nightly and 9:30 to 11 pm Sunday through Thursday. If you're feeling peckish, there's a menu of Asian-influenced dishes. RumFire also features original cocktails, signature shots, and live music. ⊠ *Sheraton Waikiki,*

2255 Kalakaua Ave. ☎808/922–4422 ⊕www.rumfirewaikiki.com.

The Study. It's tricky to find The Study at the Modern Honolulu—it's behind a huge, revolving bookcase in the lobby behind the registration desk. It's an überchic space, with intimate alcoves and oversize sofas that are both hip and inviting. The literary-themed cocktails, like the "Huckle Berry Finn" and the "War and Peace," are pricey but cool. ✉ *The Modern Honolulu, 1775 Ala Moana Blvd. ☎808/943–5800 ⊕www.themodernstudy.com.*

Tiki's Grill & Bar. Tiki torches light the way to this restaurant and bar overlooking Kuhio Beach. A mix of locals and visitors head here on the weekend to get their fill of kitschy cool. There's nightly entertainment featuring contemporary Hawaiian

MAI TAIS

Hard to believe, but the cocktail known around the world as the mai tai has been around for more than 50 years. While the recipe has changed slightly over the years, the original formula, created by bar owner Victor J. "Trader Vic" Bergeron, included 2 ounces of 17-year-old J. Wray & Nephew rum over shaved ice, ½ ounce Holland Dekuyper orange curaçao, ¼ ounce Trader Vic's rock candy syrup, ½ ounce French Garier orgeat syrup, and the juice of one fresh lime. Done the right way, this tropical drink still lives up to the name "mai tai!" meaning, "out of this world!"

musicians. Don't leave without sipping on the Lava Flow, served in a whole coconut, or noshing on the famous coconut shrimp. ✉ *Aston Waikiki Beach Hotel, 2570 Kalakaua Ave. ☎808/923–8454 ⊕www.tikisgrill.com.*

The Veranda. The Veranda at the Moana Surfrider—Waikiki's first hotel—has its own interesting history. From this location, the radio program *Hawaii Calls* first broadcast the sounds of Hawaiian music to a U.S. mainland audience in 1935. Hawaiian entertainers continue to provide the perfect accompaniment to the sounds of the waves. There's a small bar in the dining area—this space turns into the Beachhouse at the Moana for dinner—or mosey to The Beach Bar below and enjoy live Hawaiian music nightly. ✉ *Moana Surfrider, 2365 Kalakaua Ave. ☎808/922–3111 ⊕www.moana-surfrider.com.*

Waiolu Ocean View Lounge. Hawaiian bars should have two things: stellar views of the sunset over the ocean and equally awesome mai tais. Both are on offer at the Waiolu Ocean View Lounge at the posh Trump International Hotel. It's one of the few places you can get absinthe served in the traditional drip. There's live music, ranging from contemporary to Hawaiian to R&B, on Thursday, Friday, and Saturday nights, with an attractive crowd showing up around 8 pm. It's busy but not suffocating, and seats are scarce once the music starts at 7:30 pm, so reserve a table in advance. ✉ *Trump International Hotel, 223 Saratoga Rd. ☎808/683–7777 ⊕www.trumpwaikikihotel.com.*

Wang Chung's Karaoke Bar. Dubbed the "Friendliest Bar in Waikiki," this charming (read: small) karaoke bar is a must-see on any trip to the island. The positive vibe comes from owner Dan Chang, who personally welcomes his guests. (He might even hug you.) The cocktails are innovative and the list of karaoke songs is extensive. Don't be surprised if the entire bar starts singing along. ⊠ *2410 Koa Ave.* ☎ *808/921–9176* ⊕ *www.wangchungs.com.*

CLUBS

Addiction Nightclub. Traditional banquettes offer intimate seating for VIP tables, and bottle service lends a New York City nightclub feel at The Modern Honolulu. Red-velvet ropes guide you to the entrance; once inside you can dance to house and hip-hop music under a stunning ceiling installation of 40,000 round lights. But Addiction comes with a price—there's a $20 cover (if you're not on the guest list) and drinks aren't cheap. ⊠ *The Modern Honolulu, 1775 Ala Moana Blvd.* ☎ *808/943–5800* ⊕ *www.addictionnightclub.com.*

Hula's Bar and Lei Stand. Hawaii's oldest and best-known gay-friendly nightspot offers panoramic views of Diamond Head by day and high-energy club music by night. Check out the soundproof, glassed-in dance floor. Patrons have included Elton John, Adam Lambert, and Dolly Parton. ⊠ *Waikiki Grand Hotel, 134 Kapahulu Ave., 2nd fl.* ☎ *808/923–0669* ⊕ *www.hulas.com.*

Nashville Waikiki. Country music in the tropics? You bet! Dress up like a *paniolo* (Hawaiian cowboy) and mosey on out to the giant dance floor at Nashville Waikiki. There's line dancing and free dance lessons five nights a week. Look for wall-to-wall crowds on the weekend. Pool tables, dartboards, and Wii consoles keep them occupied. ⊠ *Ohana Waikiki West Hotel, 2330 Kuhio Ave.* ☎ *808/926–7911* ⊕ *www.nashvillewaikiki.com.*

DOWNTOWN HONOLULU

BARS

Gordon Biersch. This outdoor bar flanks Honolulu Harbor. Live bands serenade patrons with everything from funk to jazz to rock and roll. Those who feel inspired can strut their stuff in front of the stage, while others can enjoy a pint of the restaurant's own brew and a nice view of multimillion-dollar yachts. ⊠ *Aloha Tower Marketplace, 1 Aloha Tower Dr., Suite 1123* ☎ *808/599–4877* ⊕ *www.gordonbiersch.com.*

Murphy's Bar & Grill. On the edge of Chinatown, this bar has served drinks to such locals and visitors as King Kalakaua and Robert Louis Stevenson since the late 1800s. The kind of Irish pub you'd find in Boston, Murphy's is a break from all the tropical fruit-garnished drinks found in Waikiki, and it's definitely the place to be on St. Patrick's Day. Its block party fundraiser on that day is one of the most popular on the island. On Friday it serves some of the best homemade fruit pies around. They're so good, they sell out during lunch. ⊠ *2 Merchant St.* ☎ *808/531–0422* ⊕ *www.murphyshawaii.com.*

Nocturna Lounge. This is Hawaii's first self-described NextGen lounge, a stylish and sophisticated karaoke and gaming lounge at the Waterfront Plaza. It boasts a full bar, four private suites with state-of-the-art karaoke, and video game consoles around the lounge featuring the latest in social gaming. Play "Street Fighter" in the open lounge, perfect your moves in "Dance Central" on the Xbox Kinect in a side room, or wander through the noisy club while sipping one of Nocturna's creative cocktails with names like "Sonic Boomtini" and "Yuzu is About to Die." The crowd isn't as young as you'd expect at a club outfitted with video game consoles—in fact, you must to be at least 21 to enter. ⊠ *Waterfront Plaza, 500 Ala Moana Blvd.* ☎ *808/521–1555* ⊕ *www. nocturnalounge.com.*

thirtyninehotel. This loft and art gallery is on the cutting edge of what's hot downtown. Every three months it gets a new "art installation," where a local artist repaints and reconfigures the entire space. The bartenders and their "market-fresh" cocktails have become the stuff of local legend, using Hawaiian produce to re-create classic turn-of-the-century libations. Entertainment varies from jazz combos to DJs spinning the latest hits. ⊠ *39 N. Hotel St.* ☎ *808/599–2552* ⊕ *www. thirtyninehotel.com.*

CLUBS

M Nightclub. M Nightclub is an ultramodern venue with an urban, artsy vibe. White walls are illuminated with shades of lavender, pink, and turquoise, and the space is decked with three bars, VIP seating areas, and an elevated DJ booth spinning house music over a spacious dance floor. It's big enough to host networking mixers and fashion shows, and its location in downtown lures the after-work crowd. The suggested dress code—collared shirts and shoes—makes this a more grown-up hipster spot. ⊠ *500 Ala Moana Blvd.* ☎ *808/529–0010* ⊕ *www.mnlhnl.com.*

CHINATOWN

CLUBS

The Dragon Upstairs. In the heart of Chinatown, this cool club—formerly a tattoo parlor, hence the dragon mural—serves up classic cocktails along with loungy jazz performances most nights of the week. You'll hear local vocalists, as well as small combos, in this unique venue upstairs from Hank's Cafe Honolulu. ⊠ *1038 Nuuanu Ave.* ☎ *808/526–1411* ⊕ *www.thedragonupstairs.com.*

ALA MOANA

BARS

FAMILY **Dave & Buster's.** This restaurant features a fully stocked bar and lots of amusements ranging from classic billiards to shuffleboard and the latest in video arcade games. There's live Hawaiian music at the rooftop bar on Friday and hip-hop on Wednesday night. ⊠ *Ward Entertainment Complex, 1030 Auahi St.* ☎ *808/589–2215* ⊕ *www.daveandbusters. com.*

Fodor's Choice **Mai Tai Bar.** After a long day of shopping at Ala Moana Shopping Center, the fourth-floor Mai Tai Bar is a perfect spot to relax. There's
★ live entertainment and happy hour specials for both food and drink. There's never a cover charge and no dress code. To avoid waiting in line, get here before 9 pm. ⊠ *Ala Moana Center, 1450 Ala Moana Blvd.* ☎ *808/947–2900* ⊕ *www.maitaibar.com.*

CLUBS

Fodor's Choice **Rumours.** It may not be the hippest club in town, but Rumours prides
★ itself on its theme events and its retro vibe, spinning hits from the 1970s and 80s. It's got free *pupu* to nibble on and cages to dance inside. ⊠ *Ala Moana Hotel, 410 Atkinson St.* ☎ *808/955–4811.*

7

SOUTHEAST OAHU

BARS

Kona Brewing Co. This massive restaurant and bar on the docks of Koko Marina has long been a hot spot in east Honolulu. In addition to serving the company's signature brews, this authentic pub offers live music most nights. It's a lively spot, especially on the weekends when it's standing-room-only at the bar. ⊠ *Koko Marina Center, 7192 Kalanianiole Hwy., Honolulu* ☎ *808/396–5662* ⊕ *www.konabrewingco.com.*

The Shack. This sports bar and restaurant is one of the few late-night spots you can find in Southeast Oahu. After a day of snorkeling at Hanauma Bay, stop by to kick back, have a beer, eat a burger, or play a game of pool. ⊠ *Hawaii Kai Shopping Center, 377 Keahole St., Hawaii Kai* ☎ *808/396–1919.*

WINDWARD OAHU

BARS

Boardrider's Bar & Grill. Tucked away in Kailua Town, Boardrider's has long been the place for local bands to strut their stuff. Look for live music—reggae to rock and roll—every Friday and Saturday night. The spruced-up space includes a pool table, dartboards, and eight TVs for watching the game. ⊠ *201-A Hamakua Dr., Kailua* ☎ *808/261–4600.*

THE NORTH SHORE

BARS

Breaker's Restaurant. Just about every surf competition post-party is celebrated at this family-owned establishment. (The owner's son, Benji Weatherly, is a pro surfer.) Surfing memorabilia, including longboards hanging from the ceiling, fill the space. A tasty late-night menu is available until midnight. There's live music on Saturday. ⊠ *Marketplace Shopping Center, 66-250 Kamehameha Hwy., #G120, Haleiwa* ☎ *808/637–9898* ⊕ *www.breakersnsh.com.*

Surfer: The Bar ⊠ *Turtle Bay Resort, 57-091 Kamehameha Hwy., Kahuku* ☎ *808/293–6000* ⊕ *turtlebaysurf.com/surferthebar.*

WHERE TO EAT

Updated by
Lesa Griffith

Oahu is undergoing something of a renaissance at both ends of the dining spectrum. You can splurge on world-class contemporary cuisine at destination restaurants and explore local flavors at popular, very affordable holes in the wall. Whatever your taste and budget, you'll find places that pique your interest and palate.

You may wish to budget for a pricey dining experience at the very top of the restaurant food chain, where chefs Alan Wong, Roy Yamaguchi, George Mavrothalassitis, Chris Kajioka, and others you've seen on the Food Network and Travel Channel put a sophisticated spin on local foods and flavors. Savor dishes that take cues from Japan, China, Korea, the Philippines, the United States, and Europe, then are filtered through an Islands sensibility. Take advantage of the location and order the superb local fish—mahimahi, opakaka, ono, and opa.

Spend the rest of your food dollars where budget-conscious locals do: in plate-lunch places and small ethnic eateries, at roadside stands and lunch wagons, or at window-in-the-wall delis. Snack on a *musubi* (a handheld rice ball wrapped with seaweed and often topped with Spam), slurp shave ice with red-bean paste, or order up Filipino pork adobo with two scoops of rice and macaroni salad.

In Waikiki, where most visitors stay, you can find choices from upscale dining rooms with a view to Japanese noodle shops. When you're ready to explore, hop in the car, or on the trolley or bus—by going just a few miles in any direction, you can save money and eat like a local.

Kaimuki's Waialae Avenue, for example, is a critical mass of good eats and drinks. There you'll find an espresso bar, a Chinese bakery, a patisserie, an Italian bistro, a dim-sum restaurant, Mexican food, and a Hawaii regional cuisine standout (3660 on the Rise)—all in three blocks, and 10 minutes from Waikiki. Chinatown, 15 minutes in the other direction and easily reached by the Waikiki Trolley, is another dining (and shopping) treasure, not only for Chinese but also Vietnamese, Filipino, Malaysian, and Indian food, and even a chic little tea shop.

Outside Honolulu and Waikiki there are fewer dining options, but restaurants tend to be filled with locals and are cheaper and more casual. Cuisine is mainly American—great if you're traveling with kids—but there are a handful of Italian and Asian places worth trying as well.

OAHU DINING PLANNER

EATING-OUT STRATEGY

Where should we eat? With dozens of eateries competing for your attention, it may seem like a daunting question. But our writers and editors have done most of the legwork—the selections here represent the best dining Oahu has to offer. Search "Best Bets" for picks by price, cuisine, and experience. Or find a restaurant quickly—reviews are ordered alphabetically within their geographic area.

WITH KIDS

Hawaii is a kid-friendly destination in many regards, and many restaurants welcome the little ones. That said, there are probably a few places in Waikiki where you're better off dining sans kids and taking advantage of your hotel's child care.

SMOKING

Smoking is prohibited except in places where liquor revenues exceed food sales.

PARKING

In Waikiki, walk or take a cab; it's cheaper than parking or valet rates. Elsewhere on Oahu, free, validated, and reasonably priced parking is widely available. Exceptions: parking downtown during the day is expensive—take the trolley or TheBus; Chinatown at night is somewhat dicey—use valet parking or park in one of the many marked municipal lots.

RESERVATIONS

If you expect to dine at Alan Wong's, Chef Mavro, Roy's, or Vintage Cave Honolulu, book your table from home weeks in advance. As in any other city, new restaurants tend to be jammed during their first few months. Otherwise, reserve when you get into town.

WHAT TO WEAR

While people on Oahu dress up for dinner more than on any other Hawaiian island, casual still reigns supreme; most top restaurants abide by the "dressy casual" standard, where dark jeans are acceptable as long as they're not worn with sneakers.

HOURS AND PRICES

People dine early here—the most sought-after dinner reservations are between 6 and 7, but you can usually have your pick of tables by 8. Exceptions: sushi bars and Japanese taverns, a few 24-hour diners, and some younger-spinning restaurants. Takeout places still open at dawn and close shortly after midday. Standard tipping for good service is 20%.

8

HONOLULU

There's no lack of choices when it comes to dining in Honolulu, where everything from the haute cuisine of heavy-hitting top-notch chefs to a wide variety of Asian specialties to reliable and inexpensive American favorites can be found.

WAIKIKI

As Honolulu's tourist hub, Waikiki is dense with restaurants. There are notable steak houses and grills in Waikiki as well, serving upscale American cuisine. But thanks to the many Japanese nationals who stay here, Waikiki is blessed with lots of cheap, filling, authentic Japanese food, particularly noodle houses. Plastic representations of food in the window outside are an indicator of authenticity and a help in ordering. It's not uncommon for a server to accompany a guest outside so that the selection can be pointed to.

$$
ITALIAN
✕ **Arancino di Mare.** Arancino offers fresh seafood, hand-trimmed beef, pastas cooked to order, handmade pizza dough and bread, house-made desserts, and meats and cheeses imported from Italy. Locals as well as tourists come here to enjoy dishes that use only fresh, authentic ingredients. Customer favorites include pescatore and a pizza with shrimp and Maui onions, which is the owner's favorite pizza. There's a Beach Walk location, too, as well as a new location at the Kahala Resort. $ *Average main: $26* ⊠ *2552 Kalakaua Ave., Waikiki* ☎ *808/931–6273* ⊕ *www.arancino.com* $ *Average main: $26* ⊠ *255 Beach Walk Ave., Waikiki* ☎ *808/923–5557.*

$$$$
STEAKHOUSE
✕ **Bali Steak & Seafood.** This many-windowed, multilevel room takes delightful advantage of the restaurant's perch above the beach, facing Diamond Head. The chef creates uncomplicated contemporary cuisine—grilled fish, steaks, and chops accented with East–West fusion flavors. The experienced staff, often called on to serve the VIPs who favor this hotel, extends unruffled and gracious service. $ *Average main: $40* ⊠ *Hilton Hawaiian Village, 2005 Kalia Rd., Waikiki* ☎ *808/941–2254* ⊕ *www.hiltonhawaiianvillage.com/dining/bali-steak-and-seafood* ⌖ *Reservations essential* ⦵ *Closed Sun and Mon. No lunch.*

$$$$
STEAKHOUSE
✕ **BLT Steak.** Although celebrity chef Laurent Tourondel ended his affiliation with the BLT Steak chain just three months after this outlet opened, that hasn't diminished its status as one of the swankiest rooms in town. And Swedish chef de cuisine Johann Svensson, who came from Aquavit in New York, has kept standards high at this sleek, updated, French-inflected version of a steak house, with dishes such as a pancetta-dotted lobster Cobb salad and catch of the day with escabeche equaling (if not outshining) the meat options, which come with a choice of nine sauces. From the tables of resined Makassar ebony, striped like a zebra, to the black-leather booths, this is a place for an intimate tête-à tête over a jalapeño-cilantro margarita, while you decide to go surf or turf. Svensson's specials are always stellar. Or have a burger and oysters at the bar, where Honolulu movers and shakers can be found wheeling and dealing. $ *Average main: $42* ⊠ *Trump International Hotel Waikiki*

BEST BETS FOR
FOR OAHU DINING

Where can I find the best food the island has to offer? Fodor's writers and editors have selected their favorite restaurants by price, cuisine, and experience in the lists below. In the first column, the Fodor's Choice properties represent the "best of the best" across price categories. You can also search by area for excellent eats—just peruse our complete reviews on the following pages.

Fodor's Choice★

Alan Wong's, $$$$, p. 234
Chef Mavro, $$$$, p. 234
Honolulu Burger Co., $, p. 234
Ono Hawaiian Foods, $, p. 238
Opal Thai Food, $, p. 247
The Pig and the Lady, $$, p. 227
Salt Bar & Kitchen, $$, p. 241
Town, $$, p. 241
12th Avenue Grill, $$, p. 241
Vintage Cave Honolulu, $$$$, p. 231

By Price

$

Bac Nam, p. 229
Diamond Head Market & Grill, p. 242

Hank's Haute Dogs, p. 228
Honolulu Burger Co., p. 234
Kakaako Kitchen, p. 228
Lucky Belly, p. 227
Ono Hawaiian Foods, p. 238
Opal Thai Food, p. 247

$$

Kalapawai Café and Deli, p. 245
The Pig and the Lady, p. 227
Salt Bar & Kitchen, p. 241
Shokudo, p. 231
Vino, p. 225

$$$

Hiroshi Eurasion Tapas, p. 230
Nobu, p. 220
Roy's, p. 243

$$$$

Alan Wong's, p. 234
Chef Mavro, p. 234
Hoku's at the Kahala, p. 242
3660 on the Rise, p. 241
Vintage Cave Honolulu, p. 231

By Cuisine

CONTEMPORARY HAWAIIAN

Alan Wong's, $$$$, p. 234
Chef Mavro, $$$$, p. 234
Hoku's at the Kahala, $$$$, p. 242
Roy's, $$$, p. 243

PLATE LUNCH

Diamond Head Market & Grill, $, p. 242
Kakaako Kitchen, $, p. 228

Ono Hawaiian Foods, $, p. 238
Ted's Bakery, $, p. 247

SUSHI

Mitch's Sushi Restaurant, $$$$, p. 243
Nobu, $$$, p. 220
Sushi Sasabune, $$$$, p. 237
Yanagi Sushi, $$, p. 225

By Experience

MOST KID-FRIENDLY

Big City Diner, $, p. 229
Kalapawai Café, $$, p. 245
Ono Hawaiian Foods, $, p. 238
3660 on the Rise, $$$$, p. 241
Wailana Coffee House, $, p. 224

MOST ROMANTIC

Hau Tree Lanai, $$$$, p. 214
Hoku's at the Kahala, $$$$, p. 242
Michel's at the Colony Surf, $$$$, p. 220
Sarento's Top of the "I," $$$$, p. 222

BEST VIEW

Orchids, $$$$, p. 221
Sarento's Top of the "I," $$$$, p. 222
Top of Waikiki, $$$$, p. 223

Where to Eat in Waikiki

Arancino di Mare **25**
Bali Steak & Seafood **6**
BLT Steak **10**
Chart House Waikiki **2**
dk Steakhouse **26**
Doraku Sushi **18**
Duke's Canoe Club **21**

Hau Tree Lanai **29**
Hula Grill **22**
Hy's Steak House **24**
Il Lupino Trattoria &
Wine Bar **9**
Japengo **23**
Kai Market **16**

Kaiwa **11**
Keo's in Waikiki **8**
Michel's at the
Colony Surf **30**
Morimoto **7**
Nobu **13**
Ocean House
Restaurant **14**

Orchids **15**
Prince Court **1**
Rumfire Waikiki **17**
Sarento's Top
of the 'I' **3**
Side Street Inn
on Da Strip **31**
Singha Thai Cuisine **5**

Taormina **12**
Teddy's Bigger
Burgers **28**
Tiki's Grill and Bar **27**
Top of Waikiki **19**
Wailana Coffee
House **4**
Wolfgang's Steakhouse .. **20**

Beach Walk, 223 Saratoga Rd., Waikiki ☎ *808/683–7440* ⊕ *www.*
e2hospitality.com/blt-steak-waikiki ⊘ *No lunch.*

$$$$ ✗ **Chart House Waikiki.** Enjoy the sunset views over the yacht harbor
AMERICAN as you take in live music nightly while sipping a signature "Guy-Tai"
cocktail at this Waikiki landmark. The restaurant opened in 1969 and
the menu retains the mid-century notion of "fine dining"—oysters
Rockefeller, shrimp cocktail, and steaks (from a garlicky tenderloin to
a Wagyu New York strip), along with island nods such as ahi wont-
ons, *poke*, and macadamia-nut-crusted mahimahi. Regulars perch at
the bar, while in the dining room local families, gangs of Japanese
tourists, and aging Don Drapers feast amid the dark, cork-lined walls.
Owner Joey Cabell, a surf-world legend and onetime competitive skier,
founded the Chart House chain in 1962 in Aspen, Colorado; he sold
his interest in the business 10 years later, hanging on to the Honolulu location. ■**TIP**→ **Try to nab a table on the lanai—but you need
to book well in advance to get one.** ⑤ *Average main: $41* ✉ *1765 Ala*
Moana Blvd., Waikiki ☎ *808/941–6669* ⊕ *www.charthousehonolulu.*
com ⊘ *No lunch.*

$$$$ ✗ **dk Steakhouse.** Honolulu has its share of national chain steak houses—
STEAKHOUSE but you're in Hawaii, why not go local? D.K. Kodama's second-floor
restaurant serves Vintage Natural Beef, sourced from mainland ranchers
who use no hormones or antibiotics. Choose from wet- and dry-aged
cuts. The 22-ounce "Paniolo" (cowboy) rib-eye steak is dry-aged 30
days on the bone and seasoned with a house-made rub. The potato
au gratin, topped with Maui onions and Parmesan, is addictive. The
accommodating management even has menus for the gluten-free and
vegan (!). The restaurant shares space, but not a menu, with Kodama's Sansei Seafood Restaurant & Sushi Bar; sit at the bar perched
between the two and you can order from either menu. ⑤ *Average main:*
$55 ✉ *Waikiki Beach Marriott Resort and Spa, 2552 Kalakaua Ave.,*
Waikiki ☎ *808/931–6280* ⊕ *www.dksteakhouse.com* ⊘ *No lunch.*

$$ ✗ **Doraku Sushi.** From entrepreneur Kevin Aoki, son of Benihana
JAPANESE founder Rocky Aoki, comes this low-lighted, bells-and-whistles sushi-
roll chain (Miami, Kuala Lumpur, and Ho Chi Minh City have other
locations) aimed at a nightclubbing crowd. Order dishes such as tuna
tataki and the popular Emporer Roll, a seafood extravaganza of tuna,
crab, shrimp, and scallop crusted in panko and flash-fried. And there
is tempura everything—from lobster to brownies. The Waikiki location
caters to the visitor crowd, while locals head to the newer location on
Kapiolani Boulevard, near the Ala Moana Center (✉ *1009 Kapiolani*
Blvd., ☎ *808/591–0101).* This place is not for sushi purists, but it's per-
fect for party people. ⑤ *Average main: $25* ✉ *Royal Hawaiian Center,*
2233 Kalakaua Ave., Waikiki ☎ *808/922–3323* ⊕ *www.dorakusushi.*
com ⌕ *Reservations essential.*

$$$ ✗ **Duke's Canoe Club.** Locals often take visiting friends and family from
AMERICAN the mainland to this hotel restaurant for the beachfront setting—it's
right in front of the famed Canoes surf break in Waikiki. Named for
the father of modern surfing, and filled with Duke Kahanamoku memorabilia, Duke's is a popular open-air bar and steak-and-seafood grill.
Two words: salad bar. Duke's has one—a huge one—which gives you

8

an idea of the aim-to-please food. Pick one of the four catches of the day—such as mahimahi and opa (moonfish)—then choose one of four preparations. The prime rib and *huli huli* (rotisserie) chicken are also good options. The atmosphere can be raucous when live music by A-list Hawaiian performers fills the air. Sit back and enjoy your mai tai. ■TIP→ You can experience many of the same great flavors and pay half the price by siting in the bar. ⓢ *Average main: $28* ✉ *Outrigger Waikiki on the Beach, 2335 Kalakaua Ave., Waikiki* ☎ *808/922–2268* ⊕ *www.dukeswaikiki.com.*

$$$$
AMERICAN

✕ **Hau Tree Lanai.** The vine-like *hau* tree is ideal for sitting under, and it's said that the one that spreads itself over this beachside courtyard is the very one that shaded Robert Louis Stevenson as he mused and wrote about Hawaii. Today diners are still enjoying the shade and the view at this romantic beachside hotel restaurant. The restaurant is known for its rich, classic eggs Benedict for breakfast, papaya chicken salad at lunch, and workmanlike fresh catch of the day or steak at dinner. Dinner entrée portions are quite large. During the day you get a nice sightline of bodies beautiful prancing on Kaimana Beach. ⓢ *Average main: $48* ✉ *New Otani Kaimana Beach Hotel, 2863 Kalakaua Ave., Waikiki* ☎ *808/921–7066* ⊕ *www.kaimana.com* ⌚ *Reservations essential.*

$$
HAWAIIAN

✕ **Hula Grill.** The placid younger sister of boisterous Duke's, downstairs, this restaurant and bar resembles a plantation-period summer home: open to the air, outfitted with kitschy decor, stone-flagged floors, warm wood, and floral prints. The food is carefully prepared and familiar— standard breakfast items, steaks and grilled seafood at dinner—but with local and Asian touches that add interest. There's a fabulous Diamond Head view. ⓢ *Average main: $28* ✉ *Outrigger Waikiki on the Beach, 2335 Kalakaua Ave., Waikiki* ☎ *808/923–4852* ⊕ *www. hulagrillwaikiki.com* ☾ *No lunch.*

$$$$
STEAKHOUSE

✕ **Hy's Steak House.** If the Rat Pack reconvened for big steaks and a bigger red, they'd feel right at home at Hy's, which has changed little since it opened in 1976. The formula: prime-grade beef cooked over an open kiawe-wood fire (aka mesquite), old-style service, a men's-club atmosphere (but ladies very welcome), and a wine list recognized for excellence by *Wine Spectator.* Aside from the signature steaks, specialties include beef Wellington, Caesar salad, and those flambéed desserts rarely seen these days—the last two are prepared table-side, of course. ⓢ *Average main: $54* ✉ *Waikiki Park Heights Hotel, 2440 Kuhio Ave., Waikiki* ☎ *808/922–5555* ⊕ *www.hyshawaii.com* ⌚ *Reservations essential* ☾ *No lunch.*

$$$
ITALIAN

✕ **Il Lupino Trattoria & Wine Bar.** Il Lupino doesn't reinvent Italian cuisine here—you get pretty good renditions of tried-and-true favorites such as fried calamari, caprese salad, four-cheese pizza, *bucatini all'amatriciana,* and a grilled veal chop. But when you put all the elements together—the yellow awning, the brigade of white-shirted servers, the well-appointed wine locker, the patio seating, and long wood bar that doglegs out to the open air—not to mention the decent food—you get a well-rounded, enjoyable dining experience. The place is packed for happy hour, when you can order $7 small plates. Il Lupino even serves American breakfast—eggs Benedict, pancakes, and omelets. Reservations aren't

Continued on page 219

LUAU: A TASTE OF HAWAII

The best place to sample Hawaiian food is at a backyard luau. Aunts and uncles are cooking, the pig is from a cousin's farm, and the fish is from a brother's boat.

But even locals have to angle for invitations to those rare occasions. So your choice is most likely between a commercial luau and a Hawaiian restaurant.

Some commercial luau are less authentic; they offer little of the traditional diet and are more about umbrella drinks, spectacle, and fun.

For greater culinary authenticity, folksy experiences, and rock-bottom prices, visit a Hawaiian restaurant (most are in anonymous storefronts in residential neighborhoods). Expect rough edges and some effort negotiating the menu.

In either case, much of what is known today as Hawaiian food would be as foreign to a 16th-century Hawaiian as risotto or chow mein. The pre-contact diet was simple and healthy—mainly raw and steamed seafood and vegetables. Early Hawaiians used earth ovens and heated stones to cook seafood, taro, sweet potatoes, and breadfruit and seasoned their food with sea salt and ground kukui nuts. Seaweed, fern shoots, sweet potato vines, coconut, banana, sugarcane, and select greens and roots rounded out the diet.

Successive waves of immigrants added their favorites to the ti leaf–lined table. So it is that foods as disparate as salt salmon and chicken long rice are now Hawaiian—even though there is no salmon in Hawaiian waters and long rice (cellophane noodles) is Chinese.

AT THE LUAU: KALUA PORK

The heart of any luau is the *imu*, the earth oven in which a whole pig is roasted. The preparation of an imu is an arduous affair for most families, who tackle it only once a year or so, for a baby's first birthday or at Thanksgiving, when many Islanders prefer to imu their turkeys. Commercial luau operations have it down to a science, however.

THE ART OF THE STONE

The key to a proper imu is the *pohaku*, the stones. Imu cook by means of long, slow, moist heat released by special stones that can withstand a hot fire without exploding. Many Hawaiian families treasure their imu stones, keeping them in a pile in the backyard and passing them on through generations.

PIT COOKING

The imu makers first dig a pit about the size of a refrigerator, then lay down *kiawe* (mesquite) wood and stones, and build a white-hot fire that is allowed to burn itself out. The ashes are raked away, and the hot stones covered with banana and ti leaves. Well-wrapped in ti or banana leaves and a net of chicken wire, the pig is lowered onto the leaf-covered stones. *Laulau* (leaf-wrapped bundles of meats, fish, and taro leaves) may also be placed inside. Leaves—ti, banana, even ginger—cover the pig followed by wet burlap sacks (to create steam). The whole is topped with a canvas tarp and left to steam for the better part of a day.

OPENING THE IMU

This is the moment everyone waits for: The imu is unwrapped like a giant present and the imu keepers gingerly wrestle out the steaming pig. When it's unwrapped, the meat falls moist and smoky-flavored from the bone, looking just like Southern-style pulled pork, but without the barbecue sauce.

WHICH LUAU?

Most resort hotels have luau on their grounds that include hula, music, and, of course, lots of food and drink. Each island also has at least one "authentic" luau. For lists of the best luau on each island, visit the Hawaii Visitors and Convention Bureau website: ⊕ *www.gohawaii.com*.

MEA AI ONO
GOOD THINGS TO EAT

LAULAU

Steamed meats, fish, and taro leaf in ti-leaf bundles: fork-tender, a medley of flavors; the taro resembles spinach.

LOMI LOMI SALMON

Salt salmon in a piquant salad or relish with onions, tomatoes.

POI

Poi, a paste made of pounded taro root, may be an acquired taste, but it's a must-try during your visit.

Consider: The Hawaiian Adam is descended from *kalo* (taro). Young taro plants are called "keiki"–children. Poi is the first food after mother's milk for many Islanders. Ai, the word for food, is synonymous with poi in many contexts.

Not only that, we love it. "There is no meat that doesn't taste good with poi," the old Hawaiians said.

But you have to know how to eat it: with something rich or powerfully flavored. "It is salt that makes the poi go in," is another adage. When you're served poi, try it with a mouthful of smoky kalua pork or salty lomi lomi salmon. Its slightly sour blandness cleanses the palate. And if you don't like it, smile and say something polite. (And slide that bowl over to a local.)

Laulau

Lomi Lomi Salmon

Poi

IN FOCUS LUAU: A TASTE OF HAWAII

8

E HELE MAI AI! COME AND EAT!

Hawaiian restaurants tend to be inconveniently located in well-worn storefronts with little or no parking, outfitted with battered tables and clattering Melmac dishes, but they personify aloha, invariably run by local families who welcome tourists who take the trouble to find them.

Many are cash-only operations and combination plates are a standard feature: one or two entrées, a side such as chicken long rice, choice of poi or steamed rice and—if the place is really old-style—a tiny portion of coarse Hawaiian salt and some raw onions for relish.

Most serve some foods that aren't, strictly speaking, Hawaiian, but are beloved of kamaaina, such as salt meat with watercress (preserved meat in a tasty broth), or *akubone*

(skipjack tuna fried in a tangy vinegar sauce).

Our favorite: **Dani's Restaurant** (✉ 4201 Rice St., Lihue, ☎ 808/245–4991).

MENU GUIDE

Much of the Hawaiian language encountered during a stay in the Islands will appear on restaurant menus and lists of luau fare. Here's a quick primer.

ahi: *yellowfin tuna.*

aku: *skipjack, bonito tuna.*

amaama: *mullet; it's hard to get but tasty.*

bento: *a box lunch.*

chicken luau: *a stew made from chicken, taro leaves, and coconut milk.*

haupia: *a light, pudding-like sweet made from coconut.*

imu: *the underground oven in which pigs are roasted for luau.*

kalua: *to bake underground.*

kimchee: *Korean dish of fermented cabbage made with garlic, hot peppers, and other spices.*

Kona coffee: *coffee grown in the Kona district of the Big Island.*

laulau: *literally, a bundle. Laulau are morsels of pork, chicken, butterfish, or other ingredients wrapped with young taro leaves and then bundled in ti leaves for steaming.*

lilikoi: *passion fruit, a tart, seedy yellow fruit that makes delicious desserts, juice, and jellies.*

lomi lomi: *to rub or massage; also a massage. Lomi lomi salmon is fish that has been rubbed with onions and herbs; commonly served with minced onions and tomatoes.*

luau: *a Hawaiian feast; also the leaf of the taro plant used in preparing such a feast.*

luau leaves: *cooked taro tops with a taste similar to spinach.*

mahimahi: *mild-flavored dolphinfish, not the marine mammal.*

mai tai: *potent rum drink with orange liqueurs and pineapple juice, from the Tahitian word for "good."*

malasada: *a Portuguese deep-fried doughnut without a hole, dipped in sugar.*

manapua: *steamed chinese buns filled with pork, chicken, or other fillings.*

niu: *coconut.*

onaga: *pink or red snapper.*

ono: *a long, slender mackerel-like fish; also called wahoo.*

ono: *delicious; also hungry.*

opihi: *a tiny limpet, found on rocks.*

papio: *a young ulua or jack fish.*

poha: *Cape gooseberry. Tasting a bit like honey, the poha berry is often used in jams and desserts.*

poi: *a paste made from pounded taro root, a staple of the Hawaiian diet.*

poke: *cubed raw tuna or other fish, tossed with seaweed and seasonings.*

pupu: *appetizers or small plates.*

saimin: *long thin noodles and vegetables in broth, often garnished with small pieces of fish cake, scrambled egg, luncheon meat, and green onion.*

sashimi: *raw fish thinly sliced and usually eaten with soy sauce.*

ti leaves: *a member of the agave family. The leaves are used to wrap food while cooking and removed before eating.*

uku: *deep-sea snapper.*

ulua: *a member of the jack family that also includes pompano and amberjack. Also called crevalle, jack fish, and jack crevalle.*

required, but with the knot of people normally waiting outside the entrance, they're recommended. Ⓢ *Average main: $33* ✉ *Royal Hawaiian Center, 2233 Kalakaua Ave., Waikiki* ☎ *808/922–3400* ⊕ *www. illupino.com.*

$$$$
MODERN ASIAN

✕ **Japengo.** The trendy, spendy Japengo may set your bankroll back a bit for a night out on the town, but the food—a contemporary mix of Japanese, Chinese, and Southeast Asian flavors—gets consistently high marks from diners. You get interesting flavor combinations in dishes such as the prawn-and-mango salad with palm sugar-mint vinaigrette, Singaporean chili crab, and the Tengu roll with softshell crab, scallop, snow crab, and spicy mayo. A kids' menu is available. Ⓢ *Average main: $44* ✉ *Hyatt Regency Waikiki, 2424 Kalakaua Ave., Waikiki* ☎ *808/923–1234* ⊕ *hyatthotels.hyatt.com/corporate/restaurants/ japengo/en/waikiki.html* ⌲ *Reservations essential* ◷ *No lunch.*

$$$$
ECLECTIC

✕ **Kai Market.** A buffet in a giant resort hotel might send some discerning diners running, but the mass-market Sheraton Waikiki has pulled off this "farm-to-table" smorgasborg of island and international flavors with great aplomb. Yes, there is the obligatory prime rib carving station (locals are loco for prime rib), but there's also cilantro-laden Chinese-style steamed fish, clams in a ginger-black-bean sauce, osso bucco, and Korean-style braised short ribs. Chef Darren Demaya uses as much local produce as possible on the daily-changing dinner menu. Station chefs pluck herbs from the "living wall" as needed. And you get the added bonus of the daily open-air luau-style show a Hawaiian music duo, a hula dancer, and a fire-knife dancer. ■TIP➜ Friday and Saturday are "seafood nights" and costs $3 more; but children age five and under eat free. Ⓢ *Average main: $55* ✉ *Sheraton Waikiki Hotel, 2255 Kalakaua Ave., Waikiki* ☎ *808/922–4422* ◷ *No lunch.*

$
JAPANESE

✕ **Kaiwa.** At this anti-mom-and-pop Japanese restaurant, choose from the teppan bar, the sushi bar, the main dining room, or the sexy *zashiki* room, curtained off by strands of lights. The place is a kaleidoscope of chocolate brown tiles, understated waterfalls, and dropped ceilings of Japanese fabric. You can try *okonomiyaki,* the famous savory pancakes that are a specialty of Osaka, with mix-and-match ingredients scrambled on a griddle, then drizzled with piquant sauces. Jewel-like appetizers such as dashi gelee topped with tender abalone and sea urchin come sparkling in martini glasses. And simpler grilled dishes include kurobuta pork topped with barley miso and Japanese pumpkin with asparagus and bacon. Ⓢ *Average main: $43* ✉ *Waikiki Beach Walk, 226 Lewers St., Waikiki* ☎ *808/924–1555.*

$$
THAI

✕ **Keo's in Waikiki.** Many Islanders—and many Hollywood stars—have gotten their first taste of pad Thai noodles, lemongrass, and coconut milk curry at one of veteran restaurateur Keo Sananikone's eateries. This one, perched at the entrance to Waikiki, characterizes his formula: a bright, clean space awash in flowers with intriguing menu titles and reasonable prices. Evil Jungle Prince, a stir-fry redolent of Thai basil, flecked with chilies and rich with coconut milk, is a classic; also try the apple bananas (smaller, sweeter variety of banana) in coconut milk. The Eastern and Western breakfasts are popular. Ⓢ *Average main: $23* ✉ *2028 Kuhio Ave., Waikiki* ☎ *808/951–9355* ⊕ *keosthaicuisine.com.*

8

$$$$ ╳ **Michel's at the Colony Surf.** Consistently voted "most romantic res-
FRENCH taurant" in local publications' reader polls, Michel's is an old-school
French favorite on Waikiki's tranquil Gold Coast. You pay for the
beachside view, which you watch turn from blue to fireball orange at
sunset. (To get a window table you need to reserve at *least* a month in
advance.) Opened in 1962, the place retains a *Mad Men* feel, with lots
of wood and stone and bow-tied servers preparing things like steak
tartare table-side. Among the French classics (garlicky escargots, mus-
tard-crusted rack of lamb) are local twists, such as Kauai-raised prawns
with passion-fruit vinaigrette and Chinese-style steamed pink snapper.
Brunch is served the first Sunday of every month. ⑤ *Average main: $55*
✉ *Colony Surf, 2895 Kalakaua Ave., Waikiki* ☎ *808/923–6552* ⊕ *mi-
chelshawaii.com* ⌂ *Reservations essential* ✆ *No lunch.*

$$$$ ╳ **Morimoto.** Iron Chef Masahara Morimoto of Food Network fame is
JAPANESE a big part of the dining scene in Honolulu. He's always in town for the
annual Hawaii Food & Wine Festival, which takes place in September
and includes an Asia-Pacific night at The Modern led by Morimoto.
In the sleek white-and-chartreuse room you'll find the signature dishes
served at his restaurants around the world—like Duck Duck Duck
(duck three ways) and *ishi yaki buri bop* (yellowtail and rice cooked
at your table in a hot stone pot) along with original creations taking
cues from local cuisine, such as the chef's *loco moto* (Wagyu beef with
a sunny-side-up egg and gravy), and, of course, sushi. ■**TIP➜ Try the
tofu, which is made right at your table.** You can choose to sit at the sushi
bar, the regular bar, or at a table, but try to get a seat outside, with a
view overlooking the yacht harbor. The place is also a popular spot for
breakfast (Japanese style!) and brunch, and the lunch set menus are a
bargain. ⑤ *Average main: $41* ✉ *The Modern, 1775 Ala Moana Blvd.,
Waikiki* ☎ *808/943–5900* ⊕ *morimotowaikiki.com.*

$$$ ╳ **Nobu.** Nobu Waikiki remains a magnet for visiting celebrities and
JAPANESE local bigwigs—and lots of Japanese tourists. Part of an ever-growing
FUSION global chain, this outpost serves Nobu Matsuhisa's decades-old Japa-
nese-Peruvian signatures such as black cod lacquered with sweet den
miso, along with original dishes like *sous vide kurobuta* pork belly
with jalapeño, and ahi *poke* made with a sweet soy-mustard sauce, *ogo*
(seaweed) from Molokai, and Big Island hearts of palm. The intense
flavors can lead to unabandoned ordering—and the cost quickly adds
up. The dramatically lighted sushi bar serves some of the finest nigiri on
the island. For a quick bite and cocktails, head to the lounge for happy
hour, when pretty young things languish on the banquettes. ■**TIP➜ Glu-
ten-free diners can choose from a short but delicious special menu
that includes an addictive pepperoncini with threads of hearts of palm
standing in for the spaghetti, and wheat-free soy sauce is always avail-
able for the asking.** ⑤ *Average main: $33* ✉ *Waikiki Parc Hotel, 2233
Helumoa Rd., Waikiki* ☎ *808/237–6999* ⊕ *www.noburestaurants.com.*

$$$ ╳ **Ocean House Restaurant.** Guests are greeted on the front porch at this
SEAFOOD re-creation of a 1900s plantation home. Tables and booths are spaced
for views. The menu puts forth the bounty of the Pacific with such
dishes as Parmesan-crusted opah, coconut lobster skewers, and seared
peppered scallops. For beef lovers, there's the slow-roasted prime rib. If

Oahu Food Trucks

CLOSE UP

Lunch wagons, or "food trucks" as they are now known around the country, have been an island staple for plate lunches for decades. With the taco-truck craze and the emergence of social media, Oahu's fleet is growing, but many don't have a very long half-life.

You can check the trucks' locations and daily menus on Twitter or Instagram, or try a sampling from more than two dozen vendors at the monthly Eat the Street food-truck rally. Visit ⊕ *www.eatthestreethawaii.com* for details.

Here are some of our favorite lunch wagons:

Camille's on Wheels (⊕ *Twitter.com/Camillesonwheel*) mixes and matches global flavors to create addictive tacos like beef chimichurri and mahimahi with mirin aioli. Camille also bakes a hell of a pie—her dulce de leche and mango versions have cult followings.

Elena's (⊕ *Twitter.com/ElenasFilipino*) is an extension of the popular, family-run Filipino restaurant in Waipahu. There are three trucks, in Campbell, Mililani, and the airport area. Try the AFRO, an adobo–fried rice omelet, or the famous *lechón* (roast pork with onions and tomatoes) special.

Momo Burger (⊕ *Twitter.com/momoburgerhi*) serves up hearty burgers made with grass-fed, locally raised beef. Contemporary twists come in the form of green onion aioli on the teriyaki burger, and special "Momo sauce" and smoked Gouda on the bacon cheeseburger.

Taco Kabana (⊕ *Instagram.com/TacoKabana*) has a regular spot in a big parking lot on Kapiolani Boulevard, right near Ala Moana Center. It's open Monday through Saturday from noon to 8 pm serving classic soft tacos filled with things like carne asada and grilled chicken.

8

you're an early riser, you can also enjoy the daily breakfast or Sunday brunch offerings. Ⓢ *Average main: $32* ⊠ *Outrigger Reef on the Beach, 2169 Kalia Rd., Waikiki* ☎ *808/923-2277* ⊕ *www.oceanhousewaikiki.com* ☾ *No lunch.*

$$$$
SEAFOOD

✕**Orchids.** Perched along the seawall at historic Gray's Beach, Orchids in the luxe Halekulani resort is open all day—it's a locus of power breakfasters, ladies who lunch, celebrating families at the over-the-top Sunday brunch, and the gamut at dinner. The louvered walls are open to the breezes, sprays of orchids add color, the seafood is perfectly prepared, and the wine list is intriguing. The contemporary menu of international flavors reflects the hotel's well-traveled clientele—you can go around the world in one dinner, zigzagging from smoked duck carpaccio to marlin and Asian pear tartare to chicken tagine to steamed sesame pink snapper with shiitake mushrooms. Collared shirts are required for gentlemen. ■TIP➔ Halekulani executive chef Vikram Garg offers Table One, a custom dining experience within Orchids. He asks you your food preferences and makes culinary magic. It's not mentioned on the website—call to book. Ⓢ *Average main: $42* ⊠ *Halekulani, 2199 Kalia Rd., Waikiki* ☎ *808/923-2311* ⊕ *www.halekulani.com* ⋩ *Reservations essential.*

$$$$
ECLECTIC

✗**Prince Court.** This restaurant overlooking Ala Wai Yacht Harbor is a multifaceted success, with exceptional high-end lunches and dinners, daily breakfast buffets, weekly dinner seafood buffets, and sold-out weekend brunches (Sunday only). With a truly global mix of offerings, the overall style is Eurasian. Their ever-changing prix-fixe buffet includes offerings such as Australian rack of lamb, Kahuku prawns, and medallions of New York Angus beef. You can order à la carte as well. $ *Average main: $42* ✉ *Hawaii Prince Hotel Waikiki, 100 Holomoana St., Waikiki* ☎ *808/944–4494* ⊕ *www.princeresortshawaii.com.*

> ### PUPU
>
> Entertaining Hawaiian style means having a lot of *pupu*—the local term for appetizers or hors d'oeuvres. Locals eat these small portions of food mostly as they wind down from their workday, relax, and enjoy a couple of beers. Popular *pupu* include sushi, tempura, teriyaki chicken skewers, barbecue meat, and our favorite: *poke* (pronounced "po-keh"), or raw fish, seasoned with seaweed, shoyu, and other flavorings.

$$
ASIAN FUSION

✗**Rumfire Waikiki.** Cocktails, bite-size shareable plates, and flaming oversize torches make this place particularly popular for happy hour, when it is always packed. Eat inside, perched on ottomans in front of floor-to-ceiling windows, or outside, steps from the beach. Graze on sliced coffee-rubbed rib steak, fish tacos, or spicy Szechuan baby back ribs, as you sip concoctions such as a High Maka Mai Tai made with 23-year-old Ron Zacapa Centenario rum. At night, Rumfire is a popular club/lounge for young locals. $ *Average main: $22* ✉ *Sheraton Waikiki Hotel, 2255 Kalakaua Ave., Waikiki* ☎ *808/922–4422* ⊕ *www. rumfirewaikiki.com.*

$$$$
ITALIAN

✗**Sarento's Top of the "I".** Among restaurants with the best views in Honolulu, 30th-floor Sarento's, which looks toward the Koolau Mountains and the South Shore, is a popular special-date venue. The menu offers regional Italian cuisine, and the tiger prawn scampi and osso buco are local favorites. Meat eaters lean toward the melt-in-your-mouth filet mignon topped with Gorgonzola cream sauce. The deep wine cellar contains some gems, and there may not be more attentive service staff in the city. For a less spendy meal, you may want to opt for happy hour and order from their appetizer menu, which is filled with tasty choices. $ *Average main: $48* ✉ *Ilikai Waikiki Hotel, 1777 Ala Moana Blvd., 30th fl., Waikiki* ☎ *808/955–5559* ⊕ *www.sarentoswaikiki.com* ⚑ *Reservations essential* ⊘ *No lunch.*

$$
ECLECTIC

✗**Side Street Inn on Da Strip.** The original Hopaka Street pub is famous as the place where celebrity chefs gather after hours; this second location, also run by Colin Nishida, is on bustling Kapahulu Avenue, closer to Waikiki. Local-style bar food—salty panfried pork chops with a plastic tub of ketchup; fried rice; and passion fruit–glazed ribs—comes in huge, shareable portions. This is a place to dress any way you like, nosh all night, and watch sports on TV. *Pupu* (in portions so large as to be dinner) are served from 3 pm to 11:30 pm daily. $ *Average main: $20* ✉ *614 Kapahulu Ave., Waikiki* ☎ *808/739–3939* ⊕ *www.sidestreetinn. com* ⊘ *No lunch.*

$$
THAI
✕ **Singha Thai Cuisine.** Chai and Joy Chaowasaree's devotion to their native Thailand is evident in the gilt model of Bangkok's royal palace that graces the entryway of this restaurant just below street level on a busy Waikiki corner. Especially good is Singha Thai's way with seafood—Siamese fighting fish, a whole fish sizzling in garlic-chili oil, or fish in Thai chili, ginger, and black-bean sauce—and the contemporary additions to the menu, such as blackened ahi summer rolls. $ *Average main: $21* ✉ *1910 Ala Moana Blvd., Waikiki* ☎ *808/941–2898* ⊕ *www.singhathai.com* ☾ *No lunch.*

$$$$
ITALIAN
✕ **Taormina.** Honolulu has its share of Japanese-owned Italian restaurants, and Taormina, taking its culinary cues from Sicily, is the best. In a sleek, elegant room (there is outdoor seating, but this is one place we recommend staying indoors), the menu includes clean, well-executed classics, from grilled squid over cannellini beans to a giant veal Parmesan. Pastas include tuna-and-bottarga spaghetti and the trademark *uni* (sea urchin) with tagliatelle. The artfully presented antipasti *misti* (mixed appetizers) should not be missed. For dessert, go traditional with cannoli or contemporary with an acai granita and taro chips. The wine list is extensive. $ *Average main: $36* ✉ *Waikiki Beach Walk, 227 Lewers St., Waikiki* ☎ *808/926–5050* ⊕ *taorminarestaurant.com* ⌖ *Reservations essential.*

$
BURGER
✕ **Teddy's Bigger Burgers.** Modeled after 1950s diners, this local franchise serves classic moist and messy burgers, along with turkey and veggie burgers, as well as chicken breast and fish sandwiches. The fries are crisply perfect, the shakes rich and sweet. The original location in Waikiki combines burger shack simplicity with surf-boy cool—there's even a place to store your surfboard while you have your burger. This popular location has given birth to several others around the state. $ *Average main: $10* ✉ *134 Kapahulu Ave., Waikiki* ☎ *808/926–3444* ⊕ *teddysbiggerburgers.com.*

$$$
MODERN
HAWAIIAN
✕ **Tiki's Grill and Bar.** On the second floor of a busy hotel, Tiki's is the kind of place people come to Waikiki for: a retro–South Pacific spot designed for fun. It has a back-of-the-bar faux volcano, an open-air lounge with live local-style music, indoor-outdoor dining, and a view of the beach across the street. Despite the name, you don't get run-of-the-mill *pupus* here. Chef Ronnie Nasuti, who for years helmed the Roy's flagship, stronghold of Hawaiian regional cuisine, turns out beautifully composed plates and manages to put fresh twists on the super familiar—like a refreshing iceberg wedge salad brightened with slices of watermelon radish, pancetta chips, and a blue-cheese vinaigrette, or seared swordfish in a carrot yuzu sauce. Be sure to try one of the mai tais, which come in a variety of flavors. $ *Average main: $27* ✉ *Aston Waikiki Beach Hotel, 2570 Kalakaua Ave., Waikiki* ☎ *808/923–8454* ⊕ *tikisgrill.com.*

$$$$
MODERN
AMERICAN
✕ **Top of Waikiki.** The three-tiered, revolving Top of Waikiki has amazing 360-degree views of Honolulu (a full rotation takes one hour), but unlike most of its peers this restaurant has food to match the stunning panorama. Lance Kosaka, who was executive chef at Alan Wong's Pineapple Room, turns out contemporary American dishes with island flavor. Scallops with sweet corn pudding and pancetta and haute nachos

8

made with chorizo and Asiago béchamel are lively starters. For dinner, although they may sound basic, the seafood pasta and garlic rib eye are the most popular entrées because they're just that good. To get a sunset view, grab dinner from 5 to 6 pm, or take a seat at the bar in the center of the restaurant for happy hour–priced cocktails and appetizers. ⑤ *Average main: $40 ⊠ Waikiki Business Plaza, 2270 Kalakaua Ave., Waikiki ☎ 808/923–3877 ⊕ topofwaikiki.com.*

$ ✕**Wailana Coffee House.** Coffee
AMERICAN shops are a dying breed in Honolulu, but the 24-hour Wailana Coffee House, opened in 1969, is still going strong. Budget-conscious snowbirds, night owls with a yen for karaoke, all-day drinkers of

> ## MALASADAS
>
> Donuts without a hole, *malasadas* are a contribution of the Portuguese, who came to the Islands to work on the plantations. Roughly translated, the name means "half-cooked," which refers to the origin of these deep-fried, heavily sugared treats: they are said to have been created as a way to use up scraps of rich, buttery egg dough. A handful of bakeries specialize in malasadas (Leonard's on Kapahulu, Agnes in Kailua, Champion on Beretania); restaurants sometimes serve an upscale version stuffed with fruit puree; they're inevitable at fairs and carnivals. Eat them hot or not at all.

both coffee and the stronger stuff, hearty eaters, and post-clubbing club kids all crowd this venerable, family-run diner and cocktail lounge at the edge of Waikiki. Banana pancakes and corned beef hash at breakfast; French dips, burgers, and Salisbury steak (!) at lunch; and trademark "broasted" chicken at dinner—this place is a trip down food memory lane. Most checks are under $11, and there's a $2.50 children's menu. It's open 24 hours a day, seven days a week, 365 days a year (except Tuesday, when the restaurant closes from 10 pm to 6 am), but the place fills up, and a line forms around the corner at breakfast time, so arrive early or late. ⑤ *Average main: $12 ⊠ 1860 Ala Moana Blvd., at Ena Rd., Waikiki ☎ 808/955–1764 ⚑ Reservations not accepted.*

$$$$ ✕**Wolfgang's Steak House.** Sequestered in an upscale Waikiki mall, this
STEAKHOUSE open-air spot offers diners the opportunity to get a New York–style steak dinner with gruff New York–style service. Sound like Peter Luger's on the Pacific? Well, owner Wolfgang Zweiner was once head waiter at that legendary Brooklyn steak house. Part of a chain that originated in New York, this Honolulu outpost serves good steaks that have been dry-aged on-site. Rounding out the menu are steak-house classics such as shrimp cocktail, slabs of Canadian bacon, crab cakes, creamed spinach and the token grill fish selection. Stop by during happy hour for a prix-fixe sampler deal. ⑤ *Average main: $55 ⊠ Royal Hawaiian Center, 2201 Kalakaua Ave., Waikiki ☎ 808/922–3600 ⊕ wolfgangssteakhouse.net.*

DOWNTOWN

$ ✕**Honolulu Museum of Art Cafe.** The Honolulu Museum of Art's cool
AMERICAN courtyards and galleries filled with works by masters from Monet to Hokusai are well worth a visit and, afterward, so is this popular lunch

restaurant. The open-air café is flanked by a burbling water feature and 8-foot-tall ceramic "dumplings" by artist Jun Kaneko—a tranquil setting in which to eat your salade niçoise (featuring seared ahi) or fork-tender filet mignon sandwich with Dijon-caper relish. You'll rub shoulders with a who's who of the local art and business communities. Reservations are recommended. ⓢ *Average main: $17* ✉ *Honolulu Museum of Art, 900 S. Beretania St., Downtown Honolulu* ☎ *808/532– 8734* ⊕ *www.honolulumuseum.org* ⊘ *No dinner.*

$ ✕ **Murphy's Bar & Grill.** Located in the heart of the financial district, Honolulu's go-to Irish bar serves Guinness on tap and an Irish-American menu of pubby favorites such as spicy chicken wings, jalapeño poppers, fish-and-chips, corned beef and cabbage, and grilled New York steak—without that Waikiki price tag. But probably the most popular menu item is the Blarney Burger, gooey with Guinness-infused cheddar cheese. The restaurant has been featured on Guy Fieri's *Diners, Drive-ins and Dives* on the Food Network as a place that specializes in comfort food for the weary traveler. The dining room's booths attract business bigwigs, journalists, and staff from the nearby Kumu Kahua Theatre. Meanwhile, the young and restless play darts and shuffleboard in the bar. ⓢ *Average main: $16* ✉ *2 Merchant St., Downtown Honolulu* ☎ *808/531–0422* ⊕ *murphyshawaii.com.*

AMERICAN

$$ ✕ **Vino.** Island oenophiles make a beeline for this wine bar and restaurant, which regularly holds special tastings and dinners. Chef Keith Endo creates his take on contemporary Italian cuisine with some local accents. House-made pastas, jumbo shrimp in a resonant cioppino sauce, and Big Island smoked pork pair well with wines selected by nationally recognized Master Sommelier Chuck Furuya. He makes sure food and service are grade-A quality amid a let-your-hair-down atmosphere. You can order items from the adjacent Hiroshi's Eurasion Tapas, as they share a kitchen. ■**TIP**➜ Vino is well situated for stopping off between downtown sightseeing and a return to your Waikiki hotel. ⓢ *Average main: $25* ✉ *Waterfront Plaza, 500 Ala Moana Blvd., Downtown Honolulu* ☎ *808/524–8466* ⊕ *vinohawaii.com* ⊘ *Closed Sun.–Tues. No lunch.*

WINE BAR

8

$$ ✕ **Yanagi Sushi.** One of relatively few restaurants to serve the complete menu until 2 am (Sunday only until 10 pm), Yanagi is a full-service Japanese restaurant offering not only sushi and sashimi around a small bar, but also *teishoku* (combination menus), tempura, stews, and grill-it-yourself shabu-shabu. The fish can be depended on for freshness and variety. Try the baked volcano roll stuffed with crabmeat, the spicy shrimp tempura roll, or, if you're brave, the abalone sashimi—straight out of the tank. ⓢ *Average main: $28* ✉ *762 Kapiolani Blvd., Downtown Honolulu* ☎ *808/597–1525* ⊕ *yanagisushi-hawaii.com.*

JAPANESE

CHINATOWN

$ ✕ **Legend Seafood Restaurant.** Do as the locals do: start your visit to Chinatown with breakfast dim sum at this Hong Kong–style restaurant. If you want to be able to hear yourself think, get there before 9 am, especially on weekends. And don't be shy: use your best cab-hailing technique and sign language to make the cart ladies stop at your table

CHINESE

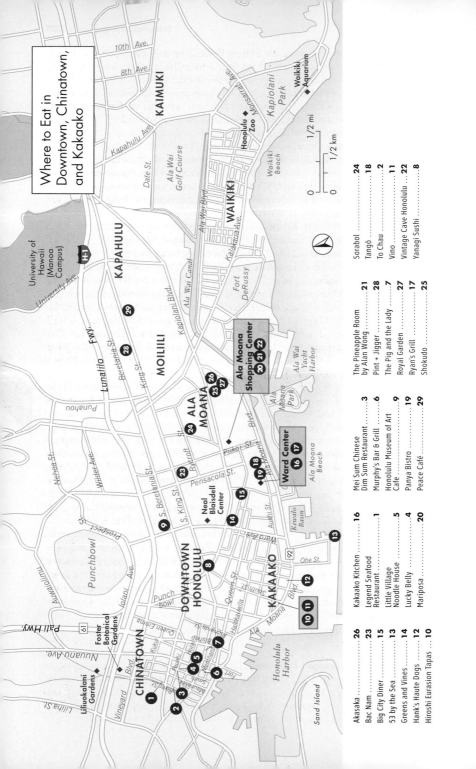

Where to Eat in Downtown, Chinatown, and Kakaako

KAIMUKI

University of Hawaii (Manoa Campus)

KAPAHULU

WAIKIKI

MOILIILI

ALA MOANA

DOWNTOWN HONOLULU

CHINATOWN

KAKAAKO

Honolulu Zoo

Waikiki Aquarium

Kapiolani Park

Ala Moana Shopping Center

Ward Center

Neal Blaisdell Center

Foster Botanical Gardens

Liliuokalani Gardens

Punchbowl

Honolulu Harbor

Sand Island

0   1/2 mi
0   1/2 km

and show you their wares. The pork-filled steamed buns, spinach dumplings, taro-and-pork *gok* (bite-size fried balls), and still-warm custard tarts are excellent pre-shopping fortification. Dim sum dishes cost $2.75 to $5.75, so knock yourself out. The place also has à la carte lunch and dinner menus. ⑤ *Average main: $13* ✉ *Chinese Cultural Plaza, 100 N. Beretania St., Suite 108, Chinatown* ☎ *808/532–1868* ⊕ *www. legendseafoodhonolulu.com.*

$ ✕ **Little Village Noodle House.** Unassuming and budget-friendly, Little Village is so popular with locals that it expanded to the space next door.
CHINESE The extensive pan-China menu is filled with crowd pleasers such as shredded beef, spinach with garlic, Shanghai noodles, honey-walnut shrimp, and orange chicken with dried green beans. Reservations are accepted for parties of five or more. ■ **TIP→ Two hours of free parking are available in the parking lot immediately to the right of the restaurant (if you can nab a space).** ⑤ *Average main: $10* ✉ *1113 Smith St., Chinatown* ☎ *808/545–3008* ⊕ *littlevillagehawaii.com.*

$ ✕ **Lucky Belly.** At Honolulu's answer to New York's Momofuku Noodle
ASIAN Bar, a hip local crowd sips cocktails and slurps familiar noodle dishes with a modern twist. Try the Belly Bowl with smoked bacon, sausage, and pork belly in a savory broth loaded with noodles. At dinner, the *pupu* menu features trendy small plates such as pork belly buns, oxtail dumplings, and steak tartare spiced with Japanese chili powder. The service here is unpretentious and attentive, and you can also order your food to go. Lucky Belly accepts dinner reservations for 5 to 6:30 pm only, so be prepared for a wait if you dine after that. ■ **TIP→ Arrive by 11:30 if you want a table for lunch; this place quickly fills up with the downtown crowd.** ⑤ *Average main: $12* ✉ *50 N. Hotel St., Chinatown* ☎ *808/531–1888* ☉ *Closed Sun.*

$ ✕ **Mei Sum Chinese Dim Sum Restaurant.** In contrast to the sprawling,
CHINESE noisy halls in which dim sum is generally served, Mei Sum is compact and shiny bright. It's open daily, one of the few places that serves dim sum from 8 am all the way to 9 pm. Be ready to guess and point at the color photos of dim sum favorites as not much English is spoken, but the charades pay off when you get your delicate buns and tasty bites. Other menu items and specials are also served. ⑤ *Average main: $11* ✉ *1170 Nuuanu Ave., Suite 102, Chinatown* ☎ *808/531–3268.*

$$ ✕ **The Pig and the Lady.** After making waves as sous chef at Chef Mavro,
MODERN ASIAN then operating pop-up nights and a noodle stand at farmers' markets
Fodor's Choice for two years—not to mention a six-month stage at San Francisco's
★   Rich Table—rising star Andrew Le opened his own place in November 2013. The Pig and the Lady is a casual noodle house by day, attracting downtown office workers, but becomes a creative contemporary restaurant by night, when serious chowhounds come out. Drawing on both his Vietnamese heritage and multicultural island flavors, the talented, playful Le is a wizard with spice and acid, turning out dishes of layered flavor such as "coffee can bread" (which is baked in Café du Monde coffee cans) with chicken liver paté, Kyoho grapes, and pink peppercorns. Another innovative dish is porchetta with pomegranate-arugula salsa verde. A young, creative crowd, craft cocktails, and affordable prices keep the DIY-chic space (Le's family and friends did everything!)

8

with exposed brick hopping. $ *Average main: $20* ⊠ *83 N. King St., Chinatown* ☎ *808/585–8255* ⊕ *www.thepigandthelady.com.*

$ ✕ **To Chau.** Wonder why people are standing in line on River Street? To

VIETNAMESE get bowls of steaming *pho* (Vietnamese beef noodle soup) at To Chau. This spot was a pho pioneer. Many Vietnamese restaurants have since opened and surpassed To Chau's quality, but eating habits die hard in this city. The divey storefront is open only until 2:30 pm, but you may be turned away if the food runs out earlier. $ *Average main: $8* ⊠ *1007 River St., Chinatown* ☎ *808/533–4549* ◬ *Reservations not accepted* ▬ *No credit cards* ☾ *No dinner.*

KAKAAKO

$$$$ ✕ **53 by the Sea.** Housed in a McVilla aimed at attracting a Japanese

CONTEMPORARY wedding clientele, this restaurant serves contemporary Continental food that focuses primarily on well-prepared standards you'd find at a reception (crab cakes in lemon puree, mahimahi with a mango beurre blanc, lamb chops in a red wine reduction)—albeit with a million-dollar view of Honolulu, from Kakaako to Diamond Head. Perched at water's edge, with famed surf break Point Panic offshore, 53 by the Sea uses its setting to great advantage—the crescent-shaped dining room faces the sea, so even if you're not at a table nestled against the floor-to-ceiling windows, you have a fine view. It's the stuff marriage proposals are made of. If you aren't proposing or dining, you can have cocktails and appetizers at the bar's little outdoor balcony and watch the city light up as the sun goes down. Sublime. $ *Average main: $50* ⊠ *53 Ahui St., Kakaako* ☎ *808/536–5353* ⊕ *www.53bythesea.com* ◬ *Reservations essential.*

$ ✕ **Hank's Haute Dogs.** Owner Henry "Hank" Adaniya is the restaura-

HOT DOG teur who gave celeb Chicago chef Grant Achatz his first big break at

FAMILY the late restaurant Trio in Evanston, Illinois. So it's no surprise that his idea of a hot dog involves things like wild boar sausage with cranapple relish. In 2006, Hank moved to his parents' home state to open this DIY chic storefront in the regentrifying neighborhood of Kakaako. Go classic with the Chicago Dog, made with the traditional fixings (including neon green relish) or gourmet with the butter-seared lobster sausage topped with garlic-relish aioli. And always get the duck-fat fries with a house-made dipping sauce (curry ketchup is a winner). Hank's now serves burgers, too. Forget cola; here you can have island-fresh drinks like hibiscus lemonade and lilikoi-lime soda. $ *Average main: $7* ⊠ *324 Coral St., Kakaako* ☎ *808/532–4265* ⊕ *www.hankshautedogs. com* ◬ *Reservations not accepted.*

$ ✕ **Kakaako Kitchen.** Russell Siu was the first of the local-boy fine dining

MODERN chefs to open a place of the sort he enjoys when he's off-duty, serving

HAWAIIAN high-quality plate lunches (he uses house-made sauce instead of from-

FAMILY a-mix brown gravy, for example). Here you can get a crab-and-avocado salad sandwich and honey-soy sauce pork chops with two scoops of either brown or white rice, and green salad instead of the usual macaroni salad. Breakfast is especially good, with combos like corned-beef hash and eggs, as well as exceptional baked goods. You order at the counter (be prepared to stand in line if you go right at noon), stake out a table, and wait for the food to come. $ *Average main: $13* ⊠ *Ward*

Centres, 1200 Ala Moana Blvd., Kakaako ☎ *808/596–7488* ⊕ *kakaakokitchen.com* ⚖ *Reservations not accepted.*

$$ ✕**Panya Bistro.** The newest location of this local chainlet is an easy-
ECLECTIC breezy café run by Hong Kong–born sisters Alice and Annie Yeung.
The crowd-pleasing menu is a mix of contemporary American (salads,
sandwiches, pastas) and Asian (Thai-style steak salad, Japanese-style
fried chicken, Singaporean *laksa*), served in a disco-tinged space (there's
also a full bar!) in the fast-developing neighborhood of Kakaako. Across
the street is the new Ward Village Shops complex housing TJ Maxx and
Nordstrom Rack. ⑤ *Average main: $18* ✉ *Hokua, 1288 Ala Moana
Blvd., Kakaako* ☎ *808/597-8880* ⊕ *www.panyagroup.com.*

$ ✕**Ryan's Grill at Ward Centre.** An all-purpose food-and-drink emporium,
AMERICAN lively and popular Ryan's has an exceptionally well-stocked bar, with 20
beers on tap, an outdoor deck, and TVs broadcasting sports. Lunch, din-
ner, and small plates are served until midnight. The eclectic menu ranges
from an addictive hot crab-and-artichoke dip with focaccia to grilled
fresh fish, pasta, salads, and sophisticated versions of local favorites, such
as the Kobe beef hamburger steak. ⑤ *Average main: $20* ✉ *Ward Centre,
1200 Ala Moana Blvd., Kakaako* ☎ *808/591–9132* ⊕ *ryansgrill.com.*

ALA MOANA

$$ ✕**Akasaka.** Step inside this tiny sushi bar tucked behind the Ala Moana
JAPANESE Hotel, and you'll swear you're in an out-of-the-way Edo neighborhood
in some indeterminate time. Don't be deterred by its location between
strip clubs or its reputation for inconsistent service. Greeted with a
cheerful *"Iraishaimase!"* (Welcome!), sink down at a diminutive table
or perch at the handful of seats at the sushi bar. It's safe to let the sushi
chefs here decide (*omakase*-style) or you can go for the grilled specialties, such as scallop *battayaki* (grilled in butter). ⑤ *Average main: $21*
✉ *1646 B Kona St., Suite B, Ala Moana* ☎ *808/942–4466.*

$ ✕**Bac Nam.** Tam and Kimmy Huynh's menu is much more extensive
VIETNAMESE than most, ranging far beyond the usual *pho* (beef noodle soup) and *bun*
(cold noodle dishes). Lamb curry, tapioca dumplings, tamarind head-
on shrimp, an extraordinary crab noodle soup, and other dishes hail
from North and South Vietnam. The no-frills atmosphere is welcoming and relaxed at this go-to spot for locals. At lunch it's packed with
people who work in the neighborhood. Reservations are not accepted
for groups fewer than six. ⑤ *Average main: $12* ✉ *1117 S. King St.,
Ala Moana* ☎ *808/597–8201.*

$ ✕**Big City Diner.** Part of a local chain of retro diners, Big City offers
AMERICAN Hawaii-style comfort favorites for breakfast, lunch, and dinner. In the
FAMILY morning you get rice instead of potatoes, option of fish or Portuguese
sausage instead of bacon, roasted macadamia nut pancakes smothered
in *haupia* (coconut) sauce—with generous portions and low prices. At
lunch and dinner you can try things like baby back ribs, kimchi fried
rice, fish with ginger-lime sauce, and burgers. ⑤ *Average main: $16*
✉ *Ward Entertainment Center, 1060 Auahi St., Ala Moana* ☎ *808/591–
8891* ⊕ *bigcitydinerhawaii.com.*

$ ✕**Greens and Vines.** Honolulu's only raw-food restaurant was an
VEGETARIAN immediate hit when it opened in 2012, having filled a healthy hole

8

in the city's dining landscape. Dishes such as the Living Lasagna, made with layers of seasoned zucchini, basil pesto, sun-dried tomato "marinara," macadamia nut "ricotta," and spinach have meat eaters convinced that raw and vegan food is delicious. The casual café also has a refrigerated case of entrées, spreads, and crackers to go. ■TIP→ Chef-owner Sylvia Thompson and her husband are oenophiles and hold periodic wine-tasting dinners. ⑤ *Average main: $15* ✉ *NineONine, 909 Kapiolani Blvd., Ala Moana* ☎ *808/536–9680* ⊕ *greensandvines.com* ✆ *Closed Sun.*

$$$ ✕ **Hiroshi Eurasion Tapas.** Founding chef Hiroshi Fukui is no longer with
ASIAN FUSION the restaurant, but the new young team continues his signature style of "West & Japan" cuisine. With an emphasis on local ingredients (one of the chefs has served tilapia that he raised himself in his backyard!) mixed with French technique, the menu always intrigues. Order a slew of small plates and share, or go with a more traditional big-plate entrée. Signatures include red wine–steamed veal cheeks, locally raised *kampachi* fish carpaccio, and *misoyaki* (marinated in a rich miso-soy blend, then grilled) butterfish. For a decadent treat, try the foie gras *sushi*. You can also order off the menu from Vino, next door, as they share a kitchen. ■TIP→ During Happy Hour, from 5:30 to 6:30, everything on the menu is half price when you sit at the bar—and the seats go fast. ⑤ *Average main: $27* ✉ *Waterfront Plaza, 500 Ala Moana Blvd., Ala Moana* ☎ *808/533–4476* ⊕ *www.hiroshihawaii.com* ✆ *No lunch.*

$$$ ✕ **Mariposa.** Yes, the popovers and the wee cups of bouillon are there
ASIAN at lunch, but in every other regard, this Neiman Marcus restaurant menu departs from the classic model, incorporating a clear sense of Pacific place. The breezy open-air veranda, with a view of Ala Moana Park, twirling ceiling fans, and life-size hula-girl murals say Hawaii. The menu at this headquarters for ladies who lunch gives the calorie and gluten info for contemporary American dishes such as braised pork belly and scallops with pickled watercress and passion-fruit brown butter, and a pork chop with sun-dried cherry port wine sauce. Make sure to leave room for the warm lilikoi pudding cake for dessert. ⑤ *Average main: $35* ✉ *Nieman Marcus, Ala Moana Center, 1450 Ala Moana, Ala Moana* ☎ *808/951–8887* ⊕ *www.neimanmarcushawaii.com/restaurant.aspx* ⚑ *Reservations essential.*

$$$ ✕ **The Pineapple Room by Alan Wong.** For some people, this restaurant is the
MODERN only reason to go to Macy's. At Alan Wong's more casual second spot
HAWAIIAN the chef de cuisine plays intriguing riffs on local food themes. Power lunchers confer over the stack-'em-high burger—made with locally raised grass-fed beef, bacon, cheddar cheese, hoisin-mayonnaise spread, avocado salsa, and a huge onion ring—it's one of the best in town. Ladies more often lean toward lighter fare like the Caesar salad with island-style grilled chicken or sesame-crusted opah (moonfish) in a yuzu ponzu sauce. Service is professional; reservations are recommended. ⑤ *Average main: $35* ✉ *Ala Moana Center, 1450 Ala Moana Blvd., Ala Moana* ☎ *808/945–6573* ⊕ *www.alanwongs.com* ✆ *No dinner Sun.*

$$ ✕ **Royal Garden.** Royal Garden is one of the best dim sum spots in town,
CHINESE and people don't mind paying a little more for the quality they get (about $4 per four-piece dish). From 10 am to 2 pm, when dim sum is

offered, just point to the steamed and baked morsels that look good; chances are, they're as good as they look. The regular menu features Hong Kong–style dishes, from the pedestrian shrimp with walnuts to the crazy poetic signature "osmanthus flower" made with dried scallops, crab, bean sprouts, and egg, and, of course, sweet, fragrant osmanthus flowers. ⑤ *Average main: $21* ✉ *Ala Moana Hotel, 410 Atkinson Dr., Ala Moana* ☎ *808/942–7788.*

$$ ✗ **Shokudo.** With a soaring ceiling, crazy red mobile sculpture, con-
JAPANESE temporary Japanese grazing plates, fruity vodka "sodas," and hungry young people, Shokudo is a culinary house of fun. Whether you go for new-wave fusion dishes such as sushi pizza (a flat, baked square of rice topped with salmon, scallop, crab, and pickled jalapeño), or more traditional noodle bowls and sushi, the food is all good. Do get the signature honey toast for dessert—a hollowed-out loaf of Japanese sandwich bread stuffed with cubes of its toasted innards and vanilla ice cream that's drizzled with honey. ■ **TIP→ Shokudo is one of Honolulu's few late-night eateries that is not a fast-food joint. Last orders are taken at 1 am.** ⑤ *Average main: $21* ✉ *Ala Moana Pacific Center, 1585 Kapiolani Blvd., Ala Moana* ☎ *808/941–3701* ⊕ *www.shokudojapanese.com.*

$$ ✗ **Sorabol.** The largest Korean restaurant in the city, this 24-hour eat-
KOREAN ery, with its tiny parking lot and maze of booths and private rooms, offers a vast menu encompassing the entirety of day-to-day Korean cuisine, plus sushi. English menu translations are cryptic at best. Still, it's great for wee hour "grinds" (local slang for food): *bi bim bap* (veggies, meats, and eggs on steamed rice), *kal bi* and *bulgogi* (barbecued meats), meat or fish *jun* (thin fillets battered with egg then fried), and kimchi pancakes. ⑤ *Average main: $24* ✉ *805 Keeaumoku St., Ala Moana* ☎ *808/947–3113* ⊕ *sorabolhawaii.com.*

$$ ✗ **Tängö.** On the ground floor of a glass-sheathed condominium, Tängö's
ECLECTIC spare contemporary setting stays humming at breakfast, lunch, and dinner. The Scandinavian decor (there are Marimekko prints on the walls) comes in the form of blond and birch woods, earthy complements to the cloud-like hanging white lamps. Finnish chef Göran Streng has a couple of nods to his heritage in unfussy dishes such as gravlax with crispy skin and mustard-dill sauce, but the menu is by and large general bistro, running from bouillabaisse to herb-crusted rack of lamb with some Asian nods. Budget gourmands come here for the bargain four-course prix-fixe menus—just $36 and $45. Reservations are only available for dinner, and don't expect a super-touristy experience—Streng caters mostly to his discriminating city-dwelling clientele. ⑤ *Average main: $25* ✉ *Hokua Building, 1288 Ala Moana Blvd., Ala Moana* ☎ *808/593–7288* ⊕ *www.tangocafehawaii.com* ⌛ *Reservations essential.*

$$$$ ✗ **Vintage Cave Honolulu.** The opening of Vintage Cave Honolulu in
CONTEMPORARY December 2012 was the most exciting culinary thing to happen on the
Fodor's Choice island in almost a decade. Billionaire Japanese developer Takeshi Seki-
★ guchi gave rising star chef Chris Kajioka, an alum of New York's Per Se and San Francisco's Aziza, carte blanche to create his dream kitchen and menu in a dark, brick-lined space that was once the storage basement of the Japanese department store Shiryokiya, which Sekiguchi also owns. (The space is also a private wine club—hence the name.) Today

8

chefs from across the country and Japan clamor to be a part of Kajioka's "collaboration dinner" program. He turns out the most progressive, enchanting food in the state, each plate in a progressive multicourse dinner a jewel-like composition that dazzles with color, texture, and, most important, flavor. Strong Japanese and French influences converge in his food, which mixes grade-A international ingredients (osetra caviar, foie gras, dry-aged organic beef, Tsukiji Market fish) from around the world with the freshest local produce (such as sea beans plucked from the banks of an ancient Hawaiian fishpond). Signature creations include a "seafood platter" of bite-size raw-fish constructions, a maple-glazed rectangle of brioche topped with caviar, and charred caraflex cabbage (grown specially for Kajioka on the Big Island) stacked in a dainty square and served in a resonant kombu-anchovy broth with a dollop of miso-crème fraîche. It's prix-fixe tasting menu only, and worth every cent of the considerable price. ⑤ *Average main: $295* ⊠ *Ala Moana Center, 1450 Ala Moana Blvd., Suite 2250, Ala Moana* ☎ *808/441–1744* ⊕ *www.vintagecave.com* ⌂ *Reservations essential.*

IWILEI

$$
AMERICAN
FAMILY

✗ **La Mariana Restaurant & Sailing Club.** The last of Honolulu's old-school tiki bars is tucked away in the industrial area of Sand Island. A mix of salty-dog sailors (the place looks out on sailboats bobbing in the Keehi Lagoon marina) and hipsters drink stiff mai tais (cocktails are all made with bottled mixers—no handcrafted anything here) sitting at the bar lighted by puffer-fish hanging lamps or in peacock chairs in the dining room. The food—breaded shrimp with cocktail sauce and fries, prime rib with mashed potatoes—is equally cast in *Mad Men* amber (frozen vegetable medley anyone?). You go for the feeling that Don the Beachcomber might walk in any minute. ■ **TIP➜** Ron Miyashiro—a blind pianist who once played at the late, great Tahitian Lanai—tinkles the ivories on Thursday nights, and amateur talents croon along. ⑤ *Average main: $20* ⊠ *50 Sand Island Access Rd., Iwilei* ☎ *808/848–2800* ⊕ *www.lamarianasailingclub.com.*

$$
SEAFOOD

✗ **Nico's at Pier 38.** Lyon-born chef Nico Chaiz's harborside restaurant is steps from the Honolulu Fish Auction, which explains his "line-to-plate" concept—super-fresh fish at a reasonable price. The signature dish is an ahi steak crusted in *furikake* (a Japanese mix of toasted nori and sesame seeds) and pan-seared, but he lets his French flag fly with steak frites and bouillabaisse, too. At lunch—when the place serves local-style plate lunches—you'll rub shoulders with a mix of rough-hewn dock workers, fishermen, office drones, and cops. Come dinner, a younger crowd arrives for beers on tap and cocktails. Try to get a table on the outside lanai. And if you're staying in a place with a kitchen, there's also a fish market selling fresh seafood, as well as prepared foods such as *poke*, soups, and stews; it's open 6:30 am to 6 pm Monday through Saturday, and 10 to 4 on Sunday. ⑤ *Average main: $21* ⊠ *1133 N. Nimitz Hwy., Pier 38, Iwilei* ☎ *808/540–1377* ⊕ *nicospier38.com* ⌂ *Reservations not accepted.*

$
DINER

✗ **Sugoi Bento & Catering.** This breakfast-and-lunch spot was among the first of a new wave of plate-lunch places to take particular care with

CLOSE UP

Oahu's Best Takeout

For lunch at the beach, or a movie night in your hotel room, do as Islanders do: get takeout. (And in the Islands, incidentally, the proper term is always takeout or to-go, never take-away.)

The universality of takeout here stems from traditions imported by plantation workers from Asia. The Chinese had their bakeries, the Japanese *okazu-ya*, Asian-style delis. Honolulu is awash in Western-style fast-food joints, Islands-style plate-lunch places, and Asian drive-ins offering Japanese sushi, Korean barbecue, Thai noodles, and Vietnamese spring rolls.

But locals particularly cherish the old-style businesses, now into the third and fourth generation, usually inconveniently located, with no parking and ridiculously quirky hours—and each with a specialty or two that no one else can quite match.

Buy a cheap Styrofoam cooler, pack it with ice to keep the goodies cool, and stop by one of these places. And remember: you'll need cash.

Fukuya Delicatessen. Get a taste of local Japanese culture at this family-run operation on the main thorough-fare in charming Moiliili, a mile or

so mauka out of Waikiki. Open since 1939, Fukuya offers takeout break-fasts and lunches, Japanese snacks, noodle dishes, even confections. Try *mochi* (sweet rice-flour cakes), *shoyu chicken*, hash patties, garlic chicken, and Asian-style salads. The folks here are particularly patient and helpful to visitors. Open 6 am to 2 pm. ⊠ *2710 S. King St., Moiliili* ☎ *808/946–2073* ⊟ *No credit cards* ☾ *Closed Mon. and Tues. No dinner.*

Mitsu-Ken. Trust us: Ignore the downscale neighborhood and the unpromising, battered exterior, and line up to order the garlic chicken (either as a plate lunch with rice and salad or the chicken only). Crispy, profoundly garlicky, and drizzled with a sweetish glaze that sets the whole thing off, Mitsu-Ken chicken will haunt your dreams. But go early; they open at 5 am, and by 1 pm they're wash-ing down the sidewalks. To avoid the wait, you can call the day before to place an order, then head to the cashier at the "phone order pickup line." It's in Kahili, not far from the Bishop Museum. ⊠ *1223 N. School St., Kapalama* ☎ *808/848–5573* ⊟ *No credit cards* ☾ *Closed Sun. and Mon. No dinner.*

8

quality and nutrition. They serve, for example, brown rice and green salad instead of the usual white rice and macaroni loaded with mayon-naise (but the proteins still aren't great options if you're monitoring your cholesterol). Sweet-and-spicy garlic chicken and *mochiko* (rice-batter-dipped and fried) chicken, adapted from traditional Japanese dishes, are specialties. Service is quick and cheerful. Primarily a takeout place, Sugoi is in a strip mall in industrial Kalihi, north of town. Pick up a bottle of their pungent garlic sauce to relive the experience back home. ⑤ *Average main: $11* ⊠ *City Square Shopping Center, 1286 Kalani St., Iwilei* ☎ *808/841–7984* ⊕ *www.sugoihawaii.com* ⟵ *Reservations not accepted* ⊟ *No credit cards* ☾ *Closed Sun. No dinner.*

MAKIKI HEIGHTS

$

BURGER

Fodor's Choice

★

✕**Honolulu Burger Co.** Owner Ken Takahashi retired as a nightclub impresario on the Big Island to become a real-life burger king. This modest storefront is the home of the locavore burger, made with range-fed beef, Manoa lettuce, and tomatoes that are all island raised—and you can taste the difference. Go classic with a single hand-shaped patty, the meat loosely packed to let the juices run free, or one of Takahashi's creations such as the Miso Kutie burger topped with red miso glaze and Japanese cucumber slices. The Korean Big Bang—braised short ribs with a spicy *ko choo jang* aioli—is as delicious as it is messy. And do get the truffle fries. There's a second location across the street from Kahala Mall (✉ *4210 Waialae Ave.,* ☎ *808/735–5202*). ⑤ *Average main: $11* ✉ *1295 S. Beretania St., Makiki* ☎ *808/626–5202* ⊕ *www. honoluluburgerco.com* ⚖ *Reservations not accepted.*

$

AMERICAN

✕**Spalding House Cafe.** In the exclusive Makiki Heights neighborhood above the city, the Honolulu Museum of Art Spalding House's casual café spills out of the ground floor of the museum onto the lush, expansive lawn with a million-dollar view of the city and Diamond Head. Sit inside when it's hot, grab an outdoor table when the trade winds are blowing. The short, Mediterranean-accented menu features items such as house-made soups, gourmet sandwiches, a hummus plate with fresh pita, and a roasted vegetable salad with curried quinoa. The café offers a $30 "Lauhala and Lunch" picnic for two, which includes a choice of sandwich or salad for each person, dessert bars, and beverage packed in a picnic basket—grab a tatami mat and lay your spread under the huge monkeypod tree on the museum grounds. ⑤ *Average main: $12* ✉ *2411 Makiki Heights Dr., Makiki* ☎ *808/237–5225* ⊘ *Closed Mon. No dinner.*

MOILIILI

$$$$

MODERN

HAWAIIAN

Fodor's Choice

★

✕**Alan Wong's Restaurant Honolulu.** Alan Wong is the undisputed king of Hawaiian regional cuisine, earning love and respect for his humble demeanor and practice as much as for his food. The "Wong Way," as it's not-so-jokingly called by his staff, includes an ingrained understanding of the aloha spirit, evident in the skilled but unstarched service, and creative and playful interpretations of Islands cuisine. Try crab mousse and lobster medallions in kudzu dashi, his signature ginger-crusted *onaga* (snapper), or, if you're feeling indulgent, the chef's tasting menu. With warm tones of koa wood, and *lauhala* grass weaving, you'll forget you're on the third floor of an office building. There's a reason the president dines here whenever he's in town. ⑤ *Average main: $38* ✉ *McCully Court, 1857 S. King St., 3rd fl., Moiliili* ☎ *808/949–2526* ⊕ *www.alanwongs.com* ⚖ *Reservations essential* ⊘ *No lunch.*

$$$$

MODERN

EUROPEAN

Fodor's Choice

★

✕**Chef Mavro.** George Mavrothalassitis, who took two hotel restaurants to the top of the ranks before opening this James Beard Award–winning restaurant in 1998, admits he's crazy. Crazy because of the care he takes to draw out the truest and most concentrated flavors, to track down the freshest fish, to create one-of-a-kind wine pairings. But for this passionate Marseilles transplant, there's no other way. He marries French technique with global flavors and local ingredients. The menu

OAHU'S BEST SHAVE ICE

Island-style shave ice (never *shaved ice*—it's a pidgin thing) is said to have been born when neighborhood kids hung around the icehouse, waiting to pounce on the shavings from large blocks of ice, carved with ultrasharp Japanese planes that created an exceptionally fine-textured granita.

In the 1920s, according to the historian for syrup manufacturer Malolo Beverages Co., Chinese vendors developed sweet fruit concentrates to pour over the ice.

The evolution continued with mom-and-pop shops adding their own touches, such as hiding a nugget of Japanese sweet bean paste in the center; placing a small scoop of ice cream at the bottom; and adding *li hing* powder (a seasoning Chinese use on preserved fruits).

There's nothing better on a sticky hot day. Here are two great places to try:

Waiola. Waiola Shave Ice, off Kapahulu Avenue, is known for its finely shaved ice and wide variety of flavors, and more recently has become famous through its regular appearances in the reboot of *Hawaii Five-0*. In real life, the service is a bit surly and the prices are slightly higher than for most other shave ice, but it's close to Waikiki. ⊠ *525 Kapahulu Ave., Kapahulu.*

Uncle Clay's House of Pure Aloha. Located in a strip mall in the residential neighborhood of Aina Haina, Uncle Clay's is a happy place. They specialize in house-made all-natural syrups made from cane sugar and locally sourced fruits. They've even got a flavor called "kalespin"—a combination of kale and spinach. ⊠ *Aina Haina Shopping Center, 820 W. Hind Dr., Aina Haina (right off Kalanianaole Hwy).*

changes quarterly, every dish (including dessert) matched with a select wine. Choose from a four- or six-course menu or the grand degustation (vegetarian and gluten-free options are available). Etched-glass windows screen the busy street-corner scene, and all within is mellow and serene with starched white tablecloths, fresh flowers, wood floors, and contemporary Islands art. This is a memorable gastronomic experience. ⑤ *Average main: $130* ⊠ *1969 S. King St., Moiliili* ☎ *808/944–4714* ⊕ *www.chefmavro.com* ⊲ *Reservations essential* ⊗ *No lunch.*

$ ✗ **Chiang Mai.** Long beloved for its Thai classics based on family recipes, such as spicy curries and stir-fries and sticky rice in woven grass
THAI baskets, Chiang Mai is a short cab ride from Waikiki. Some dishes, like the signature Cornish game hen in lemongrass and spices, show how acculturation can create interesting pairings. The cozy space is decorated with Thai fabrics and artwork. ⑤ *Average main: $25* ⊠ *2239 S. King St., Moiliili* ☎ *808/941–1151* ⊕ *808chiangmai.com* ⊗ *No lunch weekends.*

$$$ ✗ **Imanas Tei.** Nihonjin (Japanese nationals) and locals flock to this
JAPANESE tucked-away, bamboo-ceilinged restaurant for its tasteful, simple decor and equally tasteful—and perfect—sushi, sashimi, *nabe* (hot pots prepared at the table), and grilled dishes. You assemble your meal dish by dish, and the cost can add up if you aren't careful. Reservations are

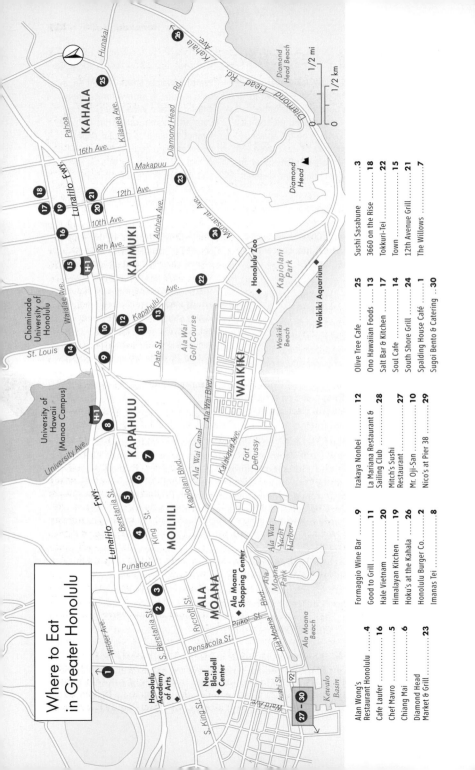

Where to Eat in Greater Honolulu

taken only for 5 to 7 pm; after that, there's always a line, so go early or very late. The parking lot is the size of a handkerchief. ⑤ *Average main: $30* ✉ *2626 S. King St., Moiliili* ☎ *808/941–2626, 808/934–2727* ☾ *Closed Sun. No lunch.*

$ | VEGETARIAN **✕ Peace Café.** This tranquil little storefront with a rustic country communal table is a nurturing sanctuary on a fast-food-loving island. Place your order at the counter, serve yourself lemon-infused water from a large glass beverage jar, and wait for your Yogini plate (a mountain of brown rice, beans, greens, and seaweed), soy soba salad, Moroccan chickpea stew, barbecue tempeh sandwich, and other vegan bites. Peace Café also has a selection of coffees, lattes, and teas—'cause you don't want to get *too* peaceful. ⑤ *Average main: $10* ✉ *2239 S. King St., Moiliili* ☎ *808/951–7555* ⊕ *www.peacecafehawaii.com* ☾ *No dinner Sun.*

$ | ECLECTIC **✕ Pint + Jigger.** Dining trends are late to arrive in Honolulu, and the gastropub phenomenon is no exception. Opened in 2012 by a group of people that includes a former Nobu Waikiki bar manager, Pint + Jigger is the best of the genre. Sit at one of the "beer garden" communal benches or perch at a high top in this welcoming wood-and-brick room for Dave Newman's farm-to-glass cocktails and craft beers. They pair well with bites such as a Scotch egg made with pork rillettes, strips of double-cut bacon spiced up with a jalapeño-corn salsa, and a burger topped with stout cheese. Plates are diverse enough to provide everything from a nibble (house-made barbecue potato chips) to a full meal (pan-seared salmon in lemon beurre blanc). After work and on weekends it is packed. ⑤ *Average main: $13* ✉ *1936 S. King St., Moiliili* ☎ *808/744–9593* ⊕ *www.pintandjigger.com* 🍴 *Reservations not accepted* ☾ *No lunch.*

$$$$ | JAPANESE **✕ Sushi Sasabune.** Be sure to get a seat at the counter (tables are for plebes) and prepare for an unforgettable sushi experience—if you behave. Part of a chainlet with locations in Los Angeles, Beverly Hills, and New York, this is the home of Seiji Kumagawa—Honolulu's sushi nazi. The way to go is the *omakase*-style (oh-*mah*-ka-*say*, roughly, "trust me"), letting the chef send out his choices of the highest-grade sea creatures for the night. The dishes are served with instructions: "Please, no shoyu on this one." "One piece, one bite." People who defy Kumagawa and go ahead and dip their nigiri in shoyu anyway have been kicked out of the restaurant mid-meal. The parade of dishes always includes the signature California baby squid stuffed with Louisiana crab. A caution: the courses come rapidly until you cry uncle. You pay by the course, which is generally two pieces of sushi or six to eight slices of sashimi, and they can add up fast. The final price depends on how far you can go. ⑤ *Average main: $115* ✉ *1419 S. King St., Moiliili* ☎ *808/947–3800* ⊕ *sushisasabune.tumblr.com* 🍴 *Reservations essential* ☾ *Closed Sun and Mon. No lunch Sat.*

$$ | HAWAIIAN **✕ The Willows.** Locals come to this buffet-only spot to celebrate things like graduations and showers, and it has its share of wedding receptions (there's a chapel on-site). It's an acre oasis of pavilions overlooking a network of ponds (once natural streams flowing from mountain to sea). The Islands-style comfort food includes the trademark chicken curry (*Joy of Cooking* style, not Indian) along with Hawaiian dishes such as

8

laulau (a steamed bundle of ti leaves containing pork, butterfish, and taro tops) and kalua pig. ⑤ *Average main: $38* ⊠ *901 Hausten St., Moiliili* ☎ *808/952–9200* ⊕ *willowshawaii.com* ⚱ *Reservations essential.*

KAPAHULU

$
AMERICAN

✕ **Good to Grill.** Specializing in grilled meats, this casual restaurant is a good choice for a full, quality meal at reasonable prices. From prime rib to melt-in-your-mouth short ribs to garlic shrimp pasta, you can count on a consistently good experience every time. It's modest but tasty and well-prepared food. The reasonable breakfasts on weekends and BYOB policy are definite pluses. No wonder Scott Caan of *Hawaii Five-0* is a repeat customer. ⑤ *Average main: $12* ⊠ *Safeway Center Kapahulu, 888 Kapahulu Ave., Suite 170, Kapahulu* ☎ *808/734–7345* ⊕ *www.goodtogrill.com* ⚱ *Reservations not accepted.*

$$$
JAPANESE

✕ **Izakaya Nonbei.** Teruaki Mori designed this pub to put you in mind of a northern inn in winter in his native Japan, and it is one of the most traditional of Honolulu's izakaya. Dishes not to miss—*aji tataki* (seared, vinegar-marinated jack mackerel topped with ginger); *karei kara-age* (delicate deep-fried flounder); *dobinmushi* (mushroom consommé presented in a teapot); fried *gobo* (burdock) chips; and crab, avocado, and bacon salad. And for a refreshing novelty, get the frozen sake. Open until 1:30 am on Friday and Saturday, it's good for a late-night bite. ⑤ *Average main: $30* ⊠ *3108 Olu St., Kapahulu* ☎ *808/734–5573.*

$
JAPANESE

✕ **Mr. Oji-san.** There's something for everyone at this compact, super-affordable ramen-sushi-curry-izakaya spot not far from Waikiki. The menu runs from down-home gravy-soaked hamburger steak to steaming ramen bowls to more elegant sashimi platters. If you're famished, go for a three-choice combination dinner, with selections such as chicken katsu, broiled salmon, and fried softshell crab. There's a decent sake lineup, too. ⑤ *Average main: $16* ⊠ *1018 Kapahulu Ave., Kapahulu* ☎ *808/735–4455* ⊕ *www.mrojisan.com* ☾ *Closed Sun. No lunch Sat.*

$
HAWAIIAN
Fodor's Choice
★

✕ **Ono Hawaiian Foods.** The adventurous in search of traditional Hawaiian food (teriyaki chicken with two scoops of rice is not traditional Hawaiian food) should head to this no-frills hangout, where residents patiently wait in line on the sidewalk. You can sample *poi* (a paste made from pounded taro root), *lomilomi* salmon (salmon massaged until tender and served with minced onions and tomatoes), *laulau* (pork wrapped in taro leaves and steamed), smoky *kalua* pork (roasted in an underground oven), and *haupia* (like coconut Jell-O). The Hawaiian word *ono* means "delicious"—and locals agree with the name. ⑤ *Average main: $15* ⊠ *726 Kapahulu Ave., Kapahulu* ☎ *808/737–2275* ⚱ *Reservations not accepted* ▭ *No credit cards* ☾ *Closed Sun.*

$$$$
JAPANESE

✕ **Tokkuri-Tei.** This is a favorite of locals for the playful atmosphere that belies the quality of the food created by chef Hideaki "Santa" Miyoshi, famous for his quirky menu names ("Nick Jagger" and "spider poke" among them); just say *omakase, kudasai* ("chef's choice, please"), and he'll order for you. Just be aware that some of the more rare seafood dishes can cost up to $45 (each). Get the ahi tartare *poke*—an unwieldly mound of tuna on a little pedestal of grilled rice topped with *tobiko* (flying fish roe) and drizzled with their house sauce made from mayo,

Izakaya

Japanese pub-restaurants, called *izakaya* (ee-ZAH-ka-ya), are sprouting up all over the Islands like *matsutake* mushrooms in a pine forest. They began as oases for homesick Japanese nationals but were soon discovered by adventurous locals, who appreciated the welcoming atmosphere, sprawling menus, and later dining hours.

Expect to be greeted by a merry, full-staff cry of "Irashaimase!" and offered an *oshibori* (hot towel), a drink, and handed a menu of dozens of small-plate, made-to-order dishes.

You can find *yakitori* (grilled dishes), tempura (deep-fried dishes), *donburi* (rice bowls), sushi and sashimi, *nabemono* and *shabu-shabu* (hot pots), noodles (both soup and fried), *okonomiyaki* (chop suey–type omelets), and a bizarre assortment of *yoshoku* dishes (Western foods prepared in Japanese style, such as hamburgers in soy-accented gravy, fried chicken with a mirin glaze, odd gratins, and even pizza).

Full bars are usual; a wide choice of lager-type beers and good-to-great sakes are universal. Many specialize in single-malt Scotch, but wine lists are generally short.

Izakaya menus are often confusing, many staff speak marginal English, and outings can get expensive fast (liquor plus small-plate prices equals eyes bigger than stomach). Prices range from $5 for a basket of edamame (steamed and salted soybeans) to $20 or more for *wafu* (seasoned, grilled steak, sliced for sharing). Start by ordering drinks and edamame or silky-textured braised *kabocha* pumpkin. This will keep the waiter happy. Then give yourself a quarter of an hour to examine the menu, ogle other people's plates, and seek recommendations. Start with one dish per person and one for the table; you can always call for more.

Imanas Tei. Go early to this cozy, out-of-the-way restaurant for its tasteful, simple decor and equally tasteful and simply perfect sushi, sashimi, *nabe* (hot pots prepared at the table), and grilled dishes; reservations are taken from 5 to 7 pm; after that, there's always a line. ⊠ *2626 S. King St., Moiliili* ☎ *808/941-2626 or 808/934-2727* ☞ *$8–$25.*

Izakaya Nonbei. Teruaki Mori designed this pub to put you in mind of a northern inn in winter in his native Japan; dishes not to miss— *karei kara-age* (delicate deep-fried flounder) and *dobinmushi* (mushroom consommé presented in a teapot). ⊠ *3108 Olu St., Kapahulu* ☎ *808/734-5573* ☞ *$7–$20.*

Tokkuri-Tei. This is a favorite of locals for the playful atmosphere that belies the excellence of the food created by chef Hideaki "Santa" Miyoshi, famous for his quirky menu names (Nick Jagger, Spider Poke); just say "Moriwase, kudasai" ("chef's choice, please"), and he'll order for you. ⊠ *611 Kapahulu Ave., Kapahulu* ☎ *808/739-2800* ☞ *$13–$25.*

Also worth a visit:

Kaiwa (⊠ *Waikiki Beach Walk, 2nd fl., 226 Lewers St., Waikiki* ☎ *808/924-1555*) for Osaka-style omelets.

Mr. Oji-san (⊠ *1018 Kapahulu Ave., Kapahulu* ☎ *808/735-4455*) for family-style *izakaya* specialties.

8

rice vinegar, soy sauce, garlic, and black pepper. $ *Average main: $40* ⊠ *449 Kapahulu Ave., Kapahulu* ☎ *808/732–6480.*

KAIMUKI

Ten minutes beyond Kapahulu is this commercial thoroughfare that runs through an old neighborhood filled with cool old craftsman bungalows (that are slowly being knocked down to make room for ticky-tacky boxes). It may have the highest and most diverse concentration of eateries on the island, from a Jamaican restaurant and a shabu-shabu house to a chic, contemporary bistro and a nougat manufacturer.

$$
ECLECTIC

✕ **Cafe Laufer.** Ten minutes from Waikiki, this is the Islands version of a Viennese café. At lunch people stop in for light options such as soups, Chinese chicken salad, and tuna sandwich. For teatime or post-movie dessert, try the classic apple tart, linzer torte, Black Forest cake, or chocolate macadamia-nut pastries. The dinner offers comfort-food entrées such as meat loaf, beef Stroganoff, duck confit, braised pork shank, and an all-natural, locally raised rib-eye steak. The café is open until 10 pm Friday and Saturday for a sweet nightcap. $ *Average main: $22* ⊠ *3565 Waialae Ave., Kaimuki* ☎ *808/735–7717* ⊕ *cafelaufer.com* ⌦ *Reservations not accepted.*

$$
WINE BAR

✕ **Formaggio Wine Bar.** All but invisible on the back side of a strip mall, this wine bar is going for an Italian catacomb feel, with dim lighting and soft, warm tones. Choose a small sip or an entire bottle from the extensive wine list, then enjoy the music and ponder the small-dish menu of pizzas, panini, and hot and cold specialties such as eggplant Napoleon and melting short ribs in red wine. $ *Average main: $17* ⊠ *Market City Shopping Center, 2919 Kapiolani Blvd., lower level in the rear, Kaimuki* ☎ *808/739–7719* ⊕ *formaggio808.com* ⌦ *Reservations not accepted.*

$
VIETNAMESE

✕ **Hale Vietnam.** One of Oahu's first Vietnamese restaurants, this neighborhood spot, popular with budget-minded college kids, expresses its friendly character with its name: *hale* (hah-lay) is the Hawaiian word for house or home. You'll find the region's expected staples—green-papaya salad, summer rolls, pho, bun (rice noodles). If you're not sure what to order, just ask. The staff is known for their willingness to help those who don't know much about Vietnamese food. Reservations are taken for larger groups only. $ *Average main: $12* ⊠ *1140 12th Ave., Kaimuki* ☎ *808/735–7581.*

$
ASIAN

✕ **Himalayan Kitchen.** Owned by a Nepalese chef who has worked in Indian restaurants, Himalayan Kitchen aims to serve all the cuisines of that high-altitude region. But the menu is largely Indian standards—curries, biriyanis, tandoori grills—that are the best in town (which isn't saying a lot in a town with few Indian restaurants). Nepalese dishes include *momo* (dumplings) and Kathmandu shrimp chili. Get a seat in the outdoor patio and don't forget to bring some ice cold beer—the place is BYOB. ⑤ *Average main: $17* ✉ *1137 11th Ave., Kaimuki* ☎ *808/735–1122.*

$$
CONTEMPORARY
Fodor's Choice
★

✗ **Salt Bar & Kitchen.** Hipsters and good-food hunters take their time grazing and drinking at this inviting two-level space, where the cocktails are crisp and the charcuterie house-cured. Sit at the bar or one of the tables on the second loft level and order small plates to share. Oxtail empanadas and grilled octopus with chorizo are perennial faves, but the offerings also include beautiful salad compositions (hearts of palm, sea asparagus, Thai basil, and charred tomato water), the charcuterie board accented with house-made pickles, or big plates like a Korean-flavored pastrami sandwich and a flatiron steak with fried egg puree. The food is innovative yet comforting at this sister of 12th Avenue Grill. ⑤ *Average main: $21* ✉ *3605 Waialae Ave, Kaimuki* ☎ *808/744–7567* ⊕ *www.salthonolulu.com* ⊘ *No lunch.*

$
SOUTHERN

✗ **Soul Cafe.** If you have a hankering for down-home southern fare with a gourmet twist and Pacific flair, chef Sean Priester has it all. Must-tries include shrimp and cheesy grits with bacon gravy, crab cake on spring greens with an Asian black bean dressing, and the best fried chicken in town. Be prepared to order extra corn bread. It's that good. ⑤ *Average main: $12* ✉ *3040 Waialae Ave., Kaimuki* ☎ *808/947–3113* ⊕ *pacific-soulhawaii.com.*

$$$$
MODERN
HAWAIIAN

✗ **3660 on the Rise.** This casually stylish eatery is a 10-minute drive from Waikiki in restaurant-packed Kaimuki. Sample Chef Russell Siu's New York Steak Alae (steak grilled with Hawaiian clay salt), the crab cakes, or the signature ahi katsu wrapped in nori and deep-fried with a wasabi-ginger butter sauce. Siu combines a deep understanding of local flavors with a sophisticated palate, making this place especially popular with homegrown gourmands. ■**TIP→** The dining room can feel a bit snug when it's full (as it usually is); go early or late. ⑤ *Average main: $37* ✉ *3660 Waialae Ave., Kaimuki* ☎ *808/737–1177* ⊕ *www.3660.com* ⊘ *Closed Mon. No lunch.*

$$
INTERNATIONAL
Fodor's Choice
★

✗ **Town.** Opened in 2005, stylish Town remains a hot spot for Honolulu's creative class and farm-to-table diners. Chef-owner Ed Kenney and his partner Dave Caldiero offer a Mediterranean-eclectic menu ranging from hand-cut pastas and refreshing composed salads (pastas and salads) to clean preparations of fish and meat (polenta with egg and asparagus or buttermilk panna cotta). Get a bunch of tasting plates to share—ahi tartare on risotto cakes and mussels in a fennel-Cinzano broth are instant winners—or go big with dishes such as opah (moon-fish) in a Meyer-lemon-butter sauce and pork belly with salsa verde and polenta. If you're a vegetarian, ask for the bountiful veggie plate, which isn't on the menu. The restaurant serves breakfast and lunch, too. ⑤ *Average main: $25* ✉ *3435 Waialae Ave., Kaimuki* ☎ *808/735–5900* ⊕ *www.townkaimuki.com* ⟡ *Reservations essential* ⊘ *Closed Sun.*

$$
MODERN
HAWAIIAN
Fodor's Choice
★

✗ **12th Avenue Grill.** Until October 2013, it was hard to get a table at this popular contemporary American spot—that's when it moved down the street to larger, airier digs with a big bar serving handcrafted cocktails. Now you have a better chance of trying chef Jason Schoonover's loca-vore, seasonal food. Bright flavors in sometimes surprising combinations mark dishes like kampachi sashimi dusted with coriander and lime and served with serrano chimichurri, and grilled chicken marinated in ginger, tarragon, honey, and mustard. The specials are always excellent, and the passion-fruit mochi cake with vanilla-ginger syrup is one of the best desserts in town. $ *Average main: $26* ⊠ *1120 12th Ave., Kaimuki* ☎ *808/732–9469* ⊕ *12thavegrill.com* ⊘ *No lunch.*

DIAMOND HEAD

$ ✕ **Diamond Head Market & Grill.** Just five minutes from Waikiki hotels is
AMERICAN   Kelvin Ro's one-stop food shop—indispensable if you have accommodations with a kitchen. Join surfers, beach bunnies, and Diamond Head hikers at the takeout window to order gourmet sandwiches and plates such as hand-shaped burgers, portobello steaks, Korean kalbi ribs, and grilled ahi with wasabi-ginger sauce, rice, and salad. The chilled shelves in the market stock wraps, Japanese bentos, and salads, as well as heat-and-eat items like soups and roasted pork with mashed potatoes. And from the bakery come giant scones and desserts like lemon crunch cake. You can also pick up wine, beer, and soft drinks. $ *Average main: $11* ⊠ *3158 Monsarrat Ave., Diamond Head* ☎ *808/732–0077* ⊕ *www. diamondheadmarket.com* ⌂ *Reservations not accepted.*

$ ✕ **South Shore Grill.** Just a couple of minutes out of Waikiki proper near
AMERICAN   the base of Diamond Head, South Shore Grill is an affordable counter-service spot. It's especially convenient if you need to refuel before or after sightseeing or beach time. The restaurant is also known for its fish tacos, and offers sandwiches (on ciabatta rolls), entrée salads, stuffed burritos, and a plate of ono (wahoo) coated with macadamia-nut pesto and served with a tangy slaw. $ *Average main: $10* ⊠ *3114 Monsarrat Ave., Diamond Head* ☎ *808/734–0229* ⊕ *www.southshoregrillhawaii. com* ⌂ *Reservations not accepted.*

KAHALA

$$$$ ✕ **Hoku's at the Kahala.** Everything about this room speaks of quality and
ASIAN FUSION   sophistication: the wall of windows with their beach views, the avant-garde cutlery and dinnerware, the solicitous staff, and the carefully constructed Euro-Pacific cuisine. The menu constantly changes, but you can count on Chef Wayne Hirabayashi to use fresh, local ingredients when possible in his innovative dishes such as braised short-rub tempura, salt-crusted rack of lamb with tomato confit, and butter-poached lobster with passion-fruit jus. It's an excellent and popular choice for special occasions or for Sunday brunch. The dress code is collared shirts, no beachwear. $ *Average main: $55* ⊠ *The Kahala Hotel & Resort, 5000 Kahala Ave., Kahala* ☎ *808/739–8760* ⊕ *www.kahalaresort.com* ⌂ *Reservations essential* ⊘ *Closed Mon. and Tues. No lunch.*

$ ✕ **Olive Tree Cafe.** An Iranian Hellenophile owns this bustling, self-serve
GREEK   café that serves the best taramasalata, falafel, and souvlaki in town. Stand in line at the counter to order while your companion tries to shanghai one of the outdoor tables. It's BYOB, and you can get good wines next door at Olive Tree's sister gourmet shop, Oliver. There's no corkage fee, and they'll even lend you a corkscrew. Located behind

Kahala Mall, this is a great option if you're headed back to town late from a day at the beach on the East Side. ⑤ *Average main: $13* ✉ *4614 Kilauea Ave., Suite 107, Kahala* ☎ *808/737–0303* ⚑ *Reservations not accepted* ▭ *No credit cards* ⊘ *No lunch.*

MAPUNAPUNA

$$$$
SUSHI
✗ **Mitch's Sushi Restaurant.** This microscopic sushi bar (15 seats) is an adjunct of a wholesale seafood market operated by gregarious South African expatriate Douglas Mitchell, who oversees the sushi chefs and keeps customers chatting. The fish, air-freighted from around the world, is ultrafresh, well cut (into huge pieces—to the regret of those who follow the one-bite rule), and nicely presented. You can spend as much or as little as you like—$56 for a half dozen pieces of prime bluefin tuna belly, or just a few dollars for pickled plum sushi. Off the beaten path even for residents, the place has a sort of cult following. ⑤ *Average main: $60* ✉ *524 Ohohia St., near Honolulu International Airport, Mapunapuna* ☎ *808/837–7774* ⊕ *www.mitchsushi.com* ⚑ *Reservations essential.*

SOUTHEAST OAHU

$$$
MODERN
HAWAIIAN
✗ **Roy's.** Roy Yamaguchi is one of the 12 founding chefs of Hawaiian regional cuisine—a culinary movement that put Hawaii on the food map back in 1991. Opened in 1988, his flagship restaurant across the highway from Maunalua Bay is still packed every night. Food-savvy visitors on a Hawaiian regional cuisine pilgrimage mix with well-heeled residents. (If you're sensitive to pressure to turn the table, it's best to visit later in the evening.) The wide-ranging and ever-interesting Hawaiian fusion menu is made up of his longtime classics, like Szechuan-spiced baby back ribs and blackened ahi with soy mustard butter sauce, and contemporary creations such as a pork chop with Hawaiian-chili chimichurri sauce and *andagi* (an Okinawan donut hole) made with poi. There's also an exceptional wine list. The Waikiki location is equally busy and has a four-course menu for vegans and gluten-free eaters. ⑤ *Average main: $34* ✉ *Hawaii Kai Corporate Plaza, 6600 Kalanianaole Hwy., Hawaii Kai, Honolulu* ☎ *808/396–7697* ⊕ *www. royshawaii.com* ⚑ *Reservations essential* ⊘ *No lunch.*

WINDWARD OAHU

$
AMERICAN
✗ **Big City Diner.** This outlet of the popular retro diner chain has outdoor lanai seating, a bar, and is across the street from a small bird sanctuary. It's a hot spot for breakfast; popular dinner items include grilled steak with onions and mushrooms, baby back ribs, meat loaf, and salads. ⑤ *Average main: $16* ✉ *108 Hekili St., Kailua* ☎ *808/263–8880* ⊕ *bigcitydinerhawaii.com.*

$
AMERICAN
✗ **Boots & Kimo's Homestyle Kitchen.** Sometimes you have to wait an hour for a table here—but no one complains once they've had a bite of the banana pancakes topped with thick macadamia-nut sauce (they've got their own cult following) at this Kailua breakfast and lunch spot.

8

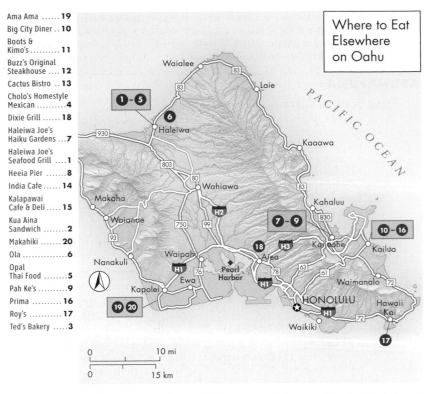

Where to Eat
Elsewhere
on Oahu

Brothers Ricky and Jesse Kiakona treat their guests like family. At lunch the signature is a plate of *pulehu* (grilled) ribs. When the operation moved from a hole in the wall in a new, larger space in 2010, the line just got longer. ⑤ *Average main: $9* ✉ *151 Hekili St., Suite 102, Kailua* ☎ *808/263–7929* 🍴 *Reservations not accepted* ⊘ *No dinner.*

$$$ ✕ **Buzz's Original Steakhouse.** Virtually unchanged since it opened in
STEAKHOUSE 1967, this neighborhood institution opposite Kailua Beach Park is filled with the enticing aroma of grilling steaks. It doesn't matter if you're a bit sandy (though bare feet are not allowed). Find a spot in the cozy maze of rooms, stop at the salad bar, and order up a steak, a burger, teriyaki chicken, or the fresh fish special. If you sit at the bar, expect to make friends. ■**TIP**→ **Be warned: the mai tais here are the strongest you'll find anywhere.** ⑤ *Average main: $35* ✉ *413 Kawailoa Rd., Kailua* ☎ *808/261–4661* ⊕ *www.buzzssteakhouse.com* 🍴 *Reservations essential.*

$$ ✕ **Cactus Bistro.** John Memering brought a whole new flavor profile to
LATIN AMERICAN Oahu when he opened this casual pan-Latin restaurant in Kailua. He puts his own island spin on duck "carnitas" with tomatillo-jalapeño marmalade, and a coconut-milk–infused *mariscada* (Brazilian seafood stew). Saffron-colored walls and frozen sangrias add to the good-time vibe. ⑤ *Average main: $21* ✉ *Davis Bldg., 767 Kailua Rd., Kailua* ☎ *808/261–1000* ⊕ *www.cactusbistro.com.*

$$ ✕ **Haleiwa Joe's Haiku Gardens.** Like its more famous sister location on
AMERICAN the North Shore, this casual, friendly Haleiwa Joe's is a seafood grill
(the chef has a daily special preparation for the day's catch that comes
straight from the Honolulu Fish Auction) and also serves turf favorites.
It's the view of the Haiku Gardens directly behind the restaurant makes
the difference at this Kaneohe location. Come for an early dinner or
fantastic Sunday brunch and enjoy the stunning views. Be sure to leave
time for a stroll around the pond and through the garden. ⑤ *Average
main: $22* ✉ *44-336 Haiku Rd., Kaneohe* ☎ *808/247–6671* ⊕ *www.
haleiwajoes.com* ⚓ *Reservations not accepted.*

$ ✕ **Heeia Pier General Store and Deli.** This shack at the end of Heeia Pier
HAWAIIAN serves a-cut-above plate lunches to a motley crew of local fishermen,
young hipsters (the owner used to be a club promoter), and tourists
who veer off the beaten track. Try the guava barbecue chicken or the
luau stew (a hearty stew made with taro leaves and beef), which are
specialties; the fish specials are always good. This place is worth a stop
if you're exploring the Windward side. ⑤ *Average main: $8* ✉ *Heeia
Pier, 46-499 Kamehameha Hwy., Kaneohe* ☎ *808/235–2192* ⊕ *www.
heeiapier.com* ⚓ *Reservations not accepted* ⊘ *Closed Mon. No dinner.*

$ ✕ **India Cafe.** At this warm, welcoming takeout storefront owned by
INDIAN Indians of Malaysian origin, you get South Asian staples such as *dosai*
(griddle breads made of rice and lentil flour filled with savory and
sweet ingredients), *daal* (lentil stew), curries, and samosas, as well as a
few Malaysian choices like shrimp sambal. It's a great choice for veg-
etarian and gluten-free diners. There are four small tables. ⑤ *Average
main: $10* ✉ *Kailua Shopping Center, 600 Kailua Rd., #129, Kailua*
☎ *808/262–1800* ⊕ *www.indiacafehawaii.com.*

$$ ✕ **Kalapawai Cafe & Deli.** Chef Jason Iwane, born and raised in Kailua,
ECLECTIC always keeps things interesting at this one-stop Mediterranean-leaning
café, wine bar, bakery, and gourmet deli. The green-and-white Kailua
landmark is a meeting spot for Windward residents. Come in on your
way to the beach for a cup of coffee and bagel and stop back for a gourmet pizza or bruschetta (how does eggplant confit, sweet peppers, honey,
and goat cheese sound?) at lunchtime. The menu changes frequently, but
at dinner you may find tempting choices such as duck ragout with dried
cherries and mushrooms, or fresh grilled fish with lemongrass risotto
and red curry aioli. ■**TIP➔ If you're staying in a Kailua vacation rental,
the is the place to pick up prepared foods such as stuffed grape leaves and
crab cakes to take home.** ⑤ *Average main: $19* ✉ *750 Kailua Rd., Kailua*
☎ *808/262–3354* ⊕ *www.kalapawaimarket.com.*

$$ ✕ **Pah Ke's Chinese Restaurant.** If you happen to be on the Windward Side
CHINESE at dinner time, this out-of-the-ordinary Chinese restaurant—named for
the local pidgin term for Chinese (literally translated this is Chinese's
Chinese Restaurant)—is a good option. Ebullient owner and chef Ray-
mond Siu, a former hotel pastry chef, focuses on healthier cooking
techniques and local ingredients. The menu offers all the usual suspects
(like kung pao chicken), but you should hone in on the "house special-
ties" such as braised short ribs rubbed with Kona coffee and curry, and
scallops with flash-fried spinach leaves. Call ahead to find out if he's
got any cool specials and to alert them to dietary restrictions—they are

8

Shrimp Snacks

No drive to the North Shore is complete without a shrimp stop. Shrimp stands dot Kamehameha Highway from Kahaluu to Kahuku. For about $12, you can get a shrimp plate lunch or a snack of chilled shrimp with cocktail sauce, served from a rough hut or converted van (many permanently parked), with picnic-table seating.

The shrimp-shack phenomenon began with a lost lease and a determined restaurateur. In 1994, when Giovanni and Connie Aragona couldn't renew the lease on their Haleiwa deli, they began hawking their best-selling dish—an Italian-style scampi preparation involving lemon, butter, and lots of garlic—from a truck alongside the road. About the same time, aquaculture was gaining a foothold in nearby Kahuku, with farmers raising sweet, white shrimp and huge, orange-whiskered prawns in shallow freshwater ponds. The ready supply and the success of the first shrimp truck led to many imitators.

Though it's changed hands, that first business lives on as Giovanni's Original Shrimp Truck, parked in Kahuku town. Signature dishes include the garlic shrimp and a spicy shrimp sauté, both worth a stop.

But there's plenty of competition—at least a dozen stands, trucks, or stalls are operating at any given time, with varying menus (and quality).

Not all of that shrimp comes fresh from the ponds; much of it is imported. The only way you can be sure you're buying local, farm-raised shrimp is if the shrimp is still kicking. Romy's Kahuku Prawns and Shrimp Hut (Kamehameha Highway, near Kahuku) is an arm of one of the longest-running aquaculture farms in the area; it sells live shrimp and prawns and farm-raised fish along with excellent plate lunches. The award-winning Mackey's serves some of the juiciest, tastiest plates on the North Shore; if you're lucky, you'll be greeted by the gregarious Mackey Chan himself.

very accommodating. $ *Average main: $22 ⊠ 46-018 Kamehameha Hwy., Kaneohe* ☎ 808/235–4505 ⊕ www.pahke.com.

$$
PIZZA
✕ **Prima.** The beautifully blistered pies are cooked in a white-tiled Ferrara wood-burning oven that you can see in the open kitchen of this bright, light pizzeria with robin's egg–blue Eames shell chairs. This is as Neapolitan as it gets on Oahu, and these are the best pizzas on the island, topped with such ingredients as soppressata, prosciutto, and spicy meatballs. At dinner, look for a short menu of chef specials, perhaps a grilled octopus salad or square of roasted pork belly. $ *Average main: $18 ⊠ Kailua Foodland Marketplace, 108 Hekili St., Kailua, Honolulu* ☎ 808/888–8933 ⊕ www.primahawaii.com.

THE NORTH SHORE

$
MEXICAN
✕ **Cholo's Homestyle Mexican.** There are a few places on the North Shore that are the area's great gathering places. Foodland is one. Another is Cholo's. Festively done up with Mexican tchotchkes, this longtime spot serves up decent rice-and-beans plates of Mexican standards (steak

fajitas, burritos, enchiladas) at affordable prices. The fish tacos are made with sashimi-grade ahi—caught just offshore and brought in from Haleiwa Pier—and the margaritas are made with locally sourced fruit. (You won't find a sweeter fresh mango margarita anywhere.) Early birds should check out the morning menu; the restaurant opens at 9 am and serves different variations of the breakfast burrito. ⑤ *Average main: $13* ⊠ *North Shore Marketplace, 66-250 Kamehameha Hwy., Haleiwa* ☎ *808/637–3059* ⊕ *www.cholos.mx.*

$$ ✕ **Haleiwa Joe's Seafood Grill.** After the long drive to the North Shore,
AMERICAN it's a treat to while away the afternoon on the covered open-air lanai at Haleiwa Joe's, scoring a couple of cute souvenir mai tai cups, watching the boats and surfers in the harbor, and munching crunchy coconut shrimp, a fish sandwich, or the fresh fish special. It's just past the Anahulu Stream Bridge. A Kaneohe location overlooks lush Haiku Gardens. ⑤ *Average main: $27* ⊠ *66-011 Kamehameha Hwy., Haleiwa* ☎ *808/637–8005* ⊕ *www.haleiwajoes.com* ⚠ *Reservations not accepted.*

$ ✕ **Kua Aina Sandwich.** This North Shore spot has gone from funky burger
BURGER shack (it first opened in 1975) to institution, with crowds of tourists and locals standing in line to order the large, hand-formed burgers heaped with bacon, cheese, salsa, and pineapples. The patties are packed tight, so they tend to be on the dry side. Kua Aina also has a Honolulu location in the Ward Centre. ⑤ *Average main: $10* ⊠ *66-160 Kamehameha Hwy., Haleiwa* ☎ *808/637–6067* ⚠ *Reservations not accepted.*

$$$ ✕ **Ola at Turtle Bay Resort.** In a rustic-beam-and-concrete-floor pavilion
MODERN literally on the sand, Ola's draw is its ocean-view location at the Turtle
HAWAIIAN Bay Resort on the North Shore. In an area where a quasi-Mexican cantina is considered a big night out, this spot with reliable Hawaiian regional cuisine is a favorite standby. Dishes such as five-spiced braised beef short ribs with corn relish or a catch of the day with a macadamia-nut pesto cream deliver bold flavors. ⑤ *Average main: $42* ⊠ *Turtle Bay Resort, 57-091 Kamehameha Hwy., Kahuku* ☎ *808/293–0801* ⊕ *olaislife.com.*

$ ✕ **Opal Thai Food.** When you go on your big adventure to the North
THAI Shore, you might want to stop at this crowded little room, which serves
Fodor's Choice the best Thai food on the island. Sanith "Opel" Sirichandhra and his
★ wife Aoy are neighborhood celebrities for their down-to-earth ways and pungent, addictive *tom kha* (coconut curry) soup, green curry, and drunken noodles. Opel (yes, the spelling is different from that of the restaurant's name) is a vegetarian, so he's tuned in to accommodating herbivores and people with food sensitivities. ⑤ *Average main: $10* ⊠ *Haleiwa Town Center, 66-197 C Kamehameha Hwy., Haleiwa* ☎ *808/637–7950* ⊙ *Closed Sun. and Mon.*

$ ✕ **Ted's Bakery.** Sunburned tourists and salty surfers rub shoulders in
AMERICAN their quest for Ted's famous chocolate *haupia* pie (layered coconut and chocolate puddings topped with whipped cream) and hearty plate lunches—like gravy-drenched hamburger steak and mahimahi. Parking spots and the umbrella-shaded tables are a premium, be prepared to grab and go. ⑤ *Average main: $9* ⊠ *59-024 Kamehameha Hwy.,*

8

Haleiwa ☎ *808/638–8207* ⊕ *www.tedsbakery.com* ⌕ *Reservations not accepted.*

CENTRAL OAHU

$ ✕ **Dixie Grill.** Casual and family-friendly, the Dixie Grill, just off the
AMERICAN freeway in Pearl City, brings a taste of the South to the Islands with
barbecue (including a variety of spicy sauces to choose from), seafood
specialties (creole mahimahi, fried catfish), shrimp and grits, gumbo,
and hush puppies. ■ **TIP→ This place is convenient if you're visiting
Pearl Harbor or the swap meet.** ⑤ *Average main: $18* ✉ *99-016 Kame-
hameha Hwy., Aiea* ☎ *808/485–2722* ⊕ *www.dixiegrill.com* ⌕ *Reservations not accepted.*

WEST (LEEWARD) OAHU

$$$$ ✕ **Ama Ama.** There's nothing Mickey Mouse about the food at the fine-
MODERN dining restaurant of this Disney resort. Chef Kevin Chong was chef de
HAWAIIAN cuisine at Chef Mavro for seven years, and his food has a brightness
and innovation not always seen in resort restaurants. Add to that the
view of the Ko Olina lagoons and Pacific Ocean—and live music by
top local performers—and you have an evening worth the pretty penny.
From a Thai seafood curry to a pork chop with a mushroom ragout,
the ingredients are largely local, but the flavors are international. And
the puffed potatoes are a fun side. If you're on a budget, skip dinner—
breakfast and lunch entrées are half the price (although menu offerings
vary). ⑤ *Average main: $40* ✉ *Aulani, a Disney Resort & Spa, 92-1185
Aliinui Dr., Ko Olina, Kapolei* ☎ *808/674–6200* ⊕ *disneyparks.disney.
go.com* ⌕ *Reservations essential.*

$$$$ ✕ **Makahiki—The Bounty of the Islands.** The buffet restaurant at Disney's
HAWAIIAN Aulani resort offers a wide variety of locally produced items, as well
FAMILY as familiar dishes from stateside and the rest of the world. You'll find
sustainable Hawaiian seafood, Asian selections, familiar grilled meats
and vegetables, and a kids' menu. If you have children, plan months
in advance to get a reservation for the Character Breakfast, as it's only
offered on select days and is always sold out. An à la carte menu is also
available. ■ **TIP→ Arrive early for dinner and have a drink at the adjacent Olelo Room, where the staff are fluent in Hawaiian; you can get a
language lesson along with your libation.** ⑤ *Average main: $43* ✉ *Au-
lani, a Disney Resort & Spa, 92-1185 Aliinui Dr., Ko Olina, Kapolei*
☎ *808/674–6200* ⊕ *resorts.disney.go.com* ⌕ *Reservations essential.*

WHERE TO STAY

Updated by
Catherine E.
Toth

As in real estate, location matters. And though Oahu is just 44 miles long and 30 miles wide—meaning you can circle the entire island before lunch—it boasts neighborhoods and lodgings with very different vibes and personalities. If you like the action and choices of big cities, consider Waikiki, a 24-hour playground with everything from surf to karaoke bars. Those who want an escape from urban life look to the island's leeward or windward sides, or the North Shore, where the surf culture creates a laid-back atmosphere.

Most of the island's major hotels and resorts are in Waikiki, which has a lot to offer within a small area—namely shopping, restaurants, nightlife—and nearly 3 miles of sandy beach. You don't need a car in Waikiki; everything is nearby, including the Honolulu Zoo and Waikiki Aquarium, the 300-acre Kapiolani Park, running and biking paths, grocery stores, and access to public transportation that can take you to museums, shopping centers, and historic landmarks around the island.

You'll find places to stay along the entire stretch of both Kalakaua and Kuhio avenues, with smaller and quieter hotels and condos at the eastern end, and more business-centric accommodations on the western edge of Waikiki, near the Hawaii Convention Center, Ala Moana Center, and downtown Honolulu.

The majority of tourists who come to Oahu stay in Waikiki, but choosing accommodations in downtown Honolulu affords you the opportunity to be close to shopping and restaurants at Ala Moana Center, the largest shopping mall in the state. It also provides easy access to the airport.

If you want to get away from the bustle of the city, consider a stay on Oahu's leeward coast. Consider the Ko Olina resort area, about 20 minutes from the Honolulu International Airport and 40 minutes from Waikiki. Here, there are great golf courses and quiet beaches and coves that make for a relaxing getaway. But you'll need a car to get off the property if you want to explore the rest of the island.

Other more low-key options are on Windward Oahu or the North Shore. Both regions are rustic and charming, with quaint eateries and coffee shops, local boutiques, and some of the island's best beaches. One of Oahu's premier resorts, Turtle Bay, is located here, too.

OAHU LODGING PLANNER

LODGING PROPERTY TYPES
HOTELS AND RESORTS

Oahu offers more accommodation choices than any other Hawaiian island, and for many visitors, staying at a top-notch resort or hotel here—such as the luxe Turtle Bay Resort on the North Shore or the posh Halekulani in Waikiki—is the ultimate island-style pampering experience.

Keep in mind that most Waikiki hotels charge $10 or more per day for parking. Consider renting a car only on the days that you wish to go exploring or factor the parking costs into your budget.

B&BS AND INNS

There are about a dozen B&Bs on Oahu, primarily located in Kailua, on the windward side of the island. Several are located within walking distance of world-famous Kailua Beach and a handful have pools. A few serve simple Continental breakfasts with pastries, coffee, and fresh island fruit and juices, while others provide breakfast items in the units for guests to enjoy at their leisure during their stay. *In addition to the listings below, check the Oahu Visitors Bureau website (⊕ www.gohawaii.com/oahu) for additional B&B options.*

CONDOS AND VACATION RENTALS

Vacation rentals give you the convenience of staying at a home away from home—and you should be able to find the perfect getaway on Oahu. Properties managed by individual owners can be found at online vacation-rental directories, as well as on the Oahu Visitors Bureau website. There also are several Oahu-based management companies with vacation rentals. Compare companies, as some offer Internet specials and free nights when booking.

RESERVATIONS

After your online research but before you book a room, try calling the hotels directly. Sometimes on-property reservationists can get you the best deals, and they usually have the most accurate information about rooms, availability, and hotel amenities. If you use a toll-free number, ask for the location of the calling center you've reached. If it's not in Oahu, double-check information and rates by calling the hotel's local number.

PRICES

The lodgings we list are the cream of the crop in each price category. Assume that hotels have private bath, phone, and TV unless we state otherwise. We always list facilities but not whether you'll be charged

9

an extra fee to use them, so when pricing accommodations, find out what's included.

HONOLULU

The vast majority of hotels in Honolulu are in Waikiki, but there are also a few in Downtown Honolulu and in the Ala Moana area between Downtown and Waikiki. Away from the hopping scene of Waikiki or busy downtown, accommodations on the rest of Oahu range from quiet and romantic bed-and-breakfasts and cottages to less expensive hotels that are a great value. There are a few luxury resorts as well, where you'll truly feel like you're getting away from it all.

For expanded hotel reviews, visit Fodors.com.

WAIKIKI

Hotels in Waikiki range from super-luxe resorts to the kind of small, beachy places where shirtless surfers hang out in the lobby. It's where the heart of the action is on Oahu. Those traveling with families might want to take into consideration easy access to the beach, restaurants, and other activities, as parking in the area can sometimes be difficult and pricey. For those looking to be slightly removed from the scene, choose accommodations on the *ewa* (west) end of Waikiki.

$ | **Aqua Aloha Surf Waikiki.** This boutique property just two blocks from
HOTEL | Waikiki Beach offers surfer chic accommodations and is a great value,
FAMILY | too. **Pros:** fun lobby; great island decor and friendly atmosphere; pool with sundeck and cabanas; on-site coin-operated laundry. **Cons:** no view; traffic noise; 10-minute walk to beach. ⑤ *Rooms from: $85* ☒ *444 Kanekapolei St., Waikiki* ☎ *866/970–4160, 808/954–7410* ⊕ *www. alohasurfhotelwaikiki.com* ↪ *202 rooms* ⓧ *Breakfast.*

$$ | **Aqua Pacific Monarch.** Previously part of the Aston chain, this boutique
RENTAL | hotel, now operated by Aqua Hospitality, is located one block from west end of Waikiki Beach. **Pros:** fantastic view from rooftop pool; hospitality lounge; the on-site Jinroku Restaurant & Bar is good. **Cons:** stairs to the pool deck are fairly steep and may be difficult for some. ⑤ *Rooms from: $183* ☒ *2427 Kuhio Ave., Waikiki* ☎ *808/923–9805, 866/940–2782* ⊕ *www.aquaresorts.com* ↪ *216 units* ⓧ *No meals.*

$ | **Aqua Palms Waikiki.** Across from the Hilton Hawaiian Village on Ala
RENTAL | Moana Boulevard, just as it curves toward Waikiki's Kalakaua Avenue, the 12-story Aqua Palms completed a $15-million transformation into a "condotel" and now offers studio and luxury one-bedroom-suite accommodations. **Pros:** excellent full kitchens in suites; comfortable furnishings; trolley stop directly in front of hotel; free WiFi. **Cons:** closest beach access is through the Hilton Hawaiian Village across the street. ⑤ *Rooms from: $129* ☒ *1850 Ala Moana Blvd., Waikiki* ☎ *808/954–7424, 866/970–4165, 808/947–7256* ⊕ *www.aquapalms. com* ↪ *262 guest rooms, 5 suites* ⓧ *No meals.*

$$$ | **Aston at the Waikiki Banyan.** Families and active travelers love the con-
RENTAL | venience and action of this hotel, just a block from Waikiki Beach and
FAMILY | bustling Kalakaua Avenue. **Pros:** many rooms have great views; walking

BEST BETS FOR OAHU LODGING

Fodor's writers and editors have selected their favorite hotels, resorts, condos, vacation rentals, and B&Bs by price and experience. Fodor's Choice properties represent the "best of the best" across price categories. You can also search by area for excellent places to stay—check out our reviews on the following pages.

Fodor'sChoice★

Ala Moana Hotel, p. 263

Halekulani, p. 257

The Kahala Hotel & Resort, p. 263

Royal Hawaiian, p. 261

By Price

$

Aqua Aloha Surf Waikiki, p. 252

Aqua Palms Waikiki, p. 252

The Breakers, p. 256

Ke Iki Beach Bungalows, p. 265

Royal Grove Hotel, p. 261

Winston's Waikiki Condos, p. 262

$$

Aston Waikiki Beach Hotel, p. 262

The Equus Hotel, p. 257

Hilton Hawaiian Village Beach Resort and Spa, p. 258

Paradise Bay Resort, p. 263

$$$

Ala Moana Hotel, p. 263

Embassy Suites Waikiki Beach Walk, p. 257

Halekulani, p. 257

Waikiki Parc, p. 262

$$$$

JW Marriott Ihilani Resort & Spa, p. 266

The Kahala Hotel & Resort, p. 263

Marriott Ko Olina Beach Vacation Club, p. 266

Moana Surfrider, p. 259

Outrigger Reef on the Beach, p. 260

The Royal Hawaiian, p. 261

By Experience

MOST KID-FRIENDLY

Aqua Aloha Surf Waikiki, $, p. 252

Aston Waikiki Beach Hotel, $$, p. 262

Embassy Suites Waikiki Beach Walk, $$$, p. 257

Hilton Hawaiian Village Beach Resort and Spa, $$, p. 258

Marriott Ko Olina Beach Vacation Club, $$$$, p. 266

BEST FOR ROMANCE

Halekulani, $$$, p. 257

JW Marriott Ihilani Resort & Spa, $$$$, p. 266

The Kahala Hotel & Resort, $$$$, p. 263

Moana Surfrider, $$$$, p. 259

The Royal Hawaiian, $$$$, p. 261

BEST HOTEL BAR

Hilton Hawaiian Village Beach Resort and Spa, $$, p. 258

JW Marriott Ihilani Resort & Spa, $$$$, p. 266

Moana Surfrider, $$$$, p. 259

Outrigger Waikiki on the Beach, $$$$, p. 260

The Royal Hawaiian, $$$$, p. 261

BEST SPA

Halekulani, $$$, p. 257

Hilton Hawaiian Village Beach Resort and Spa, $$, p. 258

JW Marriott Ihilani Resort & Spa, $$$$, p. 266

The Kahala Hotel & Resort, $$$$, p. 263

Waikiki Beach Marriott Resort & Spa, $$$$, p. 262

BEST B&BS & INNS

Diamond Head Bed and Breakfast, $, p. 257

Ke Iki Beach Bungalows $, p. 265

Paradise Bay Resort, $$, p. 263

BEST BEACH

JW Marriott Ihilani Resort and Spa, $$$$, p. 266

The Kahala Hotel & Resort, $$$$, p. 263

Marriott Ko Olina Beach Vacation Club, $$$$, p. 266

Moana Surfrider, $$$$, p. 259

The Turtle Bay Resort, $$$, p. 265

9

WHERE TO STAY ON OAHU

Neighborhood	Local Vibe	Pros	Cons
Honolulu	Lodging options are limited in downtown Honolulu, but if you want an urban feel or to be near Chinatown, look no farther.	Access to a wide selection of art galleries, boutiques, and new restaurants as well as Chinatown.	No beaches within walking distance. If you're looking to get away from it all, this is not the place.
Waikiki	Lodgings abound in Waikiki, from youth hostels to five-star accommodations. The area is always abuzz with activity and anything you desire is within walking distance.	You can surf in front of the hotels, wander miles of beach, and explore hundreds of restaurants and bars.	This is tourist central. Prices are high, and you are not going to get the true Hawaii experience.
Windward Oahu	More in tune with the local experience, here is where you'll find most of the island's B&Bs and enjoy the lush side of Oahu.	From beautiful vistas and green jungles, this side really captures the tropical paradise most people envision when dreaming of a Hawaiian vacation.	The lushness comes at a price—it rains a lot on this side. Also, luxury is not the specialty here; if you are looking to get pampered, stay elsewhere.
The North Shore	This is true country living, with one luxurious resort exception. It's bustling in the winter (when the surf is up) but pretty slow-paced in the summer.	Amazing surf and long stretches of sand truly epitomize the beach culture in Hawaii. Historic Haleiwa has enough stores to keep shopaholics busy.	There is no middle ground for accommodations; you're either in backpacker cabanas or $300-a-night suites. There is also zero nightlife, and traffic can get heavy during winter months.
West (Leeward) Oahu	This is the resort side of the rock; there is little outside of these resorts, but plenty on the grounds to keep you occupied for a week.	Ko Olina's lagoons offer the most kid-friendly swimming on the island, and the golf courses on this side are magnificent. Rare is the rainy day out here.	You are isolated from the rest of Oahu, with little in the way of shopping or jungle hikes.

distance to shops and restaurants. **Cons:** trekking to the beach (a block away) with all of your gear; no on-site restaurant. $ *Rooms from: $331* ⊠ *201 Ohua Ave., Waikiki* ☎ *808/922–0555, 877/997–6667* ⊕ *www. astonwaikikibanyan.com* ⇱ *876 units* ⏐❂⏐ *No meals.*

$$
HOTEL
FAMILY
⊟ **Aston Waikiki Beach Hotel.** A good choice for families, this large hotel is directly across the street from a protected stretch of Kuhio Beach and near Kapiolani Park. **Pros:** fun for families; great beach access. **Cons:** active lobby area and crowded elevators; no self-parking. $ *Rooms from: $229* ⊠ *2570 Kalakaua Ave., Waikiki* ☎ *808/922– 2511, 877/997–6667, 800/877–7666* ⊕ *www.astonwaikikibeach.com* ⇱ *645 rooms, 40 suites* ⏐❂⏐ *Breakfast.*

$$$$
RENTAL
⊟ **Aston Waikiki Beach Tower.** You'll find the elegance of a luxury all-suites condominium combined with the intimacy and service of a boutique

Where to Stay in Waikiki

Aqua Aloha Surf Waikiki **20**
Aqua Pacific Monarch **32**
Aqua Palms Waikiki **5**
Aqua Waikiki Joy **18**
Aston Waikiki Sunset **38**
Aston at the
Waikiki Banyan **37**
Aston Waikiki Beach **40**

Aston Waikiki
Beach Tower **36**
Aston Waikiki Circle **34**
The Breakers **9**
Castle Waikiki Shore **12**
Coconut Waikiki Hotel **17**
Diamond Head B&B **41**
Doubletree Alana Waikiki ..**6**

Embassy Suites
Waikiki Beach Walk **10**
The Equus Hotel **2**
Halekulani **14**
Hawaii Prince Hotel **1**
Hilton Hawaiian Village **7**
Hilton Waikiki Beach Hotel .**35**
Holiday Inn Waikiki
Beachcomber **23**

Hyatt Regency Waikiki **31**
Ilikai Hotel & Suites **4**
Ilima Hotel **21**
Luana Waikiki **8**
Moana Surfrider **30**
The Modern Honolulu **3**
Ohana Waikiki East **28**
Ohana Waikiki Malia **19**

Ohana Waikiki West **26**
Outrigger Reef
on the Beach **13**
Outrigger Waikiki
on the Beach **25**
Royal Grove Hotel **33**
The Royal Hawaiian **24**
Sheraton Princess
Kaiulani **29**

Sheraton Waikiki **16**
Trump International
Waikiki Beach Walk **11**
Waikiki Beach Marriott **39**
Waikiki Parc **15**
Waikiki Sand Villa **27**
Winston's Waikiki Condos ..**22**

hotel right on bustling Kalakaua Avenue. **Pros:** *very* large rooms— big enough to move into. **Cons:** no on-site restaurants; you must cross a busy street to the beach. ⑤ *Rooms from: $499 ✉ 2470 Kalakaua Ave., Waikiki ☎ 877/997–6667 ⊕ www. astonwaikikibeachtower.com ↪ 140 units ⦿ No meals.*

$ **Aston Waikiki Circle Hotel.** This
HOTEL unusual 14-story circular hotel—built to resemble a Chinese lantern—is a Waikiki landmark, though the rooms are small, with tiny bathrooms with showers only. **Pros:** unbeatable location and views; on-site surfboard lockers and complimentary beach gear. **Cons:** small rooms; interior design, though charming to some, may feel dated to others. ⑤ *Rooms from: $151 ✉ 2464 Kalakaua Ave., Waikiki ☎ 808/923–1571, 877/997–6667 ⊕ www.astonwaikikicircle.com ↪ 104 rooms ⦿ No meals.*

$ **Aqua Waikiki Joy Hotel.** A trellised open-air lobby of Italian marble,
HOTEL a koi pond, and a guava smoothie greet you on arrival at this Lewers Street hideaway, now run by Aqua Hospitality, about a five-minute stroll from Kalakaua Avenue and through one of the many public-access ways to the beach. **Pros:** a bit of old Waikiki; rooms are spotless; attentive staff; karaoke lounge in the lobby. **Cons:** rooms are slightly dated; valet parking only. ⑤ *Rooms from: $175 ✉ 320 Lewers St., Waikiki ☎ 808/923–2300, 866/767–4528, 808/441–7781 ⊕ www. aquawaikikijoy.com ↪ 50 rooms, 44 suites ⦿ Breakfast.*

$$ **Aston Waikiki Sunset.** This 38-story high-rise condominium resort is
RENTAL near Diamond Head, one block from Waikiki Beach and on the city's bus line. **Pros:** spectacular views; in-room Wi-Fi; heated swimming pool; lots to do within walking distance. **Cons:** noise from outdoor activities can be a distraction. ⑤ *Rooms from: $227 ✉ 229 Paoakalani Ave., Waikiki ☎ 808/922–0511, 877/997–6667 ⊕ www.astonwaikikisunset. com ↪ 435 units ⦿ No meals.*

$ **The Breakers.** Despite an explosion of high-rise construction all around
RENTAL it, the low-rise Breakers continues to offer a taste of 1960s Hawaii in this small complex a mere half block from Waikiki Beach. **Pros:** intimate atmosphere; great location. **Cons:** a bit worn down; parking space is limited though free. ⑤ *Rooms from: $140 ✉ 250 Beach Walk, Waikiki ☎ 808/923–3181, 800/426–0494 ⊕ www.breakers-hawaii.com ↪ 64 units ⦿ No meals.*

$$$ **Castle Waikiki Shore.** Nestled between Fort DeRussy Beach Park and
RENTAL the Outrigger Reef on the Beach, this is the only condo hotel directly on Waikiki Beach. **Pros:** great security; great views; great management; free high-speed Wi-Fi available in rooms. **Cons:** beach out front is kind of thin; two-night stay minimum; no on-site dining. ⑤ *Rooms from: $270 ✉ 2161 Kalia Rd., Waikiki ☎ 808/952–4500, 800/367–5004 ⊕ www. castleresorts.com/Home/accommodations/waikiki-shore ↪ 168 units.*

$ **Coconut Waikiki Hotel.** Overlooking the Ala Wai Canal, this reasonably
HOTEL priced boutique hotel is more residential than a typical resort, with a

cobblestone driveway, a lobby with rattan living room–style furnishings, a wall of French doors that open up to a gazebo garden, and a tiny swimming pool tucked in a backyard. **Pros:** a small and economical hotel in Waikiki; free Wi-Fi throughout hotel; coin-operated laundry on site. **Cons:** the walk through busy Waikiki gets tiring when you're carrying all of your beach equipment; valet-only parking. $ *Rooms from: $129 ⊠ 450 Lewers St., Waikiki ☎ 866/974–2626, 808/923–8828 ⊕ www.jdvhotels.com ➔ 81 rooms ⦿ Breakfast.*

$
B&B/INN

📷 **Diamond Head Bed and Breakfast.** Many travelers and residents would love to own a home like this art-filled B&B at the base of Waikiki's famous Diamond Head crater, one of the city's most exclusive neighborhoods; however, there are only three rooms available, so you may have to work a bit to stay here. **Pros:** secluded and peaceful; very homey. **Cons:** small and therefore difficult to book; doesn't accept credit cards; no air-conditioning. $ *Rooms from: $130 ⊠ 3240 Noela Dr., Waikiki ☎ 808/923–3360, 800/262–9912 reservations ⊕ www.diamondheadbnb.com ➔ 2 rooms, 1 suite ☰ No credit cards ⦿ Breakfast.*

$$
HOTEL

📷 **Doubletree Alana Waikiki.** Its location—a 10-minute walk from the Hawaii Convention Center—and its 24-hour business center and gym meet the requirements of the Doubletree's global business clientele. **Pros:** free Wi-Fi in lobby; professional staff; pleasant public spaces; walk-in glass showers with oversize rain showerheads. **Cons:** it's a 10-minute walk to the beach. $ *Rooms from: $209 ⊠ 1956 Ala Moana Blvd., Waikiki ☎ 808/941–7275 ⊕ doubletree3.hilton.com ➔ 317 rooms ⦿ No meals.*

$$$
RESORT
FAMILY

📷 **Embassy Suites Waikiki Beach Walk.** In a place where space is at a premium, the only all-suites resort in Hawaii offers families and groups traveling together a bit more room to move about, with two 21-story towers housing one- and two-bedroom suites. **Pros:** great location next to Waikiki Beach Walk and all of its shops and restaurants; great vibe; nice pool deck; complimentary hot breakfast served daily. **Cons:** no direct beach access. $ *Rooms from: $319 ⊠ 201 Beachwalk St., Waikiki ☎ 800/362–2779, 808/921–2345 ⊕ www.embassysuiteswaikiki.com ➔ 300 1-bedroom suites, 69 2-bedroom suites ⦿ Breakfast.*

$$
HOTEL

📷 **The Equus Hotel.** This small hotel has been completely renovated with a Hawaiian country theme that pays tribute to Hawaii's polo-playing history. **Pros:** casual; fun atmosphere; attentive staff; nicely furnished rooms. **Cons:** on a very busy road you must cross to get to the beach. $ *Rooms from: $190 ⊠ 1696 Ala Moana Blvd., Waikiki ☎ 808/949–0061, 800/669–7719 ⊕ www.equushotel.com ➔ 66 rooms, 1 suite ⦿ No meals.*

$$$
RESORT
Fodor's Choice
★

📷 **Halekulani.** The luxurious Halekulani exemplifies the translation of its name—the "house befitting heaven"—and from the moment you step into the lobby, the attention to detail and impeccable service wrap you in privilege at this beachfront location away from Waikiki's bustle. **Pros:** location on small (private-feeling) beach; heavenly interior spaces; wonderful dining opportunities in-house; world-class service; artsy perks. **Cons:** might feel a bit formal for Waikiki; pricey. $ *Rooms from: $500*

9

✉ *2199 Kalia Rd., Waikiki* ☎ *808/923–2311, 800/367–2343* ⊕ *www. halekulani.com* ⇆ *411 rooms, 43 suites* ⦿| *No meals.*

$$$$
HOTEL
⛝ **Hawaii Prince Hotel & Golf Club Waikiki.** This slim high-rise with 538 oceanfront rooms including 57 luxury suites fronts Ala Wai Yacht Harbor at the *ewa* (west) edge of Waikiki. **Pros:** fantastic views; all very elegant; easy exit from complicated-to-maneuver Waikiki; smoking and non-smoking rooms available. **Cons:** no free Internet; no beach access. ⑤ *Rooms from: $415* ✉ *100 Holomoana St., Waikiki* ☎ *888/977–4623, 808/956–1111* ⊕ *www.hawaiiprincehotel.com* ⇆ *481 rooms, 57 suites* ⦿| *No meals.*

$$
RESORT
FAMILY
⛝ **Hilton Hawaiian Village Beach Resort and Spa.** Location, location, location: this megaresort and convention destination sprawls over 22 acres on Waikiki's widest stretch of beach, with the green lawns of neighboring Fort DeRussy creating a buffer zone to the high-rise lineup of central Waikiki. **Pros:** activities and amenities can keep you and the kids busy for weeks; stellar spa. **Cons:** ongoing renovations and construction noise might be a problem; oceanfront rooms in the Rainbow Tower may have obstructed views as the hotel is repairing its famous mural; size of property can be overwhelming; the hotel charges a resort fee of $30 (plus tax) per room, per night. ⑤ *Rooms from: $239* ✉ *2005 Kalia Rd., Waikiki* ☎ *808/949–4321, 800/774–1500* ⊕ *www. hiltonhawaiianvillage.com* ⇆ *3,616 rooms, 244 suites, 639 condominiums* ⦿| *No meals.*

$$
HOTEL
⛝ **Hilton Waikiki Beach Hotel.** Two blocks from Kuhio Beach, this 37-story high-rise, located on the Diamond Head end of Waikiki, is great for travelers who want to be near the action, but not right in it. **Pros:** good value; central location; very helpful staff; pleasant, comfortable public spaces. **Cons:** a bit of a distance to the beach; very few rooms with views. ⑤ *Rooms from: $219* ✉ *2500 Kuhio Ave., Waikiki* ☎ *808/922–0811, 888/370–0980* ⊕ *www3.hilton.com* ⇆ *601 rooms, 8 suites* ⦿| *No meals.*

$$$
HOTEL
FAMILY
⛝ **Holiday Inn Waikiki Beachcomber Resort.** Located almost directly across from the upgraded Royal Hawaiian Center, next door to the International Marketplace, and 300 steps from the beach, the Holiday Inn is a well-situated family-friendly hotel. **Pros:** lots of freebies; in the thick of Waikiki action. **Cons:** very busy area; no direct beach access; no on-site cultural activities. ⑤ *Rooms from: $319* ✉ *2300 Kalakaua Ave., Waikiki* ☎ *808/922–4646, 877/317–5756* ⊕ *www.waikikibeachcomberresort. com* ⇆ *491 rooms, 5 suites* ⦿| *No meals.*

$$$
RESORT
FAMILY
⛝ **Hyatt Regency Waikiki Resort and Spa.** Though it's across the street from Kuhio Beach, the Hyatt is actually considered oceanfront, as there's no resort between it and the Pacific Ocean. **Pros:** public spaces are open; elegant and very professional spa; kid-friendly; close to the beach. **Cons:** in a very busy and crowded part of Waikiki; on-site pool is quite small; can feel a bit like you're staying in a shopping mall. ⑤ *Rooms from: $300* ✉ *Hyatt Regency Waikiki Resort and Spa, 2424 Kalakaua Ave., Waikiki* ☎ *808/923–1234, 800/633–7313* ⊕ *www.hyattregencywaikiki. com* ⇆ *1,230 rooms, 18 suites* ⦿| *No meals.*

$$$$
RESORT
⛝ **Ilikai Hotel and Suites.** At the *ewa* (west) edge of Waikiki overlooking the Ala Wai Small Boat Harbor, this high-rise resort has both standard

rooms and units with full kitchens, which can save you some money if you dine in occasionally. **Pros:** views of sunset from most rooms on the *ewa* (west) side; comfortable beds; central location. **Cons:** very slow elevators; in need of renovations. ⑤ *Rooms from: $400* ✉ *1777 Ala Moana Blvd., Waikiki* ☎ *808/949–3811, 866/406–2782* ⊕ *www.ilikaihotel.com* ↝ *728 rooms, 51 suites* ☝☉ *No meals.*

ASK FOR A LANAI

Islanders love their porches, balconies, and verandas—all wrapped up in a single Hawaiian word: lanai. You may not want to look at a parking lot, so when booking, ask about the lanai and be sure to specify the view (understanding that top views command top dollars). Also, check that the lanai is not merely a step-out or Juliet balcony, with just enough room to lean against a railing—you want a lanai that is big enough for patio seating.

$$
RENTAL
☝ **Ilima Hotel.** Tucked away on a residential side street near Waikiki's Ala Wai Canal, this locally owned 17-story condominium-style hotel is a gem. **Pros:** big rooms are great for families; free parking in Waikiki is a rarity; on-site coin-operated laundry facilities; smoking rooms available. **Cons:** limited hotel parking, and street parking can be difficult to find; not the most luxurious accommodations; 10-minute walk to the beach. ⑤ *Rooms from: $215* ✉ *Ilima Hotel, 445 Nohonani St., Waikiki* ☎ *808/923–1877, 800/801–9366* ⊕ *www.ilima.com* ↝ *99 units* ☝☉ *No meals.*

$$$
HOTEL
☝ **Luana Waikiki.** At the entrance to Waikiki near Fort DeRussy is this welcoming hotel offering both rooms and condominium units, and in January 2014 it came under the umbrella of Aqua Hospitality. **Pros:** on-site full service spa; sundeck with barbecue grills (rare for Waikiki); walking distance to shops and restaurants; on-site coin-operated laundry; free Wi-Fi. **Cons:** no direct beach access. ⑤ *Rooms from: $265* ✉ *2045 Kalakaua Ave., Waikiki* ☎ *808/955–6000, 866/940–2782* ⊕ *www.aqualuanawaikiki.com* ↝ *225 units* ☝☉ *No meals.*

$$$$
RESORT
☝ **Moana Surfrider, A Westin Resort & Spa.** Outrageous rates of $1.50 per night were the talk of the town when the "First Lady of Waikiki" opened her doors in 1901; today, this historic beauty—the oldest hotel in Waikiki—is still a wedding and honeymoon favorite with a sweeping main staircase and period furnishings in its historic Moana wing. **Pros:** elegant; historic property; best place on Waikiki Beach to watch hula and have a drink; can't beat the location. **Cons:** you'll likely dodge bridal parties in the lobby; the hotel now charges a mindboggling resort fee of $31.41 per room, per day. ⑤ *Rooms from: $570* ✉ *2365 Kalakaua Ave., Waikiki* ☎ *808/922–3111, 866/500–8313* ⊕ *www.moanasurfrider.com* ↝ *750 rooms, 46 suites* ☝☉ *No meals.*

$$$$
HOTEL
☝ **The Modern Honolulu.** Gen Xers will immediately feel at home in this edgy hotel with an eye to slick design. **Pros:** excellent design; unpretentious feel; great bars and restaurants; nice spa. **Cons:** not kid-friendly; on the outer edge of Waikiki; direct beach access a five-minute walk away. ⑤ *Rooms from: $450* ✉ *1775 Ala Moana Blvd., Waikiki* ☎ *808/943–5800, 866/970–4161* ⊕ *www.themodernhonolulu.com* ↝ *353 rooms; 30 suites* ☝☉ *No meals.*

9

$$$ ⌕ **Ohana Waikiki East.** If you want
HOTEL   to be in central Waikiki and don't
want to pay beachfront lodging
prices, consider the Ohana Waikiki
East. **Pros:** close to the beach and
reasonable rates; decent on-site eat-
eries, including a piano bar. **Cons:**
some rooms with no lanai; very
basic public spaces. ⑤ *Rooms from:
$279* ✉ *150 Kaiulani Ave., Waikiki*
📞 *808/922–5353, 866/956–4262*
⊕ *www.ohanahotelsoahu.com/
ohana_east/* ↪ *403 rooms, 38
suites* ⍥ *No meals.*

$$ ⌕ **Ohana Waikiki Malia.** Close to
HOTEL   the *ewa* (west) end of Waikiki,
this older hotel comprises a pair
of buildings, one with standard
rooms, the other with one-bedroom
suites that have kitchenettes. **Pros:**
central to shopping and dining
in Waikiki; on-site coin-operated

laundry facilities. **Cons:** views not much to speak of. ⑤ *Rooms from:
$259* ✉ *2211 Kuhio Ave., Waikiki* 📞 *808/923–7621, 866/956–4262*
⊕ *www.ohanahotelsoahu.com/ohana_waikiki_malia/* ↪ *285 rooms,
47 suites* ⍥ *No meals.*

$$ ⌕ **Ohana Waikiki West.** This economical hotel offers a third-floor pool
HOTEL   and sundeck overlooking all the action of busy Kuhio Avenue. **Pros:**
clean rooms; centrally located. **Cons:** no bathtubs; a walk to the beach.
⑤ *Rooms from: $209* ✉ *2330 Kuhio Ave., Waikiki* 📞 *808/922–5022,
866/956–4262* ⊕ *www.ohanahotels.com* ↪ *645 rooms, 16 suites*
⍥ *No meals.*

$$$$ ⌕ **Outrigger Reef on the Beach.** Multimillion-dollar renovations have
HOTEL   drastically updated this beachfront property, adding a new entrance
FAMILY   that incorporates a Hawaiian voyaging design theme; expanded guest
rooms; larger and more contemporary bathrooms; and a new signature
restaurant—the poolside Kani Ka Pila Grille, with nightly live music
by legendary Hawaiian entertainers—though the Shore Bird Restau-
rant & Beach Bar and Ocean House Restaurant also remain. **Pros:** no
resort fees; on beach; direct access to Waikiki Beach Walk. **Cons:** views
from non-oceanfront rooms are uninspiring; can be pricey. ⑤ *Rooms
from: $489* ✉ *2169 Kalia Rd., Waikiki* 📞 *808/923–3111, 866/956–
4262* ⊕ *www.outriggerreef-onthebeach.com* ↪ *631 rooms, 38 suites*
⍥ *No meals.*

$$$$ ⌕ **Outrigger Waikiki on the Beach.** Renovated in 2012, this star of Out-
RESORT   rigger Hotels & Resorts sits on one of the finest strands of Waikiki
Beach. **Pros:** no resort fee; the best bar on the beach is downstairs; free
Wi-Fi in lobby; on-site coin-operated laundry. **Cons:** the lobby feels
a bit like an airport with so many people using it as a throughway
to the beach. ⑤ *Rooms from: $489* ✉ *2335 Kalakaua Ave., Waikiki*

☎ *808/923–0711, 808/956–4262* ⊕ *www.outriggerwaikikihotel.com* ↪ *479 rooms, 30 suites* ⦿ *No meals.*

LOOKING FOR A PRIVATE BEACH?

The Royal Hawaiian Hotel and Moana Surfrider—the two oldest hotels on Oahu—are the only hotels in Waikiki with property lines that extend out into the sand. They have created private roped-off beach areas that can be accessed only by hotel guests. The areas are adjacent to the hotel properties at the top of the beach.

$ **Royal Grove Hotel.** Two genera-
HOTEL tions of the Fong family have put their heart and soul into the operation of this tiny (by Waikiki standards), pink six-story hotel that feels like a throwback to the days of boarding houses, where rooms were outfitted for function, not style, and served up with a wealth of home-style hospitality at a price that didn't break the bank. **Pros:** very economical Waikiki option; lots of character. **Cons:** no air-conditioning in some rooms; rooms are dated; no on-site parking. ⑤ *Rooms from: $70* ✉ *151 Uluniu Ave., Waikiki* ☎ *808/923–7691* ⊕ *www.royalgrovehotel.com* ↪ *80 rooms, 7 suites* ⦿ *No meals.*

$$$$ **The Royal Hawaiian, a Luxury Collection Resort.** There's nothing like
RESORT the legendary Pink Palace of the Pacific, and an $85 million face-lift
Fodor'sChoice in 2009, the iconic hotel set on 14 acres of prime Waikiki Beach is a
★ unique blend of luxury and tradition. **Pros:** can't be beat for history; mai tais and sunsets are amazing; there's a doctors-on-call service. **Cons:** history is not cheap; you'd better like pink; resort fee of $36.65 per room per day. ⑤ *Rooms from: $765* ✉ *2259 Kalakaua Ave., Waikiki* ☎ *808/923–7311, 866/716–8110* ⊕ *www.royal-hawaiian.com* ↪ *495 rooms, 33 suites* ⦿ *No meals.*

$$$ **Sheraton Princess Kaiulani.** This hotel sits across the street from its
HOTEL upscale sister property, the Moana Surfrider. **Pros:** in the heart of everything in Waikiki; on-site surfboard storage (for a fee). **Cons:** no direct beach access; kids' activities off-site; pool closes early; no spa; hotel charges a resort fee of $26.18 tax inclusive, per room per day. ⑤ *Rooms from: $310* ✉ *120 Kaiulani Ave., Waikiki* ☎ *808/922–5811, 866/716–8109* ⊕ *www.princess-kaiulani.com* ↪ *1,142 rooms, 14 suites* ⦿ *No meals.*

$$$$ **Sheraton Waikiki.** If you don't mind crowds, this could be the place for
HOTEL you: towering over its neighbors on the prow of Waikiki's famous sands, the enormous Sheraton Waikiki is center stage on Waikiki Beach. **Pros:** location in the heart of everything. **Cons:** busy atmosphere clashes with laid-back Hawaiian style. ⑤ *Rooms from: $515* ✉ *2255 Kalakaua Ave., Waikiki* ☎ *808/922–4422, 866/716–8109* ⊕ *www.sheraton-waikiki.com* ↪ *1,634 rooms and suites* ⦿ *No meals.*

$$$$ **Trump International Hotel Waikiki Beach Walk.** One of the chicest hotels
HOTEL on the Waikiki scene, Trump has been drawing rave reviews since its opening in November 2009. **Pros:** beautifully appointed rooms; on the edge of Waikiki so a bit quieter; great views of Friday fireworks. **Cons:** must cross street to reach the beach; pricey. ⑤ *Rooms from: $509* ✉ *223 Saratoga Rd., Waikiki* ☎ *808/683–7777, 877/683–7401*

9

⊕ *www.trumphotelcollection.com/waikiki/* ➷ *305 rooms, 127 suites* ⦿ *No meals.*

$$$$
RESORT

⊞ **Waikiki Beach Marriott Resort & Spa.** On the eastern edge of Waikiki, this flagship Marriott sits on about 5 acres across from Kuhio Beach and close to Kapiolani Park, the Honolulu Zoo, and Waikiki Aquarium. **Pros:** stunning views of Waikiki; professional service; airy

tropical public spaces; unbeatable location. **Cons:** large impersonal hotel; Kalakaua Avenue can be noisy. ⑤ *Rooms from: $390* ✉ *2552 Kalakaua Ave., Waikiki* ☎ *808/922–6611, 800/367–5370* ⊕ *www.marriottwaikiki.com* ➷ *1,175 rooms, 135 suites* ⦿ *No meals.*

$$$
HOTEL

⊞ **Waikiki Parc.** In contrast to the stately vintage-Hawaiian elegance of her sister hotel, the Halekulani, the Waikiki Parc makes a contemporary statement, offering the same attention to detail in service and architectural design but lacking the beachfront location and higher prices. **Pros:** modern; great access to Waikiki Beach Walk. **Cons:** no direct beach access. ⑤ *Rooms from: $285* ✉ *2233 Helumoa Rd., Waikiki* ☎ *808/921–7272, 800/422–0450* ⊕ *www.waikikiparc.com* ➷ *297 rooms* ⦿ *No meals.*

$
HOTEL

⊞ **Waikiki Sand Villa.** Families and those looking for an economical rate without sacrificing proximity to Waikiki's beaches, dining, and shopping return to the Waikiki Sand Villa year after year. **Pros:** fun bar; fitness center; economical choice. **Cons:** the noise from the bar might annoy some; 10-minute walk to the beach. ⑤ *Rooms from: $165* ✉ *2375 Ala Wai Blvd., Waikiki* ☎ *808/922–4744, 800/247–1903* ⊕ *www.sandvillahotel.com* ➷ *214 rooms* ⦿ *No meals.*

$
RENTAL

⊞ **Winston's Waikiki Condos.** This five-story condominium complex specializing in monthly rates is just off Kuhio Avenue near the International Marketplace and two blocks from Waikiki Beach. **Pros:** the owner is a slice of 1960s Hawaii; suites are all unique; careful attention to details. **Cons:** not many suites; credit cards not accepted for payment (only to hold reservations); two blocks from the beach; parking not available at the condo and can be pricey elsewhere. ⑤ *Rooms from: $79* ✉ *417 Nohonani St., Waikiki* ☎ *808/924–3332, 800/545–1948* ⊕ *www.winstonswaikikicondos.com* ➷ *10 units* ⦿ *No meals.*

DOWNTOWN HONOLULU

$$
HOTEL

⊞ **Aston at the Executive Centre Hotel.** Downtown Honolulu's only hotel is an all-suites high-rise in the center of the business district, within walking distance of the historic Capitol District, museums and Honolulu's Chinatown and a 10-minute drive from Honolulu International Airport. **Pros:** central to downtown businesses, transportation, and sights; great restaurant—Hukilau—in the lobby. **Cons:** no beach within walking distance; area businesses shut down early on weekdays and usually close on weekends; parking is very expensive. ⑤ *Rooms from: $260* ✉ *1088*

Bishop St., Downtown Honolulu ☎ *808/539–3000, 877/997–6667* ⊕ *www.astonhotels.com* 🛏 *116 suites* ᴼⅼ *Breakfast.*

ALA MOANA

$$$
HOTEL
Fodor'sChoice
★

🖵 **Ala Moana Hotel.** A great value in a pricey hotel market, this well located and nicely appointed hotel is connected to Oahu's largest mall, the Ala Moana Center, by a pedestrian ramp, and is a 10-minute walk to Waikiki. **Pros:** great value; adjacent to Ala Moana Center and all of its shops and restaurants; rooms nicely appointed; quick walk to the beach. **Cons:** outside the heartbeat of Waikiki; not right on the beach; large, impersonal hotel. ⑤ *Rooms from: $289* ✉ *410 Atkinson Dr., Ala Moana* ☎ *808/955–4811, 866/956–4262* ⊕ *www.alamoanahotelhonolulu.com* 🛏 *1,090 studios, 44 suites* ᴼⅼ *No meals.*

> ### CONDO COMFORTS
>
> The local **Foodland** (✉ Market City, 2939 Harding Ave., near intersection with Kapahulu Ave. and highway overpass, Kaimuki ☎ 808/734–6303 ✉ Ala Moana Center, 1450 Ala Moana Blvd., ground level, Ala Moana ☎ 808/949–5044) grocery-store chain has two locations near Waikiki. A smaller version of larger Foodland, **Food Pantry** (✉ 2370 Kuhio Ave., across from Miramar hotel, Waikiki ☎ 808/923–9831) also has apparel, beach stuff, and tourist-oriented items.

KAHALA

$$$$
RESORT
Fodor'sChoice
★

🖵 **The Kahala Hotel & Resort.** Hidden away in the upscale residential neighborhood of Kahala (on the other side of Diamond Head from Waikiki), this elegant oceanfront hotel has played host to celebrities, princesses, the Dalai Lama, and nearly every president since Lyndon Johnson as one of Hawaii's very first luxury resorts. **Pros:** away from hectic Waikiki; beautiful rooms and public spaces; heavenly spa; pet-friendly. **Cons:** Waikiki is a drive away. ⑤ *Rooms from: $495* ✉ *5000 Kahala Ave., Kahala* ☎ *808/739–8888, 800/367–2525* ⊕ *www.kahalaresort.com* 🛏 *306 rooms, 32 suites* ᴼⅼ *No meals.*

WINDWARD OAHU

$$
B&B/INN

🖵 **Paradise Bay Resort.** If you're looking for an alternative to staying in Waikiki and you aren't fussy about amenities, consider Paradise Bay Resort, located 30 minutes from both Waikiki and the North Shore. **Pros:** great views of Kaneohe Bay; cooler temps on this side of the island; pet-friendly. **Cons:** not all units are beside the bay; rental car is a necessity. ⑤ *Rooms from: $195* ✉ *47-039 Lihikai Dr., Kaneohe* ☎ *800/735–5071, 808/239–5711* ⊕ *www.paradisebayresort.com* 🛏 *57 units* ᴼⅼ *Breakfast.*

Condotels

One popular alternative in vacation lodging is a hybrid that encompasses aspects of both the condominium vacation rental and the full-service hotel. Today, many people invest in hotel condominium units as vacation homes and then rent them out when they are not in residence.

Unlike many single-family condos, these units can be rented out easily and require less maintenance, since the units are managed by hotel companies. Condotels give both owners and renters the spaciousness, convenience, and privacy of a vacation home along with the amenities of full-service hotel resorts. Just consider the possibilities: amenities can include pre-arrival grocery-delivery service, daily maid service, a newspaper at your doorstep each morning, Wi-Fi, DVD entertainment systems, big flat-screen TVs, and in-room massage and spa treatments. Concierges can assist with restaurant reservations, sightseeing tours, and car rentals.

No longer is it just you, your condo, and a swimming pool. At many of these properties, you have access to golf courses, tennis courts, horse stables, hot tubs, spas, and fitness centers. Forget mere barbecue pits—you may have access to private cabanas, where you can dine with a view. You can do your laundry on property, or even in your own unit's washer and dryer, or send it out. There's typically 24-hour front-desk and business services, if you just can't keep the office at bay.

Consider what your needs are in terms of location, size of unit, bedding, family desires, amenities, architectural style, and character. Ask about views, private lanai, the complex's family-friendly vibe, and proximity to the beach.

Since condotel units have individual owners and are rented out through management companies, inquire when booking about furniture and decor standards. Some units are individually furnished and decorated while others are defined by the condotel management. Also inquire as to bedding configurations. Will you be sleeping in regular beds or on a pullout sofa? If your unit has a kitchen or kitchenette, consider which appliances and equipment you need. Some kitchens come furnished with as little as a tiny microwave and mini-refrigerator, but fancy full-service ones might contain convection ovens, wine coolers, dishwashers, and wet bars.

Many of Waikiki's older hotels are enjoying resurgences as they've been transformed into hotel condominiums.

THE NORTH SHORE

$ **Backpackers Vacation Inn and Plantation Village.** Laid-back Haleiwa
B&B/INN surfer chic at its best, Backpackers is spartan in furnishings, rustic in amenities, and definitely very casual in spirit. **Pros:** friendly, laid-back staff who can offer recommendations; prices you won't find anywhere else. **Cons:** many rooms are plainly furnished. $ *Rooms from: $62* ⊠ *59-788 Kamehameha Hwy., Haleiwa* ☎ *808/638-7838* ⊕ *www.backpackers-hawaii.com* ⤳ *25 rooms* ⦿ *No meals.*

9

$ ⊞ **Ke Iki Beach Bungalows.** At this 1½-acre sloped beachfront lot with
RENTAL   six duplex bungalows, you can choose from studios to one- or two-
bedroom units outfitted with breezy beach-house furnishings, individual
grills, hammocks and picnic tables, and access to a 200-foot strand of
sugary white-sand beach running between the North Shore's famous
Waimea Bay and Ehukai Beach (Banzai Pipeline). **Pros:** helpful and
friendly staff; great prices; steps to the beach. **Cons:** a bit far from
restaurants and shopping. ⑤ *Rooms from: $135* ⊠ *59-579 Ke Iki Rd.,
Haleiwa* ☎ *808/638–8829, 866/638–8829* ⊕ *www.keikibeach.com*
↳ *11 units* ⦿ *No meals.*

$$$ ⊞ **The Turtle Bay Resort.** Sprawling over 880 acres of natural landscape
RESORT   on the edge of Kuilima Point in Kahuku, the Turtle Bay Resort boasts
spacious guest rooms averaging nearly 500 square feet, with lanai that
showcase stunning peninsula views. **Pros:** great open, public spaces
in a secluded area of Oahu; beautiful two-level spa. **Cons:** renovation
work planned for 2014 may cause disruptions; very far from anything
else—even Haleiwa is a 20-minute drive; hotel charges a $25 per night
resort fee. ⑤ *Rooms from: $289* ⊠ *57-091 Kamehameha Hwy., Box
187, Kahuku* ☎ *808/293–6000, 800/203–3650, 866/827–5321 reser-
vations* ⊕ *www.turtlebayresort.com* ↳ *397 rooms, 40 suites, 42 beach
cottages, 56 ocean villas* ⦿ *No meals.*

WEST (LEEWARD) OAHU

$$$$
RESORT
FAMILY

🛏 **Aulani, A Disney Resort & Spa.** In September 2011, Disney opened its first property in Hawaii, an elaborate, full-service complex in the resort area of Ko Olina about a 40-minute drive from Waikiki on Oahu's leeward side. **Pros:** tons to do on premise; very kid-friendly; a 1,500-square-foot teens-only spa with a private entrance, yogurt bar, and teen-specific treatments. **Cons:** a long way from Waikiki; "character breakfasts" are often sold

WORD OF MOUTH

"I would suggest you stay up at the North Shore for a few nights and then maybe spend a few nights in lovely Kailua, or vice versa depending on the availability. You can drive from Kailua up the leeward side to North Shore in about an hour if you decided to just stay down there." —Tomsd

out. $ *Rooms from: $480* ✉ *92-1185 Aliinui Dr., Ko Olina, Kapolei* ☎ *714/520–7001, 808/674–6200, 866/443–4763* ⊕ *resorts.disney.go.com/aulani-hawaii-resort* ⟿ *359 rooms, 16 suites, 481 villas* ⏍ *No meals.*

$$$$
RESORT

🛏 **JW Marriott Ihilani Resort & Spa.** Forty-five minutes and a world away from the bustle of Waikiki, this sleek, 17-story resort anchors the Ko Olina Resort and Marina on Oahu's Leeward coastline. **Pros:** beautiful property; impeccable service; pool is stunning at night. **Cons:** a bit of a drive from Honolulu; rental car a must; there's a daily resort fee of $25. $ *Rooms from: $545* ✉ *92-1001 Olani St., Ko Olina, Kapolei* ☎ *808/679–0079, 800/626–4446* ⊕ *www.ihilani.com* ⟿ *351 rooms, 36 suites* ⏍ *No meals.*

$$$$
RENTAL
FAMILY

🛏 **Marriott Ko Olina Beach Vacation Club.** Though primarily a time-share property, Marriott Ko Olina also offers nightly rentals, which range from hotel-style standard guest rooms to expansive and elegantly appointed one- or two-bedroom guest villa apartments. **Pros:** suites are beautifully decorated and have ample space for families; full kitchens; nice views; fairly private lagoon; on-site weekly Polynesian dinner show. **Cons:** at least a half-hour drive to Honolulu $ *Rooms from: $349* ✉ *92-161 Waipahe Pl., Ko Olina, Kapolei* ☎ *808/679–4700, 800/307–7312* ⊕ *www.marriottvacationclub.com* ⟿ *544 units* ⏍ *No meals.*

TRAVEL SMART
OAHU

GETTING HERE AND AROUND

Visitors to Oahu can navigate by orienting themselves to a few major landmarks. Oahu is made up of two extinct volcanoes, which form the island's two mountain ranges: Waianae and Koolau. The Waianae range curves from Kaena State Park, on the island's westernmost point, past Makaha, Waianae, and Nanakuli to Ko Olina on the sunny leeward shore. The extinct craters of Diamond Head and Koko Head are usually visible from anywhere along the island's leeward coast. The Koolau Range forms a jagged spine that runs from the island's eastern tip along the windward coast to the famous surfing center on the North Shore.

▌AIR TRAVEL

Flying time to Oahu is about 10 hours from New York, 8 hours from Chicago, and 5 hours from Los Angeles.

All of the major airline carriers serving Hawaii fly direct to Honolulu; some also offer nonstops to Maui, Kauai, and the Big Island, though most flights to the latter two come from the west coast only. Honolulu International Airport, although open-air and seemingly more casual than most major airports, can be very busy. Allow extra travel time during busy mornings and afternoons.

Plants and plant products are subject to regulation by the Department of Agriculture, both on entering and leaving Hawaii. Upon leaving, you'll have to have your bags x-rayed and tagged at the airport's agricultural inspection station before you proceed to check-in. Pineapples and coconuts with the packer's agricultural inspection stamp pass freely; papayas must be treated, inspected, and stamped. All other fruits are banned for export to the U.S. mainland. Flowers pass except for gardenia, rose leaves, jade vine, and mauna loa. Also banned are insects, snails, soil, cotton, cacti, sugarcane, and all berry plants.

Bringing your dog or cat with you is a tricky process and not something to be done lightly. Hawaii is a rabies-free state and requires animals to pass strict quarantine rules, which you can find online at ⊕ hdoa.hawaii.gov/ai/aqs/. Most airlines do not allow pets to travel in the cabin on flights to Hawaii (though Alaska Airlines and Hawaiian Airlines are notable exceptions). If specific pre- and post-arrival requirements are met, most animals qualify for a five-day-or-less quarantine.

Airline Security Issues Transportation Security Administration ☏ 808/831–2755 ⊕ www.tsa.gov.

Air-Travel Resources in Oahu State of Hawaii Airports Division Offices ☏ 808/836–6413 ⊕ www.hidot.hawaii.gov/airports.

AIRPORTS

Honolulu International Airport (HNL) is 20 minutes (9 miles) west of Waikiki, and is served by most of the major domestic and international carriers. To travel to other islands from Honolulu, you can depart from either the interisland terminal or the commuter-airline terminal, located in two separate structures adjacent to the main overseas terminal building. A free Wiki-Wiki shuttle bus operates between terminals.

Airport Information Honolulu International Airport (HNL) ☏ 808/836–6413 ⊕ hawaii.gov/hnl.

GROUND TRANSPORTATION

Some hotels have their own pickup and drop-off service, though it may be for a fee, so check when you book accommodations.

Taxi service is available on the center median just outside baggage-claim areas. Look for the taxi dispatchers wearing green shirts, who will radio for a taxi. The fare to Waikiki runs approximately $35 to $40, plus 35¢ per bag, and tip, with a maximum of four passengers. An oversize baggage fee may apply.

Another option is to take a private shuttle service like Roberts Hawaii. The company will greet you at the arrival gate, escort you to baggage claim, and take you to your hotel. Call ahead for the service, which costs $13 per person for one-way service, $24 round-trip.

TheBus, the municipal bus, will take you into Waikiki for only $2.50, but you are allowed only one bag, which must fit on your lap.

Contacts Roberts Hawaii ☎ 808/539–9400 ⊕ www.robertshawaii.com. **TheBus** ☎ 808/848-5555 ⊕ www.thebus.org.

FLIGHTS FROM THE U.S. MAINLAND

From the U.S. mainland, Alaska Airlines, American, Delta, Hawaiian, US Airways, and United serve Honolulu.

Contacts Alaska Airlines ☎ 800/252-7522 ⊕ www.alaskaair.com. **American Airlines** ☎ 800/433-7300 ⊕ www.aa.com. **Continental Airlines** ☎ 800/523-3273 for U.S. and Mexico reservations, 800/231-0856 for international reservations ⊕ www.continental.com. **Delta Airlines** ☎ 800/221-1212 for U.S. reservations, 800/241-4141 for international reservations ⊕ www.delta.com. **Hawaiian Airlines** ☎ 800/367-5320 ⊕ www.hawaiianairlines.com. **United Airlines** ☎ 800/864-8331 for U.S. reservations, 800/538-2929 for international reservations ⊕ www.united.com. **US Airways** ☎ 800/428-4322 ⊕ www.usairways.com.

CHARTER FLIGHTS

Two bigger companies provide charter flights between the Islands. go! Airlines offers nonstop charter service from Oahu to Lanai and Maui. The company also serves the Big Island, Kauai, and Molokai. Mokulele Airlines, once merged with go!, also operates its own charter flights depending on the time of year and how busy commercial flight schedules are.

Contacts go! Airlines ☎ 888/435-9462 ⊕ www.iflygo.com. **Pacific Wings** ☎ 888/575-4546 ⊕ www.pacificwings.com.

INTERISLAND FLIGHTS

If you've allotted more than a week for your vacation, you may want to consider visiting one of the other Hawaiian Islands. From Honolulu, flights depart almost hourly from early morning until evening. Since each flight lasts only 30 to 60 minutes, you can watch the sunrise on Oahu and sunset on the Big Island, Kauai, Lanai, Maui, or Molokai. To simplify your vacation, schedule your return flight to Oahu so that it coincides with your flight home.

In addition to Hawaiian Airlines (see ⇨ Flights from the U.S. Mainland) and go! Airlines (see ⇨ Charter Flights), Island Air and Mokulele Airlines operate regular service between the Islands, so be sure to compare prices. All have frequent-flyer programs that entitle you to rewards and upgrades. A number of wholesalers offer Neighbor Islands packages including air, hotel, rental car, and even visitor attractions or activities.

Interisland Flights Mokulele Airlines ☎ 866/260-7070 ⊕ www.mokuleleairlines.com. **IslandAir** ☎ 800/652-6541 ⊕ www.islandair.com.

■ BOAT TRAVEL

FERRIES

No ferries serve Oahu at this writing or offer interisland transportation from Oahu.

CRUISES

For information about cruises, see Chapter 1, Experience Oahu.

When Pan Am's amphibious *Hawaii Clipper* touched down on Pearl Harbor's waters in 1936, it marked the beginning of the end of regular passenger-ship travel to the Islands. From that point on, the predominant means of transporting visitors would be by air, not by sea. Today, however, cruising to Hawaii is a delightful way to experience the beauty and majesty of the Pacific Ocean and Hawaiian Islands. While several major cruise lines offer seasonal cruises to and from the Hawaiian Islands, only Norwegian Cruise Line offers interisland cruises from Honolulu aboard its ship *Pride of America*.

Contacts Norwegian Cruise Line ☎ *866/234–7050* ⊕ *www.ncl.com.*

■ BUS TRAVEL

Getting around by bus is an affordable option on Oahu, particularly in the most heavily touristed areas of Waikiki. In addition to TheBus and the Waikiki Trolley, Waikiki has brightly painted private buses, many of them free, that shuttle you to such commercial attractions as dinner cruises, garment factories, and the like.

You can travel around the island or just down Kalakaua Avenue for $2.50 on Honolulu's municipal transportation system, affectionately known as TheBus. It's one of the island's best bargains. Buses make stops in Waikiki every 10 to 15 minutes to take passengers to nearby shopping areas.

You're entitled to one free transfer, so ask for one when boarding. Exact change is required, and dollar bills are accepted. A four-day pass for visitors costs $35 and is available at ABC convenience stores in Waikiki and in the Ala Moana Shopping Center. Monthly passes cost $60.

The company's website has timetables, route maps, and real-time bus tracking, or you can download the free DaBus app for your smartphone. You also can find privately published booklets at most drugstores and other convenience outlets. The important route numbers for Waikiki are 2, 8, 13,19, 20, and 42. If you venture farther afield, you can always travel back on one of these buses.

The Waikiki Trolley has three lines and dozens of stops that allow you to plan your own itinerary while riding on brass-trimmed, open-air buses that look like trolleys. The Historic Honolulu Sightseeing Tour (Red Line) travels between Waikiki and downtown Honolulu and includes stops at Aloha Tower, Ala Moana Shopping Center, and the State Capitol and Iolani Palace. The Waikiki/Ala Moana Shopping Shuttle (Pink Line) runs from the DFS Galleria Waikiki to Ala Moana and back, stopping at various Waikiki locations. The Scenic Diamond Head Sightseeing Tour runs through Waikiki and down around Diamond Head. A one-day pass costs $18 to $32, four-day passes are $54, and seven-day passes are $59. There are often money-saving online deals.

Contacts TheBus ☎ *808/848–5555* ⊕ *www.thebus.org.* **Waikiki Trolley** ☎ *808/593–2822* ⊕ *www.waikikitrolley.com.*

■ CAR TRAVEL

Except for one area around Kaena Point, major highways follow Oahu's shoreline and traverse the island at two points. Rush-hour traffic (6:30 to 9:30 am and 3:30 to 6 pm) can be frustrating around Honolulu and the outlying areas. Winter swells also bring traffic to the North Shore, as people hoping to catch some of the surfing action clog the two-lane Kamehameha Highway. Parking along many streets is curtailed during these times, and tow-away zones are strictly enforced. Read curbside signs before leaving your vehicle, even at a meter.

Asking for directions will almost always produce a helpful explanation from the locals, but you should be prepared for an island term or two. Instead of using compass directions, remember that Hawaii residents refer to places as being either *mauka* (toward the mountains) or *makai* (toward the ocean). Other directions depend on your location: in Honolulu, for example, people say to "go Diamond Head," which means toward that famous landmark, or to "go *ewa*," meaning in the opposite direction. A shop on the *mauka*–Diamond Head corner of a street is on the mountain side of the street on the corner closest to Diamond Head. It all makes perfect sense once you get the lay of the land.

GASOLINE

Gasoline is almost always more expensive on Oahu than on the U.S. mainland.

ROAD CONDITIONS

Oahu is relatively easy to navigate. Roads, although their names are often a challenge for the tongue, are well marked; just watch out for the many one-way streets in Waikiki and downtown Honolulu. Keep an eye open for the Hawaii Visitors and Convention Bureau's red-caped King Kamehameha signs, which mark major attractions and scenic spots. Ask for a map at the car-rental counter. Free publications containing helpful maps are found at most hotels throughout Waikiki.

ROADSIDE EMERGENCIES

In case of an accident, pull over if you can. If you have a cell phone, call the roadside assistance number on your car-rental contract or AAA Help. If your car has been broken into or stolen, report it immediately to your rental-car company. If it's an emergency and someone is hurt, call 911 immediately.

Contacts **AAA Help** ☎ *800/222-4357* ⊕ *www.hawaii.aaa.com.*

RULES OF THE ROAD

Be sure to buckle up, as Hawaii has a strictly enforced mandatory seat-belt law for front- and backseat passengers. Children under four must be in a car seat (available from car-rental agencies), and children ages four to seven must be seated in a rear booster seat or child restraint such as a lap and shoulder belt. Hawaii also prohibits texting or talking on the phone (unless you are over 18 and using a hands-free device) while driving. The highway speed limit is usually 55 mph. In-town traffic moves from 25 to 40 mph. Jaywalking is not uncommon, so watch for pedestrians, especially in congested areas such as Waikiki and downtown Honolulu. Unauthorized use of a parking space reserved for persons with disabilities can net you a $250 to $500 fine.

Oahu's drivers are generally courteous, and you rarely hear a horn. People will slow down and let you into traffic with a wave of the hand. A friendly wave back is customary. If a driver sticks a hand out the window in a fist with the thumb and pinky sticking straight out, this is a good thing: it's the *shaka*, the Hawaiian symbol for "hang loose," and is often used to say "thanks."

CAR RENTALS

Hotel parking garages charge upwards of $20 per day, so if you're staying in Waikiki you may want to rent a car only when you plan to sightsee around the island. You can easily walk or take public transportation to many of the attractions in and around the area.

If you are staying outside Waikiki, your best bet is to rent a car. Even though the city bus is a wonderfully affordable way to get around the island, you'll want the flexibility of having your own transportation, especially if you're planning lots of stops.

■TIP➜ Make sure that a confirmed reservation guarantees you a car. Agencies sometimes overbook, particularly for busy weekends and holiday periods.

You can rent anything from an econobox and motorcycle to a Ferrari while on Oahu. Rates are usually better if you reserve through a rental agency's website. It's wise to make reservations far in advance, especially if visiting during peak seasons.

Rates in Honolulu begin at about $25 a day for an economy car with air-conditioning, automatic transmission, and unlimited mileage. This does not include the airport concession fee, general excise tax, rental-vehicle surcharge, or vehicle-license fee. When you reserve a car, ask about cancellation penalties and drop-off charges, should you plan to pick up the car in one location and return it to another. Many rental companies offer coupons for discounts at various attrac-

Car Rental Resources

Automobile Associations		
AAA	☎ 800736–2886	⊕ www.aaa.com
National Automobile Club	☎ 650/294–7000	⊕ www.thenac.com (CA residents only)
Major Agencies		
Alamo	☎ 800/462–5266	⊕ www.alamo.com
Avis	☎ 800/331–1212	⊕ www.avis.com
Budget	☎ 800/527–0700	⊕ www.budget.com
Hertz	☎ 800/654–3131	⊕ www.hertz.com
National Car Rental	☎ 800/227–7368	⊕ www.nationalcar.com
Thrifty Car Rental	☎ 888/400–8877	⊕ www.thrifty.com

tions that could save you money later on in your trip.

In Hawaii you must be 21 years of age to rent a car, and you must have a valid driver's license and a major credit card. Those under 25 will pay a daily surcharge of $10 to $25. Request car seats and extras such as GPS when you make your reservation. Hawaii's Child Restraint Law requires that all children three years and younger be in an approved child safety seat in the backseat of a vehicle. Children ages four to seven must be seated in a rear booster seat or child restraint such as a lap and shoulder belt. Car seats and boosters range from $11 to $12 a day with a cap of $60 per rental.

In Hawaii your unexpired mainland driver's license is valid for rental for up to 90 days.

Be sure to allow plenty of time to return your vehicle so that you can make your flight. Traffic in Honolulu is terrible during morning and afternoon rush hours. Give yourself about 3½ to 4 hours before departure time to return your vehicle if you're traveling during these peak times; otherwise plan on about 2½ to 3 hours.

▌TAXI TRAVEL

Taxis can be found at the airport, in the more popular resort areas, or by calling local taxi companies. Rates are $3.10 at the drop of the flag and each additional mile is $3.20. Drivers are generally courteous and the cars are in good condition; many of them air-conditioned. In addition, taxi and limousine companies can provide a car and driver for half-day or daylong island tours, and a number of companies also offer personal guides. Remember, however, that rates are quite steep for these services, ranging from $100 to $200 or more per day.

Contacts TheCAB Hawaii ☎ *808/422–2222* ⊕ *www.thecabhawaii.com.* **Carey Hawaii Chauffeured Services** ☎ *888/405–1792, 800/336–4646* ⊕ *www.carey.com/Carey/ cities/US/Hawaii.* **Charley's Taxi & Limousine** ☎ *808/233–3333* ⊕ *www.charleystaxi.com.* **Elite Limousine Service** ☎ *800/776–2098, 808/735–2431* ⊕ *www.elitelimohawaii.com.*

ESSENTIALS

■ BUSINESS SERVICES AND FACILITIES

The Hawaii Convention Center, located at the entrance to Waikiki, is a gorgeous facility that captures the spirit of Hawaii through its open-air spaces, tropical gardens, and soaring forms that resemble Polynesian canoes. The center also boasts a $2-million art collection featuring the work of dozens of local artists. The Hawaii Visitors & Convention Bureau's website has a directory of products and services.

Contacts Hawaii Convention Center ✉ *1801 Kalakaua Ave., Waikiki, Honolulu* ☎ *808/943–3500* ⊕ *www.hawaiiconvention. com.*

■ COMMUNICATIONS

INTERNET

Most of the major hotels and resorts offer high-speed access in rooms and lobbies. Check with your hotel in advance to confirm that access is wireless; if not, ask whether in-room cables are provided. In some cases there will be an hourly or daily charge. If you're staying at a small inn or B&B that doesn't have Internet access, ask about the nearest café or coffee shop that does.

Contacts Cybercafes. Cybercafes lists more than 4,000 Internet cafés worldwide. ⊕ *www. cybercafes.com.* **JiWire.** JiWire features a directory of Wi-Fi hotspots around the world. ⊕ *v4.jiwire.com/search-hotspot-locations.htm.*

■ EMERGENCIES

To reach the police, fire department, or an ambulance in an emergency, dial 911.

A doctor, laboratory-radiology technician, and nurses are always on duty at Doctors on Call. Appointments are not necessary. Dozens of medical insurance plans are accepted, including Medicare, Medicaid, and most kinds of travel insurance.

Kuhio Pharmacy is Waikiki's only pharmacy and handles prescriptions Monday through Saturday until 7 pm (it's closed on Sunday). Longs Drugs is open evenings at its Ala Moana location and 24 hours at its South King Street location (a 15-minute drive from Waikiki). Pillbox Pharmacy, located in Kaimuki, will deliver prescription medications for a small fee.

Doctors and Dentists Doctors on Call ✉ *Sheraton Princess Kaiulani Hotel, 120 Kaiulani Ave., Waikiki, Honolulu* ☎ *808/971–6000.*

General Emergency Contacts Coast Guard Rescue Center ☎ *808/842–2600.*

Hospitals and Clinics Castle Medical Center ✉ *640 Ulukahiki St., Kailua* ☎ *808/263–5500* ⊕ *castlemed.org.* **Kapiolani Medical Center for Women and Children** ✉ *1319 Punahou St., Makiki Heights, Honolulu* ☎ *808/983–6000.* **Queen's Medical Center** ✉ *1301 Punchbowl St., Downtown Honolulu, Honolulu* ☎ *808/538–9011.* **Straub Clinic** ✉ *888 S. King St., Downtown Honolulu, Honolulu* ☎ *808/522–4000.*

Pharmacies Longs Drugs ✉ *Ala Moana Shopping Center, 1450 Ala Moana Blvd., 2nd level, near the Ewa wing expansion, Ala Moana, Honolulu* ☎ *808/949–4010* ✉ *2470 S. King St., Moiliili, Honolulu* ☎ *808/947–2651.* **Kuhio Pharmacy** ✉ *1922 Kalakaua Ave., between McCully St. and Niu St., Waikiki, Honolulu* ☎ *808/942–1922 Kalakaua location* ⊕ *www.kuhiopharmacy.com* ✉ *Ohana Waikiki West Hotel, 2330 Kuhio Ave., Waikiki, Honolulu* ☎ *808/923–4466.* **Pillbox Pharmacy** ✉ *1133 11th Ave., Kaimuki, Honolulu* ☎ *808/737–1777.*

■ HEALTH

Hawaii is known not only as the Aloha State, but also as the Health State. The life expectancy here is 81.2 years, the longest in the nation. Balmy weather makes it easy to remain active year-round, and the low-stress attitude contributes to the general well-being. When visiting the Islands, however, there are a few health issues to keep in mind.

The Hawaii State Department of Health recommends that you drink 16 ounces of water per hour to avoid dehydration when hiking or spending time in the sun. Use sunblock, wear UV–reflective sunglasses, and protect your head with a visor or hat. If you're not acclimated to warm, humid weather, you should allow plenty of time for rest stops and refreshments. When visiting freshwater streams, be aware of the tropical disease leptospirosis, spread by animal urine and carried into streams and mud. Symptoms include fever, headache, nausea, and red eyes. If left untreated it can cause liver and kidney damage, respiratory failure, internal bleeding, and even death. To avoid this, don't swim or wade in freshwater streams or ponds if you have open sores and don't drink from any freshwater streams or ponds.

On the Islands, fog is a rare occurrence, but there can often be "vog," an airborne haze of gases released from volcanic vents on the Big Island. During certain weather conditions, such as "Kona Winds," the vog can settle over the Islands and wreak havoc with respiratory and other health conditions, especially asthma or emphysema. If susceptible, stay indoors and get emergency assistance if needed.

The Islands have their share of insects. Most are harmless but annoying. When planning to spend time outdoors in hiking areas, wear long-sleeve clothing and pants and use mosquito repellent containing DEET. In damp places you may encounter the dreaded local centipedes, which are brown and blue and measure up to eight inches long. Their painful sting is similar to those of bees and wasps. When camping, shake out your sleeping bag and check your shoes, as the centipedes like cozy places. When hiking in remote areas, always carry a first-aid kit.

▍ HOURS OF OPERATION

Even people in paradise have to work. Generally local business hours are weekdays 8 to 5. Banks are usually open Monday to Thursday 8:30 to 4 and until 6 on Friday. Some banks have Saturday-morning hours.

Many self-serve gas stations stay open around the clock, with full-service stations usually open from around 7 am until 9 pm. U.S. post offices generally are open weekdays 8:30 or 9 to 4:30 or 5 and Saturday 8:30 or 9 to noon or 2. On Oahu, the Ala Moana post office is the only branch, other than the main Honolulu International Airport facility, that stays open until 4:15 pm on Saturday.

Most museums generally open their doors between 9 and 10 and stay open until 5 Tuesday to Saturday. Many museums operate with afternoon hours only on Sunday and close on Monday. Visitor-attraction hours vary, but most sights are open daily with the exception of major holidays such as Christmas. Check the local newspaper upon arrival for attraction hours and schedules if visiting over holiday periods. The local daily carries a listing of "What's Open/What's Not" for those time periods.

Stores in resort areas sometimes open as early as 8, with shopping-center opening hours varying from 9 to 10 on weekdays and Saturday, a bit later on Sunday. Bigger malls stay open until 9 weekdays and Saturday and close at 5 on Sunday. Boutiques in resort areas may stay open as late as 11.

▍ MONEY

Prices here are given for adults. Substantially reduced fees are almost always available for children, students, and senior citizens.

ATMS AND BANKS

ATMs, for easy access to cash, can be found at many locations throughout Oahu, including shopping centers, convenience and grocery stores, and hotels and resorts, as well as outside most bank branches.

CREDIT CARDS

It's a good idea to inform your credit-card company before you travel. Otherwise, the credit-card company might put a hold on your card owing to unusual activity—not a good thing halfway through your trip. Record all your credit-card numbers—as well as the phone numbers to call if your cards are lost or stolen—in a safe place, so you're prepared should something go wrong. Both MasterCard and Visa have general numbers you can call (collect if you're abroad) if your card is lost, but you're better off calling the number of your issuing bank, since MasterCard and Visa usually just transfer you to your bank; your bank's number is usually printed on your card.

Reporting Lost Cards American Express ☎ *800/528–4800 in the U.S.* ⊕ *www. americanexpress.com.* **Diners Club** ☎ *800/234–6377 in the U.S.* ⊕ *www. dinersclub.com.* **Discover** ☎ *800/347–2683 in the U.S.* ⊕ *www.discover.com.* **Master-Card** ☎ *800/627–8372 in the U.S.* ⊕ *www. mastercard.com.* **Visa** ☎ *800/847–2911 in the U.S.* ⊕ *www.visa.com.*

▌PACKING

Oahu is casual: sandals, bathing suits, and comfortable, informal clothing are the norm. In summer synthetic slacks and shirts, although easy to care for, can be uncomfortably warm.

There's a saying that when a man wears a suit during the day, he's either going for a loan or he's a lawyer trying a case. Only a few upscale restaurants require a jacket for dinner. The aloha shirt is accepted dress on Oahu for business and most social occasions. Shorts are acceptable daytime attire, along with a T-shirt or polo shirt. There's no need to buy expensive sandals on the mainland—here you can get flip-flops (locals call them slippers) for a couple of dollars and off-brand sandals for $20. Golfers should remember that many courses have dress codes requiring a collared shirt; call courses you're interested in for details. If you're not prepared, you can pick up appropriate clothing at resort pro shops. If you're visiting in winter or planning to visit a high-altitude area, bring a sweater or light- to medium-weight jacket. A polar fleece pullover is ideal, and makes a great impromptu pillow. If you're planning on doing any hiking, a good pair of boots is essential.

SHIPPING LUGGAGE AHEAD

Imagine globe-trotting with only a carry-on in tow. Shipping your luggage in advance via an air-freight service is a great way to cut down on backaches, hassles, and stress—especially if your packing list includes strollers, car seats, etc. There are some things to be aware of, though.

First, research carry-on restrictions; if you absolutely need something that isn't practical to ship and isn't allowed in carry-ons, this strategy isn't for you. Second, plan to send your bags several days in advance to U.S. destinations and as much as two weeks in advance to some international destinations. Third, plan to spend some money: it will cost at least $100 to send a small piece of luggage, surfboard, or a golf bag to a domestic destination, much more to places overseas.

Some people use Federal Express to ship their bags, but this can cost even more than air-freight services. All these services insure your bag (for most, the limit is $1,000, but you should verify that amount); you can, however, purchase additional insurance for about $1 per $100 of value.

Contacts Luggage Concierge ☎ *800/288–9818* ⊕ *www.luggageconcierge.com.* **Luggage Free** ☎ *800/361–6871* ⊕ *www.luggagefree. com.* **Luggage/Sports Express.** Luggage/ Sports Express ships luggage and sports equipment including golf clubs and surfboards. ☎ *800/357-4174* ⊕ *www.sportsexpress.com.*

▌ SAFETY

Oahu is generally a safe tourist destination, but it's still wise to follow the same common-sense safety precautions you would normally follow in your own hometown. Rental cars are magnets for break-ins, so don't leave any valuables in the car, not even in a locked trunk. Avoid poorly lighted areas, beach parks, and isolated areas after dark as a precaution. When hiking, stay on marked trails, no matter how alluring the temptation might be to stray. Weather conditions can cause landscapes to become muddy, slippery, and tenuous, so staying on marked trails will lessen the possibility of a fall or getting lost.

Women traveling alone are generally safe on the Islands, but always follow the safety precautions you would use in any major destination. When booking hotels, request rooms closer to the elevator, and always keep your hotel-room door and balcony doors locked. Stay away from isolated areas after dark; camping and hiking solo are not advised. If you stay out late visiting nightclubs and bars, use caution when exiting nightspots and returning to your lodging.

▌**TIP➔** Distribute your cash, credit cards, IDs, and other valuables between a deep front pocket, an inside jacket or vest pocket, and a hidden money pouch. Don't reach for the money pouch once you're in public.

Contact Transportation Security Administration (*TSA*). ⊕ *www.tsa.gov.*

▌ TAXES

Since 2010, there is a 9.25% tax added onto your hotel bill. A $3-per-day road tax is also assessed on each rental vehicle.

▌ TIME

Hawaii is on Hawaiian Standard Time, five hours behind New York, and two hours behind Los Angeles.

When the U.S. mainland is on daylight saving time, Hawaii is not, so add an extra hour of time difference between the Islands and U.S. mainland destinations. You may also find that things generally move more slowly here. That has nothing to do with your watch—it's just the laid-back way called Hawaiian time.

▌ TIPPING

As this is a major vacation destination and many of the people who work in the service industry rely on tips to supplement their wages, tipping is not only common, but expected.

TIPPING GUIDELINES FOR OAHU	
Bartender	$1 to $5 per round of drinks, depending on the number of drinks
Bellhop	$1 to $5 per bag, depending on the level of the hotel and whether you have bulky items like golf clubs and surfboards
Hotel Concierge	$5 or more, depending on the service
Hotel Doorman	$1 to $5 if s/he helps you get a cab or helps with bags, golf clubs, etc.
Hotel Maid	$1 to $3 a day (either daily or at the end of your stay, in cash)
Hotel Room-Service Waiter	$1 to $2 per delivery, even if a service charge has been added
Skycap at Airport	$1 to $3 per bag
Taxi Driver	15% to 20%, but round up the fare to the next dollar amount
Tour Guide	10% of the cost of the tour
Valet Parking Attendant	$1 to $3, each time your car is brought to you
Waiter	15% to 20%, with 20% being the norm at high-end restaurants; nothing additional if a service charge is added to the bill

TOURS

GUIDED TOURS

One way to manage several Hawaiian Islands on the same trip is to take a guided tour that includes all your travel arrangements in the Islands, including hotels, interisland transfers, and some sightseeing.

Globus has three Hawaii itineraries that include Oahu, one of which is an escorted cruise on Norwegian Cruise Line's *Pride of America* that includes four days on the island. Tauck and Trafalgar offer several land-based Hawaii itineraries that include nights on Oahu. Both companies offer similar itineraries with visits to the USS *Arizona* Memorial National Park and plenty of free time to explore the island. Tauck offers an 11-night "Best of Hawaii" itinerary. Highlights of the Oahu portion of the trip include a Waikiki outrigger canoe trip and a private dinner at Iolani Palace. Trafalgar has 7- to 12-night multi-island tours.

Atlas Cruises & Tours, sells more than a dozen Hawaii trips ranging from 8 to 13 days, operated by various guided tour companies including Globus, Tauck, and Trafalgar.

Contacts Atlas Cruises & Tours ☎ 800/942–3301 ⊕ www.atlastravelweb.com. **Globus** ☎ 866/755–8581 ⊕ www.globusjourneys.com. **Tauck Travel** ☎ 800/788–7885 ⊕ www.tauck. com. **Trafalgar** ☎ 866/544–4434 ⊕ www. trafalgar.com.

SPECIAL-INTEREST TOURS
BIRD-WATCHING

More than 150 species of birds live in the Hawaiian Islands. For about $4,575 per person double-occupancy, Field Guides has a three-island (Oahu, Kauai, and the Big Island), 10-day, guided bird-watching trip that includes accommodations, meals, ground transportation, and interisland air.

Victor Emanuel Nature Tours, the largest company in the world specializing in birding tours, has two nine-day "Fall Hawaii" and "Spring Hawaii" trips to

FODORS.COM CONNECTION

Before your trip, be sure to check out what other travelers are saying in "Travel Ratings" and "Talk" on www.fodors.com.

Oahu, Kauai, and the Big Island that cost around $3,895 and include accommodations, meals, interisland air, ground transportation, and guided excursions.

Contacts Field Guides ☎ 800/728–4953 ⊕ www.fieldguides.com. **Victor Emanuel Nature Tours** ☎ 800/328–8368 ⊕ www. ventbird.com.

CULTURE

Elderhostel, a nonprofit educational travel organization running tours under the name Road Scholar, offers several guided Hawaii tours for adults 50 and over that provide in-depth looks into the culture, history, and beauty of the Islands.

Contacts Road Scholar ☎ 800/454–5768 ⊕ www.roadscholar.org.

HIKING

Sierra Club Hawaii offers regular guided hiking tours, outings, botanical gardens visits, and cleanup and community service efforts on Oahu that you can join in on during your visit.

Contacts Sierra Club Hawaii ☎ 808/538–6616 ⊕ www.sierraclubhawaii.com.

TRIP INSURANCE

Comprehensive trip insurance is valuable if you're booking a very expensive or complicated trip (particularly to an isolated region) or if you're booking far in advance. Comprehensive policies typically cover trip cancellation and interruption, letting you cancel or cut your trip short because of illness, or, in some cases, acts of terrorism in your destination. Such policies might also cover evacuation and medical care. Some also cover you for trip delays because of bad weather or mechanical problems, as well as for lost or delayed luggage.

Another type of coverage to consider is financial default—that is, when your trip is disrupted because a tour operator, airline, or cruise line goes out of business. Generally you must buy this when you book your trip or shortly thereafter, and it's available to you only if your operator isn't on a list of excluded companies.

Always read the fine print of your policy to make sure that you're covered for the risks that most concern you. Compare several policies to be sure you're getting the best price and range of coverage available.

Insurance Comparison Info Insure My Trip ☎ 800/487-4722 ⊕ www.insuremytrip.com. **Square Mouth** ☎ 800/240-0369 ⊕ www. squaremouth.com.

Comprehensive Insurers Allianz Global Assistance ☎ 800/884-3556 ⊕ www. allianztravelinsurance.com/. **CSA Travel Protection** ☎ 800/711-1197 ⊕ www. csatravelprotection.com.**Travel Guard** ☎ 800/826-4919 ⊕ www.travelguard.com. **Travelex Insurance** ☎ 888/228-9792 ⊕ www.travelexinsurance.com. **Travel Insured**

International ☎ 800/243-3174 ⊕ www. travelinsured.com.

▌VISITOR INFORMATION

Before you go to Hawaii, contact the Oahu Visitors Bureau (OVB) for a free vacation planner and map. The OVB website has online listing of accommodations, activities and sports, attractions, dining venues, services, transportation, travel professionals, and wedding information. For general information on all of the Islands, contact the Hawaii Visitors & Convention Bureau. The HVCB website has a calendar of local events that will be taking place during your stay.

Contacts Hawaii Visitors & Convention Bureau ☎ 800/464-2924 for brochures ⊕ www.gohawaii.com. **Oahu Visitors Bureau** ☎ 877/525-6248 ⊕ www.gohawaii.com/oahu.

ONLINE RESOURCES
Contacts Hawaii Beach Safety ⊕ oceansafety.ancl.hawaii.edu. **Hawaii Department of Land and Natural Resources** ⊕ hawaii.gov/dlnr. **Hawaii Tourism Authority** ⊕ www.travelsmarthawaii.com.

HAWAIIAN VOCABULARY

Although an understanding of Hawaiian is by no means required on a trip to the Aloha State, a *malihini*, or newcomer, will find plenty of opportunities to pick up a few of the local words and phrases. Traditional names and expressions are widely used in the Islands. You're likely to read or hear at least a few words each day of your stay.

With a basic understanding and some uninhibited practice, anyone can have enough command of the local tongue to ask for directions and to order from a restaurant menu. One visitor announced she would not leave until she could pronounce the name of the state fish, the *humuhumunukunukuāpua'a*.

Simplifying the learning process is the fact that the Hawaiian language contains only eight consonants—H, K, L, M, N, P, W, and the silent *'okina*, or glottal stop, written '—plus one or more of the five vowels. All syllables, and therefore all words, end in a vowel. Each vowel, with the exception of a few diphthongized double vowels such as *au* (pronounced "ow") or *ai* (pronounced "eye"), is pronounced separately. Thus *'Iolani* is four syllables (ee-oh-la-nee), not three (yo-la-nee). Although some Hawaiian words have only vowels, most also contain some consonants, but consonants are never doubled.

Pronunciation is simple. Pronounce *A* "ah" as father; *E* "ay" as in weigh; *I* "ee" as in marine; *O* "oh" as in no; *U* "oo" as in true.

Consonants mirror their English equivalents, with the exception of W. When the letter begins any syllable other than the first one in a word, it is usually pronounced as a V. *'Awa*, the Polynesian drink, is pronounced "ava," *'ewa* is pronounced "eva."

Almost all long Hawaiian words are combinations of shorter words; they are not difficult to pronounce if you segment them. *Kalaniana'ole*, the highway running east from Honolulu, is easily understood as *Kalani ana 'ole*. Apply the standard pronunciation rules—the stress falls on the next-to-last syllable of most two- or three-syllable Hawaiian words—and Kalaniana'ole Highway is as easy to say as Main Street.

Now about that fish. Try *humu-humu nuku-nuku āpu a'a*.

The other unusual element in Hawaiian language is the *kahakō*, or macron, written as a short line (ˉ) placed over a vowel. Like the accent (´) in Spanish, the kahakō puts emphasis on a syllable that would normally not be stressed. The most familiar example is probably *Waikīkī*. With no macrons, the stress would fall on the middle syllable; with only one macron, on the last syllable, the stress would fall on the first and last syllables. Some words become plural with the addition of a macron, often on a syllable that would have been stressed anyway. No Hawaiian word becomes plural with the addition of an *s*, since that letter does not exist in the language.

What follows is a glossary of some of the most commonly used Hawaiian words. Hawaiian residents appreciate visitors who at least try to pick up the local language.

'a'ā: rough, crumbling lava, contrasting with *pāhoehoe*, which is smooth.

'ae: yes.

aikane: friend.

āina: land.

akamai: smart, clever, possessing savoir faire.

akua: god.

ala: a road, path, or trail.

ali'i: a Hawaiian chief, a member of the chiefly class.

aloha: love, affection, kindness; also a salutation meaning both greetings and farewell.

'ānuenue: rainbow.

'a'ole: no.

'apōpō: tomorrow.

'auwai: a ditch.

auwē: alas, woe is me!

'ehu: a red-haired Hawaiian.

'ewa: in the direction of 'Ewa plantation, west of Honolulu.

hala: the pandanus tree, whose leaves (*lau hala*) are used to make baskets and plaited mats.

hālau: school.

hale: a house.

hale pule: church, house of worship.

ha mea iki or **ha mea 'ole:** you're welcome.

hana: to work.

haole: ghost. Since the first foreigners were Caucasian, *haole* now means a Caucasian person.

hapa: a part, sometimes a half; often used as a short form of *hapa haole*, to mean a person who is part-Caucasian.

hau'oli: to rejoice. *Hau'oli Makahiki Hou* means Happy New Year. *Hau'oli lā hānau* means Happy Birthday.

heiau: an outdoor stone platform; an ancient Hawaiian place of worship.

holo: to run.

holoholo: to go for a walk, ride, or sail.

holokū: a long Hawaiian dress, somewhat fitted, with a yoke and a train. Influenced by European fashion, it was worn at court, and at least one local translates the word as "expensive mu'umu'u."

holomū: a post–World War II cross between a *holokū* and a mu'umu'u, less fitted than the former but less voluminous than the latter, and having no train.

honi: to kiss; a kiss. A phrase that some tourists may find useful, quoted from a popular hula, is *Honi Ka'ua Wikiwiki*: Kiss me quick!

honu: turtle.

ho'omalimali: flattery, a deceptive "line," bunk, baloney, hooey.

huhū: angry.

hui: a group, club, or assembly. A church may refer to its congregation as a *hui* and a social club may be called a *hui*.

hukilau: a seine; a communal fishing party in which everyone helps to drive the fish into a huge net, pull it in, and divide the catch.

hula: the dance of Hawai'i.

iki: little.

ipo: sweetheart.

ka: the. This is the definite article for most singular words; for plural nouns, the definite article is usually *nā*. Since there is no *s* in Hawaiian, the article may be your only clue that a noun is plural.

kahuna: a priest, doctor, or other trained person of old Hawai'i, endowed with special professional skills that often included prophecy or other supernatural powers; the plural form is kāhuna.

kai: the sea, saltwater.

kalo: the taro plant from whose root *poi* (paste) is made.

kamā'aina: literally, a child of the soil. It refers to people who were born in the Islands or have lived there for a long time.

kanaka: originally a man or humanity, it is now used to denote a male Hawaiian or part-Hawaiian, but is occasionally taken as a slur when used by non-Hawaiians. *Kanaka maoli,* originally a full-blooded Hawaiian person, is used by some Native Hawaiian rights activists to embrace part-Hawaiians as well.

kāne: a man, a husband. If you see this word on a door, it's the men's room. If you see *kane* on a door, it's probably a misspelling; that is the Hawaiian name for the skin fungus tinea.

kapa: also called by its Tahitian name, *tapa,* a cloth made of beaten bark and usually dyed and stamped with a repeat design.

kapakahi: crooked, cockeyed, uneven. You've got your hat on *kapakahi*.

kapu: keep out, prohibited. This is the Hawaiian version of the more widely known Tongan word *tabu* (taboo).

kapuna: grandparent; elder.

kēia lā: today.

keiki: a child; *keikikāne* is a boy, *keiki-wahine* a girl.

kona: the leeward side of the Islands, the direction (south) from which the *kona* wind and *kona* rain come.

kula: upland.

kuleana: a homestead or small plot of ground on which a family has been installed for some generations without necessarily owning it. By extension, *kuleana* is used to denote any area or department in which one has a special interest or prerogative. You'll hear it used this way: If you want to hire a surfboard, see Moki; that's his *kuleana*.

lā: sun.

lamalama: to fish with a torch.

lānai: a porch, a balcony, an outdoor living room. Almost every house in Hawai'i has one. Don't confuse this two-syllable word with the three-syllable name of the island, Lāna'i.

lani: heaven, the sky.

lau hala: the leaf of the *hala*, or pandanus tree, widely used in handicrafts.

lei: a garland of flowers.

limu: sun.

lolo: stupid.

luna: a plantation overseer or foreman.

mahalo: thank you.

makai: toward the ocean.

malihini: a newcomer to the Islands.

mana: the spiritual power that the Hawaiian believed inhabited all things and creatures.

manō: shark.

manuwahi: free, gratis.

mauka: toward the mountains.

mauna: mountain.

mele: a Hawaiian song or chant, often of epic proportions.

Mele Kalikimaka: Merry Christmas (a transliteration from the English phrase).

Menehune: a Hawaiian pixie. The *Menehune* were a legendary race of little people who accomplished prodigious work, such as building fishponds and temples in the course of a single night.

moana: the ocean.

mu'umu'u: the voluminous dress in which the missionaries enveloped Hawaiian women. Now made in bright printed cottons and silks, it is an indispensable garment. Culturally sensitive locals have embraced the Hawaiian spelling but often shorten the spoken word to "mu'u." Most English dictionaries include the spelling "muumuu."

nani: beautiful.

nui: big.

ohana: family.

'ono: delicious.

pāhoehoe: smooth, unbroken, satiny lava.

Pākē: Chinese. This *Pākē* carver makes beautiful things.

palapala: document, printed matter.

pali: a cliff, precipice.

pānini: prickly pear cactus.

paniolo: a Hawaiian cowboy, a rough transliteration of *español*, the language of the Islands' earliest cowboys.

pau: finished, done.

pilikia: trouble. The Hawaiian word is much more widely used here than its English equivalent.

puka: a hole.

pupule: crazy, like the celebrated Princess Pupule. This word has replaced its English equivalent in local usage.

pu'u: volcanic cinder cone.

waha: mouth.

wahine: a female, a woman, a wife, and a sign on the ladies' room door; the plural form is *wāhine*.

wai: freshwater, as opposed to saltwater, which is *kai*.

wailele: waterfall.

wikiwiki: to hurry, hurry up (since this is a reduplication of *wiki*, quick, neither *w* is pronounced as a *v*).

Note: Pidgin is the unofficial language of Hawai'i. It is a Creole language, with its own grammar, evolved from the mixture of English, Hawaiian, Japanese, Portuguese, and other languages spoken in 19th-century Hawai'i, and it is heard everywhere.

INDEX

PHOTO CREDITS

Front cover: Rick Doyle/Corbis [Description: Waimea Bay]. 1, santonius silaban/iStockphoto, 2, Eddy Galeotti/Shutterstock, 5, cunningham-photos.com. Chapter 1: Experience Oahu: 8-9, Grant Studios/ eStock Photo. 10 (top), Ken Ross/vies-tiphoto.com. 10 (bottom), Oahu Visitors Bureau. 11 (top left), Oahu Visitors Bureau. 11 (top right), Corbis. 11 (bottom), Michael S. Nolan/age fotostock. 13 (left and right), SuperStock/age fotostock. 16 (left), Douglas Peebles Photography/Alamy. 16 (top right), David Franzen/Doris Duke Foundation for Islamic Art. 16 (bottom center), Tor Johnson/Photo Resource Hawaii/Alamy. 16 (bottom right), Deborah Davis/Alamy. 17 (top left), Oahu Visitors Bureau. 17 (bottom left), David L. Moore/Alamy. 17 (right), Hawaii Tourism Authority (HTA)/Tor Johnson. 18 (left), Hawaii Tourism Authority (HTA)/Tor Johnson. 18 (top right), Ablestock.com/Thinkstock. 18 (bottom right), IMG_6266 by takaokun (http://www.flickr.com/photos/takaokun/5017244988/) (Attribution License). 19 (left), Hawaii Tourism Authority (HTA) / Tor Johnson. 19 (right), Photo Resource Hawaii/ Alamy. 23 (left), Oahu Visitors Bureau. 23 (right), Stephanie Horrocks/iStockphoto. 25, Tor Johnson/ Photo Resource Hawaii/Alamy. 27 (left), Corbis. 27 (right), Jay Spooner/iStockphoto. 29, Andre Seale / Alamy. 31 (left), Luca Tettoni/viestiphoto.com. 31 (right), SuperStock/age fotostock. 32, Jose Gil/ Shutterstock. 33 (left), Cheryl Casey/Shutterstock. 33 (right), Katja Govorushchenko/iStockphoto. 34, Oahu Visitors Bureau. 35 (left), Starwood Hotels & Resorts. 35 (right), Amanda Ostrom-Eckelbarger, Fodors.com member. 36, Ray Kachatorian/Starwood Hotels & Resorts. 37 (left), iStockphoto. 37 (right), muhawi001/Flickr, 38, Michael Brake/iStockphoto. Chapter 2: Exploring Oahu: 39, iStockphoto. 40, lmaronic/Shutterstock. 41, Tor Johnson/Photo Resource Hawaii/Alamy. 51, Library of Congress Prints & Photographs Division. 53 (top), Corbis. 53 (bottom), USS Arizona Memorial Photo Collection/NPS. 54, Army Signal Corps Collection in the U.S. National Archives. 54 (inset), USS Missouri Memorial Association. 55, USS Bowfin Submarine Museum & Park. 57, Doug- las Peebles/eStock Photo. 59, Ken Ross/viestiphoto.com. 66, David L. Moore/Alamy. 72, SIME/Giovanni Simeone/eStock Photo. 74, Corbis. 82, Kenny Williams/Alamy. 84, Blaine Harrington/age fotostock. 85, Pierre Tostee. 86 and 87, ASP Tostee. 88, cunninghamphotos. com. 92, Alan Seiden/Oahu Visitors Bureau. Chapter 3: Beaches: 95, J.D. Heaton/age fotostock. 96, Dhoxax/Shutterstock. 100, David Schrichte/Photo Resource Hawaii/Alamy. 103, 105, and 107. SuperStock/age fotostock. 109, Chuck Babbitt/iStock Photo. 111 and 112, Photo Resource Hawaii/Alamy. Chapter 4: Water Sports & Tours: 115, Dave Bjorn/ Photo Resource Hawaii/Alamy. 116, Kato Inowe/Shutterstock. 118 and 121, Photo Resource Hawaii/ Alamy. 126, Douglas Peebles/eStock Photo. 129, J.D. Heaton/age fotostock. 132, Photo Resource Hawaii/Alamy. 133, Ron Dahlquist/ HVCB. 134, SuperStock/age fotostock. 136 (top), SPrada/iStockphoto. 136 (bottom), Gert Vrey/iStockphoto. 137, sweetlifephotos/iStockphoto. 139, Photo Resource Hawaii/Alamy. 143, Karen Wilson/ASP Tostee. 145, Douglas Peebles/ eStock Photo. Chapter 5: Golf, Hiking & Outdoor Activities: 147, Photo Resource Hawaii/Alamy. 148, Preferred Hotel Group. 149, Blue Hawaiian Helicopters. 151, Jon McLean/Alamy. 153, Luca Tettoni/viestiphoto.com. 154, KauaI Visitors Bureau. 155, Jack Jeffrey. 160, Tor Johnson/Aurora Photos. 164, Photo Resource Hawaii/Alamy. Chapter 6: Shops & Spas: 169, Beauty Photo Studio/age fotostock. 170, The Leading Hotels of the World. 177 (top), Linda Ching/HVCB. 177 (bottom), Sri Maiava Rusden/ HVCB. 178, Michael Soo/ Alamy. 179 (top), leisofhawaii.com. 179 (2nd from top), kellyalexanderpho- tography.com. 179 (3rd, 4th, and 5th, from top), leisofhawaii.com. 179 (bottom), kellyalexanderpho- tography.com. Chapter 7: Entertainment & Nightlife: 189, Polynesian Cultural Center. 190, Jose Gil/Shutterstock. 192, Ann Cecil/ Photo Resource Hawaii/Alamy. 196, Hawaii Visitors & Convention Bureau. 197, Thinkstock LLC. 199, Hawaii Visitors & Convention Bureau. Chapter 8: Where to Eat: 207, David L. Moore/Alamy. 208, Joshua Rainey Photography/Shutterstock. 215, Polynesian Cultural Center. 216 (top), Douglas Peebles Photography. 216 (top center), Douglas Peebles Photography/Alamy. 216 (center), Dana Edmunds/Polynesian Cultural Center. 216 (bottom center), Douglas Peebles Photography/Alamy. 216 (bottom), Purcell Team/Alamy. 217 (top, top center, and bottom center), HTJ/HVCB. 217 (bottom), Oahu Visitors Bureau. Chapter 9: Where to Stay: 249, Waikiki Parc Hotel. 250, The Kahala. Back cover (from left to right): SergiyN/Shutterstock; Oahu Visitors Bureau/Shutterstock; David Franzen/ Doris Duke Foundation for Islamic Art. Spine: Bennyartist/Shutterstock.

ABOUT OUR WRITERS

James Cave is a writer, editor, and founder of the *Offsetter*, an arts and culture website in Honolulu. He has covered the arts, entertainment, and culture of Honolulu for publications such as the *Honolulu Weekly*, *HI Luxury*, *Waikiki Magazine*, and *Honolulu Magazine*. For this edition, James updated our Entertainment and Nightlife chapter.

Born and raised on Oahu, **Lesa Griffith** also spent childhood years in Ghana, the Congo, Jordan, and Indonesia—which she believes developed her no-flavors-barred palate. A freelance food writer, she lives in Honolulu and equally enjoys a good *laulau* (sprinkled with chili pepper water) and Iranian caviar. She updated Where to Eat for this book.

Trina Kudlacek fell in love with Hawaii while on vacation 20 years ago. She now has the best of all possible worlds as she splits her time between her home in Hawaii, where she is a lecturer at the University of Hawaii, and Italy, where she is a tour guide. For this edition, she updated Beaches, Water Sports and Tours, and Golf, Hiking, and Outdoor Activities.

U.K.-born **Chris Oliver** has been a resident of Oahu for 30 years. As a reporter and travel editor for *The Honolulu Advertiser* she wrote about the Hawaiian Islands, as well as national and international destinations, with an eye for what visitors would most enjoy on a visit to Hawaii. Coming from a different country, climate, and culture has given her an enthusiasm for the exotic. She currently edits a newsletter, writes for *Hawaii* magazine, and divides her time between Hawaii and the United Kingdom. She updated Shopping for this edition.

Born and raised on Oahu, **Catherine E. Toth** has worked as a newspaper reporter in Hawaii since 2004 and continues to freelance—in between surfing, hiking, and eating everything in sight—for such print and online publications as *Forbes Travel Guide*, *Alaska Airlines Magazine*, *HAWAII*, and *Modern Luxury Hawaii*. For this edition, she updated Where to Stay and Spas.

Writer and multimedia journalist **Anna Weaver** is a sixth-generation *kamaaina*, born and raised in Kailua, Oahu, when it was a bit sleepier than it is now that the president takes his winter break there. She can never get enough Spam *musubi*, *malassadas*, or hiking time in her home state. Anna has written for *Slate*, as well as such Hawaii publications as *The Honolulu Advertiser* (now *Star-Advertiser*), *Honolulu Magazine*, and *Pacific Business News*. She updated the Exploring and Travel Smart chapters for this edition.